Faithful to Secularism

RELIGION, CULTURE, AND PUBLIC LIFE

Religion, Culture, and Public Life
Series Editor: Katherine Pratt Ewing

The resurgence of religion calls for careful analysis and constructive criticism of new forms of intolerance as well as new approaches to tolerance, respect, mutual understanding, and accommodation. To promote serious scholarship and informed debate, the Institute for Religion, Culture, and Public Life and Columbia University Press are sponsoring a book series devoted to the investigation of the role of religion in society and culture today. This series includes works by scholars in religious studies, political science, history, cultural anthropology, economics, social psychology, and other allied fields whose work sustains multidisciplinary and comparative as well as transnational analyses of historical and contemporary issues. The series focuses on issues related to questions of difference, identity, and practice within local, national, and international contexts. Special attention is paid to the ways in which religious traditions encourage conflict, violence, and intolerance and also support human rights, ecumenical values, and mutual understanding. By mediating alternative methodologies and different religious, social, and cultural traditions, books published in this series will open channels of communication that facilitate critical analysis.

For complete list of books in the series, see page 265

Faithful to Secularism

THE RELIGIOUS POLITICS OF DEMOCRACY IN IRELAND, SENEGAL, AND THE PHILIPPINES

David T. Buckley

COLUMBIA UNIVERSITY PRESS

NEW YORK

Columbia University Press
Publishers Since 1893
New York   Chichester, West Sussex
cup.columbia.edu

Copyright © 2016 Columbia University Press
All rights reserved

Library of Congress Cataloging-in-Publication Data
Names: Buckley, David T., author.
Title: Faithful to secularism : the religious politics of democracy in Ireland,
Senegal, and the Philippines / David T. Buckley.
Description: New York City : Columbia University Press, 2017. |
Series: Religion, culture, and public life |
Includes bibliographical references and index.
Identifiers: LCCN 2016023863 | ISBN 9780231180061 (cloth : alk. paper)
Subjects: LCSH: Secularism—Ireland. | Secularism—Senegal. | Secularism—Philippines. |
Religion and politics—Ireland. | Religion and politics—Sengal. | Religion and politics—
Philippines. | Democracy—Religious aspects.
Classification: LCC BL2747.8 .B83 2017 | DDC 322/.1—dc23
LC record available at https://lccn.loc.gov/2016023863

Columbia University Press books are printed on permanent and durable acid-free paper.
Printed in the United States of America

Cover Design: Martin Hinze

For Mom and Dad,
Christine and James Buckley

CONTENTS

List of Figures and Tables   ix
Acknowledgments   xi

Introduction   1

1. Benevolent Secularism:
A Theory of the Religious Politics of Democracy   9

2. Secular Emergence in Ireland:
Home Rule and Rome Rule?   42

3. Secular Evolution in Ireland:
Religion and Post-Catholic Politics   62

4. Secular Emergence in Senegal:
Laïcité in Translation   84

5. Secular Evolution in Senegal:
Sopi and Institutional Change 106

6. Secular Emergence in the Philippines:
Beyond the Malolos Stalemate 133

7. Secular Evolution in the Philippines:
People Power and Pluralization 154

Conclusion: The Future of Religion and Secular Democracy 183

Notes 201
Bibliography 235
Index 253

FIGURES AND TABLES

FIGURES

1.1. Benevolent secularism and secular emergence.   34
1.2. Benevolent secularism and institutional change.   34

TABLES

I.1. Overview of Cases   6
1.1. Variation in Religion and Democracy   15
1.2. Dimensions and Indicators of Benevolent Secularism Versus Passive and Assertive Secularism   25
1.3. Institutional Effects within Coalition Blocs   30
1.4. Case Configuration during Secular Emergence   38
1.5. Summary of Types of Qualitative Evidence Used   39
2.1. Assessing Benevolent Secularism in Ireland at Independence   51
2.2. Preference Effects of Benevolent Secularism in Ireland   57
3.1. Summary of Secular Evolution in Ireland   67
3.2. Secularism and Public Opinion in Ireland: Question Wording   78

3.3. Ireland Topline Results by Religious Tradition and Attendance   79
3.4. Testing Benevolent Secular Consensus in Ireland   80
4.1. Assessing Benevolent Secularism in Senegal   93
4.2. Preference Effects of Benevolent Secularism in Senegal   99
5.1. Summary of Secular Evolution in Senegal   113
5.2. Secularism and Public Opinion in Senegal: Question Wording   126
5.3. Senegal Topline Results by Religious Tradition   127
5.4. Testing Benevolent Secular Consensus in Senegal   128
5.5. Religious Traditions and Interfaith Engagement in Senegal   129
6.1. Assessing Benevolent Secularism in the Philippines   143
6.2. Preference Effects of Benevolent Secularism in the Philippines   148
7.1. Summary of Institutional Change in the Philippines   165
7.2. Benevolent Secularism and Public Opinion in the Philippines: Question Wording   176
7.3. Philippines Topline Results by Religious Tradition   178
7.4. Testing Benevolent Secular Consensus in the Philippines   179
7.5. The Born-Again Catholic Difference?   180

ACKNOWLEDGMENTS

Over the course of writing this book, I have incurred more debts than I can possibly hope to repay. My first thanks go to Tom Banchoff, who has been an ideal mentor, balancing critical engagement with intellectual freedom. José Casanova was a constant source of comparative insights and encouragement for the geographic scope of the project. Clyde Wilcox has been an enthusiastic guide in religion and public opinion research, both for this project and for others. Al Stepan's trailblazing work on the "twin tolerations" was in many ways the foundation my research, and it was an honor to have his energetic input.

The project would not have been possible without the generous support of the Social Science Research Council (SSRC) Dissertation Proposal Development Fellowship, the Cosmos Club Foundation, and the Center for Asian Democracy at the University of Louisville. Vincent Pecora and Jonathan Sheehan convened a fantastic group of young scholars through the SSRC's After Secularization group, which contributed significantly to this project's development. It was my pleasure to have their input, particularly when that input came in southern California.

Research centers in each field site were essential to my work. The West Africa Research Center (WARC) in Dakar, the Ateneo Center for Asian Studies (ACAS) at the Ateneo de Manila University, and the Irish School of Ecumenics

(ISE) at Trinity College Dublin were all ideal homes for periods of visiting fellowship, combining intellectual support with a welcoming scholarly environment. Ousmane Sene and the late Mame Coumba Ndoye at WARC, the late Lydia Yu-Jose and Anne Candelaria at ACAS, and Gillian Wylie and Geraldine Smyth at ISE were incredibly generous hosts and interlocutors. Brian and Avegrace Marana as well as Nick and Emily Johnson can bunk with me anytime. Generous professional colleagues helped me with interview sampling in each field site, especially Etienne Smith and Assane Diagne in Dakar and Eleanor Dionisio, Jayeel Cornelio, and Jonathan Chow in Manila. Each of my interview subjects contributed significantly to the project's success. The interviews simply could not have succeeded without their candor, good humor, and flexible schedules. I am thankful to the archivists and staff at the Archives nationales du Sénégal, the Filipiniana Section of the Rizal Library at the Ateneo de Manila University, Trinity College Library Dublin, and the Archives of the Archdiocese of Dublin. Mahar Mangahas of Social Weather Stations in Quezon City, Philippines; Babaly Sall of Groupe d'études et de recherches constitutionnelles et politiques at the University of Gaston Berger in St. Louis, Senegal; and Greg Smith of the Pew Research Group were quite generous with their assistance in locating relevant public opinion data.

Colleagues in the Department of Political Science at the University of Louisville have been a great source of wisdom as this project moved to completion. I am particularly humbled by the support of those who have established the Paul Weber Endowed Chair in Politics, Science, and Religion in memory of their beloved mentor, friend, and family member. Beyond Louisville, many have helped the project with critical engagement, especially Ruthie Braunstein, Michael Driessen, Anna Grzymala-Busse, Nader Hashemi, Ahmet Kuru, Cecelia Lynch, Jeremy Menchik, Dan Philpott, and Grace Yukich. Students and faculty at the Institute for Qualitative and Multimethod Research gave invaluable feedback on the project's design. The guidance of James Guth, Bud Kellstedt, and Corwin Smidt at Calvin College's Henry Institute Workshop in Religion and Public Opinion laid the foundation for the survey analysis in this book. The Institut für die Wissenschaften vom Menschen's Summer School on Religion and Public Life in Cortona, Italy, was an ideal setting, both intellectually and geographically, to develop the project with friends. In many ways, the project originated in the University of Virginia's Program in Political and Social Thought under the engaging guidance of Michael J. Smith.

My colleagues and friends at Georgetown played a special part in shaping this project. Peter Henne, Luis Felipe Mantilla, and Hesham Sallam share an interest in the dynamics of religious-secular relations, and all read several versions of the project's core argument over time. Andy Bennett, Matt Carnes, Jocelyne Cesari, Desha Girod, Marc Morjé Howard, Michael Kessler, Dan

Nexon, and Hans Noel played an important role in developing aspects of the research design over time. Georgetown's Berkley Center for Religion, Peace, and World Affairs was an ideal spot to gather intellectual energy and engage in quiet writing. E. J. Dionne's energy and passion for issues of religion and democratic life make him an inspiration, and his friendship was significant to the project's success. Supportive friends in the Georgetown Department of Government doctoral program are too many to name individually, but special thanks go to the entering class of fall 2007 and all who bought a round along the way.

I am fortunate to owe my deepest thanks closest to home. My parents, James and Christine Buckley, have modeled the kind of home and professional lives to which I aspire. My wife, Jessica Belue Buckley, is a joyful partner; I thank her for all of the life she has given to those around her. My daughter, Sarah, and son, Xavier, tolerated neglect and absences tied to this book in good spirits and raised my own along the way. They, even more than the rest listed here, cannot reasonably be held responsible for any deficiencies in the manuscript.

Faithful to Secularism

Introduction

On September 30, 2010, a prayer service at Manila Cathedral broke with formal rites. With the mayor of Manila and Catholic bishops present, local tour guide and activist Carlos Celdran interrupted an ecumenical service to denounce the role of the Catholic Bishops' Conference of the Philippines in debates on a reproductive health bill. Celdran won himself a place on the news and a spot in jail for violation of Philippine laws protecting religious worship.

The incident captures the dynamic relationship between religion and democracy in the Philippines and beyond. On the one hand, Celdran played his role in keeping with long-established patterns of Philippine politics. He appeared dressed as José Rizal, the Filipino nationalist author who opposed the power of Spanish friars more than a century ago, and holding a placard bearing the name "Damaso," the unsavory friar at the center of Rizal's most famous novel, *Noli me tángere*. At the same time, Celdran's protest had an unmistakably modern feel. He was not arguing for official disestablishment of the Catholic Church; even the bishops gathered in the cathedral advocate for basic church–state differentiation. Rather, Celdran protested the extent of church influence over particular issue areas of public policy. The grounds of religion–state disputes have evolved in the Philippines and elsewhere.

This project examines how actors become and remain "faithful to secularism" even in the face of contention over religion's role in public life. Why do what Alfred Stepan has termed the "twin tolerations" between religion and state emerge in seemingly unlikely places,[1] in particular places such as Ireland, Senegal, and the Philippines, where a religious majority has significant influence in public life? This general question raises two more precise puzzles that this book takes up in turn. First, why do the twin tolerations emerge at critical junctures such as national independence? Why, for example, did independence from British colonial administration not lead to an established Catholic state in Ireland? Second, why do the twin tolerations endure during periods of change or crisis? Why, for example, has Senegal's version of *laïcité* survived manipulations by the regime of former President Abdoulaye Wade? In both phases, the argument foregrounds the importance of institutional conditions, or what I call "benevolent secularism," in explaining why key actors accept the twin tolerations and how alliances crossing religious-secular and interfaith divides preserve the twin tolerations over time. Benevolent secularism's most distinctive feature is the cooperative role it encourages for religious actors in public life. It is, in its ideal type, a consensual model of secularism, in which public religion need not lead to sectarian division.

Distinguishing between periods of emergence and those of evolution rests on historical institutionalist insights regarding critical junctures in institutional development.[2] Periods of secular emergence, occurring regularly after war, revolution, or independence from colonial rule, provided unique opportunities to recast the religion–state relationship in cases as diverse as France, Turkey, and India.[3] These junctures provide unusual moments of indeterminacy in the shape of political institutions and set enduring boundaries on the religion–state relationship. However, historical legacies do not eliminate future jockeying over religion and politics.[4] Indeed, the question facing path-dependent accounts is what mechanisms explain the endurance of institutions over time, even in the face of challengers. Distinguishing institutional emergence from evolution is particularly important to the study of religion and democracy, which too often treats founding documents as definitive statements of future outcomes rather than as only one force structuring future political contention.

Carlos Celdran's protest in Manila Cathedral is just one example of a broader reality: religion and democracy continue to make tense bedfellows. Some religious actors, across a range of faith traditions, openly advocate for restrictions on minority rights and clash with more secular elites in public life. Modernizing nationalists from Nehru to Atatürk have seen religion as in tension with social progress and political development. Others, writing in Thomas Hobbes's shadow, argue that religion is particularly conflict prone and that religious actors are incapable of engaging in the compromise required of democratic politics. Such tensions between religious and secular actors came to a tragic end in Algeria's descent into civil war in the 1990s. Unease between religion and political participation looms just beneath the surface much more broadly, from fairly successful democracies such as Indonesia and India to divided societies such as Nigeria and Sri Lanka. Today, the challenge may be greatest in the Arab world as Islamists at times gain influence through elections and political transitions destabilize the place of religion in democratic life.[5]

This tension between religion and democracy can fuel a "secularism trap"—that is, the breakdown of democracy due to the decision of either religious or secular elites to pursue maximalist demands related to the place of religion in democratic politics.[6] Democracy opens politics to a range of new competitors, from labor unions to women's movements. In highly religious societies, this competition raises the specter of political domination by religious parties over dissenters of various stripes. Both religious and secular elites have incentives to make maximalist demands, especially amid founding elections and constitution drafting. However, if either group does so, democracy fails because either religious demands undercut rights protections or secularist restrictions cut off political participation by religious actors. To use U.S. Assistant Secretary of State Edward Djerejian's famous phrasing regarding Algeria: "One person, one vote, one time."[7] In such contexts, a trap looms. Democracy could empower an antidemocratic religious majority, but limits on that majority would cut off any meaningful democratization. Fear of religious domination provokes a backlash as antireligious forces exclude religious movements from public life and in the process cut short democratic participation. The secularism trap can spring from either end. On some occasions, religious actors actually manage to capture state institutions, initially through democratic means, and proceed to violate rights protections and break down the autonomy of state institutions. More commonly, fear of this outcome springs the trap from the other side as authoritarian regimes use antireligious fears to clamp down on political participation. In either case, the secularism trap has short-circuited the prospect for robust democratic politics.

In spite of fears, research suggests that the secularism trap is not inevitable. From Asia to Latin America, politically active religious majorities coexist with democratic politics. Scholarship from the authoritarian Middle East suggests that participation at times produces moderation of religious actors.[8] Vali Nasr has argued that in more democratic environments such as Indonesia and Turkey, "Muslim democracy" is coming to parallel the earlier history of Christian democracy in Europe.[9] This research emerges at the same time that scholars are noting the diversity in institutions of religion–state relations and the consequences that this variation has for democratic politics.[10] Given the clear compatibility between religion and democracy in some settings, scholars need to get beyond the secularism trap and explore the conditions under which the politics of religion threatens (or does not threaten) democratic politics. This book takes up that task by analyzing the existence of the "twin tolerations" between religion and democracy—that is, the mutual accommodation in which the state tolerates the private and public freedom of religious actors and religious actors tolerate the authority of the state to autonomously formulate and implement public policy.[11]

The first phase of this argument highlights the relationship between religion and politics during the period of *secular emergence*. What explains why religious and secular actors sometimes support the twin tolerations at critical junctures but at other times threaten the kind of political decay that culminated in Algeria's civil war? This research question focuses attention on junctures such as postcolonial independence when the institutional relationship between religion and state is up for grabs and actors have significant leeway in setting institutions in founding documents such as constitutions. The very indeterminacy of these junctures makes the secularism trap seem highly threatening as political actors push their institutional preferences during fairly rare moments of institutional flux. Why is it, for instance, that even in the face of a devout religious majority at political independence, the secularism trap never truly operated as Ireland became an independent democracy? Understanding how religious majorities come to support Stepan's twin tolerations is a central step in understanding why states become faithful to secularism.

The second phase shifts from critical junctures to institutional *evolution*: How do actors demonstrate their faithfulness to the twin tolerations over time, even in the face of challengers and institutional alternatives? The relationship between state and religion, frequently settled during early periods of state formation, has demonstrated significant variation in recent years across a range of cases. What Peter Berger has termed the "desecularization of the world"[12] challenges the stability of existing institutions of secularism. Historical context alone cannot account for these contemporary patterns of change. And yet some states see gradual evolution in the religion–state relationship, within historical boundaries, whereas others see the breakdown of historical patterns and their replacement by an alternative institutional configuration. Understanding how actors preserve the twin tolerations when they are threatened is the second stage in understanding why states become faithful to secularism.

I propose an institutional theory that addresses both the emergence and the evolution of religion's place in democratic politics. I argue that institutions of "benevolent secularism" can prove central in balancing majority participation with minority rights, particularly when one religion enjoys a clear demographic majority. I define benevolent secularism as a variety of institutional relationship between religion and state that combines three dimensions: differentiation of religious and state bodies, cooperation between religious and state actors, and state maintenance of what Rajeev Bhargava has termed "principled distance" from all religious communities.[13] Benevolent secularism stands in contrast not only to forms of religious establishment but also to more assertive forms of secularism found in France and Turkey. Public religion is not only tolerated but also encouraged, which brings consequences not likely under other varieties of secularism. Benevolent secularism increases the likelihood of the twin tolerations at critical junctures by affecting preferences within religious and secular blocs about the appropriate place of religion in democratic politics, thus building internal support for the twin tolerations.

If institutional structure explains the emergence of the twin tolerations at critical junctures, it also shapes their evolution over time. The twin tolerations endure even in the face of challenges by promoting ties between key actors: bridging religious-secular divides and strengthening interfaith relations. Even when the twin tolerations seem threatened by changing demographics or bursts of religious "outbidding,"[14] institutional structure reinforces the mutual credibility of religious and secular commitments to the twin tolerations, encouraging a diverse coalition to stabilize religion's role in public life. In this institutional environment, jockeying among coalition allies can result in secular evolution, but within the general bounds set by historical precedent.

I test this argument about the effect of benevolent secularism in three cases: Ireland, Senegal, and the Philippines. At the critical juncture in modern independence, each of these cases made a likely candidate for the secularism trap. And yet after contestation each secured the twin tolerations in part because of the institutional structure of benevolent secularism. Since these critical junctures, the cases have diverged in many regards, with distinct challenges to the twin tolerations emerging. Senegal has seen calls to increase the Islamic character of state institutions and an unprecedented threat to the twin tolerations from the administration of President Abdoulaye Wade. Ireland has experienced an explosion of anticlerical hostility in response to cover-ups of clerical sex abuse as well as the rapid deterioration of Catholic influence over public and private life. And religious pluralization in the Philippines has complicated the relationship between religion and state, while violence in Muslim-majority parts of Mindanao has raised serious questions about the even-handedness of state institutions. In each case, I first examine historical evidence of the role of institutional structure in the *emergence* of the twin tolerations and then turn to contemporary interview and survey evidence that institutional structure is responsible for the *evolution* of religious politics over time. Table I.1 summarizes the central time periods under consideration in each case. The initial stage of secular emergence in each is centered on a focused period of constitutional deliberation, and secular evolution takes place over a more extended timeframe.

TABLE I.1. OVERVIEW OF CASES

Case	Secular Emergence			Secular Evolution	
	Event		Date	Source of Challenge	Time Range
Senegal	Independence from French rule		1960	Administration of President Wade	2000–2012
Philippines	Commonwealth Constitution deliberations		1934	Marcos regime; new pluralism	1975–present
Ireland	Debates over post–Free State Constitution		1937	Collapse of "Catholic Ireland"	1972–present

This argument carries implications beyond these three diverse cases, including implications for policy makers tasked with analyzing the place of religion in international politics. Three stand out. First, questions of fundamental religious liberty are a relatively limited portion of contemporary religious politics. Policy makers, particularly in the United States, have prioritized religious liberty through bodies such as the U.S. Commission on International Religious Freedom and have done important work documenting and promoting freedom of religion around the world. However, much of the action in these cases is several steps removed from fundamental threats to religious liberty. To make sense of religious politics of democracy, policy analysts should cast a wider net, including patterns of religious-secular cooperation or competition in party politics, social welfare provision, and policy consultation. Second, the political role of religion results from debates *within* religious communities as much between them. The traditions studied in this book, whether Senegalese Sufism or Irish atheism, are internally diverse, and these internal divisions shape political life. Understanding these internal debates may present obstacles to policy makers but is essential in coming to grips with the religious politics of democracy. Finally, policy makers should not overestimate the appeal of religious politics. It is too often assumed that believers have an essential desire to merge religion and state and that elites desire such influence above all things. This mistake is made by some who welcome political religion as well as by others who prefer to confine religion strictly to the private sphere. The reality is less clear. Religious populations show broad support for limiting religion's influence on politics, and religious elites frequently understand the limits of religious appeals in politics.[15] Policy makers should understand these limits as well and in turn not overstate the challenge posed by religious actors to democratic institutions.

Assessing the relationship between religion and democracy is a pressing task for scholars of comparative politics. In the argument I present here, I build an empirical case meant to challenge assumptions about the meaning of secularism and the impact of religion on democratic politics. Although serious obstacles emerged in reconciling religion and democracy in each of the states I examine, my argument is basically optimistic about the prospects for these cases and others. Divisions between religious and secular actors or along interfaith lines are not inevitable. And putting religion on the democratic agenda need not sharpen such divisions and promise sectarian division. This general optimism is not to deny highly contentious issues that may continue to vex the religion–state relationship. Throughout the book, I attempt to do justice to troubling aspects of benevolent secularism, from minorities who may not be party to the state's benevolence to the effect of benevolence on common flashpoints such as family law and regulation of human sexuality. Studying the implications of benevolent secularism makes significant progress in understanding how even religious devout populations remain faithful to secularism as well as the tensions likely to endure in such settings.

OUTLINE OF THE STUDY

The book moves forward first by setting out a theoretical framework that establishes expectations about the influence of benevolent secularism and then by moving to the main case studies. Two chapters per state take up the two questions at the center of the project: How do the twin tolerations emerge in seemingly least-likely cases, and how do institutions of benevolent secularism evolve over time in changing political environments?

Ireland's period of secular emergence demonstrates the role of benevolent secularism in altering the preferences of a powerful Catholic clerical elite. It was only the conjunction of differentiation, cooperation, and principled distance that simultaneously reassured small religious minorities while gaining assent from politically powerful Catholic clerics. The period of emergence also highlights the difficulties in maintaining principled distance given Catholic dominance. Ireland's secular evolution tells a dramatically different story of the end of religious hegemony and the rise of an anticlerical movement with less interest in a cooperative relationship between religion and state. That benevolent secularism has evolved in this environment rather than breaking down entirely demonstrates the significant influence of coalition alliances shaped during the Irish critical juncture.

Secular emergence in Senegal clarifies the impact of benevolent secularism both on a group of political elites interested in political stability and on Muslim leaders negotiating political institutions with the departure of French colonial authority. President Léopold Sédar Senghor plays a crucial role here as both a state elite dedicated to developing *laïcité* and a Roman Catholic operating in a Muslim-majority country. The period of emergence also demonstrates ambiguity in the extent of religion–state cooperation as family law became a stumbling block even among coalition allies. Senegal's secular evolution differs sharply from that in Ireland; the challenge is the rising call for integrating religion and state rather than the growth of anticlericalism. After his election in 2000, President Wade weakened dimensions of benevolent secularism in an attempt to win a portion of the Muslim leadership over to his political camp. The evolution of Senegalese *laïcité* to meet this challenge is testament to robust interfaith relations, and the enduring commitment to *laïcité* among Senegal's Sufi brotherhoods.

Benevolent secularism emerged in the Philippines after sequential Spanish and American colonial rule. Independence leaders arrived at benevolent secularism as an alternative to both the official establishment of Catholicism under Spanish colonialism and the rather strict separation of church and state that characterized the early years of American rule. With the adoption of benevolent secularism, sharp historical debates between Masonic political elites and the Catholic hierarchy diminished in importance. Secular evolution has gone through two distinct stages in the Philippines. The first corresponded to the bid to break down benevolent secularism by the dictatorship of Ferdinand Marcos in the 1970s and 1980s. The second has resulted from recent pluralization in religious leadership, which has encouraged contention over equal status of Muslim citizens, reproductive health legislation opposed by many Catholic elites, and the rise of pastor-politicians on the campaign trail.

1. *Benevolent Secularism*

A THEORY OF THE RELIGIOUS POLITICS OF DEMOCRACY

This book engages long-standing debates about the relationship between religion and democracy. As an empirical project, it builds on recent institutionalist scholarship documenting the varieties of secularism compatible with democratic governance. It places special emphasis on explicitly benevolent forms of secularism and the impact that such cooperation has on public life. It advances institutional research in focusing on the effects that political institutions have on the preferences within religious and secular blocs and on the coalitions that often form among these blocs, even across religious-secular or interfaith divides. The argument highlights normative tensions within both religious and secular communities over the place of religion in democratic politics as well as the diverse coalitions that stabilize religion's public role. This chapter sets out the book's theoretical framework in more depth and explains the research design used to test its empirical expectations.

Until recently, leading empirical accounts of democracy paid limited attention to debates over the place of religion in democratic life. Classic works in modernization theory assumed that the same process of social development that caused democracy would reduce the strength of religious institutions and individual faith; Daniel Lerner's analysis of changing social authority in Balgat remains paradigmatic in this regard.[1] This strand of political research is closely tied to sociological theories of "secularization," in which economic development drives "the process by which sectors of society and culture are removed from the domination of religious institutions and symbols."[2] Even as scholars of democratization moved away from the most teleological versions of modernization theory, leading work showed limited systematic attention to the nature of the institutional relationship between religion and democratic polities. As Alfred Stepan has noted, classic works from Robert Dahl and Arend Lijphart leave the institutional place of religion in democracy largely unaddressed, although they do pay some attention to the presence of religious political parties.[3] Guillermo O'Donnell and Philippe Schmitter make significant progress in noting the role of some religious actors in "resurrecting civil society" in opposition to authoritarian rule but pay less attention to the institutional rules that will structure religion's place in post-transition democratic politics.[4] Religion exists on the periphery of core institutional dilemmas about economic redistribution and political participation for former authoritarian elites.

A second wave of scholarship refocused on the place of religion in democracy, largely through attention to the threat that religious divisions may pose to democracy. In his classic work, Seymour Martin Lipset worries that unresolved religious divisions could pose a major "crisis of legitimacy" as the place of religion in democratic life turns (presumably tractable) debates over economic distribution into "a deep-rooted conflict between God and Satan."[5] These fears of religious threat endure in more recent forms. Adam Przeworski worries that "the resurgence of the political power of the church" will undercut the "particular form of suspension of belief" necessary for enduring democracy.[6] Stathis Kalyvas points to credible commitments problems in contexts where "contrary to typical transitions, compromise is hindered by the challengers' religious identity."[7] Assumptions of religious irrationality and threat in the West are rooted in the "religious wars" of early-modern Europe, but in contemporary scholarship are also motivated by the rise of political Islam in electoral contexts. John Waterbury most clearly distills this concern, arguing that "religious political groups (Islamic and non-Islamic) are non-democrats of a particular kind. . . . Where the scriptures are both holy and explicit, as is the case in Islam, pragmatic compromise will be very difficult."[8] Conflicts between Islamists and other members of Arab political oppositions since the Arab Spring have lent further energy to scholars who view religion as uniquely resistant to the compromise necessary for democratic institutions.

Other, less-pessimistic scholarship has recently contended that political institutions can mitigate the tensions between religion and democratic politics. This view is in keeping with the broad turn to institutions in political science and has in general produced more optimistic readings of the relationship between religion and democracy. Although Daniel Philpott acknowledges the "political ambivalence of religion," he makes a case for institutional independence between religion and state as summoning the better angels from religious actors in democratic life.[9] Stepan's research has demonstrated the diverse institutional conditions compatible with the "twin tolerations," from liberal forms of religious establishment to more pluralistic systems in India and elsewhere.[10] Jeffrey Haynes has documented the nuanced relationship between religion, democracy, and development in much of the developing world, particularly in sub-Saharan Africa.[11] Much institutional scholarship stresses the importance of historical critical junctures—for instance, Ahmet Kuru's persuasive case that early institutional variation among France, Turkey, and the United States shapes current political outcomes.[12] Institutions can have an effect because, to borrow from Stepan, religious movements are "multivocal." Diverse political norms coexist within seemingly singular religious communities, and institutions can affect these internal debates. This sort of institutionalist argument has extended to the analysis of Islamist movements, with the "inclusion–moderation hypothesis" arguing that the institutional conditions of political participation may change behavior or norms within religious movements.[13] This scholarship has made important progress in "taking religion seriously" while noting the diverse empirical impact that religious actors have actually had on democratic politics in recent decades.

This recent scholarship is in many ways a significant advance on earlier assumptions of religion's irrelevance or inherent threat to democracy. However, it raises several subsequent questions about the impact of political institutions on religious politics. First, how do institutions shape the "multivocality" of religious groups? What are the relevant "multivocal" blocs within a given religious community, and what mechanisms explain how institutions have an impact on these internal dynamics? Second, how do institutions shape politics not only *within* religious communities but also *between* religious majorities, religious minorities, and secular movements? Why do divisions along religious-secular lines or between faith groups feared by many scholars *not* emerge, and how are institutions linked to religious-secular or interfaith cooperation? And third, if historical legacies matter so much for the place of religion in democracy, what explains patterns of institutional change in religion–state relations? Why do institutions sometimes endure revisionist challengers, and why does the place of religion in democracy seem simultaneously path dependent *and* highly dynamic?

In answering each of these questions, this book traces institutional effects both at traditional critical junctures, or "secular emergence," and through periods of institutional change, or "secular evolution." This division draws on recent theories of institutional change, in particular what James Mahoney and Kathleen Ann Thelen call "gradual institutional change."[14] Dividing periods of emergence from periods of evolution provides significant benefits in making sense of the relationship between religion and democracy. Emergence is undeniably important because the basic rules of the political game are open for debate, whether due to revolution or to postcolonial independence. However, the institutional relationship between religion and democracy remains dynamic beyond these junctures. Ignoring periods of secular evolution overstates the continuity of the religion–democracy relationship. Understanding when this dynamism leads to subtle patterns of institutional change rather than to a full collapse of existing institutions is essential to making sense of the impact of periods of new religious mobilization on democracies from Latin America to the Muslim-majority world.

Although this argument is primarily empirical, the findings come with implications for ongoing debates among theorists of religion and democracy. Richard Rorty's classic claim that religion is a "conversation stopper" has come under scrutiny from a range of philosophers and theologians in the past decade.[15] Thinkers as diverse as Jürgen Habermas, Jeffrey Stout, Émile Perreau-Saussine, and Abdullahi an-Na'im have imagined more extensive public roles for religion in democratic politics.[16] Some, reviving Tocqueville's evaluation of religion in American democratic culture, have argued for the normative contributions of religion to democracy, whereas others have at the very least tried to chasten liberal voices most skeptical of religion's involvement in democratic debates. Several questions drive this recent research in political theory, philosophy, theology, and law. Do religious claims impede democratic deliberation? What would be lost by the liberal tradition if religion were driven entirely from democratic politics? And how does the trajectory of what Charles Taylor has dubbed the West's "secular age" compare with dynamics of religion and society elsewhere? These theoretical questions are pressing, but they all also come with empirical implications. Throughout this volume, empirical findings demonstrate both the flexibility of democratic polities in incorporating religion into public life and the conditions that encourage broader religious-secular cooperation than is often found among Western theorists.

ASSESSING THE OUTCOMES OF INTEREST

What does it mean to assess the place of religion in democratic politics? The question is of practical importance. For instance, should the existence of religious political parties such as Ennahda in Tunisia at a critical juncture in regime transformation be taken as evidence of the secularism trap? And once we decide how to evaluate the status of the relationship between religion and democracy at critical junctures, how should we evaluate the endurance of secular institutions over time? Does the lack of any recent amendment to the U.S. Constitution related to religion indicate that no institutional change has taken place in the United States in the past half-century or more? Clear understandings of the outcomes at critical junctures and the nature of institutional change over time are needed before evaluating theories of how secular democracy emerges and evolves.

At critical junctures, three outcomes are possible for the relationship between religion and democracy. First, religious actors could coexist with democratic politics and minority rights protections. This outcome is what Stepan defines as the "twin tolerations" between religion and democratic politics. Stepan defines his tolerations as a kind of mutual accommodation between religion and state institutions that cuts two ways. First, "democratic institutions must be free, within the bounds of the constitution and human rights, to generate policies. Religious institutions should not have constitutionally privileged prerogatives that allow them to mandate public policy." State institutions must be autonomous and effective, able to form and implement policy without quasi-judicial veto from religious institutions. Second, toleration falls on the state in the protection of religion: "At the same time, individuals and religious communities . . . must have complete freedom to worship privately. In addition, as individuals and groups, they must be able to advance their values publicly in civil society and to sponsor organizations and movements in political society."[17] As Stepan acknowledges, a wide range of empirical arrangements between religion and state meets his standards; there is no particular assumption that a strict exclusion of religion from democratic politics is a necessary characteristic of democracy.

If this mutual accommodation constitutes one outcome at critical junctures in regime formation, then political breakdown through the secularism trap provides the other two. The secularism trap can spring from the religious side, when a religious majority uses a moment of political opening to seize control of state institutions, in the process excluding religious minorities from equal protection and enshrining power for religious institutions in constitutional law that violates the twin tolerations. This outcome has path-dependent implications by linking religious institutions to the coercive apparatus of an antiliberal political regime. This dynamic took place over the course of the Iranian Revolution, with long-lasting results.

A third outcome is important to remember as well. The secularism trap can spring from the secular side, with political elites using fears of religious takeover to legitimate the repression of religious institutions. This occurred most dramatically in the lead-up to the Algerian civil war but has also occurred at various points in time in authoritarian regimes' manipulations in Turkey and Egypt, among other states. In these cases, state officials' tolerance of religious institutions breaks down, resulting in violation of religious liberty, forced privatization of religious practice, or the coercive incorporation of religious institutions within the state bureaucracy. Although liberal democrats tend to worry about the religious side of the secularism trap, the empirical record suggests that the twin tolerations regularly, perhaps more regularly, break down from the secular authoritarian side.

Assessing the existence of the twin tolerations obviously requires careful evaluation of comparative political institutions. Looking at a constitution for the existence of a state church, for instance, is only a first step. Some established state churches—for example, the Church of England—are generally compatible with the twin tolerations, whereas some states that seem to provide for freedom of religious belief, such as China, may violate the twin tolerations in practice. This means that assessing the twin tolerations takes attention to more than the most basic features of constitutions. It also requires tracing the implementation of constitutional provisions through legislation, jurisprudence, and policy formation.

In contrast to the critical junctures that characterize secular *emergence*, periods of secular *evolution* vary between those that result in gradual institutional renegotiation and those that lead to the breakdown and replacement of political institutions. Will institutions concretized during critical junctures evolve gradually over time or go through a more dramatic process of breakdown and replacement? Secular evolution is a process of institutional change other than formal replacement; it is characterized by variation *within* existing institutional boundaries as institutions vary in application. Evolution is a more gradual process in which religious and state actors push the boundaries of existing institutions without breaking down those institutions and replacing them with an institutional alternative. The institutional change captured by secular evolution has become a major focus of comparative institutionalist scholarship in the past decade. Institutionalist work from James Mahoney and Kathleen Thelen, Jacob Hacker, and others has observed that much institutional change does not result from the wholesale replacement of an existing institution by another contender but rather from the different operation of the same formal institution within a changed social or political context.[18] Although *replacement*—that is, the formal shift from one typological space to another—is one path of change, it is not the exclusive option and perhaps not the most likely one.[19]

In practice, the precise nature of secular evolution can vary quite widely after institutions take shape at critical junctures. In some instances, evolution may appear either more permissive or restrictive—for instance, as the state allows greater or lesser public influence to religious actors as a whole. In other cases, evolution would be more accurately described as hierarchical or egalitarian as states either privilege one religious community or take steps to treat all religious communities more even-handedly. What unites these varieties of evolution is that none constitutes a move across typological space or the breakdown of existing institutions. It is crucial to study such evolution both because it has real impact on the democratic politics of religion and because it constitutes the dominant form of institutional change in the area of state secularism. Because of these nuanced patterns of change, the study of secular evolution lends itself to qualitative analysis that places a premium on thorough evidence collection in cases over time.

Highlighting secular evolution opens a whole field of unexamined institutional dynamism to scholarship. If one simply examines institutional breakdown and replacement, secular settlements appear nearly stagnant, overdetermined by historical legacies that leave no room for individual agency. However, within these historical bounds, it is clear that meaningful institutional change is a regular occurrence. Actors push the boundaries of existing institutions, reshaping them to meet their changing preferences and to reflect altered demographic landscapes.

Table 1.1 summarizes the two types of variation in the realm of religion and democratic politics. In the theoretical sections that follow, I examine leading explanations for this variation and then set out my own institutional framework.

TABLE 1.1. VARIATION IN RELIGION AND DEMOCRACY

Outcome	*Indicators*
Secular Emergence	
Twin Tolerations	1. State institutions free to formulate and implement policy without formal religious veto. AND 2. Religious actors free to practice in private and organize in public.
Secularism Trap	1. Religious capture of state institutions. OR 2. State repression of public or private religion.
Secular Evolution	
Institutional Evolution	Change within the boundaries of existing institutions of religion–state relations
Institutional Replacement	Change through the breakdown of existing institutions and formal replacement with another variety of religion–state relations

APPROACHES TO RELIGION AND DEMOCRACY

The contentious relationship between religion and democracy has attracted substantial scholarly attention in recent years. Especially as the Arab Awakening has brought both excitement and anxiety among advocates of democratization, scholars have sought to explain how religious mobilization might coexist with democratic politics. In this section, I set out three contrasting approaches to this subject. Within each, I distinguish, as much as possible, predictions regarding secular emergence and secular evolution. Although I critique each, this critique is not meant to imply that these traditions provide no help in understanding the relationship between religion and democracy. To the contrary, each approach has important insights. But each is hampered by limitations, in particular a general inattention to the ways in which institutional structure shapes the preferences of actors contesting the relationship between religion and democracy.

MODERNIZATION THEORY AND THE FADING OF RELIGION

In its purest form, modernization theory expects that the process of development decreases individual religiosity and weakens the hold of religious institutions over public life. As Peter Berger put it in his classic formulation, "Secularization manifests itself in the evacuation by the Christian churches of areas previously under their control or influence."[20] Expanding beyond Christian Europe, Karl Deutsch argued half a century ago that "maharajas, sultans, sheikhs and chieftains all are quite unlikely to cope with these new problems, and traditional rule by land-owning oligarchies or long established religious bodies most often is apt to prove equally disappointing in the face of new needs."[21]

Of course, as both Deutsch and Samuel Huntington observed, parts of the modernization package may not move in sync, creating gaps in which social mobilization outstrips the capacity of state institutions and thus encourages unrest or state breakdown.[22] In this scenario, the secularism trap may loom when political participation expands before the breakdown of religious loyalty. The solution, then, would be the exclusion of religious actors until further secularization occurs. This argument plays quite comfortably into the hands of authoritarian regimes in economically underdeveloped societies.

Secularization theory, like its cousin modernization theory, is generally deterministic in its predictions about both the emergence and evolution of secular institutions: development brings reduced individual religiosity and increased confinement of religion in the private sphere. The twin tolerations should emerge, then, in economically advanced societies. Secular evolution should be unidirectional, with more restrictive forms of secularism emerging over time as religious institutions lose legitimacy and fade to the margins of public life.

Ultimately, this approach is unsatisfying in making sense of the relationship between religion, democracy, and economic development. During the period of secular emergence, democracies from India to Senegal and the Philippines demonstrate that the conjunction of underdevelopment, political mobilization, and high religiosity need not condemn a country to the secularism trap. And over time, secular evolution has hardly proven unidirectional. Even within highly developed states of western Europe, for instance, sharp debates have recently broken out over the scope of accommodation to religious minorities from eastern Europe and the Arab world. In the developing world, periods of economic growth in China and India have heightened religion–state tensions rather than leading to the smooth separation of the two. There is every reason to think that by increasing state capacity, development will increase friction between religion and state.[23]

A prime weakness of secularization theory is that its focus on structural changes in the economy overlooks the agency that shapes religion–state relations. The weakening of religious institutions in the face of economic development is taken for granted in this approach, so it is relatively unimportant to trace bargaining among coalition partners or the ways in which institutions may shape that bargaining over time. However, the empirical record does not bear out this claim. Economic development has facilitated the urban preaching of Pentecostal ministers in Latin America and permitted Islamist elites to distribute their views through new technology. Development has an undeniable impact on religion–state relations, but its causal role is less deterministic than secularization theory claims.

THE UNDUE PESSIMISM OF RATIONALIST THEORIES

A spate of recent rationalist scholarship argues that tensions between religion and democracy are a product either of the demographic structure of the religious marketplace or of bargaining breakdowns across the religious-secular divide. The secularism trap is in many ways a rationalist construction at its core. It is assumed that religious actors, like others in politics, have a preference for power maximization, and even if such actors claim alternative preferences, these commitments are noncredible to smaller minority communities. The very existence of a politically active religious majority provokes anticlericalism and the secularism trap. Religion's relationship with democracy, on this telling, is shaped by material competition among actors whose preferences closely resemble any firm or interest group.

From this basic starting point, rationalist theories of secular emergence develop in a number of specific ways. For rationalists such as Anthony Gill, the twin tolerations are most stable in religiously fragmented societies such as the United States, where religious institutions prefer a form of state secularism that protects their liberty to compete in the private sphere rather than any form of state religion.[24] Religion and democracy most easily coexist when a sort of hurting stalemate among religious groups makes secular governance an appealing outcome. Others such as Stathis Kalyvas argue that religion and democracy coexist when hierarchical religious institutions can deliver credible commitments to secular elites. Kalyvas's comparison of Belgium and Algeria suggests that Catholicism, with its cohesive authority structure, provides firmer ground for harmonizing religion and democracy than does horizontally organized Islam.[25] Of course, neither religious fragmentation nor hierarchical religious structures are subject to easy manipulation, so these rationalist theories present little reason for optimism about the relationship between religion and democracy in a wide range of cases.

Major rationalist thinkers such as Gill and Kalyvas have dedicated less time to the evolution of secular institutions over time. Gill does argue in his framework that dominant religious majorities will respond to new religious competitors by using the state to exclude them from the religious marketplace. This argument is in keeping with his focus on religious institutions' preference for material maximization and their general competition as they behave like firms in a marketplace. If we extend this framework further, secular institutions should evolve when it suits the material interests of the dominant religious community, while institutions break down and are formally replaced when a hegemonic religion fades from the scene and a fragmented religious marketplace arises.

In contrast to the functionalism of modernization theory, rationalist theories make a substantial contribution in focusing attention on the role of actors in contesting institutional boundaries. In rationalist frameworks, new players in the religious marketplace destabilize existing institutions by provoking existing religious communities to use the state to put up barriers to new religious competition. Gill points to the Russian Orthodox Church's use of the Russian state to exclude competing minorities as exemplifying this trend. Rationalists are right to focus on new religious pluralism as a major cause of secular evolution. However, their assumptions about fairly zero-sum competition and noncredible commitments between religious groups are overly bleak, in part because they choose to assume largely material interests even among religious actors. This assumption sells short the complex interests that drive the bargaining around religion–state relations. For instance, Irish Catholic elites have generally responded to the growing Irish Muslim minority not as a threat but as a partner in Irish public life.

This lack of attention to preferences and to the way preferences may be influenced by the structure of political institutions makes rationalist theories unduly pessimistic about how democracies can manage religious mobilization. Zero-sum competition and noncredible commitments along religious-secular or interfaith boundaries are not as sharp as often supposed; a coalition that crosses these divides may not take an act of divine intervention. The structure of political institutions can further reduce potential divides and build credible commitments to secularism even in unlikely cases.

THE IMPRECISION OF RELIGIOUS MODERATION

A final approach to explaining the relationship between religion and democracy has seized scholarly imagination in recent years: religious moderates secure the twin tolerations. On this telling, religious actors may be capable of living with the twin tolerations, but only after adopting a set of liberal values or political theology. This discourse is prominent in discussions of political Islam, especially in light of the Arab Awakening, with commentators eager to identify "moderate Muslims" who can be reconciled to secular state authority.[26] These arguments bear echoes of debates about the inclusion of leftist European parties in post–World War II democratic politics.[27]

There is a certain appeal in these arguments, and religious liberals can play a role in the emergence of the twin tolerations. The attention to specifying actor preferences is also an advance over the competition-driven bargaining of rationalist analysis. However, a comparative look at religious participants in democratic politics makes it clear that any concept of "moderation" should be used carefully. A first weakness is that one person's moderate is another's closet theocrat. The credible-commitment problems highlighted by rationalist analysis do not disappear simply because religious moderates affirm liberal political theology at critical junctures of secular emergence. Events since the fall of the Mubarak regime in Egypt have crystallized this point. In some settings, Muslim Brotherhood leaders regularly expressed "moderate" views on the record on topics such as protections for Coptic Christians. Yet minorities worried that this moderation was not genuine or that in the future Islamist activists might have a theological change of heart.

Second, the very term *moderation* sheds more heat than light because the content of moderate beliefs needs further specification. Must moderates agree to keep religion privatized within houses of worship? Or sign on to international human rights standards for religious minorities and women? Or perhaps even affirm the political philosophy of liberal philosophers such as John Rawls? Although studying the content of theological beliefs related to religion and politics is an important task, the blunt label *moderation* only begs the question of what aspect of belief must be moderated.

Finally, even if moderates play a role in some settings, liberal religious values are clearly not the only path to accepting the twin tolerations. Those who predict that moderate religious values must precede democratization underestimate the ability of the twin tolerations to emerge even in highly orthodox societies.[28] Religious communities have various reasons for accepting the twin tolerations during critical junctures, and even decidedly "immoderate" religious elites may decide that their own goals are best met by maintaining a certain distance from the political fray.

Religious moderates may also play a more complex role in the process of secular evolution over time than advocates of moderation assume. Theories of religious moderation seem to assume that the growth in the number of religious liberals will tame religious passions and stabilize the place of religion in democratic politics over time. Secular evolution will proceed less contentiously in a world where religious liberals come to enjoy more influence. However, this claim is open to empirical challenge. Religious liberals are frequently rivals of more orthodox religious institutions, and so the promotion of religious liberalism may actually provoke a reaction from traditionalist believers who perceive a threat in the growth of the number of supposed moderates. Something like this dynamic emerged in the United States in the years before the emergence of the Religious Right as communities of religious traditionalists who had traditionally shunned political life mobilized in the face of what they perceived as an expansion of liberalism in both religious and social life.[29] This is not to say that religious liberalism will necessarily threaten the twin tolerations. Rather, its presence refocuses our attention on the broader coalition politics that stabilize the twin tolerations.

Although these limits are significant, it is important to acknowledge the progress that religious moderation theory makes in highlighting religious actors' preferences and in paying attention to the ways in which political theology shapes the bargaining among religious and state blocs. However, in spite of this approach's strongest claims, card-carrying religious liberals are neither a necessary nor a sufficient condition for building the twin tolerations or for encouraging secular evolution. They are not necessary because orthodox religious groups may have their own sound reasons for accepting the twin tolerations, especially to preserve religion's autonomy from the state. Religious moderates are not sufficient because they may actually touch off counterreactions from more orthodox religious communities, making it more difficult to stabilize the relationship between religion and democracy.

One thing shines through in each of these alternatives: the general absence of institutional structure in analyzing the twin tolerations. Modernization theory pays little attention to the variety of institutional arrangements that coexist even within the developed West. Existing rationalist theories underemphasize institutional design's impact on bargaining. And focusing on religious moderation overlooks the varied institutional settings within which actors work.

THEORY: INSTITUTIONAL STRUCTURE AND COALITION POLITICS

In contrast to these alternative approaches, I argue that institutional structure plays a central role in managing tensions between religion and democracy, even in countries with a politically active religious majority. In making this institutional argument, I build on recent work from Stepan, Kuru, Jonathan Fox, and others on the multiple secularisms compatible with democratic government.[30] Expanding on their work, I identify an institutional type, what I call "benevolent secularism," that can prove central in harmonizing religion with democratic politics in cases where leading alternative theories predict limited prospects for the twin tolerations. This form of secularism rests on a cooperative, public role for religion in democratic life rather than on the exclusion of religion to a purely private sphere. This institutional structure increases the likelihood of the twin tolerations because of its impact on the coalition politics related to religion. The structure of benevolent secularism shapes the preferences of three groups during critical junctures: secular elites, the religious majority, and religious minority communities. Over time, this institutional impact on actor preferences stabilizes secular evolution through encouraging coalition ties: reducing the severity of religious-secular divides and strengthening interfaith relations. By shaping actor preferences and promoting a coalition that cross-cuts major social divisions, benevolent secularism reduces the likelihood of the secularism trap at critical junctures and promotes secular evolution over time.

In this section, I advance a two-part argument. First, I flesh out the concept of benevolent secularism and distinguish it from alternative institutional configurations of religion–state relations. Second, I detail the coalitional effects through which benevolent secularism operates both at critical junctures and during periods of secular evolution. By shaping actor preferences and encouraging partnerships across the religious-secular and interfaith divides, benevolent secularism promotes the twin tolerations not only at critical junctures but also over time as demographic shifts and revisionist movements bring new tensions to the relationship between religion and democratic politics.

CONCEPTUALIZING BENEVOLENT SECULARISM

Benevolent secularism is one variety of institutional relationship between religion and state. I define benevolent secularism as an institutional configuration that (1) maintains *differentiation* of religious and state institutions, (2) institutionalizes *cooperation* between religious and state actors in the democratic public square, and (3) establishes what Rajeev Bhargava has called a *"principled distance"* between the state and diverse religious communities.[31]

Benevolent secularism features a basic differentiation between religious and state institutions. Differentiation rules out one officially recognized state church, as in the Church of England. Such establishments may in some cases be compatible with the twin tolerations but constitute a different institutional place for religion in democracy. Differentiation comes with concrete implications in areas such as employment: religious appointments are not subject to state veto, and state appointments are not subject to a religious test. Bans on religious tests for office in the U.S. Constitution are thus a concrete indicator of differentiation. Because the state is not tied to one religious community, differentiation also implies protection of religious liberty. States may not restrict individuals' or groups' religious liberty because such restrictions would break down the supposed differentiation between state institutions and the religious sphere. In differentiating religion and state, benevolent secularism shares some ground with what Kuru calls "passive and assertive secularism."[32] On this dimension, benevolent secularism stands in clearest contrast with patterns of formal religious establishment.

Aside from this similarity, however, there are serious differences among benevolent secularism and Kuru's two institutional varieties, passive and assertive secularism. The clearest difference is in the cooperation that benevolent secularism institutionalizes between state and religious actors. Some forms of cooperation are largely material and financial. Tax breaks for religious associations are a basic signal of material cooperation. Most benevolent secular states, however, go beyond this form of cooperation. Material support frequently takes the form of funding for religious education. Cooperation in provision of religious education is a core feature of benevolent secularism in the Philippines, for example, and Senegal recently increased the presence of religious instruction in public schools for both the Muslim majority and Christian minorities. Similar cooperation may exist in areas of social service provision, in particular health care and poverty alleviation; Catholic institutions are major players in health care in the Philippines as well as in a range of other international cases, including the United States. Cooperation can also extend to religious activities such as pilgrimages, religious festivals, and public religious celebrations. Until recent budget cuts, Ireland provided state support to low-income families for religious celebrations.

Another indicator of cooperation moves from material support to policy consultation. Benevolent secularism includes religious institutions in formalized policy-consultation processes that signal a cooperative relationship between religion and state actors. Family law is among the most common areas of consultation, for example, with religious arbitrators playing some role in custody and inheritance disputes within the Muslim community in the Philippines under the Code of Muslim Personal Laws. In practice, the areas of consultation range far beyond family law, from worker-protection policy to development strategies—for instance, anti-HIV/AIDS campaigns throughout sub-Saharan Africa, including in Senegal. Such policy consultation grants religious actors a voice in public debates without violating the state's capacity to formulate and implement policies independent of religious authorization. This last point is important to note. *Cooperation* between religion and state does not equate to state *capitulation* to any and all religious interests. Religious actors have no veto over the formation of state policy; to enshrine such prerogatives would violate religious authorities' toleration of the state's autonomy in policy implementation.

Finally, benevolent secularism maintains a *principled distance* between the state and the various religious communities in its borders. Principled distance refers to a kind of even-handedness in state dealings with religious communities, but one that "rests on a distinction between equal treatment and treating everyone as an equal."[33] Bhargava's distinction here approximates the division between equality of opportunity and equality of outcome; all religions will *not* engage in precisely identical relationships with the state, but all should have had similar opportunities to do so. Principled distance distinguishes benevolent secularism from "hegemonic religion" and its troubling consequences that Jocelyne Cesari analyzes in much of the modern Middle East.[34] In the context of benevolent secularism, principled distance primarily means that the cooperation between religion and state must be available on a basically equal basis to all religions. Thus, when the Senegalese state makes pilgrimage funding available to Muslims, it should provide similar opportunities to its Catholic minority. Principled distance should extend to the patterns of policy consultation as well. Such consultations do not necessarily need to include all religions, but any religious actors able and willing to participate should have that opportunity. Again, *equal* participation in policy consultation may not be required. In a consultation related to AIDS policy, for instance, it would be in keeping with the state's principled policy goal to consult more closely with religious groups most active in that area of social ministry.

Maintaining principled distance also relates to state authorities' intervention in religious affairs. May states intervene in religious communities' practices, or should they instead provide religious exemptions from generally applicable civil laws? Again, principled distance "cannot antecedently decide that it will always refrain from interfering in religions or that it will interfere in each equally."[35] The state may deem intervention necessary in some cases but grant exemptions in others. Bhargava insists that such interventions and exemptions must be guided by "nonsectarian motives" if they are to rise to the standard of principled distance.[36] Relevant exemptions may be grounded in explicit constitutional guarantees of the autonomy of religious communities—for example, Article 19 of Senegal's Constitution guarantees that "religious institutions and communities regulate and administer their own affairs in an autonomous manner." Exemptions are a matter of principled distance because they regularly protect religious communities that would unintentionally bear the brunt of generally applicable civil laws. For example, Philippine courts have exempted Jehovah's Witnesses from certain marital requirements, and Ireland's Jewish community received exemption from certain commercial regulations related to the Sabbath. As the state's regulatory power has grown over the past century in combination with increasing religious pluralism in both cases, claims to exemption have become a dominant flashpoint in the evolution of benevolent secularism.[37]

This three-part conceptualization distinguishes benevolent secularism from other institutional configurations of religion–state relations. Differentiation of religion and state distinguishes benevolent secularism from even relatively liberal forms of official religious establishment found in places such as the United Kingdom. Benevolent secularism also stands apart from Kuru's assertive and passive secularisms. Whereas his assertive secularism "mean[s] that the state excludes religion from the public sphere" and passive secularism "requires that the secular state play a 'passive' role in avoiding the establishment of any religion,"[38] benevolent secularism explicitly promotes cooperation among state and religious bodies. Cooperation between religion and state sets off benevolent secularism from passive secularism's more laissez-faire approach to the religious marketplace. Benevolent secular institutions do not simply let religious forces jockey among themselves for privately available funding and support. Cooperation and principled distance contrast benevolent secularism with assertive secularism, which subordinates religion to state and coerces religious institutions. Assertive secularism in Turkey permitted material funding of religious

TABLE 1.2. DIMENSIONS AND INDICATORS OF BENEVOLENT
SECULARISM VERSUS PASSIVE AND ASSERTIVE SECULARISM

	Benevolent	Passive	Assertive
Dimension 1: Differentiation			
Disestablishment	Yes	Yes	Yes
Dimension 2: Cooperation			
Material Support (e.g., for education)	Yes	No	Yes
Policy Consultation (e.g., on family law)	Yes	No	No
Dimension 3: Principled Distance			
Impartial Access to Public Support	Yes	Yes	No
Religious Exemptions/Autonomy	Yes	No	No

institutions, for example, but there was no autonomy of these institutions from state control.

Table 1.2 summarizes this conceptualization of benevolent secularism. The combination set out earlier is an ideal type; a concrete case may blend varieties of secularism. Indeed, one could argue that secularism in the United States, especially in areas related to state funding of religious nonprofits, has become more benevolent in recent years. The concrete cases that ground this book are themselves imperfect matches to the benevolent ideal type at times, as discussed in more detail later. Although a match may be imperfect, concrete cases can still approximate the benevolent model, and this particular configuration of religion–state relations has unique implications for the preferences of relevant actors both at critical junctures and over time.

INSTITUTIONAL EFFECTS: LINKING BENEVOLENT SECULARISM TO ACTORS AND COALITIONS

Saying that institutions matter begs the question of how these institutions have a causal effect on the place of religion in democratic politics. This question is implicit in path-dependent accounts of political institutions but is largely unexamined in the context of religion–state relations. I argue that institutions matter in shaping the interests of a diverse, three-part coalition: secular elites in state and civil society, the religious majority, and religious minority groups. Institutions increase the likelihood of the twin tolerations during both periods of secular emergence and evolution. First, at critical junctures of secular emergence, benevolent secularism shapes preferences within each of these blocs by empowering those most disposed to accept the twin tolerations. Second, during periods of secular evolution, benevolent secularism reduces the likelihood of institutional breakdown by promoting alliances *across* elite blocs, bridging religious-secular and interfaith divides. Institutions have this effect by encouraging iterated interactions across these divides that transmit information, build normative consensus, and promote shared interests. The secularism trap largely presupposes sharp divides among these groups at the elite level, but benevolent secularism reduces divisions and builds mutually credible commitments to the twin tolerations over time.

In the context of a single predominant religious community, we can think of three blocs bargaining about the relationship between religion and democracy: the majority religion, secular state and civil society elites, and smaller religious minorities. Benevolent secular institutions give each bloc in this coalition a reason to stick with the twin tolerations. Although the effects are distinct, they in general encourage a "mutual self-limitation"; neither religious nor secular blocs will use their full material capabilities to violate the twin tolerations.[39] Benevolent secularism's precise impact within each bloc is distinct. In what follows, I trace these internal effects and then illustrate how these *within*-group effects shape alliances *across* the diverse parts of this coalition by bridging religious-secular divides and improving interfaith relations.

Institutions can shape preferences because, to borrow from Stepan's work, religious traditions are "multivocal."[40] That is to say, even in the context of a single predominant religious community, there are inevitable internal divisions regarding the appropriate public role for that community. These kinds of internal divisions also exist on the side of political elites, some of whom have anticlerical beliefs, whereas others are more open to a collaborative role for religion in democratic life. Within each bloc, benevolent institutions empower those willing to seek the twin tolerations. Multivocality thus provides a crucial condition for disarming the secularism trap. Each of these groups—religious majority, minorities, and political elites—faces distinct material and normative incentives to accept the institutional bargain of a benevolent secularism.[41]

Within the majority religion, benevolent institutions shape preferences by empowering "pious secularists"—that is, those who are personally religious but prefer to maintain distance between religion and state. Members of the religious majority do not need to be enthusiastic liberals to find this bargain appealing. Rather, pious secularists are "[those] hostile to worldliness and the kinds of compromise which the established [religion] has to make with the state."[42] This skepticism of state authority makes formal religious establishment less appealing precisely because state authority is likely to corrupt the religious community's legitimacy. This religious orientation to the political exists in a range of religious traditions. As Charles Hirschkind describes Egypt's Muslim pietist revival, "Opinions in regard to the state [range] from outright condemnation, to distrust and ambivalence, to indifference."[43] David Martin points out that pietist movements are vibrant in Christian-majority states as well, with Pentecostalism "indigenizing" the pietist tradition in Latin America.[44] Other pious secularists may simply be risk averse and realize that religious control of state institutions may quickly morph into state control of religious bodies or empower alternative centers of religious power to challenge the pious secularists' own clerical authority.[45] Benevolent secularism preserves a role for what José Casanova has called "public religion" and reassures religious elites that state leaders will not turn anticlerical and use state power to repress religious institutions.[46] In its combination of cooperation and differentiation, benevolent secularism strengthens the hand of these pious secularists within the majority faith community by diminishing religious fears of anticlerical repression and preserving a public role for religion in democratic life.

The pious secularists' gains come at the expense of religious integralists within the majority. The latter group would seek formal religious establishment and the breakdown of any principled distance among religious communities. For example, the Comité islamique pour la réforme du Code de la famille au Sénégal (CIRCOFS) builds its advocacy around a closer integration of Senegal's family law with aspects of the Islamic legal tradition. However, in the context of benevolent secularism, such integralism seems unnecessary even to a predominant majority. After all, religious establishment ties religious institutions to the mire of day-to-day political life and thus poses a threat to religious legitimacy. Religious establishment comes with a range of costs, from the risk that political elites will use establishment to control religious institutions to the threat of religious complicity in corrupt state institutions. Rationalist assumptions that a religious majority will push for control of state institutions underestimate these costs. Integralism comes with its own costs, and its advocates must make their case within the religious majority. Benevolent secular institutions empower those religious actors who prefer the state at arm's length. As time passes, benevolent secularism promotes a generation of religious leaders who have learned to cooperate with state institutions while respecting the twin tolerations. Thus, even if religious integralist movements emerge, the most prominent religious elites have normative and material interests in protecting the benevolent terms of the secular bargain.

Benevolent secular institutions affect debates among secular state and civil society elites in a different manner. This bloc is made up of elected officials, members of the state bureaucracy, as well as policy advocates who work on areas related to the religion–state relationship but are not themselves representatives of a religious community. These individuals frequently are state officials in some way, but they may also operate in civil society. This bloc can be a center of anticlericalism,[47] but it may also contain accommodationists who have no hostility to religion as such. Accommodationists hold a stronger hand under conditions of benevolent secularism for two reasons. First, differentiation diminishes the risk of religious capture of state institutions. Although differentiation is partially symbolic, it plays an important role in addressing the credible commitment problem highlighted by rationalist theorists such as Kalyvas. Differentiation was important to political elites drafting the Commonwealth Constitution of 1935 in the Philippines, for instance, not because of its immediate material consequences but because it sent a credible signal that the Catholic Church intended to respect the autonomy of state institutions. Second, the cooperation encouraged by benevolent secularism commits religious communities to iterated interactions with the state, wherein they negotiate a public place for religion without seeking formal control of the policy process. Cooperation between government and religious charities can aid in the provision of social services and build effectiveness for low-capacity states.

Benevolent secularism reduces support for anticlericalism among the secular state and civil society bloc because the forcible repression of the religious community seems like an unnecessary expenditure of state resources. Again, anticlericalism comes with its own costs even to secularists, whether in the form of coercion of the religious majority, international disapproval of such exclusion, or the less-coercive but similarly costly decision to take on tasks such as education and health-care provision without contributions from the religious community. As institutions evolve, the state sinks significant costs into these collaborations, so even anticlerical elites face obstacles in overturning benevolent institutional structures. Those in Ireland who wish to eliminate the religious influence on primary education, for instance, face substantial material obstacles after decades of religion–state cooperation in areas such as curricular design and teacher training. Under such conditions, strong material incentives strengthen patterns of cooperation as states sink costs into religion–state cooperation. Anticlericalism becomes a luxury rather than a necessity for secular elites.

For religious minorities, benevolent secularism affects the internal strategic debate between those who back interfaith engagement and those who advocate defensive separatism from public life. Although minorities find themselves in somewhat vulnerable positions in the context of a predominant religious majority, their leaders still have agency in their response to this social location. Should they withdraw from public life or engage with the religious majority? Benevolent secularism empowers advocates of interfaith engagement by drawing minority leaders into public partnerships and cementing their place in democratic life over time.[48] The principled distance that benevolent secularism maintains among religious communities gives minorities solid footing for legal claims if discrimination arises. Discriminatory policies would violate constitutionally guaranteed rights protections, and benevolent secularism gives minorities firmer standing for appeals for justice. For example, as Muslims in Ireland push for legal accommodation, they draw on a long history of Irish rights protections for small religious minorities to make their case to both policy makers and courts. Moreover, benevolent secular institutions build the minority community's social visibility and promote its shared interests with members of the religious majority around issues such as social service provision. Including minorities in state policy consultations—for example, Senegal's ongoing state–Muslim–Catholic collaboration to fight the transmission of HIV/AIDS—reinforces the place of multiple religions in the commonweal and builds partnerships among religious activists. Minorities remain in a vulnerable position, of course, but benevolent secularism strengthens their legal claims to protection and promotes elite interfaith cooperation.

Minority advocates of interfaith engagement face an internal challenge from those advancing defensive separatism in public life. Defensive separatists worry, often with historical precedent, that the opening of democratic politics will empower the religious majority and inevitably lead to a curtailing of the minority's religious liberty. When the separatists' view carries the day, an alliance between minorities and secularists substantially increases the likelihood of the secularism trap as secular elites promise the minority protection in exchange for the minority's support of their nondemocratic rule. However, benevolent secularism emphasizes the costs that this posture brings to minority communities. The turn to defensive separatism leaves a minority in a vulnerable social position, open to charges of collusion with antidemocratic opponents of the religious majority. Under conditions of benevolent secularism, this cost seems less justifiable. A turn to defensive separatism would also cut minority communities off from cooperation with state institutions that is both materially rewarding and in keeping with the ethical priorities of many minority elites. Again, minorities may face an unpalatable choice, but benevolent secularism offers strong material and normative incentives for advocates of interfaith engagement.

Table 1.3 summarizes these institutional effects within coalition blocs. Each effect corresponds to a testable hypothesis about the impact of institutional

TABLE 1.3. INSTITUTIONAL EFFECTS WITHIN COALITION BLOCS

Coalition Partner	Institutional Effect	Example
Religious Majority	Empower pious secularists and weaken religious integralists	Acceptance of disestablishment from Ireland's Catholic hierarchy in Constitution of 1937
Secular Elites	Empower accommodation and weaken anticlericals	Diminished anti-Catholicism during debates over Philippine's Commonwealth Constitution of 1935
Religious Minorities	Empower interfaith engagement and weaken defensive isolation	Engagement of Senegal's Catholic hierarchy in development of postindependence laïcité

design within coalition blocs at critical junctures. For instance, benevolent secular institutions should cause a decline in anticlerical sentiment among secular elites. Similar institutions should correspond with the growth of pious secularism among the religious majority. These hypotheses flow in the other direction as well. For example, institutional steps away from benevolent secularism should distress minority communities and drive them out of public partnerships into more separatist postures.

A key claim of this theory is that similar effects, in the context of a single dominant religious community, are less likely under other institutional varieties of secularism. More assertive secularism is likely to empower integralists within the majority religious community and thus render the secularism trap more likely. Even more passive takes on state secularism, however, are unlikely to have the same internal effects. It is the explicitly positive cooperation between religion and state that draws the religious community into supporting the twin tolerations. Furthermore, it is the cooperation between religion and state that promotes a generation of both state and religious elites who have a vested interest in maintaining mutual restraint between religion and state. Benevolent secularism plays a unique institutional role in building religious and state advocates for the twin tolerations.

It is reasonable to ask if these institutional effects operate only within certain preexisting conditions. One may accept Stepan's arguments about multivocality while also pointing to limits on internal diversity within religious and secular communities. Surely there are some internal religious debates that political institutions cannot decisively swing. Do the effects of benevolent secularism depend on the preexisting dominance of pious secularists among the religious majority, for example, or on the preexisting weakness of anticlericalism among secular elites in the state and civil society? This is a serious question, with both theoretical and real-world implications. It is likely that certain preexisting conditions would limit institutional effects on securing the twin tolerations. To a certain extent, research design responds to this challenge; choosing least likely cases for the twin tolerations foregrounds cases where blocs of both religious and secular elites demonstrated an interest in religious integralism or anticlericalism, respectively, and permits a tracing of institutional effects over time even on those who seemed resistant to the twin tolerations. In other words, it is important to study cases in which the twin tolerations did not seem a predetermined outcome either to actors at critical junctures in history or according to leading alternative explanations. At another level, the challenge of preexisting conditions should be seen as an opportunity for further research into the coalition politics of religion and democracy. Making sense of instances where institutions fail to operate would mark further progress in understanding debates within both religious and secular blocs as well as the mechanisms linking institutions to these debates. Maintaining this sort of focus on internal debates and links between institutions and actor preferences would mark significant progress in the ongoing research agenda of making sense of the place of religion in modern democratic politics.

These within-group institutional effects are central to secular emergence, but the structure of benevolent secularism remains a central force shaping political outcomes as the relationship between religion and democracy moves to phases of secular evolution. The relative flexibility of secular institutions decreases the likelihood of institutional collapse, but benevolent secularism remains vulnerable to various challenges, from intensified anticlericalism to unexpected religious pluralization. Institutional features such as differentiation, cooperation, and principled distance require constant interpretation in application to concrete political cases. The structure of benevolent secularism plays an independent role in promoting the future stability of these institutions during periods of secular evolution. Institutions have this effect by promoting iterated interactions that transmit information, build normative consensus, and promote shared material interests across these divides.

Benevolent secularism structures periods of institutional change because the within-group effects on actor preferences at critical junctures in turn encourage cross-cutting coalition alliances that increase mutual credibility of commitments to the twin tolerations over time. Two alliances are most important in stabilizing institutions as they face new challenges: bridging potential religious-secular divides and improving interfaith relations. Although these alliances may exist in an initial form during the critical juncture of secular emergence, they are especially important in analyzing the periods of institutional change that take place after the critical juncture draws to a close. By promoting these alliances, benevolent secularism takes on its path-dependent nature over time, even in the face of challenges from new pluralism, religious revivals, or a burst of anticlericalism.

Promoting diverse coalition alliances is crucial as existing institutions face new challenges. A range of recent scholarship has highlighted the threat posed by religious-secular divisions, using such fissures to explain anti-Americanism, authoritarian resilience, variation in social service structure, and the emergence of religious political parties.[49] Fox's "religious-secular competition perspective" has traced the importance of such tensions in a wide range of settings in the past quarter century.[50] Although a sharp religious-secular divide has serious political consequences, benevolent secularism can reduce its extent over time. With pious secularists in control of the religious majority and the most vocal anticlericals out of influence among political elites, the religious-secular divide becomes quite manageable. This alliance forms through the concrete workings of benevolent secularism, particularly in the patterns of cooperation between the religious majority and parts of the state bureaucracy. Material cooperation in the educational realm, for example, requires extensive bureaucracies that draw on both religious leaders and members of the state bureaucracy to transmit information, build confidence, and develop shared interests. Consultation in the policy realm builds networks of both religious and secular policy experts accustomed to the combination of differentiation, cooperation, and principled distance that makes up benevolent secularism. Cooperation on public-health projects in Senegal, for instance, built networks of religious and state experts who later put their expertise to work on newer challenges such as AIDS responsiveness and also served as voices protecting benevolent secularism when it came under threat in the past decade. In this institutional context, even when challenges arise, these groups have a strong interest in working together to have religion–state institutions evolve rather than in encouraging institutional breakdown and replacement.

The second coalition alliance operates in a similar but distinct manner to stabilize institutions during periods of secular evolution. Because pious secularists among the religious majority see differentiation between religion and state as beneficial to religion itself, they are less likely to advance state policies that discriminate against religious minorities. Members of the religious minority prefer pious secularists to more integralist portions of the religious majority and have an incentive to cultivate warm relations with this portion of the majority community. Cooperation in policy consultations builds relationships across religious boundaries that strengthen interfaith relations as a whole. For instance, many of the same religious actors who consult with the Senegalese state on matters of good governance are also practitioners of nonpolitical Islamic–Catholic dialogue outside of these state consultations. Benevolent secularism furthermore gives religious minorities incentive to seek strong interfaith relations because allies in the religious majority can be important bridge builders with political elites. The Irish Muslim community, for instance, has benefitted from its generally strong ties to the Catholic Church as Catholic authorities have encouraged the state to fund Muslim education. The arrival of new religious minorities is one of the stiffest challenges to the stability of secular institutions. Strong interfaith relations encourage secular institutions to evolve and manage new pluralism rather than allow pluralism to bring about institutional breakdown.

Of course, over time it is possible that these coalition alliances can deteriorate in spite of the general effect of benevolent secular institutions. Institutional structure should fortify these alliances over time, but my argument is not deterministic. After critical junctures, forces exogenous to institutional structure, such as rapid social change, the collapse of a coalition bloc, and even interstate war, could weaken coalition alliances and hamper secular evolution. If coalition alliances cease to operate, we should expect that secular institutions will not successfully evolve in the face of new challenges but will rather be formally replaced by some other variety of religion–state relations. In this case, coalition dynamics would be causally responsible for institutional breakdown.

These claims about the role of institutional structure in driving secular evolution generate observable implications. First, in the presence of a minimal religious-secular divide and strong interfaith relations, challenges to benevolent secularism should result in secular evolution rather than in institutional breakdown and formal replacement. The converse expectation should be true as well. If religious-secular divides grow and interfaith relations break down, challenges to benevolent secularism should lead to institutional breakdown and the replacement of some or all of benevolent secularism's three components by some alternative institutional configuration. Second, the strength of religious-secular and interfaith ties should, in part, be due to the workings of benevolent secularism, in particular its role in structuring elite relationships that result in iterated interactions, exchange of information, and cultivation of shared norms regarding the place of religion in public life.

Although the hypotheses regarding secular emergence and evolution generated from this institutional approach are focused on elite-level politics, they also imply claims about support for benevolent secularism among the general public. Each of the elite hypotheses set out in table 1.3, for instance, comes with observable implications in public opinion data, if such data were available from critical junctures of secular emergence. During periods of secular evolution, the coalition alliances by which secular institutions evolve in the contemporary period have similarly observable implications for opinion among the general public. For example, the hypothesized minimal religious-secular divide could be traced by comparing opinion on questions of religion–state relations among both the devout and the nonreligious. Likewise, the hypothesized role of strong interfaith relations in facilitating secular evolution should be visible in the general public. Religious majorities and minorities should actually share common ground in their opinion of principled distance and differentiation. The empirical chapters in this book make an initial attempt at testing these hypotheses with public opinion data as well as with elite sources.

Figures 1.1 and 1.2 succinctly summarize this theoretical account of benevolent secularism's effects on the politics of religion. They illustrate the argument's core logic, although it should be understood as making probabilistic rather than determinate claims. All else equal, benevolent secular institutions should be expected to make certain outcomes more likely, during both periods of secular emergence and periods of evolution. At critical junctures when the secularism trap seems most threatening, benevolent secularism is one institutional option for the future of religion–state relations. Choosing benevolent secularism has effects within each part of the secular coalition and in turn encourages alliances that bridge the religious-secular divide and improve interfaith relations even after critical junctures. Institutions have a direct effect on actor preferences at

Initial condition	Benevolent secularism?	Within-group effect	Outcome
Critical juncture (political transition and mobilized religious majority)	Yes	Pious secularists / Secular accommodation / Engaged minorities	Twin tolerations
	No	Religious integralists / Anticlericalism / Defensive minorities	Secularism trap

FIGURE 1.1. BENEVOLENT SECULARISM AND SECULAR EMERGENCE.

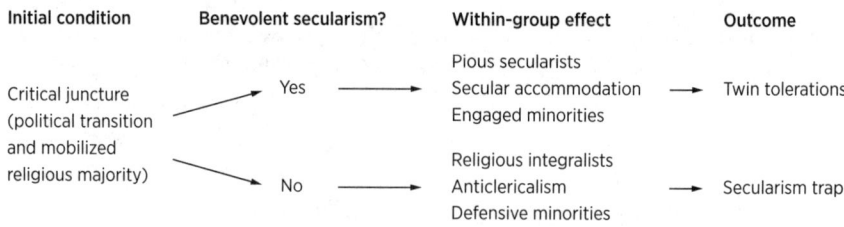

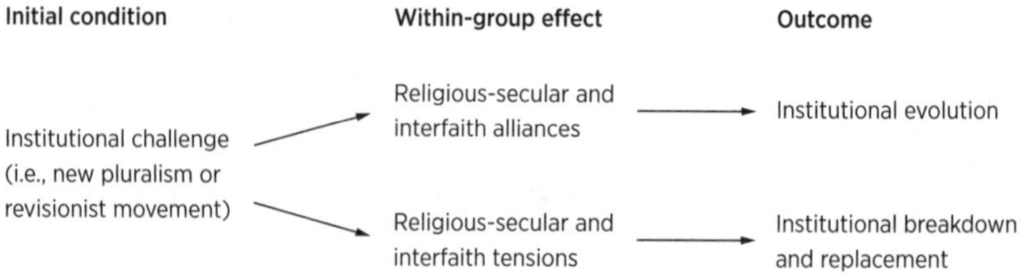

FIGURE 1.2. BENEVOLENT SECULARISM AND INSTITUTIONAL CHANGE.

critical junctures and are indirectly responsible for secular evolution over time through their impact on coalition alliances.

CASE SELECTION AND ASSESSING THE IMPACT OF INSTITUTIONAL STRUCTURE

Given this argument, how might one assess evidence of institutional influence on the relationship between religion and democracy? I employ two case-selection strategies to test the framework both at critical junctures and over the course of secular evolution. Regarding the critical juncture of secular emergence, I select least likely cases for the twin tolerations according to the leading alternative theories described earlier in this chapter. In other words, these cases are ones that would have seemed to many to be unpromising candidates for reconciling religion and democracy but that share the institutional characteristics of benevolent secularism.[51] During the period of secular evolution, these cases have faced distinct threats to the stability of the twin tolerations. On a global scale, religion has seized scholarly attention for a variety of reasons, from rising anticlericalism in some areas to religious fundamentalism in others. It is both theoretically and empirically important to understand how institutions have responded to a diverse set of challenges. I draw on three states—Ireland, Senegal, and the Philippines—to meet these two selection goals. As discussed in the substantive chapters that follow, each of these states approximates the three dimensions of benevolent secularism, although each imperfectly fulfills the ideal type. Ireland, for example, is weakest in its maintenance of differentiation. Principled distance in the Philippines has not always been robust, particularly when it comes to the Muslim community. On the whole, these differences are ones of degree rather than type. Each stands as an example of benevolent secularism.

Although empirical evidence is presented from across these three countries, the logic of inference more closely resembles that of within-case process tracing.[52] As Alexander George and Andrew Bennett summarize this within-case approach, "[Inference] focuses not on the analysis of variables across cases, but on the causal path in a single case."[53] Within each case, I present evidence documenting first the mechanisms through which benevolent secularism shapes dynamics within religious and secular blocs during periods of secular emergence and then how institutions have an impact on the strength of religious-secular and interfaith ties over time. To give one concrete example, evidence indicates that preferences within Ireland's Catholic hierarchy toward religion's place in the Constitution of 1937 were different before and after benevolent secular institutions were proposed in negotiations.

One further goal motivates this case selection. The Philippines, Ireland, and Senegal vary in their majority religious community (Catholic, Catholic, and Muslim, respectively), and yet they all have managed to stabilize the twin tolerations for extended periods of time. Comparing benevolent secularism's impact across the cases provides insight into how similar institutions may operate across civilizational boundary lines. The comparison builds on Casanova's suggestion that the twentieth century's *aggiornamento* between Catholicism and democracy may have parallels in today's religion–state dynamics in the Muslim-majority world.[54]

A brief orientation about these countries helps crystallize their place in the research design. In Ireland, the critical juncture of secular emergence is the late Free State period as the country moved to full independence in the years leading up to the Constitution of 1937. During this time, political institutions of all types, including those structuring the relationship between religion and state, were in flux, and many worried that the Catholic majority would use independence to violate minority rights and establish Catholicism as a state religion. The period of secular evolution in Ireland has been more extended, stretching from a constitutional amendment in 1972 to the present day, with a focus on institutional developments since the revelation of clergy sex abuse and the rapid decline of the Irish Catholic Church. How have political institutions endured the growing appeal of anticlericalism in modern Ireland?

In Senegal, the critical juncture of secular emergence took place as the country moved to full independence with the breakup of France's West African empire after World War II. Debates came to a head around 1960 as President Léopold Sédar Senghor consolidated his rule. During this juncture, the Muslim majority enjoyed significant public influence, and some clerics pushed for the official incorporation of sharia into civil law. The period of secular evolution in Senegal peaked during the rule of President Abdoulaye Wade, who came to power in 2000 and ruled until 2012. During this period, Wade mounted an unprecedented challenge to benevolent secularism in an attempt to build his own political power base. How have institutions in Senegal endured a period of religious vitality and renewed calls for religious integralism and a breakdown in principled distance?

In the Philippines, secular emergence focused on the late American colonial period, in particular the Commonwealth Constitutional Convention of 1934. The Catholic Church had enjoyed official religious establishment until 1898 under Spanish colonialism, and many worried that political independence would bring with it a return to the fusion of religion and state. The more gradual process of secular evolution in the Philippines began with the religious opposition to the dictatorship of Ferdinand Marcos in the mid-1980s and continues to this day. Muslims in Mindanao have claimed religious discrimination by the Catholic majority; Charismatic Christian preachers have diversified the religious landscape; and reproductive health legislation has divided Catholic and secular advocacy groups. How have institutions responded to this fragmentation of the Philippine religious landscape?

At the critical juncture of secular emergence, the Philippines, Ireland, and Senegal were all least likely cases for arriving at the twin tolerations according to the three alternative explanations set out earlier. They thus provide tough tests for the impact of benevolent secular institutions. For rational choice theorists, each had a dominant religion that could have used state institutions to freeze out potential competition. Catholicism in Ireland and the Philippines at independence and Islam in Senegal after World War II commanded the allegiance of more than four out of five citizens.[55] Theories of religious moderation would also point to the likelihood of the secularism trap. In each, a significant bloc of political elites worried that democracy could inadvertently lead to a kind of theocracy. Catholic elites in Ireland and the Philippines shared a pre–Vatican II skepticism of liberalism, and the Sufi brotherhoods that dominated Senegalese Islamic life were centered in rural heartlands removed from the more liberal, urbanized portions of the Senegalese population. Predictions flowing from modernization theory would be similarly bleak for these states at independence, as each struggled with underdevelopment and limited state provision of social services. Religiosity was high in each, and economic development had made no progress in weakening the authority of religious institutions. In short, if ever the secularism trap was set, it should have been in Dublin of the 1930s, Manila of the 1930s, and Dakar of the 1950s.

Although the cross-case research design increases confidence in my hypothesized institutional effects, the causal impact of institutional structure on actor preferences during secular emergence is tested by careful within-case process tracing. Archival and secondary-source research into these periods can test whether institutional debates during these junctures had the hypothesized effects on each of the three blocs: the religious majority, political elites, and religious minorities. In short, we should observe the coalition effects set out in table 1.3 as elites in each case considered alternatives to benevolent secularism during the critical juncture.

If the cases are all least likely for the twin tolerations at secular emergence, they have come under diverse challenges since the critical juncture came to a close. Thus, the analysis of secular evolution across these cases shows how coalition alliances across the religious-secular divide and interfaith boundaries have responded to an array of challenges to the mutual credibility of commitments to the twin tolerations. Senegal's recent history demonstrates the challenges posed by partisan manipulation of a predominant religious community. Ireland's past quarter century, in contrast, highlights the response of a coalition

TABLE 1.4. CASE CONFIGURATION DURING SECULAR EMERGENCE

	Secular Emergence		
Case	Religion–State Institutions	Alternative Explanations	Outcome of Interest
Senegal	Benevolent Secularism	Modernization: low development Rational Choice: dominant religious majority Moderation: weak religious liberals	Twin Tolerations
Philippines	Benevolent Secularism	Modernization: low development Rational Choice: dominant religious majority Moderation: weak religious liberals	Twin Tolerations
Ireland	Benevolent Secularism	Modernization: low development Rational Choice: dominant religious majority Moderation: weak religious liberals	Twin Tolerations

to revived anticlericalism. And in the Philippines, the post-Marcos consensus between religion and state has given way to the pluralization of religious leaders and social tensions among Muslim, Catholic, and secular elites. These cases, then, which shared many characteristics at independence, illustrate how coalition mechanisms have responded to diverse opportunities for institutional breakdown and replacement.

Table 1.4 summarizes the place of each case at secular emergence. Although a different set of cases would be appropriate to test the causes of complete breakdown in the twin tolerations, careful comparative analysis and within-case tracing of the hypothesized institutional effects demonstrates the effect of benevolent secularism on the tense relationship between religion and democracy, even in a challenging set of cases.

DATA COLLECTION

This project brings a diverse array of empirical evidence to bear in documenting the hypothesized effects of benevolent secularism. Overall, archival and secondary sources provide qualitative data to examine the impact of benevolent secularism at historical critical junctures, and interviews and survey data test the hypothesized impact of benevolent secularism on religious-secular and interfaith alliances over time. In practice, there is overlap between the categories of qualitative research. Interviews point to useful historical archives and data sources, and modern archives from nongovernmental organizations (NGOs) provide important evidence of contemporary secular evolution. Although I describe the data sources as distinct, I have used them in a similar manner throughout the project: to document the effect of institutions on actor preferences and coalition alliances. Table 1.5 summarizes the qualitative sources in the project. I collected archival and interview materials in Senegal in the summer of 2010, in the Philippines in the summer of 2010 and the summer of 2014, and in Ireland in the summer of 2011.

Archival research is especially important in documenting dynamics during periods of secular emergence. Secondary case studies provide information on the case-based histories of religion–state relations, in particular on how the boundary between the state and religious institutions changed at critical

TABLE 1.5. SUMMARY OF TYPES OF QUALITATIVE EVIDENCE USED

Source	State	Religious	Civil Society
Archival Materials	Records of constitutional debates and legal cases *Example*: Journal of the Philippine Constitutional Commission of 1986	Religious elite correspondence with political bodies *Example*: McQuaid Papers, Archives of the Archdiocese of Dublin	Documentation of programs linking with religious actors *Example*: Meeting notes of the Assises nationales, Senegal
Elite Interviews	Elected officials and policy makers in religion-related policy areas *Example*: "Among Ed" Panlilio, former governor, Pampanga, Philippines	Religious elites active in public affairs and relations to state *Example*: Most Reverend Diarmuid Martin, archbishop of Dublin	Organizations involved in policy areas relevant to religious communities *Example*: Boubacar Seck, executive director, Conseil des ONG d'appui au développement, Dakar

junctures of secular emergence. Primary-source archival research provides important additional evidence, specifically more detailed documentation of relevant debates than most secondary sources. Information from correspondence between elites, for example, provides unique evidence that institutions are having their hypothesized effect within and across coalition blocs. Although the risk of data mining still exists, adding archival work to secondary historiography increases confidence in data reliability throughout the project. Some highlights from archival research in the Philippines illustrate the contribution of archival work to the study. The records of the Constitutional Convention of 1934 and the Constitutional Commission of 1986 document extended debates regarding the place of religion within the Philippine Republic. Delegates debated the separation between the Catholic Church and the state, the place of religion in the educational system, and the freedom of individual conscience. A Jesuit priest, Father Joaquin Bernas, served on the Constitutional Commission of 1986, and his notes on the proceedings shed light on the internal divisions among Catholic leaders on the commission as well as patterns of agreement and disagreement among Catholic, Muslim, and Protestant commission delegates. In each case, archival materials, in particular the more recent archives of civil society organizations working on issues that touch on religion's place in public life, also contributed to the study of secular evolution.

Elite interviews provide crucial data to test the coalition alliances that drive secular evolution. The field interview sample consists of three groups that roughly correspond to the three parts of the secular coalition: religious leaders from majority and minority groups, judicial/governmental officials responsible for policy development in this area, and members of civil society organizations that work on policy issues related to the religious community. Each of these groups is relevant to testing distinct hypotheses related to secular emergence and evolution. In addition to this particular goal, interviews gathered material to distinguish between the various alternative explanations of how institutions of secularism emerged and have developed over time. Court cases or policy decisions may give a sense of how institutions of secularism have evolved over time, but interviews provide the most appropriate strategy for assessing the causes of such institutional development. Interviews proved immensely useful in understanding how several alternative explanations may actually interrelate in a given case—for instance, how the impact of economic development has actually been channeled through coalition alliances.

The final data source turns from qualitative methods to statistical survey research. The survey analysis in each case provides a test of whether the coalition effects traced at the elite level have any analogue among the general population. How popular are the values of benevolent secularism with the general population? Is there evidence that religious-secular and interfaith alliances documented in elite interviews exist within the broader public? Within the broader research design, public opinion analysis tracks the social conditions that are shaped by and in turn exert influence on the institutional relationship between religion and state. To test the framework's implications among the general public, I turn to analysis of existing public opinion data from Ireland, the Philippines, and Senegal. As I discuss when introducing the public opinion analysis in each case, the International Social Survey Programme (ISSP) and the Pew Forum on Religion and Public Life have conducted polling that directly investigates attitudes on minority rights, religious pluralism, and the appropriate role of religious actors in public debates.

2. Secular Emergence in Ireland

HOME RULE AND ROME RULE?

Among the papers of Archbishop John Charles McQuaid in Dublin is a slim volume signed simply "To Q, From Éamon de Valera."[1] Many have noted McQuaid's relationship with Ireland's preeminent independence leader, so the book, among the papers related to the Constitution of 1937, is no particular surprise. What de Valera sent to his clerical colleague is more unusual: a copy of the Constitution of the United States of America. Why would a Catholic prelate compared to Ayatollah Khameini by an *Irish Times* columnist in 2009 appreciate the gift of a secular constitution from a Protestant-majority state?[2]

A careful understanding of the secularity of Ireland's Constitution of 1937, which McQuaid advised (to mixed effect) and de Valera counted among his greatest achievements, offers some insight into this gift. Although it would clearly be inaccurate to equate Irish secularism with French *laïcité*, it is no truer to argue that Irish secularism was a facade for theocracy.[3] Irish elites instead instituted a version of benevolent secularism, with its characteristic combination of differentiation, cooperation, and principled distance, as the country transitioned to full independence from colonial rule. As Bill Kissane puts it, "The balance between religious and secular influences was not a case of either/or for the [Irish] constitutional drafters."[4] Benevolent secularism influenced preferences about the relationship between religion and politics in independent

Ireland, in particular giving firmer footing to pious secularists within the Catholic community and drawing minorities into public life. These institutions remained open to manipulation in implementation, and calls for integration of church and state persisted within Irish Catholicism. Nonbelievers in particular had good cause to complain that the state made an effort to accommodate religious minorities but had a less-coherent approach to nonreligious individuals. With that said, on the whole the institutions proposed in the Constitution of 1937 cemented a diverse coalition of political elites, Catholic clerics, and religious minorities that continues to stabilize the twin tolerations in Ireland nearly a century later. In comparative context, Ireland at independence serves as an important reminder that religious elites need not be religious liberals to consent to benevolent secularism. Moreover, postindependence tensions in Ireland indicate that benevolent secular institutions do have a dark side. They remain subject to manipulation and are certainly no cure-all for contention over religion and politics.

This chapter focuses on the emergence of Irish secularism and on how the dimensions of benevolent secularism shaped preferences among a coalition of political elites, Catholic prelates, and religious minorities. The period leading up to 1937 provided a critical juncture because institutional links between religion and state were up for grabs after centuries of British rule.[5] The British had gradually increased the freedom of the Catholic majority in legislation from the Catholic Relief Act of 1829 up to the Act for the Disestablishment of the Irish Church of 1869. Many worried that a move to full independence would bring Catholic retribution for past British abuses, enshrining Catholicism as a state religion so that "Home Rule means Rome Rule." The Irish Free State's Constitution of 1922 did no such thing but was crafted under more direct British influence through subordination to the Anglo-Irish Treaty of 1921. Surely, the skeptics worried, a document written without Britain's guiding hand would threaten religious minorities and break down state secularism. As Éamon de Valera consolidated his political power in the mid-1930s and made it clear that he and his supporters intended to draft a new constitution, these questions about the nature of religion–state relations in a fully independent Ireland came to a head. How could independent Ireland possibly secure the twin tolerations?

This chapter takes up this question and argues that the structure of benevolent secularism in Ireland helps to explain why the twin tolerations emerged and the secularism trap did not spring. The cooperative dimension of benevolent secularism appealed to Catholic elites, while differentiation and promises of principled distance alleviated anxieties among secular elites and religious minorities. The chapter moves forward in five parts. After a brief overview of the religious landscape in Ireland, I describe the main institutional dimensions of the secularism that emerged in Ireland around independence and argue that they featured the conjunction of differentiation, cooperation, and principled distance that corresponds to benevolent secularism.[6] Third, I demonstrate the effect that this institutional structure had on the preferences held by actors involved in religion–state relations. Fourth, I consider how leading alternative explanations of the twin tolerations contribute to understanding this period of secular emergence. Finally, I close with an episode that demonstrates the tensions within the institutions of the Constitution of 1937 tied to maintaining principled distance between religious communities: the Mother and Child Crisis around 1950. This event demonstrated the greatest challenge to the twin tolerations in Ireland over time: Would the social predominance of Catholicism mean that benevolent secularism simply set the stage for its de facto establishment as Ireland's state religion?

IRELAND'S RELIGIOUS LANDSCAPE

As Ireland approached independence in the interwar period, the Catholic Church was the predominant presence on the Irish religious landscape. Approximately 85 percent of the general population continues to self-report as Catholic, and although weekly mass attendance has substantially declined in the past quarter century, it remains significantly higher than in most of continental Europe. If anything, Catholic predominance during the independence period would have been a bit larger; the census of 1936 reported 93 percent of the population as Catholic.[7] Data from the ISSP wave in 2008 shows a higher percentage of Catholics in rural areas (roughly 90 percent) than in Dublin as well as higher mass attendance among country residents, but even in urban areas self-reported Catholics make up more than 80 percent of the general population.[8] This demographic dominance is only part of the story of Irish secularism, but it was certainly a central part in building what Tom Inglis has called the "moral monopoly" of the Irish Catholic Church in the first half of the twentieth century.[9]

The Catholic Church's role in public life rests not only on aggregate population numbers but also on its vast institutional network. The Irish Catholic Bishops' Conference is headquartered in Maynooth, outside of Dublin, and speaks for the hierarchy on matters of public life. In addition to the official hierarchy, the church's network of social service agencies, particularly in education and health care, is essential to making sense of the church's influence over both the population and the state as independence approached. As discussed in depth later in this chapter, the Catholic Church controls the patronage of the vast majority of schools in Ireland. The major institutions of the health-care sector show similar Catholic influence.[10] In both of these sectors, religious orders both male and female—organized through the Conference of Religious of Ireland—play as important a role as diocesan priests and the Bishops' Conference. Lay associations such as the St. Vincent de Paul Society and the Knights of Columbanus are a final piece of Catholic organizational life. These groups, although related to the hierarchy, have come to play a more independent role in the religion–state relationship through the second half of the twentieth century.

For all of the importance of Ireland's Catholic community, small but politically influential religious minorities have been a feature of Irish life since well before independence. Early nationalists such as Charles Stewart Parnell were often of Protestant stock, and even as nationalism became more closely aligned with Catholicism, nearly 200,000 Protestants were counted in the census of 1936. Many continue to come from one of the traditional Protestant churches, in particular the (Anglican) Church of Ireland, the Presbyterian Church in Ireland, and the Methodist Church in Ireland. In addition, a small Jewish community predated independence and has played an important role in the jurisprudence of religious liberty discussed in this chapter. With more recent economic growth, Ireland has attracted new religious diversity, notably a Muslim community that now approaches 50,000 in number. These minority communities, although certainly less politically visible than the Catholic community, have played a central role in the development of Irish secularism since independence. It is no great exaggeration to say that without Protestants both in Ireland and in Northern Ireland, the Constitution of 1937 may not have been secular at all.

A final demographic group that requires attention is made up of Irish who do not identify with a particular religious tradition. As will become apparent in chapter 3, today this group has come to play an unprecedented role in the development of Irish secularism. Census data from 1936 do not track forms of nonbelief or atheism, although the approximately 7,000 "others" likely included some humanists. Closer to the present, the ISSP's research in 2008 identified 8 percent of the population as having "no religion," and the census of 2006 revealed 180,000 with "no religion" and another 70,000 with "none stated," or approximately 7 percent.[11] This growth is remarkable and has political implications that I consider at length in chapter 3. However, at secular emergence, those who fell entirely outside of traditional religious denominations were of less importance in shaping constitutional institutions.

In sum, as Ireland moved to full independence, the Catholic Church's demographic and institutional dominance was unmistakable. However, even during this period of relative Catholic hegemony, Protestant minorities, a Jewish community, and even humanists were active presences in public life. It remained an open question how independence leaders would balance majority rule with the mutual restraint that characterizes the twin tolerations.

ASSESSING BENEVOLENT SECULARISM IN IRELAND

As in Senegal and the Philippines, the institutions of religion–state relations in Ireland at independence approximated benevolent secularism and its three dimensions: differentiation, cooperation, and principled distance. Stepan's twin tolerations were generally upheld, with state and religious bodies accepting a level of mutual distance well short of theocracy. At the same time, the secularism in Ireland bore little resemblance to the assertive *laïcité* of France or to its Kemalist cousin in Turkey. Moreover, the state did not simply remove itself from religious affairs in a passive manner. Rather, institutions of benevolent secularism actively supported the practice of religion in a variety of ways and explicitly charged the state with engaging religious institutions in public life.

While Ireland lurched to independence in the late 1920s, the official establishment of the Catholic Church as the one faith of independent Ireland was a live possibility. An initial constitutional draft "acknowledged . . . the Church of Christ as the Catholic Church."[12] As Justice Gerard Hogan points out, in 1937 the United Kingdom gave broad privileges to the Church of England; Norway forbade Jesuits from entering its territory; a range of Catholic countries formally privileged the Catholic Church; and anti-Semitism raged on the continent.[13] Religious establishment was a very real option during this period.

In spite of that possibility, the institutions that de Valera offered to the key actors in preparation for the Constitution of 1937 affirmed a basic differentiation of religion from state authority. Article 44.2.2 explicitly states, "The State guarantees not to endow any religion," which is an intentional echo of the Endowment Clauses of earlier British-directed documents, such as the Government of Ireland Act of 1920. Although the Endowment Clause is not a direct analogue to the Establishment Clause in the U.S. Constitution, its general effect ensured a similar basic differentiation of state and religious institutions.[14] The Irish state provides for religious ministry in prisons and the military but may not make "permanent financial provision out of taxation or otherwise."[15] This prohibition extends not only to single endowment of the Catholic Church but also to what Supreme Court justice Ronan Keane has called "concurrent endowment"—that is, endowing a set number of different religious denominations.[16]

A basic right to religious liberty for minorities accompanies the nonendowment provisions of the Constitution of 1937. Again, the language borrows heavily from earlier documents, in particular the Free State Constitution of 1922. Article 44.2.1 guarantees citizens "freedom of conscience and free profession and practice of religion [subject to public order]," and Article 44.2.3 forbids the state from imposing "any disabilities or any discrimination on the grounds of religious profession, belief or status." In 1937, Irish Protestants were particularly anxious to have their liberty of conscience protected in the Constitution, but these protections have also extended to Jews, Muslims, and others. As early as 1948, state orders regulating the sale of meat made exemptions for the Jewish community in consideration of kosher practice, and a variety of smaller minorities, including Muslims, have enjoyed religious liberty protections more recently.[17] Both in the letter of the Constitution of 1937 and in legal practice, the Irish state has protected basic religious liberty for both Catholics and smaller religious minorities.[18]

Although differentiation should not be taken for granted, particularly given the illiberal European climate in 1937, it only begins to capture Irish secularism. A more complete account must incorporate the other two dimensions of benevolent secularism: cooperation between religious and state institutions and the principled distance maintained between the state and the various religious communities. Cooperation between religion and state was central to de Valera's proposals in advance of the Constitution of 1937. In contrast to the Free State Constitution of 1922, which barely mentioned religion outside of endowment and liberty of conscience, the Constitution of 1937 institutionalized religion–state cooperation in both symbolic and material ways. Religious institutions are exempted from taxation, and Article 44.2.5 guarantees that "every religious denomination shall have the right to manage its own affairs." The state cooperates with religion not only in its charitable forms but even in the details of devotionalism. High Court justice Gavan Duffy defended the tax-deductible status of "a testamentary gift to found a convent for the perpetual adoration of the Blessed Sacrament" as, "beyond all doubt, a gift charitable at common law, because it is a gift to God" and thus in keeping with the state's constitutional obligations.[19] In short, de Valera's Constitution of 1937 went out of its way to avoid comparisons with anticlerical republican documents in continental Europe. The secular state was in part legitimized because of its cooperative relationship with religious institutions.

This cooperative understanding of secularism showed most concretely in two areas of the Constitution of 1937.[20] First of all, the educational realm in Ireland was by constitutional mandate deeply linked to religious communities.[21] Article 42.4 obligates the state to provide for free primary education "with due regard . . . especially in the matter of religious and moral formation." In application, this obligation has led to a system of primary education in which the state funds religiously owned and operated schools. While specific statistics fluctuate from year to year, more than 90 percent of the primary schools are Catholic in ethos, another 6 percent belong to various Protestant communities, and there are scattered Jewish and Muslim primary schools.[22] A small, but growing, share of schools are under the multidenominational Educate Together model, which is discussed in chapter 3. Religious education takes place during school hours, and teacher-training colleges such as the Mater Dei Institute are administered largely by the Catholic Church. Primary-school teachers must be willing to teach religious education in many settings, and the Employment Equality Acts of 1998–2008 permit religious institutions to discriminate in the hiring of teachers in order to preserve a school's religious ethos.[23] Although Article 44.2.4 allows children to attend religious schools while opting out of religious instruction, Irish courts have consistently held that the "religious ethos" of denominational schools may extend beyond the formal religious education sessions. The "integrated curriculum" means that religion may appear throughout the school day, as deemed in keeping with the school's religious ethos.

Second, cooperation between religion and state in the Constitution of 1937 showed through in the grounding of constitutional rights guarantees, particularly in the language regarding human dignity and the family. Article 41.1, on the family, begins by "recognizing the Family as the natural primary and fundamental unit group of Society, and as a moral institution possessing inalienable and imprescriptible rights, antecedent and superior to all positive law." In its original form, the article then went on to charge the state to "protect [the family] against attack" and to forbid any law "providing for the grant of a dissolution of marriage" (41.3). In Article 42, the acknowledgment of "the Family" as the "primary and natural educator of the child" protected by "inalienable right and duty" is a further example of the priority on the family that rests on natural law arguments so central to the Catholic social tradition. John Henry Whyte points out that the Constitution's provisions forbidding dissolution of marriage actually went beyond the Catholic Church's canon law position, which allowed annulments in certain circumstances.[24] Although the particular provisions regarding divorce have changed (as discussed in chapter 3), the role of Catholic thought in shaping the Constitution of 1937 still sheds light on the distinguishing features of secular institutions in independence-era Ireland: cooperative in treatment of religion, though barely maintaining principled distance among religious communities, given significant Catholic influence over political decisions.

Constitutional provisions regarding marriage are the most obvious religious influence, but it would be a mistake to reduce religious cooperation to issues tied up in the "culture war" in the United States. Whyte points out that the foundations of a range of rights enumerated in Articles 40–45 of the Constitution of 1937 "were obviously marked by Catholic thought."[25] These rights include, of course, the constitutional obligation to protect the human life of the unborn but also the obligation to build "a social order in which justice and charity shall inform all the institutions of social life." In 1937, debates about property rights and economic justice raged across Europe, and substantial religious influence shows through in constitutional provisions in areas related to the economic structure of Irish society. The treatment of private property in Article 43 owes much to the Catholic middle way between socialism and unrestrained liberal capitalism, with its recognition of "the natural right, antecedent to positive law, to the private ownership of external goods," coupled with the injunction that this right ought "to be regulated by the principles of social justice" and conducted in accordance with "the exigencies of the common good."[26]

Cooperation with religion extended from the Constitution's abstract principles to concrete patterns of policy consultation. In the years around independence, religious authorities exercised substantial influence on matters of policy formation related to morality. These matters included the Censorship of Publications Act of 1929 and the Public Dance Halls Act of 1935.[27] As Hogan points out, "Despite the occasional protests of certain non-Catholic members of the *Dáil* and Senate," such provisions easily passed into the laws in the generally conservative social climate of the time.[28] It is important that Catholic leaders frequently made common cause with Protestant colleagues in these moral crusades. The Censorship Board, for instance, included four Catholics and one Protestant,[29] and at a time of broad social conservatism the institutional Protestant churches were not about to expend their public sway advocating pornography.

Although formal differentiation and cooperation are easily traceable in the newly independent Ireland, the Irish state's principled distance among its religious communities was more tenuous. Article 44 toed the line of breaking down the principled distance between the Irish state and all of its religious communities. Section 1.2 is particularly important to quote in its entirety because those objecting to sectarianism in de Valera's constitution most typically cite it. It reads: "The State recognizes the special position of the Holy Catholic Apostolic and Roman Church as the guardian of the Faith professed by the great majority of the citizens." Section 1.3 then goes on to "recognize the Church of Ireland, the Presbyterian Church in Ireland, the Methodist Church in Ireland, the Religious Society of Friends in Ireland, as well as the Jewish Congregations and the other religious denominations existing in Ireland at the date of the coming into operation of this Constitution." Similarly, the preamble invokes "the Most Holy Trinity" and "acknowledges all our obligations to our Divine Lord, Jesus Christ." The Constitutional Review Group of 1996 pointed out that these clauses had little (if any) juridical force (even in 1937 Jews were explicitly recognized in the Constitution, notwithstanding their views on the "Most Holy Trinity").[30] This was de Valera's solution to the establishment puzzle: sociological and symbolic recognition of the Catholic Church that had no particular juridical effect but ensured that the Vatican would not oppose his constitution.[31] Although Article 44 weakened principled distance at independence, it would be a mistake to read that article in its original form as de facto establishment.

Those most justified in doubting the principled distance of independent Ireland were nonbelievers of various stripes. It is fair to say that although de Valera's constitution aspired to a kind of pluralism in its support for various religious traditions, it was not meant to be neutral between belief and nonbelief. Article 40.6.i prohibits "blasphemous" speech, and judges and the president took a generic theistic oath of office.[32] De Valera's institutional proposal in 1937 clearly aspired to principled distance among believers, but it remained unclear how that aspiration would extend to nonbelievers of different kinds. The empirical record finds much less attention given to this issue during the independence period than to treatment of religious minorities, but the place of nonbelievers in Irish public life would become a central driver of the secular evolution described in chapter 3.

The development of religion and education policy indicates the real, if imperfect, nature of principled distance around independence. As High Court justice Mary Laffoy has noted, Article 42 "in its entirety is imbued with the concept of parental freedom of choice," and protection of parental choice may not be limited simply to the majority-faith community.[33] Article 44.2.4 explicitly states, "Legislation providing State aid for schools shall not discriminate between schools under the management of different religious denominations," and so Church of Ireland, Methodist, Presbyterian, Jewish, and (today) Muslim schools have formed in areas where these minorities have sufficient critical mass to sustain a school. Of course, scattered minorities living in rural areas receive less service from such schools, a challenge that remains central in the education-reform debates detailed in chapter 3. Special financial support for boarding was previously available to Protestant secondary-school students,[34] but at the primary level minorities usually exempted themselves from religious instruction and hoped for flexible school administrators. Maintaining principled distance, in education and other areas, remained the least-stable dimension of benevolent secularism in Ireland.

Some contend that Ireland was never a secular state and thus that the institutions of the Constitution of 1937 are appropriately understood as an effective establishment of state Catholicism. This argument, although appealing to many who highlight de Valera's personal piety, holds only if one equates "state secularism" with institutions on the French or American model. Formal establishment was a policy option on the table in independence-era Ireland and was intentionally avoided. Early drafts of the Constitution, influenced in part by McQuaid (not yet an archbishop at this time), "acknowledge[d] that the Church of Christ is the Catholic Church" and made no particular mention of rights protections for Protestant communities.[35] De Valera took serious risks in his recognition of non-Catholic religions and did not simply capitulate to every piece of advice that came in from clerical advisers. Basic minority protections, in law and usually in practice, were extant from 1937 on, and cooperation with the state extended beyond the Catholic majority. Conservative Catholics would continue to agitate for official establishment through the middle of the twentieth century, indicating that, to them anyway, the Irish state was disappointingly secular in nature.

Table 2.1 provides a snapshot of the various dimensions of benevolent secularism in Ireland during the critical juncture around the Constitution of 1937. State-supported schools were owned and operated by religious orders. The Constitution provided Europe's first explicit constitutional guarantee of and protection for rights for Jews. It also acknowledged the Most Holy Trinity. Such was the nature of secularism in Ireland at independence in 1937. While these institutions are benevolent in their treatment of religion, they maintain a differentiation between state and religious institutions and protect the basic rights of minorities in the midst of "Catholic Ireland." At the same time, the principled distance among religious communities was imperfectly realized,

TABLE 2.1. ASSESSING BENEVOLENT SECULARISM IN IRELAND AT INDEPENDENCE

Indicator	Evidence
Differentiation	
Disestablishment	Nonendowment Clause, Article 44, Irish Constitution of 1937
Religious Freedom	Minority constitutional recognition, Article 44, Irish Constitution of 1937
Religion–State Cooperation	
Material Support	Denominational education structures
Policy Consultation	Constitutional recognition of the family, Article 41, Irish Constitution of 1937
Principled Distance	
Impartial Access to Public Support	Protestant school boarding vouchers
Provision of Religious Exemptions	Exemption of Jews from store closing laws, Supreme Court decision in *Quinn's Supermarket*

with the Catholic Church formally recognized as sociologically dominant and informally enjoying far more influence than minority communities. As we will see, this particular institutional combination came with consequences for the preferences that key actors expressed in debates over religious politics as Ireland moved to full independence.

THE EFFECTS OF BENEVOLENT SECULARISM

The secularity of de Valera's constitutional proposal certainly would have surprised many who had opposed Irish sovereignty since the nineteenth century. Protestants in Ireland, Britain, and even the United States had frequently worried that "Home Rule means Rome Rule" and had used these fears to justify delays in Irish sovereignty.[36] This begs the question of how Ireland's benevolent secularism managed to avoid the trap of Catholic establishment. In short, the institutions proposed in the Constitution of 1937 altered preferences on the religion–state relationship among key actors, who, for diverse reasons, consented to the twin tolerations. It is fair to say that no actors received their first preference for the Constitution's treatment of religion, but all came to an accommodation around de Valera's shrewd proposal of benevolent secularism. As Kissane summarizes, "The Catholic Church was not satisfied with the outcome, but any vestiges of secular republicanism among de Valera's ministers were also suppressed."[37]

The terms proposed in drafts of this constitution permitted a diverse coalition to sign up to the twin tolerations. All interested actors, whether republican state builders such as de Valera, Catholic clerics such as Dr. McQuaid, or Protestant elites such as Reverend Dr. J. A. H. Irwin, coalesced around a shared institutional bargain: benevolent secularism and its combination of differentiation, cooperation, and principled distance. This section documents how this institutional configuration affected elites' preferences within the three crucial coalition blocs: secular political elites, Catholic clerics, and religious minorities. Cooperation assured Catholics that Irish secularism would not turn against religion's public presence; differentiation undercut the potential growth of anticlericalism among secular elites; and principled distance engaged minorities in public life. Evidence from elite communications related to the Constitution of 1937 documents these shifts in preferences and ties them to the particular dimensions of benevolent secularism.

Within the Catholic community, the structure of benevolent secularism empowered pious secularists, who were content to permit the differentiation of religious and state institutions so long as cooperation allowed religion to have significant public influence. Again, official establishment in a country of Catholic majority remained the "ideal type" of institutional arrangement, and conservative Catholic nationalists such as the Jesuit Edward Cahill pushed for this option. At the same time, even integralists such as Cahill recognized that a "confessedly Catholic" state "may at present not be feasible" or particularly necessary if Irish secularism were characterized by cooperation between religion and state.[38] The McQuaid Papers in the Archives of the Archdiocese of Dublin show a similar dynamic. Dr. McQuaid clearly preferred establishment, in one place vigorously crossing out draft constitutional language regarding religious liberty and nonendowment.[39] Yet in the scope of his substantial correspondence, this deletion pales in comparison to the amount of attention he paid to advocating a Catholic conception of natural rights, the primacy of the family, and the church's role in education.[40] In other words, the dimension of cooperation appealed to Catholic elites even though the dimension of differentiation departed from official Catholic teaching.[41] Pious secularists could also point to constitutional protection of religion from state coercion through guarantees of religious institutional autonomy (Article 44.2.5) and property rights (Article 44.2.6). Pious secularists accepted what Whyte calls "aloofness between Church and State in Ireland," and there was "no criticism either from the hierarchy" in response to the lack of formal establishment in the Constitution of 1937.[42]

The most vivid evidence of the role of institutional structure in empowering pious secularists within the Catholic Church comes from a meeting at the Vatican between Irish officials and Cardinal Secretary of State Eugenio Pacelli (the future Pope Pius XII). Evidence indicates that the proposed combination of cooperation with differentiation persuaded Pacelli to remain silent on the official preference for religious integralism and instead to adopt a position consistent with pious secularism. De Valera was worried enough about Catholic hardliners rejecting benevolent secularism that he dispatched a top lieutenant, Joseph Walshe, to the Vatican to make sure that Vatican authorities would not openly oppose his draft constitution. Walshe eventually avoided condemnation from Pacelli precisely because of the cooperative dimension of benevolent secularism, even without establishing Catholicism as the state religion. Walshe's notes record the "smiling" Pacelli as observing that, certainly, Irish secularism was heretical, but "the Church would not take the heresy too seriously." Walshe explicitly contrasted the cooperative dimension of proposed Irish institutions with the "continental sense" of anticlerical liberalism and used this contrast to secure the Vatican's acquiescence to the proposals.[43] This was crucial because, as Cardinal Pacelli stressed to Irish envoy Charles Bewley in 1931, "the Holy See disapproves of [priests taking part in politics] in principle," unless threatened by anticlerical actors.[44] Without the benevolent structure of de Valera's institutions, Ireland would have faced a much bleaker choice between McQuaid's initial desires for religious integralism and a confrontation with the Catholic hierarchy.

With benevolent secularism as an institutional option, pious secularism carried the day, and Irish Catholic elites came to support a secular state. That said, however, religious integralism clearly maintained a foothold in elite Catholic circles, which would become especially evident in episodes that tested the Catholic dedication to principled distance, taken up in the close of this chapter.

The structure of benevolent secularism shaped the preferences of leaders of various religious minorities in a different manner, generally empowering those who sought interfaith engagement and weakening calls for minorities' defensive retreat from public life. Such a defensive retreat was an option facing minorities after Protestant disestablishment in 1869 and the failure of missionary efforts to diminish Catholic numerical dominance by the late nineteenth century. Church of Ireland bishop John Gregg wrote of a "tendency towards defeatism" among Irish Protestants that threatened to drive them from the public stage entirely.[45] The *Christian Irishman*, a Protestant periodical, summed up this position when it opined that protections given to minorities were nothing but "the toleration we all accord to the dead."[46] Given the demographic realities of Irish religion, Protestants were understandably concerned that democratization in independent Ireland would unavoidably threaten "a minority viewed with jealous hostility by elements of the population."[47]

In spite of the potential to withdraw into a defensive posture, the institutional structure of benevolent secularism strengthened minority elites with a preference for public engagement. When Gregg, now archbishop, gave vocal support to the Free State and eventually the Republic of Ireland, he was living out his maxim, "In our prayers, above all, there must be reality."[48] Clerical leaders such as Church of Ireland bishop William Plunket conceded that the colonial-era Protestant establishment had been a "tottering wall," and he would eventually join with Catholic bishops in opposing the partition of Ireland into a smaller Free State.[49] Archbishop Gregg was consulted on the wording of language on Protestant denominations in the Constitution,[50] and Reverend J. A. H. Irwin, former Presbyterian moderator of Ireland, was a close ally of de Valera, traveling with him throughout the United States in 1920 to build support for Irish independence and serving as an adviser on the religion-related provisions of the Constitution of 1937.[51] W. H. Massey, leader of the Methodist Church, wrote to de Valera that he was "quite satisfied" with the special-position clause and that later mentions of minority communities "remove any doubt on this point."[52] De Valera likewise engaged Ireland's Jewish leaders in the project, with Chief

Rabbi Isaac Herzog expressing strong approval for the inclusion of Jewish communities among those constitutionally protected in 1937.[53] The combination of differentiation and principled distance in De Valera's proposed institutions served these minorities fairly well, with schools funded, property protected, and communities constitutionally recognized. Minorities would remain in a precarious position, to be sure, but the structure of the institutions in the Constitution of 1937 enhanced the standing of those who advocated continued engagement as minority partners in democratic life.

In a different manner, the structure of benevolent secularism shaped the preferences of Ireland's secular-minded political elites, empowering those who sought accommodation with religious actors and limiting anticlericalism. There was a significant legacy of republican anticlericalism in de Valera's nationalist circles that could have fed confrontations between religion and state in an independent Ireland. During the Irish Civil War, Irish bishops "condemned in unequivocal terms the actions of the Éamon de Valera–led anti-Treatyites."[54] This condemnation fueled resentment of the hierarchy among many in the republican movement, even if de Valera himself endeavored to maintain correct relations with Catholic authorities. The strength of anticlerical resistance was directly related to the proposed institutional relationship between religion and state in the Constitution of 1937. Gerald Boland, a secular-minded Catholic member of de Valera's inner circle, voiced strong disapproval of initial proposals for explicit establishment of Catholicism as Ireland's state religion. Boland wrote that such institutional conditions "would be equivalent to the expulsion from our history of great Irishmen," and he threatened to emigrate with his family "under such a sectarian constitution."[55] Without institutionalized differentiation and minority protections, views such as Boland's could have grown into a broader anticlericalism.

The differentiation of religion and state in de Valera's constitutional proposals instead assuaged such concerns and promoted more accommodation-minded secular elites. Accommodation came with several material benefits. It brought political stability. De Valera knew that his constitution and his elected leadership of an independent Ireland would be unlikely to survive direct opposition from either the Irish Catholic hierarchy or the Vatican, so the Constitution of 1937 provided a middle ground that kept the country from plunging back into civil war. Second, the state would benefit from the low-cost labor provided by religious employees in denominational schools. Even if some republicans had more anticlerical tendencies, benevolent secularism gave significant incentives to cooperate in a time of low state capacity. Third, maintaining differentiation brought secular-minded elites around de Valera some credibility among those concerned to assuage Protestants both in the newly independent Ireland and in the six counties of Northern Ireland. W. B. Yeats's famous speech before the Free State Seanad (upper house of the Irish legislature) in 1925 captured this incentive: "If you show that this country, Southern Ireland, is going to be governed by Catholic ideas and by Catholic ideas alone, you will never get the North. You will create an impassable barrier between South and North.... You will put a wedge into the midst of this nation."[56] De Valera and Yeats agreed on that basic point at least. This set of incentives combined to undercut the appeal of anticlerical hostility among the secular state builders of independence-era Ireland.

The most direct evidence of the failure of anticlericalism to gain a serious electoral foothold in Irish politics lies in the effective nonexistence of anticlerical mass politics during this period. Catholic predominance meant that even those with reformist inclinations like de Valera had no incentive to adopt an anticlerical form of republicanism. The rather excitable Jesuit Edward Cahill may have fretted about the influence of "Freemasons of the very highest degrees" among the Irish judiciary,[57] but by the standards of continental Europe or even of Great Britain anticlericalism was a weak political force in Ireland at this time. The political party Fianna Fáil may have had a reputation as "dangerously revolutionary" or prone to socialism, but by its rise to electoral power in 1932 its leaders were siblings of clergy, members of the Knights of Columbanus, and pals of the papal nuncio.[58] De Valera and his main political opponent, William Cosgrave and the Cumann na nGaedheal party, tried to outdo one another in piety, and Fianna Fáil's enthusiastic performance at the Eucharistic Congress in 1932 accentuated the lack of anticlericalism among mainstream Irish republicans. Even the smaller Irish Labour Party was largely content with the moral conservatism that came with benevolent secularism.[59] With little electoral home for serious anticlericalism, accommodation with religion became the dominant preference among Ireland's secular elites.

As de Valera and his closest advisers circulated the institutional outlines of the religion–state relationship in his constitution, the proposals shaped ongoing debates within Catholic, minority, and state elite blocs about the place of religion in Irish public life. Table 2.2 summarizes the impact of institutional structures on preferences within each bloc. For most of the Catholic hierarchy, formal establishment was an unnecessary distraction if the religion–state relationship were sufficiently cooperative. For de Valera and other state builders, the church's institutions were helpful in providing services and in securing their own electoral futures. For religious minorities, benevolent secularism, even with fairly weak principled distance, seemed a least-bad option and drew them into public partnerships. The Constitution of 1937 remained controversial in some quarters, but this core coalition sustained it for decades to come.

TABLE 2.2. PREFERENCE EFFECTS OF
BENEVOLENT SECULARISM IN IRELAND

Coalition Partner	Hypothesized Within-Group Effect	Evidence in Ireland
Religious Majority	Empower pious secularists	Meeting with Cardinal Pacelli at the Vatican regarding the Constitution
Secular Elites	Weaken anticlericals and empower accommodation	Lack of anticlerical political party
Religious Minorities	Promote engaged minorities	De Valera's ties with Rabbi Herzog

ALTERNATIVE EXPLANATIONS OF IRISH SECULARISM

The argument linking the institutional structure of Irish secularism to the emergence of the twin tolerations at independence through secularism's impact on elite preferences stands apart from other theoretical approaches to explaining institutional religion–state relationships. How can alternative explanations—secularization theory, religious moderation theory, and rational choice theory—contribute to understanding Ireland's religious politics during this period?

First, secularization theorists might contend that institutional secularism is a by-product of economic development and the decline of individual religiosity. Secularization theory seems correct that Ireland's low levels of economic development at independence contributed to high religiosity and the influence of religious institutions. However, this high religiosity did not doom the state to theocracy; in fact, it likely contributed to the Catholic Church's willingness to accept benevolent secular institutions.

Partition into the Free State was an economic shock to the newly independent territories, and Irish economic strategy continued to struggle after 1937. Such modernization as did take place—for instance, the growth in institutions of universal education—tended to reinforce religious communities' institutional influence. Moreover, if economic development had weakened Catholic institutions, clerical elites might have been more insecure in their social standing and less confident that benevolent secularism would meet their needs. Regardless, the general lack of development at Irish independence should have set the stage for fusion of religious and state institutions rather than their differentiation.

Likewise, the argument that secularism is the result of religious moderation is little help in explaining de Valera's constitution. In the lead-up to that document's approval, the Catholic Church hosted a wildly successful international Eucharistic Congress, won legislative victories on any number of matters from public health to media censorship, and was far from liberal in its view of rights or political authority. Vatican II reforms regarding the relationship between religion and state and religious liberty were still decades in the future, and the notes from Catholic leaders such as Drs. Cahill and McQuaid show more attention to Thomist theology than to liberal philosophy. If religious liberalism on the part of the majority community is a necessary condition for secular institutions, de Valera's middle path would have been rejected by all of the major Catholic voices in public life. If there was moderation on the part of clerical elites such as McQuaid, it was in response to the institutional conditions of de Valera's constitution, not independent of them.

Rationalist explanations merit more extended attention in relation to the emergence of Irish twin tolerations. Religious elites and elected officials certainly demonstrated a good bit of strategic behavior during this critical juncture. For instance, the Protestant calculation that, with British support flagging, they should extract the best deal they could from the dominant majority seems a basically rational decision rooted in self-preservation. Likewise, de Valera's coziness with the Catholic hierarchy could be the simple result of a self-interested politician who cannily exploited the most powerful social institution in his country to help secure his electoral standing. And the Catholic Church's strategy of giving up on a formal establishment fight in favor of enshrining various substantive goals in constitutional law could also fit a loosely rationalist definition of organizational interests driving institutional development.

But most rational choice theory goes beyond the simple claim that actors pursue their preferences. As Anthony Gill proposes, "Hegemonic religious will prefer high levels of government regulation (i.e., restrictions on religious liberty) over religious minorities,"[60] a prediction with fairly clear implications for independence-era Ireland. Gill points to Catholic promotion of religious liberty in Russia but promotion of religious restrictions in Latin America to prove his point that demographics shape destiny in explaining religion–state relations. This prediction does not export well to Dublin during this juncture. The Catholic Church was hegemonic by any standard, and in an atmosphere of high political competition de Valera had every incentive to give church leaders exactly what they wanted in institutional negotiations. Moreover, given the fact that legal discrimination from the colonial power had targeted the Catholic Church in the past, Catholic elites should have been particularly keen to use the levers of state power to favor their own institutional interests in the independent Ireland.

And yet the Constitution of 1937 did not establish the Catholic Church as the state religion, involved active consultation with minority faith communities, and centered on issues of moral concern such as defining the role of families in education much more than using state resources to exclude religious competitors. What happened? In short, preferences mattered. The Catholic Church's priorities focused on the family and the undercutting of anticlericalism, and thus these areas were of more importance to Catholic negotiators in the drafting process in 1937. Catholic–Protestant relations may not have been extremely warm, but legal discrimination against Protestants would have been an unnecessary pursuit. Institutional structure affected actor preferences and resulted in a secular state even in the context of a demographic majority.

HINTS OF INSTABILITY: THE MOTHER AND CHILD CRISIS

The three dimensions of benevolent secularism facilitated passage of the Constitution of 1937 with support from a diverse coalition. However, one episode in the early postindependence period illustrates the consequences of the tenuous status of principled distance in independent Ireland. Known as the Mother and Child Crisis, this debate centered on the development of national health-care policy. It paralyzed legislation, played a role in bringing down a government, and brought Éamon de Valera back into office. More importantly for this argument, it revealed the effect of weakened principled distance on relations between Catholic, Protestant, and secular elites as well as the unresolved debates between religious integralists and pious secularists among Ireland's Catholic leadership. Although this episode revealed short-term tensions over the institutions of Irish secularism, its longer-term lessons reinforced the claims of pious secularism within the Catholic majority.

In many ways, the Mother and Child Crisis crystallized the tenuous status of principled distance at independence. What constituted an unacceptable violation of the state's principled distance from all religious communities, given the reality of Catholic demographic dominance? When the government floated plans for health-care reform in the 1940s, it was not entirely surprising that Catholic leaders would engage in the debate; in fact, such policy consultation is characteristic of benevolent secularism. However, although state officials did take care to circulate the health proposals to "the heads of all Churches, including all bishops, both Catholic and Protestant," there can be no doubt that this fight was picked by the Catholic hierarchy on behalf of distinctive features of Catholic social teaching.[61] Unlike in debates over pornography censorship, for instance, little ecumenical common cause was made on this issue; unvarnished appeals were instead made to the principles of Catholic social thought as set out in papal encyclicals. Members of the Catholic hierarchy critiqued the public-health plans as intruding on the autonomy of the family guaranteed in the Constitution, primarily through provisions related to maternal education and health screenings.[62] As tensions mounted, the policy proposals were jettisoned along with the advocating cabinet official. The standoff was eventually resolved after de Valera's return to office and some creative ambiguity in application of the legislation.

This weakening of principled distance came with implications for relations among the diverse actors who supported the secularism of the Constitution of 1937. Religious-secular tensions quickly peaked; the *Irish Times* complained that the bishops were "trespass[ing] on the domain and seek[ing] to usurp the powers of the legitimate civil authority."[63] One Catholic periodical indicted the *Irish Times* for representing "the Cromwellian traditions in Ireland [in] endeavouring to drive the Catholic Church out of the life of the country."[64] This combative turn is characteristic of a weakening of benevolent secularism; anticlericals and integralists came to have greater influence among secular and Catholic elites, respectively.

Perhaps most importantly, the Mother and Child Crisis illustrated not the political strength of Irish Catholicism, but rather the cost to the religious majority that would come with a breakdown in benevolent secularism. The crisis showed that religious integralists still enjoyed some support within the Catholic hierarchy. Critics of the proposed legislation made no secret of their desire to have Catholic principles privileged in state policy, and they won some short-term victories. However, there is no escaping the fact that the legislation that eventually passed largely mirrored core state proposals from the late 1940s that vocal elements of the hierarchy had once rejected. Moreover, as most of the statesmen advancing these proposals were themselves Catholic, the hierarchy and Catholic press had to confront "their evident failure to convince Catholic opinion on the mother and child issue."[65] Indeed, the Irish hierarchy withdrew a final letter objecting to de Valera's plans due to its likely futility and adverse consequences within the church.[66] In highlighting the costs of religious integralism, the Mother and Child Crisis ultimately served as another stage in the development of pious secularism among the Irish Catholic majority.

The institutions proposed in the Constitution of 1937 had all the dimensions of benevolent secularism: differentiation, cooperation, and principled distance. This chapter documents that institutional structure and traces its impact on preferences of different blocs: secular political elites, the Catholic majority, and religious minority communities. The benevolent structure of Irish secularism explains why this case, which seemed so prone to the secularism trap, came to secure Stepan's twin tolerations at independence. Although principled distance was especially vulnerable to manipulation and advocates of religious integralism persisted within Irish Catholicism, it was no small achievement to secure the twin tolerations in newly independent Ireland.

One ought not overlook the dark side of religion and public life in independent Ireland that benevolent secularism did not eliminate. The religion–state relationship was essentially communal or denominational in nature. Individuals who fell outside of a major faith tradition or couples who crossed denominational lines faced, at times, real legal obstacles. Homosexual persons lived with legal discrimination, although this treatment, of course, was not unique to Ireland at the time. Most devastatingly, organizations involved in cooperation between religion and state were later linked to systematic patterns of physical and sexual abuse and subsequent cover-ups by religious and state authorities that have rocked Irish public life in the past quarter century. Some have argued that benevolent secularism was in part responsible for these failures. It is difficult to know what independent impact the structure of benevolent secular institutions had on these outcomes; sex abuse and its being covered up, for instance, were tied to deeply conservative social values and high levels of deference to clerical authority that predated the Constitution of 1937. Empirically, the dark side of religion and politics in independent Ireland often resulted from areas in which Ireland *deviated from* the benevolent secular ideal type, particularly in weak maintenance of principled distance from all religious communities. Chapter 3 focuses on the actions of a diverse set of reformers to address those deviations, drawing Irish religion–state relations closer to the benevolent ideal type but without adopting a more exclusionary model of secularism in the process.

As the Mother and Child debates revealed, the benevolent nature of Irish secularism was already under challenge by midcentury. Should a more modern republic reserve a cooperative role for religious actors in democratic politics? And would Catholic elites truly abandon prior calls to integrate church and state? These questions were largely tabled after the Mother and Child episode, but only for a time. By the early 1970s, as church authority changed along with Irish politics, Ireland's take on benevolent secularism showed unmistakable signs of evolution.

3. Secular Evolution in Ireland

RELIGION AND POST-CATHOLIC POLITICS

During a parliamentary debate in July 2011 over the Catholic Church's cover-up of sexual abuse allegations, Ireland's *taoiseach*, Enda Kenny, railed against the "dysfunction, disconnection, elitism, and narcissism" of the Vatican.[1] These are strong words from any head of government—and unprecedented in Ireland. The Irish press generally praised Kenny's anti-Vatican outburst, and the World Atheist Convention held its global convocation in Dublin in June of that year, with Irish senator Ivana Bacik warning of "creeping fundamentalists" in Irish life.[2] Archbishop of Dublin Diarmuid Martin shocked many when he said at Cambridge University in 2011, "The Catholic Church in Ireland will inevitably become more a minority culture."[3] Amid declining church attendance rates, increasing diversity, and ongoing revelations of sexual abuse and cover-ups of that abuse in state-funded Catholic institutions, the nature of religion–state relations in contemporary Ireland appeared to be in flux, and the stage seemed set for a breakdown of Ireland's benevolent secularism.

And yet on May 19, 2011, just two weeks before the atheists came to town, a range of faith leaders met with Taoiseach Kenny and other elected officials at Dublin's government buildings. The agenda included consultations on economic recovery, European integration, and immigration policy. More than

90 percent of Irish primary schools continue to be denominational in ethos. The Constitution still charges the state to "respect and honour religion" (44.1). Radio Television Éireann (RTÉ) continues to broadcast the angelus, although in a new form meant to appeal to a more religiously diverse audience. In these ways and others, Irish church–state relations seem broadly constant since Éamon de Valera guided his constitution to ratification in 1937.

Religion's place in Irish life has changed utterly in the past quarter century. In particular, the unequal influence enjoyed by the Catholic bishops through the mid-twentieth century is largely a thing of the past. But benevolent secularism has generally endured this period of turmoil. If anything, Irish institutions now more closely approximate the ideal type as principled distance and differentiation are far more robust. This change has not required a breakdown and replacement of benevolent secularism. Secular evolution, not a turn to strict *laïcité*, has taken place. As Kissane aptly summarizes, "In the contemporary Irish context, state neutrality can only be construed as even-handed intervention in the religious sphere, and there is little prospect of a separation of church and state on the American model."[4] In comparative perspective, developments in Irish secularism illustrate the ability of benevolent secularism to adjust in a context of rapid social secularization. Even in a context of high economic development and declining religious participation, Ireland's distinct historical trajectory has made its religious politics stand out from other European states facing similar demographic changes.

This pattern of institutional evolution is owing to the coalitional ties promoted by benevolent secularism, in particular religious-secular partnerships and strong interfaith relations, at both the elite level and in public opinion data. In the past quarter century, pious secularists within the Catholic community worked with political elites and religious minorities to strengthen principled distance while maintaining the cooperative dimension of benevolent secularism. As Ireland became more religiously diverse in the wake of waves of immigration, faith groups worked together to bring new minorities into the state's benevolent bargain. This period of change has peaked in recent years, but it began much earlier, with Catholic politicians such as Taoiseach Garret FitzGerald and his calling of the New Ireland Forum.

This chapter examines developments in Irish benevolent secularism in four main parts. First, I document the changes that have swept Ireland's religious landscape in the past quarter century; the growth in nonbelievers and collapse of Irish Catholic dominance could have constituted major threats to settled patterns of religion–state interaction. Second, I trace changes in institutions of benevolent secularism across the three dimensions of differentiation, cooperation, and principled distance. Here, the most significant institutional evolution is in principled distance and differentiation, which have become much more robust since independence. Third, I argue that this evolution in benevolent secularism, rather than its replacement by an alternative institutional arrangement, is owing to the coalition ties across religious-secular and interfaith boundaries that benevolent secularism helps to foster. Fourth, I turn to public opinion data to document that the coalitional consensus shown in elite interviews is also reflected in the general population.

THE RELIGIOUS LANDSCAPE OF POST-CATHOLIC IRELAND

As in Senegal and the Philippines, significant demographic shifts have challenged the religion–state relationship institutionalized in Ireland at independence. Ireland has experienced the collapse in the social dominance of the Catholic majority and an undeniable uptick in religious nonaffiliation and religious minority communities. With the weakening of Catholic Ireland, Irish institutions face the possibility of more assertive secularization, closer to Paris than to Dakar.

Although forms of humanism have a long history in Ireland, the number of Irish who claim unaffiliated or nonreligious status has grown significantly only in the past quarter century. The 2011 census showed 270,000 Irish who listed no religion, in addition to more than 70,000 who did not respond to the question.[5] This number has tripled since 1981, with the "No Religion" category in particular ballooning by 450 percent. Self-identifying atheists are a smaller demographic of 4,000, but the rapid growth of those without a religion just in the past five years is remarkable. Nearly 50 percent more Irish identified as nonreligious in 2011 as did in 2006. Church attendance rates have similarly cratered among those who claim an affiliation, which may indicate that the tide of nonaffiliation in Ireland has not crested.

It is important to note that the unaffiliated in Ireland are not necessarily anticlerical in their views of the role of religion in public life. There is diversity within this group. With that said, a portion of the unaffiliated demographic does clearly hold more anticlerical preferences. A civil society association called Atheist Ireland puts the most public face on this trend. Among its campaigns: public blasphemy to intentionally violate Ireland's protection of religious sentiment and a "Be Honest to Godless!" campaign encouraging Irish to declare their nontheism on the census. Atheist Ireland's leader, Michael Nugent, explicitly challenges the pattern of cooperation between religion and state at the core of the Irish tradition of religion–state relations. As he put it to me, "We don't want a slice of the religious-ceremonial pie."[6] Rather, they seek to significantly alter the religion–state cooperation that characterizes benevolent secularism.

Within Irish Catholicism, the past quarter century has coupled demographic weakness with the growing predominance of pious secularism *within* the Catholic population. The basic demographic changes have already been covered, but in addition to the aggregate declines in religious affiliation and church participation, the numbers of both male and female religious vocations have steeply declined. During this period of weakness, a larger share of Irish Catholicism has come to adopt preferences of pious secularism, believing that older forms of unequal Catholic influence over state authority undermined Catholicism's religious legitimacy. This solidifying of pious secularism was in part a result of international developments in the political theology of the post–Vatican II Catholic Church. By the late 1970s, Vatican II had transformed Catholic theology of church–state relations. *Dignitatis humanae*, the council's declaration on religious liberty, not only affirmed the basic human right to religious freedom but also made no effort to insist on any kind of legal establishment of Catholicism even when it is in the majority. The change was so thorough-going that Archbishop Cahal Daly would sound classic pious secularist themes before the New Ireland Forum in 1984, testifying, "The Catholic Church totally rejects the concept of a confessional state. . . . We believe that the alliance of Church and State is harmful for the Church and harmful for the State."[7] This trend to pious secularism continues with the current archbishop of Dublin, Diarmuid Martin. Archbishop Martin acknowledges that an "unhealthy closeness between ecclesiastical and political figures" in Irish history contributed both to the tragedy of child abuse and to the broader process of weakening the Catholic Church's public credibility.[8]

Pious secularists also drew strength from dissatisfaction with clerical influence over politics. As Sister Ethna Regan of Dublin's Mater Dei Institute put it, Catholic domination in midcentury Ireland gave rise to an "underlying resentment" that in time served to discredit Catholic teaching authority, particularly around issues of sexuality and the family.[9] As Professor Linda Hogan of Trinity College Dublin summed up, the church became more reluctant to make explicitly theological interventions in public because "they could not be confident that these values were shared in their congregations."[10] The ongoing fallout of sexual abuse scandals in some ways seals the Catholic argument in favor of pious secularism. The unquestioned authority of church clerics that developed in the decades around independence ultimately contributed to the abuse and its cover-up. As Father Gerry O'Hanlon, S.J., of the Jesuit Centre for Faith and Justice put it to me, "State used the church, and the church allowed it."[11] This is in many ways a central claim of pious secularism: deviations from the dimensions of benevolent secularism will ultimately undermine the interests even of a predominant religious majority. As Archbishop Martin put it in a lecture in March 2011, "The Church respects the autonomy of the secular sphere . . . [provided] Caesar does not play God and does not try to banish God out of the reality of society."[12]

In addition to these shifts within the Catholic majority, Ireland's religious landscape has been transformed by new religious diversity. Although minorities as a whole continue to make up a relatively small slice of Ireland's religious landscape, census data from 2011 show that the nature of those minority groups has changed substantially in the past quarter century. Non-Catholic Christians now include a substantial Orthodox community, numbering more than 45,000 in the 2011 census, as well as 14,000 Pentecostals and more than 40,000 nondenominational Christians. The Hindu community now exceeds 10,000 members, and the Buddhist community is nearly as large.[13] Each of these demographics saw substantial growth just in the five years since the previous census, in particular the Orthodox and Pentecostal Christian communities.

A particularly important example of this new diversity is the growth of Islam in Ireland. Ireland's Islamic community has existed for decades in the form of students who came to Dublin for schooling, but it has grown into a significant public presence only in the past quarter century with the rise of the Celtic Tiger economy. Even with that Tiger's humbling, the 2011 census counted nearly 50,000 Muslims in Ireland, up from approximately 30,000 in 2006. This community is small by continental European standards but is noticeable on the streets of Ireland's larger cities, where mosques and halal butchers are a common sight.

TRACKING INSTITUTIONAL CHANGE: CLOSER TO THE BENEVOLENT IDEAL

These combined demographic changes could have easily marked the end of Irish benevolent secularism, and its replacement by more assertively separationist institutions like those found in France. And yet the basic dimensions of benevolent secularism still exist in Irish constitutional law, legislation, and patterns of political life. In this section, I document the evolution of benevolent secularism in Ireland in recent decades, focusing on the concrete areas of change summarized in table 3.1. The most dramatic changes have led not to the collapse in benevolent secularism but instead to a closer resemblance to the ideal type. This change is in fact a sign of the overall vitality of the benevolent bargain in Ireland in spite of the rapid coalitional shifts of the past quarter century.

TABLE 3.1 SUMMARY OF SECULAR EVOLUTION IN IRELAND

Area of Change	Institutional Outcome	Coalition Influence
1. Decline of Catholic Hegemony	More robust principled distance and differentiation	Religious-secular partnership through Catholic pious secularists at New Ireland Forum
2. Reform of Educational Patronage	Continuation of cooperative model	Religious-secular partnership through Forum on Patronage
3. Growth of Muslim Minority	Accommodation through cooperation and principled distance	Interfaith partnerships with Irish Muslim elites

THE END OF CATHOLICISM'S "MORAL MONOPOLY"

The most substantial change in institutions of Irish religion–state relations has moved it closer to the ideal type of benevolent secularism. Although the early Irish state extended cooperation and rights protections to other religious traditions, there is no disputing the fact that the Catholic Church enjoyed unique influence. Differentiation and principled distance were tenuous. The Constitution of 1937 recognized the sociological fact of Catholicism's "special position" as the majority faith in Ireland, even if this recognition had no legal effect. De Valera consulted widely with religious leaders, but only a Catholic hierarch such as Archbishop John McQuaid could have checked a governmental initiative such as the Mother and Child proposals.

This extensive influence for the Catholic Church has faded and been replaced by a more robust differentiation and principled distance. This shift has been a gradual process of institutional evolution and taken on a number of judicial, legislative, and popular fronts. Although the large size of the Catholic community still secures it substantial access to political leaders and informal social influence, the Irish state now maintains a more genuinely principled distance among its religious communities.

The most obvious indication of this evolution was the removal of the "special position" clause from Article 44 of the Constitution in 1972. Recall that this clause had been de Valera's way of acknowledging Catholic influence without resorting to formal establishment. By the late 1960s, however, many saw even this recognition of Catholicism to be unnecessary and sectarian. With tension escalating in Northern Ireland, Irish leaders were particularly eager to avoid charges of discrimination against minorities in the Republic of Ireland. The Committee on the Constitution reported in 1967 that "[Article 44] gives offence to non-Catholics and is also a useful weapon in the hands of those who are anxious to emphasise the differences between North and South."[14] The committee thus proposed removing both the special acknowledgment of the Catholic Church as well as the recognition of various Protestant and Jewish communities. The initiative went to a popular referendum and passed comfortably. As Reverend Dr. Trevor Morrow, former rector of the Presbyterian Church in Ireland, told me, "Today, it would be anathema to run to the bishop's palace before legislating in the Dáil."[15]

The old version of Article 44 was, however, just one part of the unique influence afforded to Catholicism by the Irish state.[16] The more concrete Catholic influence was seen in constitutional prohibitions on divorce and legal restrictions on contraceptive sales, homosexuality, and adoption by "mixed" religious marriages. When reformers critiqued Ireland's sectarian legal system, it was with these provisions, which held less appeal beyond the Catholic community, in mind. Over the past quarter century, reformers have altered these provisions one by one, in the process strengthening the differentiation and principled distance of Irish benevolent secularism.

The first major break occurred with restrictions on contraception. The sale of contraception had been illegal since before 1937, and although creative couples could circumvent the law through importation, discussion of liberalizing state law received a sharp rebuke from an aging Archbishop McQuaid as "a curse upon our country."[17] However, in *McGee v. Attorney General*, the Irish Supreme Court in 1974 begged to differ. The four-to-one decision, which rested largely on the marital right to privacy, invalidated the restrictions on contraception instituted in 1935. Importantly, Justice Brian Walsh argued, "In a pluralist society such as ours, the Courts cannot as a matter of constitutional law be asked to choose between the differing views, where they exist, of experts on the interpretation by the different religious denominations of either the nature or extent of these natural rights as they are to be found in the natural law."[18]

Contraception was in many ways the opening skirmish in what Taoiseach FitzGerald termed his "constitutional crusade" to reform Irish legal institutions. In the wake of the *McGee* decision and in response to the deteriorating situation in Northern Ireland, FitzGerald set out to review Ireland's foundational laws. The New Ireland Forum was the centerpiece of this effort, and its records provide unique insight into the process of undoing any hierarchy in state treatment of religious communities in Ireland. The forum's report in 1983 acknowledged, "Despite the implicit separation of Church and State in the 1937 Constitution, many unionists hold the view that the Catholic ethos has unduly influenced administration in the South and that the latter, in its laws, attitudes and values has not reflected a regard for the ethos of Protestants living there."[19] When the forum's report insisted that "civil and religious liberties and rights must be guaranteed . . . and government must be sensitive to minority beliefs and attitudes and seek consensus,"[20] the clear implication was that a growing segment of Irish political elites thought that Irish institutions fell short of this standard.

The New Ireland Forum did not have authority to change Irish laws, but its proceedings document just how quickly the Irish state was developing more substantial differentiation and more robust principled distance among Irish religious communities. FitzGerald's constitutional crusade was in the short run derailed by partisan politics, but in the longer term the evolved interpretation of religion–state relations in the forum's recommendations has carried the day in Ireland.[21]

This general trend continues in the realm of lesbian, gay, bisexual, and transgender (LGBT) rights, first in the Civil Partnerships Act of 2010 and then in the marriage equality referendum of 2015. The Civil Partnerships Act provided to homosexual couples rights similar to rights in marriage in areas such as inheritance, tax filings, and property ownership, and the referendum amended the Irish Constitution to provide full marriage equality to homosexual couples. These changes mark the latest stage in the process of overcoming legal barriers facing homosexuals, which has progressed since the legalization of homosexuality under European Court of Human Rights pressure in 1990. It was particularly notable that the civil partnerships debate was characterized by a general lack of mobilization from the hierarchy or conservative Catholic associations, compared with their presence in earlier divorce referenda. In multiple interviews with both liberals and conservatives, the weakness of Catholic integralists was a consistent theme. Church leaders could not even convince Fianna Fáil leadership to allow a "free vote," allowing conservative legislators to oppose party leadership without punishment for dissenting from the party line. Even the mention of religious objections caused the leader of the Green Party, John Gormley, to retort, "I thought we had left the era of Church interference behind."[22] The extension of LGBT rights is likely to pose an ongoing challenge to benevolent secularism in Ireland, particularly in that it raises claims for exemption on grounds of religious conscience. This issue is discussed further in the chapter's concluding section.

The amendment of Article 44, the *McGee* decision, the New Ireland Forum, the divorce and marriage equality referenda all add up to an important evolution in Irish benevolent secularism.[23] Both in formal constitutional language and in patterns of policy influence, the Irish state now maintains more robust differentiation and principled distance among its increasingly diverse religious communities.

COOPERATION AND REFORMING EDUCATIONAL PATRONAGE

Although Catholicism's moral monopoly has faded in contemporary Ireland, there is general continuity in the cooperative dimension of benevolent secularism, in spite of the demographic changes outlined earlier. Education reform (known as "patronage reform") is especially appropriate for documenting this element of institutional evolution. Ireland's primary schools, as described in chapter 2, are the most prominent example of the cooperative dimension of benevolent secularism. Amid increased religious diversity, the Department of Education and Skills convened the Forum on Patronage and Pluralism in the Primary Sector to gather input for adjusting religious control over educational institutions. Although these reforms are ongoing, indications are that the cooperation at the core of benevolent secularism will endure the process. True, institutions are changing to reflect new demographic realities in Ireland. However, reformers are basically advocating a continuation of the denominational system characterized by cooperation between religious and state institutions in educating the republic's citizens. As Kissane puts it, "What these changes imply is less a process of secularisation, and more a variation on the main theme of denominational schooling."[24]

In 2011, Minister for Education and Skills Ruairi Quinn launched the Forum on Patronage and Pluralism in the Primary Sector with this charge: "I see the objective for this Forum as being a very simple one. As a society, the patronage of our primary schools should reflect the diversity within our population."[25] This seemingly clear goal, of course, is complex in application.[26] At the primary level, there is a small share of what might be considered "secular" schools—that is, those not under the patronage of a religious institution.[27] At a time of declining religious attendance and increased religious diversity, patronage reform is at its core an attempt to move some schools away from Catholic control to reflect more diverse parental preferences. The Forum on Patronage has gathered input from teachers' unions, religious institutions, parents' associations, and a range of other interested stakeholders.

Patronage reform marked a serious challenge to benevolent secularism. A strict separationist position calling for dramatic reduction (and perhaps elimination) of denominational education does exist in Ireland and has attracted some attention and support. As Dr. Eoin Daly argues, "The concrete effect of the patronage model is that families in many areas of the State have little choice but to avail of denominational primary schools which are committed to beliefs contrary to their own."[28] Daly emphasizes that the denominational system, particularly in rural areas, is practically impossible to square with today's pluralism.[29] Michael Nugent of Atheist Ireland repeatedly stressed in our conversation that although dissenting students may be exempted from formal religious instruction, the "integrated curriculum" allows for a school's religious ethos to permeate the school day, and schools may account for religion in admissions decisions.[30] Daly, Nugent, and the leaders of associations such as Atheist Ireland and the Humanist Association of Ireland rightly point out that this kind of trade-off would likely not be acceptable to courts operating with an American understanding of secularism.

Patronage reform is an incomplete process; concrete change has been slow. However, insofar as change has occurred, it can be characterized as evolution within the general bounds of the cooperative religion–state relationship. Professor John Coolahan, chair of the Patronage Forum and noted education researcher, has insisted, "Pluralism is not a threat to existing practice."[31] A small handful of schools has changed patronage, moving away from both Catholic and Protestant control, but there seems little elite appetite for the wholesale removal of religious patronage from the Irish educational scene. When the Department of Education studied parent preferences about religion in education, for instance, the goal was to understand more accurately the relative demand for religious and secular educational options rather than to gauge support for ending public funding of religious education altogether. Patronage reform is centered on adjusting the existing model in response to diminished Catholic numbers and increased diversity. The Irish religion–state relationship must be pluralized, and Catholic predominance reduced. These reforms are unlikely to overturn the basically denominational nature of Irish primary education. They are, in fact, a way to bring Irish institutions in line with European Union human rights standards while preserving the cooperative dimension of benevolent secularism in Ireland.

Even the nondenominational schools favored by many secular-minded reformers reflect the Irish benevolence in treatment of religious institutions. Educate Together (ET) schools, which have expanded rapidly in recent years, serving 13,000 primary pupils with a multidenominational curriculum, can hardly be called antireligious. The ET schools themselves grew out of believers, including Catholics, who desired multidenominational education to promote broader social integration in Ireland in the late 1970s. In an interview, John Holohan, head of communications for ET schools, outlined the place of religious education, as opposed to faith formation, in the ET curriculum and the fact that faith formation still takes place, but outside of official school hours. As Holohan put it, "There's not much appetite for a totally secular state school in Ireland."[32] ET officials have worked to build relationships with local bishops, particularly to ensure that their Catholic students can still receive the sacraments after faith formation at the ET schools. ET has taken on a significant share of newer schools in Ireland; Holohan pointed out, "We are one of the few games in town" that can step in quickly to take on primary schools. Even as the program expands, it preserves something of the cooperation between religions and state that characterizes benevolent secularism.

IRISH MUSLIMS AND BENEVOLENT SECULARISM

Although Irish benevolent secularism had long incorporated Protestant and Jewish minority groups, the growth of Ireland's Muslim community has raised new questions about institutional evolution. Would the opportunities for cooperation with the Irish state afforded to Protestant, Catholic, and Jewish leaders be extended to Muslim elites? On the whole, Irish benevolent secularism has evolved to accommodate this growing minority.

This evolution shows through in several concrete accommodations made for the Muslim minority in recent years. Provisions have been made for Muslim women to wear the *hijab* in passport photos, and a Muslim burial area has been reserved within a Dublin cemetery. Hospitals, many of which are denominational, will make provision for Muslim ministry, although worship spaces are not as inclusive as the Health Research Board would like.[33] Ali Selim of the Islamic Cultural Centre of Ireland pointed out that state officials are "doing the best they can" in more complex areas, such as money lending.[34] Imams can conduct marriages, Muslim institutions have tax-exempt status, and halal butchering is legal and thriving to judge by the signs on Dublin's grocery stores. Muslim leaders are a part of government consultations and regularly submit briefs on issues ranging from abortion policy to education reform. Muslim groups' submissions to the Patronage Forum, for example, were made alongside those from the Catholic Church and the Church of Ireland. As Dr. Oliver Scharbrodt, director of the History of Islam in Ireland Project at University College Cork, put it to me, all these accommodations flow "without controversy as a consequence of the denominational model [of religion–state relations] in Ireland."[35]

The incorporation of the Muslim minority into benevolent secularism is especially visible in education policy. Recall that various Protestant denominations and the Jewish community run schools with state financial support and that Article 44.2.4 of the Constitution forbids state "discriminat[ion] between schools under the management of different religious denominations." With this firm legal footing, Muslim leaders began negotiations with the Department of Education in 1988, and the first state-backed Muslim primary school opened in 1990.[36] As Claire Hogan, an attorney with expertise in Islam and Irish law, put it to me, "State neutrality needs to be credible."[37] This school has since moved to Clonskeagh, home of the Islamic Cultural Centre of Ireland, and welcomed President Mary Robinson for its reopening. She remarked that it was "only natural" that Muslims would desire schools in keeping with the Irish denominational model.[38] Ali Selim stressed the importance of this school as "showing a level of trust" from state authorities in the Muslim community and pointed out that many of the school's teachers and administrators are non-Muslims.[39]

Of course, many Muslim children cannot attend this school and find themselves in other, predominantly Catholic primary schools. In contrast to the reaction to veiling in much of continental Europe, their attendance at these schools has not generated substantial controversy about veiling in Ireland. In 2008, a principal in County Wexford did request more guidance on the matter from the Department of Education, and he decided to allow the *hijab* in the particular case in his school. The Department of Education declined to give a definitive ruling, instead stressing the importance of local school autonomy and the obligation not to exclude certain students by constructing a restrictive uniform policy.[40] A standing-room-only consultation on the issue held by the Irish Council for Civil Liberties in May 2011 set out very limited circumstances where the *hijab* could be restricted, such as physical education classes if necessary for the student's health and safety. To this point, the *hijab* noncontroversy provides more evidence that benevolent secularism in Ireland has evolved fairly smoothly in response to the Muslim minority.

COALITION TIES AND INSTITUTIONAL EVOLUTION

The major dimensions of benevolent secularism (differentiation, cooperation, and principled distance) have become more robust in Ireland in the decades since independence. This strengthening has taken place in spite of massive changes to the Irish religious landscape, including the collapse of Catholicism's social dominance, the growth of anticlericalism, and the arrival of new religious minority communities. What accounts for institutional evolution in an environment that seems so ripe for more dramatic change? As I argue in chapter 1, benevolent secularism proves so stable because its structure encourages coalition ties that promote more gradual patterns of institutional change. Two particular partnerships have been crucial in stabilizing benevolent secularism in Ireland in the past quarter century: strong interfaith relations and a general religious-secular consensus on the need for institutional evolution. The strength of these two sets of partnerships also helps explain the failure of actors who have attempted to advance more dramatic forms of institutional change.

INTERFAITH RELATIONS AND SECULAR EVOLUTION

A central reason why benevolent secularism has evolved in spite of religious turbulence is the active interfaith partnerships between the Catholic majority and various religious minority communities. This has been especially true for the integration of Islam into Irish public life, but it also extends more broadly. Interfaith relations have improved markedly in the past quarter century as the ecumenical movement within Christianity has encouraged dialogue and laid the groundwork for more interfaith efforts in the recent past. Robust interfaith relations help explain the Catholic Church's support for the growing principled distance of the Irish state from its religious communities. When the New Ireland Forum took up its work, it did so with general support from the Catholic hierarchy. As Archbishop Cahal Daly testified at the New Ireland Forum in 1984 "What [the Catholic bishops] do here and now declare, and declare with emphasis, is that we would raise our voices to resist any constitutional proposals which might infringe or imperil the civil and religious rights and liberties cherished by Northern Protestants." Daly went on to "support the determination of most of the Protestant communities in the Republic, particularly the Church of Ireland, to retain their own denominational schools, and urge that the State should give these schools even more preferential treatment than they already receive."[41] Daly's testimony reflects the generally strong state of ecumenical relations by the early 1980s and the role it played in building meaningful principled distance into Irish benevolent secularism. Interfaith ties have played a part in patronage reform as well. As Professor Coolahan remarked at the Patronage Forum's public hearings, "The Education Body of the Church of Ireland is conscious and proud of the pattern of diversity which exists in many of their schools," and "[the Catholic Church], while concerned to uphold the denominational character of [its] schools, [has] a diverse pupil population and seek[s] to be as inclusive as possible."[42]

The centrality of interfaith relations in driving secular evolution shows through most clearly in the state's incorporation of its growing Muslim minority into the benevolent secular model. When Irish Muslims began a serious campaign to open a primary school, one of the most important markers of inclusion within the Irish religion–state relationship, they found active supporters in the Catholic hierarchy and among many Protestant leaders. When the Muslim national school at the Islamic Cultural Centre of Ireland expanded in 1996, leading Catholic and Church of Ireland clerics were in attendance for the festivities.[43] More recently, Archbishop Diarmuid Martin of Dublin has visited the school, and Ali Selim approvingly noted his suggestion of "mutual visits [by religious leaders] to offer mutual support [as a means of] strengthening interfaith relations."[44] This kind of interfaith cooperation from both Protestant and Catholic leaders helps to explain why Ireland's newfound religious diversity has not destabilized benevolent secularism. Strong interfaith relations help integrate new communities into the benevolent bargain.

Muslims and non-Muslims regularly cited the benevolence of Irish secularism as a reason for the generally positive relations between Islam and the Irish state. Polling of Irish Muslims is fairly limited, but a survey carried out by the *Irish Independent* and RTÉ in 2006 found that nearly 80 percent of Irish Muslims considered themselves fully integrated and felt accepted in Irish society.[45] Ali Selim spoke at length about how Ireland has "learned from Europe's mistakes" in managing relations with Muslims and how the general social respect shown to religion in Ireland contrasts sharply with the antireligion and anti-Islam sentiment on the continent.[46] As Patsy McGarry, the *Irish Times* religion reporter, put it recently, "The great monolith that was the Catholic Church in Ireland now seems more content to take its place as a partner among other Christian denominations and faiths, while Protestants feel more confident in the Republic than at any time since the foundation of the State."[47] This interfaith cooperation is both a result of benevolent secularism and an explanation of institutional stability even in the face of rapid religious change.

RELIGIOUS-SECULAR TIES AND SECULAR EVOLUTION

The second mechanism by which benevolent secularism stabilizes itself over time is also apparent in recent history: the promotion of ties that minimize potential religious-secular divides. A general religious-secular consensus exists that Irish religion–state relations need to evolve; many of the most vocal reformers have been Catholics themselves. In response to religious change in Ireland and in particular to criticisms of the extent of Catholic influence in public life, networks of elected officials, policy elites, and religious leaders have acted to preserve Ireland's benevolent secularism. This activity is especially visible in ongoing patterns of religion–state policy consultation and in religious-secular cooperation tied to the reform of educational patronage.

Although it is true that anger at the Catholic hierarchy has peaked in Ireland in the wake of sexual abuse scandals, it is also important to note that much of this criticism comes from within the Catholic community itself. Commonly cited evidence of rabid anticlericalism, such as Taoiseach Kenny's lambasting of the Vatican that opened this chapter, is not necessarily evidence of a vast religious-secular divide. Kenny himself is a Catholic, and mere months after his famous remarks in the Dáil he reported to the legislature on the importance of the "structured dialogue" process with religious leaders "to achieve mutual respect and understanding between the civil authorities and those who lead our churches, faith communities and non-confessional bodies."[48] In another high-profile example, Minister of Education and Skills Ruairi Quinn, Ireland's most prominent elected nonbeliever, was careful to insist in 2011, "I'm not in the business, nor is the Government, of trying to bankrupt any religious congregation. . . . [T]hey gave an awful lot of care to all of us growing up, and I'm one of them."[49]

Religious-secular ties show through in various forms of policy consultation in the past quarter century. Diverse religious actors took part in "Social Partnership" negotiations that set wage and employment policy until 2009,[50] and a broader "Structured Dialogue" between religious and state actors has touched on a range of policy issues. The timing of these initiatives shows religious and secular elites' efforts to maintain benevolent secularism in the face of growing diversity and secularization. As Taoiseach Bertie Ahern put it in his remarks launching the Structured Dialogue in 2007, "It would be an irony of history if Catholic, Protestant and Dissenter, having each experienced exclusion at some phase in our history, should now be bound together in a shared feeling of indifference from a secularized state. . . . There is a form of aggressive secularism which would have the State and State institutions ignore the importance of this religious dimension. . . . It would be a betrayal of the best traditions of Irish Republicanism to create such an environment."[51] In another address, Ahern went on to state that the cooperation through Structured Dialogue would include not only policy discussions but also state support for "high-quality theological reflection on many of the issues that are central to public debate in the Ireland of today."[52] In precisely the years of greatest threat to benevolent secularism, political elites and religious leaders rallied to its defense through this process of mutual engagement.

Evidence of the importance of religious-secular elite ties shows through in patronage reform debates as well. Cooperation can endure through the reform process. Minister Quinn has pointed out frequently that even Archbishop Diarmuid Martin has called for patronage to more accurately reflect popular demand, and, indeed, the Catholic Schools Partnership has generally cooperated with the Patronage Forum. The Irish Human Rights Commission (IHRC) hearing on religion and Irish education on May 25, 2011, highlighted the religious-secular alliances that have preserved benevolent secularism in this area.[53] Although the IHRC's report constantly notes the need for policy evolution, its "overarching recommendation[,] diversity in provision of school type[,] . . . which reflects the diversity of religious and non-religious convictions now represented in the State," is hardly a call to arms to overthrow the existing denominational system.[54]

The report, although technically neutral on denominational education, clearly assumes that reform within the existing collaborative religion–state model is possible. The launchers of the report personify religious-secular ties. A notable presence among the reports' backers, alongside a range of education reformers, was Professor William Binchy, a leading Catholic thinker from Trinity College Dublin who could never be accused of being anticlerical.[55] The partnerships between Catholics such as Binchy and more secular-minded human rights reformers exemplify the general religious-secular cooperation that has stabilized benevolent secularism during a time of great turmoil in Ireland.

In sum, in a time of great religious turbulence, religious-secular and interfaith partnerships stabilized and even fortified benevolent secularism. Catholic elites grew quite critical of earlier patterns of Catholic influence, the Muslim minority generally found allies in existing religious communities, and leading secularists were generally willing to work with religious actors to update, rather than overturn, existing institutions.

RELIGION–STATE CONSENSUS IN PUBLIC OPINION

The evidence given in the preceding section documents the role of elite ties in preserving benevolent secularism in Ireland, even in the face of significant changes in the Irish religious landscape. Does evidence exist in public opinion that these patterns of elite consensus have any analogue among the general public? The evidence on elites generates two empirical hypotheses that can be tested with public opinion data. First, there should be no significant differences across the religious-secular divide on matters related to differentiation of religion and state. Second, there should be no significant differences across interfaith divides on matters related to principled distance. Data from the ISSP's Religion and Politics module allow us to examine these mechanisms as they relate to two of the dimensions of benevolent secularism: differentiation of religious and state institutions as well as the principled distance between the state and religious communities.[56] In sum, the data reveal high aggregate levels of popular support for both differentiation and principled distance. The hypothesized religious-secular consensus on differentiation is particularly strong. One interesting division among the general population does stand out that qualifies support for the second hypothesis: although there is *interfaith* agreement on equal treatment of all religions, the religiously unaffiliated are significantly less supportive of this position.

In the analysis that follows, I focus on two questions as dependent variables that at least roughly correspond to two of the three dimensions of benevolent secularism: differentiation and principled distance. Question 1 in table 3.2 captures public attitudes to differentiation in relation to elections. The question asks about religious leaders' impact on voting decisions; although this measure is rather blunt, it provides some insight into public support for distinctions among state and religious spheres. Question 2 examines attitudes to principled distance by asking whether respect is owed to all religions. Although the idea of principled distance as developed by Rajeev Bhargava is more complex than this survey question, the question gives some sense of respondents' attitudes to religious pluralism and the place of diverse religious communities in public life. Unfortunately, existing polling is particularly weak in assessing attitudes toward cooperation between religion and state.

Table 3.3 reports aggregate results, broken down by major religious traditions and distinguishing the most regularly practicing Catholics from others. These results show nearly equal levels of very high support across religious traditions for differentiating religious elites from voting decisions. Catholics as a whole are only two points lower than the unaffiliated in expressing such support, and even respondents with the highest church attendance among the Catholic community show little less support. There is more variation between the religious traditions when examining results related to respect for all religions. Here, the widest

TABLE 3.2. SECULARISM AND PUBLIC OPINION IN IRELAND: QUESTION WORDING

Variable	Question Wording	Source/Country	Coding
Differentiation			
1. Religious Leaders Elections	How much do you agree or disagree with the following? Religious leaders should not try to influence how people vote in elections.	ISSP Religion III Module (Ireland; Philippines)	1 (Strongly Disagree) to 5 (Strongly Agree)
Principled Distance			
2. Equal Respect	How much do you agree or disagree with the following statement? We must respect all religions.	ISSP Religion III Module (Ireland; Philippines)	1 (Strongly Disagree) to 5 (Strongly Agree)

Source: International Social Survey Programme Research Group, *International Social Survey Programme (ISSP): Religion III* (Cologne, Germany: GESIS, 2008).

TABLE 3.3. IRELAND TOPLINE RESULTS BY
RELIGIOUS TRADITION AND ATTENDANCE

	N	Support for Statement: "Religious Leaders Should Not Influence Voting" (%)	Agreement with Statement: "We Must Respect All Religions" (%)
Total	2,047	78	84
All Catholics	1,795	78	85
Catholics Who Attend Church Weekly or More	899	75	88
Catholics Who Attend Church Less Than Weekly	896	79	81
Unaffiliated	144	80	75
Religious Minorities	107	76	92

Source: ISSP Research Group, ISSP: Religion III.

gaps are actually between religious minorities, who, perhaps unsurprisingly, are most supportive of this statement, and the unaffiliated, who come in far below the population as a whole. The division among Catholics is also worth noting. As a whole, Catholics are more supportive of respect for all religions than are the unaffiliated, although not quite as strongly supportive of it as religious minorities. However, within the Catholic population, differences emerge, with more observant Catholics more supportive of universal respect for religions.

Multivariate analysis controlling for major demographic factors alongside measures of religious belonging reinforces these topline results. I report two models for each question. First, I report the simple religious identification models, with the Irish nonreligious community and Irish religious minorities compared to the Catholic majority baseline. Second, I control for major demographic factors, including religious attendance. The most important results in these more complex models are still those that compare the group of respondents with no religious tradition and members of religious minority groups to the Catholic baseline category. Catholic respondents are the omitted reference category in these models, so the coefficients for the nonreligious and the religious minorities should be interpreted relative to the Catholic majority. The results are shown in table 3.4.

With respect to a question related to differentiation in the context of elections (Models 1 and 2), evidence confirms consensus across Catholic, minority, and unaffiliated boundaries. The nonreligious in Ireland are only modestly distinct from Irish Catholics and Irish religious minorities even in the simplest models with no controls. However, more complete models eliminate this distinctiveness; once socioeconomic status, gender, and religious attendance are controlled for, there is no statistically significant difference among Catholics, minorities, and the unaffiliated on religious leaders' influence on voting. This finding indicates that among the general public, as among the elites interviewed, both Catholic *and* unaffiliated Irish support the differentiation of religion and state institutions. It also indicates that *within* the Catholic community

TABLE 3.4. TESTING BENEVOLENT SECULAR CONSENSUS IN IRELAND

	Differentiation		Principled Distance	
	Religious Leaders' Impact on Vote		Respect All Religions	
	Model 1	Model 2	Model 3	Model 4
No Religion	0.28*	0.099	−0.34***	−0.31**
	[0.16]	[0.18]	[0.13]	[0.14]
Religious Minority	−0.07	−0.12	0.23*	0.22
	[0.15]	[0.15]	[0.14]	[0.14]
Sex		0.066		0.16**
		[0.064]		[0.061]
Age		0.0018		0.0025
		[0.002]		[0.002]
Education		0.03*		0.025
		[0.017]		[0.017]
Religious Attendance		0.057***		−0.0014
		[0.018]		[0.016]
N	1,997	1,990	2,001	1,992

Note: All coefficients standardized (*** $p < 0.01$, ** $p < 0.05$, * $p < 0.1$). Ordered Probit Models with robust standard errors in brackets.
Source: ISSP Research Group, ISSP: Religion III.

the pious secularism that showed through at the elite level around the New Ireland Forum and the school patronage debate is mirrored in the general population.

If Model 2 demonstrates religious-secular consensus on preserving differentiation, Models 3 and 4 turn to the question of maintaining principled distance among all religious communities. Here, the elite evidence indicates that interfaith ties prove central in maintaining principled distance, particularly in the integration of the Irish Muslim minority into benevolent secular institutions. The findings in Models 3 and 4 confirm the consensus between minorities and the Catholic majority on respect of all religious traditions. Even without controls in Model 3, minorities are only modestly more supportive of religious respect than Catholics, and in Model 4 the result drops from statistical significance. This result is quite striking because one would suspect that religious minorities have a stronger reason to respect all religions than the predominant Catholic majority does. The relatively strong Catholic support for equal respect demonstrates that the warm interfaith relations discussed by both Archbishop Diarmuid Martin and Ali Selim of the Islamic Cultural Centre of Ireland exist among the general population as well.

The most dramatic difference regarding support for principled distance comes through in examining the nonreligious respondents. Here, the unaffiliated are significantly less supportive of universal respect for religion than both religious minorities and the Catholic majority. This finding is interesting and suggests that the relatively smooth adaptation of principled distance to Ireland's growing Muslim, Orthodox, and Pentecostal minorities rests on strong interfaith grounds rather than on alliances between the unaffiliated and the minority communities. Among the general population, anyway, there seems to be raw material for religious-secular division in this area, but interfaith consensus nevertheless remains robust. This finding raises the interesting prospect that the two mechanisms of coalition ties traced throughout this argument may at times come to work independently of one another.

These public opinion results generally confirm the hypothesized parallels between elite cooperation and popular opinion. Religious-secular divides are minimal on matters of differentiation, and interfaith similarities show through in the responses to questions related to principled distance, providing another part of the explanation of why benevolent secularism has proven durable even in the face of Catholicism's ongoing collapse in Ireland. On questions of differentiation, many Irish Catholics have become deeply disenchanted with religious leaders' influence on politics and actually share the views of the nonreligious. In contrast, on matters of principled distance, Ireland's religious minorities are actually quite close to the Catholic majority, who have proven willing allies in extending public respect for religion to the relative newcomers.

This chapter demonstrates the role of coalition ties, both interfaith partnerships and general religious-secular cooperation, in causing the period of institutional change in Irish religion–state relations to be one of evolution rather than a broader breakdown in benevolent secularism. The collapse of Catholic Ireland made conditions seem open to a major revolution in religion–state relations. However, developments from the New Ireland Forum to the Forum on Patronage demonstrate that the core dimensions of benevolent secularism—differentiation, cooperation, and principled distance—endure in Ireland. In fact, insofar as there has been institutional evolution, it has made Irish religion–state relations even closer to the benevolent secular ideal type. This evolution in Irish institutions has been driven by the coalition ties that benevolent secularism promotes: strong interfaith relations and a minimal religious-secular divide. These mechanisms are observable at the elite level through debates about patronage reform and legal status of the Irish Muslim minority and in the general population through public opinion analysis.

The relationship between coalition alliances and institutional structure demonstrates the general argument concerning the path-dependent nature of benevolent secularism. In Ireland, the critical juncture around the Constitution of 1937 established the basic rules by which religion and state interacted with one another. Patterns of differentiation, cooperation, and principled distance encouraged the formation of a diverse coalition of political elites, Catholic clerics, and religious minorities in favor of benevolent secularism. That coalition has now become the source of benevolent secularism's stability in Ireland, even in the face of the rapid decline in Catholic dominance. Key partnerships across the religious-secular divide and bridging interfaith gaps have undercut attempts to overturn benevolent secularism and instead have encouraged Irish institutions to evolve a robust principled distance in a more pluralistic republic.

Benevolent secularism in Ireland will likely remain contentious, especially in areas of religious exemption from generally applicable laws. In the interest of the "free profession and practice of religion" protected by Article 44.2.1, Irish courts have historically carved out religious exemptions from certain generally applicable laws, including exemptions meant to preserve the "religious ethos" of bodies such as schools. As discussed in chapter 2, the *Quinn's Supermarket* decision held that Jewish butchers should be exempted from general restrictions on opening hours that would have unfairly burdened their businesses. The High Court held in *Fitzpatrick v. K* in 2008 that religious exemptions to blood transfusions must be honored, provided that the patient has the mental capacity to make such a decision for herself.[57] However, claims to conscience exemption are not guarantees of legal success in contemporary Ireland. In the Dáil debates regarding the civil partnerships bill of 2010, conservative legislators called for individual conscience exemptions, primarily for civil magistrates who for religious reasons objected to certifying homosexual partnerships.[58] Their point failed to carry the day. David Quinn, columnist for the *Irish Independent* and director of the traditionalist Iona Institute, argues that refusing such exemptions and related exemptions for pharmacists who object to dispensing certain contraceptives in effect amounts to hanging a "No Christians Need Apply" sign on certain modern professions.[59] The Irish government is currently in the process of revisiting exemptions for religious organizations provided in the Employment Equality Acts of 1998 and 2004.[60] Conscience exemptions have been an element of Irish benevolent secularism since independence, but their future, especially when linked to the realm of LGBT rights, is uncertain.

Ruairi Quinn famously called Ireland "post-Catholic" more than a decade ago. Time may prove him right on the demographics, but he has already been vindicated in the realm of state secularism. The unique advantages afforded Catholicism in the postwar era are largely a thing of the past, worn away by changes in demographics and discontent with the clergy's political role in the state. What has evolved, however, retains the basic benevolence in treatment of religion that has characterized Irish secularism since the independence period. These institutions continue to be contested by an array of actors, both religious and political, some of whom want to replace Ireland's tradition of secular pluralism with a more separationist model of religion–state relations. However, these revisionists face significant resistance from both religious and secular parties to the benevolent Irish bargain.

4. Secular Emergence in Senegal

LAÏCITÉ IN TRANSLATION

"La République du Sénégal est laïque, démocratique et sociale." From the first words of Article 1, Senegal's Constitution of 2001 foregrounds the *laïque* nature of the religion–state relationship. The wording has remained largely unchanged since the immediate postcolonial period, in spite of substantial constitutional developments through that same time. How did Senegal, a highly devout Muslim-majority country, emerge as a secular republic after independence from France in 1960? And what does the term *laïcité* mean in its Senegalese translation? This chapter analyzes the institutions of state secularism in Senegal and their role in promoting the twin tolerations at independence. As French colonial administration drew to a close, local actors with diverse views regarding the appropriate place of religion in politics jockeyed for influence. In this uncertain environment, Léopold Sédar Senghor proposed an institutional relationship between religion and state that closely matched the ideal type of benevolent secularism. These institutions played a central role in securing the twin tolerations during this critical juncture by affecting key actors' preferences. Religion would play a substantial role in public life without provoking either pole of the secularism trap.

The wording of the phrase from Article 1 of Senegal's Constitution offers an almost direct parallel to wording in Article 1 of the French Constitution of

1958, which declares France a "république indivisible, laïque, démocratique et sociale." As with many of Senghor's institutional proposals, elements of the religion–state relationship were indeed influenced by patterns from French history. However, although the formalities of constitutional wording echo French documents, Senghor's proposed institutionalization of *laïcité* was substantially different in its Senegalese translation. French Third Republic statesman Léon Gambetta quipped in an earlier era that anticlericalism was not an item for export, which was confirmed in the Senegalese configuration of *laïcité*. *Laïcité* in France is a version of what Ahmet Kuru has called "assertive secularism," subordinating religion to the state and forcibly cleansing the public sphere of religious influence.[1] *Laïcité* takes on a different institutional shape in Senegal, characterized by the three dimensions of benevolent secularism: differentiation, cooperation, and principled distance.

Studying secular emergence in Senegal is an important corrective to essentialist arguments about the incompatibility between Islam and secular democracy. Senegal provides clear evidence that in certain conditions Islamic authorities have been happy to uphold the twin tolerations and indeed have been skeptical of efforts to further integrate religion and state. This accommodation has not necessarily required adoption of liberal religious norms or the decline of religious belief but instead has rested on norms within Senegal's Sufi elites regarding the appropriate relationship between religion and state and on generally strong ties between Muslim and Catholic elites.

This chapter focuses on the critical juncture around Senegal's independence from French Sudan in 1960, President Léopold Sédar Senghor's political victory over Mamadou Dia, his once partner and later rival, in 1962, and Senghor's reelection as president in 1963. This period parallels the end of the Free State in Ireland; colonial imposition of political institutions drew to a close, and local elites had the opportunity to set new institutions in place to configure the relationship between religion and state. This window of indeterminacy in Senegal attracted a wave of bargaining, with groups such as the Conseil supérieur des chefs religieux (High Council of Religious Leaders) pushing for a state that enforced Islamic law. Senghor's institutionalization of *laïcité* ultimately united a diverse coalition in support of the twin tolerations in the newly independent republic.

This chapter progresses in four parts. First, I provide an overview of Senegal's religious landscape. Second, I document the benevolent dimensions of Senegalese secularism, cataloging differentiation, cooperation, and principled distance in Senegalese political institutions. Third, I demonstrate the impact of this institutional configuration on the preferences of key actors whose interactions shaped the place of religion in independence-era Senegal: the Muslim majority, secular elites wielding state power, and the Catholic minority. After considering alternative explanations of the twin tolerations in Senegal, I close by examining an episode of instability in Senegalese secularism around the Code de la famille (Family Code). Contestation in this area highlights unresolved differences even among defenders of the twin tolerations that would later drive secular evolution.

SENEGAL'S RELIGIOUS LANDSCAPE

It is easy enough to see that Senegal is a Muslim-majority country characterized by vibrant religious observance. Any walking trip near downtown Dakar's mosques on a Friday afternoon encounters sidewalks crowded with prayer mats. Islam reached Senegal, along with sub-Saharan neighbors Niger and Mali, only in the second millennium c.e., well after the initial waves of Islamic conversion in North Africa. Wholesale conversion did not take place until the nineteenth century. But the country has since largely converted, with 90 to 95 percent of the population currently identifying as Muslim in survey research. The coexistence of such an overwhelming Muslim majority with religious liberty and secular democracy sets Senegal apart from Muslim-majority dictatorships in the Arab world, although, as Alfred Stepan and Graeme Robertson have convincingly demonstrated, not from other Muslim-majority democracies such as Indonesia and Bangladesh.[2]

Although it is tempting to see Senegal as a homogeneously Sunni Muslim society, this view obscures the substantial diversity within Senegalese Islam. Sufi Islam predominates in Senegal, and various brotherhoods play an important role in public life. This is not the place for an extended discussion of Sufism in Senegal, but it is generally characterized by devotional religious practice and membership in an organized brotherhood, or *tariqa*. Sufi brotherhoods in Senegal feature close relationships between adepts, or *taalibes*, and Sufi leaders, or *marabouts*. The *taalibe–marabout* relationship may be less constraining since large-scale urbanization, but it continues to exercise substantial influence on personal behavior. Because this relationship is individualized, membership in Sufi brotherhoods is not precisely analogous to that in a mainline Protestant denomination. There is division not only among the brotherhoods but also between different groups of *marabouts* within each brotherhood.

Although demographics would tell you that Senegal is more than 90 percent Muslim, this assessment masks the relative balance among a range of Sufi brotherhoods in the country. Two deserve particular attention here: the Mouridiyya (Mourides) and Tidjanniyya (Tidjanns). Mourides make up a bit more than 30 percent of the overall population, and the Tidjanns constitute nearly 50 percent.[3] The Tidjann *tariqa* began in North Africa and spread to the area of contemporary Senegal under the leadership of al-Hajj Umar Tall in the mid–nineteenth century. Although Umar Tall adopted a largely hostile pattern of relations with animist and French forces, later Tidjann leaders, notably al-Hajj Malik Sy, were less militant.[4] The Tidjanns spread through the country, notably in the area around Tivaouane, and had an urban presence across the Quatre communes (Saint Louis, Gorée, Dakar, and Rufisque) at the heart of French Senegal before the Mourides. Political life in the early twentieth century centered on these communes, and thus the Tidjanns acquired significant influence among the emerging political class. In part because of this social prominence, the *tariqa* became a tempting target for internal factionalization, and rivalries between distinct lines within the Tidjann community became pronounced. Such rivalry remains the case to this day and is frequently cited as a reason why the Tidjanns have seen their political influence wane in comparison with relative newcomers to Senegal's Sufi landscape, the Mourides.

The Mourides are the youngest of the major Sufi *tariqa*s in Senegal and yet have rapidly acquired symbolic and material power. Sheikh Amadou Bamba Mbacké, founder of the Mourides, is a national symbol of independence and uprightness. Amadou Bamba was twice exiled by French colonial authorities, who feared his rising social influence in the late nineteenth century, and even after his return in 1907 he lived under French suspicion. The Mourides grew rapidly as independence approached, drawing many members from other Sufi communities. The Mouride focus on the link between religious discipline and physical labor has promoted commercial success in the peanut-based rural economy and in various urban commercial enterprises such as bus transportation and manufacturing. By reputation, the Mourides are more united than the fractious Tidjanns, and Mouride *marabout*s are assumed to have a particularly powerful sway over their followers. The Mouride heartland is Touba, now Senegal's second-largest city and entirely owned by the family of the current *khalife* of the order. As I discuss at length in the sections that follow, the Mourides have translated the social respect for Sheikh Amadou Bamba into wide influence on politics and even symbolism of Senegalese nationhood.[5]

Although the Muslim community predominates, Senegal is also home to a small but influential Christian minority. This group, overwhelmingly Roman Catholic and approximately 5 percent of the population, is one legacy of French colonial rule, particularly in the Quatres communes that were the centers of colonial influence. Various Catholic religious orders played a prominent role in health and education during the French period, and the Cathédrale du souvenir africain, French West Africa's first cathedral, remains a downtown Dakar landmark. Perhaps most importantly for the study of Senegalese secularism, Senegal's postindependence leader, Léopold Sédar Senghor, was a Catholic.

Senghor's personal views on relations among religions and the relationship between religion and state remain central to understanding *laïcité* in Senegal and receive attention later in this chapter. The Catholic community is spread across family and ethnic lines, which may help explain the generally peaceful state of interfaith relations. Both formal interviews and informal conversations routinely referenced families that contain both Catholic and Muslim members. Catholic educational institutions such as the elite Cours Sainte-Marie de Hann are another central site of interfaith integration. Smaller Protestant communities also exist across Senegal, particularly in Dakar, but play a less-prominent public role than do Catholic clergy and laity.

The relatively recent predominance of the Sufi brotherhoods and the Catholic minority means that traditional African religions had substantial social influence in the recent past and continue to shape Senegalese norms regarding tolerance and pluralism. More than one conversation about religion in Senegal contained the observation, "We are 95 percent Muslim, 5 percent Christian, and 100 percent animist." By the time of independence, however, the organizational influence of traditional religious leaders had been significantly weakened by colonial rule and the growth of Islamic and Christian communities. Accounting for traditional African religion remains a challenge to institutions of benevolent secularism; as discussed later, the public role preserved for Islamic and Christian leaders generally does not typically extend to representatives of traditional religions.

ASSESSING *LAÏCITÉ* AS BENEVOLENT SECULARISM

As sketched in the introduction, Senegal has substantially altered the understanding of *laïcité* associated with the state–religion relationship in France.[6] The institutions of secularism in Senegal, from the independence period to the present day, demonstrate the dimensions of benevolent secularism: (1) differentiation of religious and state institutions, (2) cooperation between religion and state in the public square, and (3) principled distance between the state and religious communities. As Senegalese scholar Djibril Samb puts it, "*Laïcité* essentially signifies separation, but not antagonism, of political and religious power."[7] Although basic even-handedness among religious traditions is a key value, there is no assumption that substantive state support for a religious community need violate that neutrality. In this section, I set out the three dimensions of Senegalese secularism, or what former president Abdou Diouf called "laïcité bien comprise," or *laïcité* properly understood.[8] My description of these dimensions includes evidence from central documents such as the Constitution as well as the implementation of those documents in policy formation and less-formal patterns of elite behavior.

Senegalese *laïcité* stands in contrast not only with the understanding of *laïcité* in early-twentieth-century France but also with American separationism, which views even nonpreferential state support for religious institutions as an inevitable source of discrimination. In typological terms, Senegalese secularism closely resembles benevolent secularism. In contrast to assertive secularism, it does not allow for the coercive priority of the state over religious communities, as in French *laïcité* or Kemalist Turkey.[9] In contrast to passive secularism, Senegal does not feature the "wall of separation" that is so familiar in American political discourse. Cooperation between religion and state in Senegal is extensive and takes place in both material support and policy consultations.

The basic differentiation of religious and state institutions features prominently in the Constitution. Religious and state institutions are constitutionally distinct, and because the state is not representative of any one religion, religious liberty is protected for citizens. As noted earlier, the republic is described as *laïque* even before it is described as *démocratique*, and there is absolutely no attempt to establish an official religion along the lines of Muslim-majority republics such as Egypt or of the established churches that endure across much of Europe. Article 6 does declare the sanctity of the human person but gives no exclusively religious basis for this statement. Sovereignty rests with the people, not with any religious community, and when Article 1.2 references "one faith" (*une foi*), there is no particular linkage to a religion. Free exercise is just as prominently declared as disestablishment. Article 1 guarantees equality under the law regardless of religion; Article 4 prohibits religious discrimination; and Article 19 guarantees "liberty of conscience, the profession and the free practice of religion." There are no religious tests for office. Loi 65-60, the Penal Code of 1965, sets out a range of specific punishments for inhibition of free exercise, including fines and prison sentences for interrupting religious services (Article 231) or preventing a minister from completing his worship functions (Article 233).[10]

At independence, differentiation showed through in electoral institutions as well, specifically in the form of prohibitions on religious political parties. Senegal explicitly outlawed religious political parties in the constitutional revisions of 1978, "forbid[ding] political parties identified with a race, ethnic group, sex, religion, sect, or region." This general prohibition had been in place since the postindependence period, when political competition was broadly constrained.[11] The most important Sufi leaders did not support forming religious political parties, although less-prominent Muslim leaders did push the boundary. Maintaining differentiation in party politics proved challenging in practice. As multiparty competition has expanded in the past quarter century, a range of *marabouts politiques* has entered the partisan fray, notably Kara Mbacké's Parti de la vérité pour le développement (PVD). The PVD and other parties like it receive extensive attention in chapter 5. For the purposes of documenting differentiation, it is enough to note that the ban on religious parties contributed to sharpened distinctions between state and religious institutions.

Although differentiation is central to Senegalese secularism, its benevolent structure comes with two other dimensions: the cooperation between state and religions and the principled distance among religious communities. As Samb puts it, "The Senegalese secular republic does not isolate God or condemn God to exile."[12] As is common in benevolent secular states, material cooperation shows through in education. The explicitly acknowledged role of religious actors in education (Article 17) reinforces the nonhostile sense of disestablishment in the Senegalese setting. The state provides bursaries in support of religious education, most of which are paid to Muslim parents sending their children to Catholic schools. Cooperation in education extends beyond the primary level. The state has also funded foreign study at major Arabic educational centers such as al-Azhar in Cairo.[13]

This pattern of religion–state cooperation extends beyond education to what Donal Cruise O'Brien has termed the "contrat social sénégalais," or Senegalese social contract.[14] Here, cooperation moves from constitutional language to daily interactions in public life. Cruise O'Brien's "social contract" involves mutual exchange between political elites and the various Sufi brotherhoods and touches on matters as diverse as development planning and agricultural policy. The Sufi brotherhoods encourage electoral participation and the collection of tax revenue in exchange not only for relative autonomy from the state but also for receiving substantial material concessions from the state in the form of tax exemptions, land grants, and development assistance. As Cruise O'Brien points out, this cooperation extends to symbols of endorsement, such as political attendance at religious festivals.[15] Although these patterns of exchange led more than one interview subject to remark that Senegal is not really a secular state, they are not inconsistent with the dimension of cooperation that characterizes benevolent secularism.

State cooperation with religious institutions extends to policy consultation in addition to these patterns of material exchange. At secular emergence, family law was the epicenter of this consultation. As in Ireland and the Philippines, in Senegal religious elites had a special interest in law related to the family, in particular marriage and inheritance, and political elites at independence realized that this area required careful consultation with a variety of elite *marabouts*. In 1961, Prime Minister Dia convened a commission to study the matter, sending hundreds of questionnaires about existing personal law customs throughout Senegal.[16] Other consultations have been less thorough, but the basic consultative pattern has existed more broadly. Over time, it has included agricultural policy related to the pricing of the key peanut crop, the meeting of key development milestones such as the Millennium Development Goals, and cooperative strategies to limit the spread of HIV/AIDS. This regularized pattern of policy consultation constitutes a clear indicator of the cooperative dimension of benevolent secularism. These consultations are not without controversy and do not necessarily resolve all differences. The family law consultations, as described later, remain contested. As Senegalese philosopher Souleymane Bachir Diagne has observed, such controversies reveal that cooperation between religion and state "cannot be taken for granted but must be pursued as a perpetual goal."[17]

The final dimension of benevolent secularism, the state's principled distance among religious communities, also characterizes the institutional relationship between religion and state in Senegal. Article 1.1 of the Constitution closes by stating that the republic "respects all beliefs" regardless of particular religious identification. Khadim Mbacké, a Mouride scholar at the Institut fondamental d'Afrique Noire, pointed out to me that *laïcité* means "equal support for all religious communities" in proportion to the demands that communities make of the state.[18] As Étienne Smith notes, however, there is a certain "proportionality" in this process, with larger movements receiving more attention from state actors.[19] In the area of material support, the state provides funds for construction and maintenance of houses of worship on an interfaith basis. The massive mosque in Touba, the spiritual capital of the Mouride brotherhood, was completed in 1963 with state support, and renovations of the Cathédrale du souvenir africain were enabled by 10 million (West African) francs at nearly the same time.[20] Such support also extends to the realm of pilgrimages and festivals. The state pays for a large hajj pilgrimage each year and in the interest of maintaining a principled distance funds a Catholic pilgrimage to Rome or the Holy Land as well. The state provides substantial infrastructural support for the grand Sufi festivals, in particular the Grand Magal pilgrimage that brings more than a million pilgrims to the Mouride heartland each year. Although no identically massive Christian festival requires state support, there are a range of Christian state holidays, including a popular Pentecost celebration that brings a large pilgrimage to the Marian prayer site at Popenguine.[21]

The principled distance of the state from its religious communities also motivates a set of exemptions from generally applicable laws. These exemptions rest on the Article 19 guarantee that religious institutions may "regulate and administer their affairs in an autonomous manner." President Senghor and his *marabout* allies interpreted autonomy broadly, including land concessions and regulatory exemptions for the Mourides in the agricultural realm.[22] Abdou Lahatte Mbacké, *khalife* of the Mourides from 1968 to 1989, obtained his two-thousand-acre personal farm from government-protected forest and turned it into a center of agricultural development.[23] Mouride peanut producers were allowed exemption from state-controlled price cooperatives and thus received a higher price for their peanuts by selling directly to Dakar-based merchants. This basic pattern has continued even after urbanization in Touba as various trade and taxation laws apply differently there, making its markets a key driver of Mouride international commerce. These exemptions can be quite controversial, and the sense under the administration of President Wade that they no longer maintained a principled distance among religious groups spurred the secular evolution analyzed in chapter 5.

It is worth noting that *laïcité* is largely a matter of executive practice in Senegal. Souleymane Bachir Diagne, Senegalese philosopher and former political adviser to President Abdou Diouf, frames *laïcité* as more of a "system of practice" than a "bureaucratic code," from its earliest days under Senghor to the present.[24] In contrast to the kinds of judicial battles over religious parties that have regularly occurred in Turkey, for instance, or the extensive jurisprudence on religion–state relations in Ireland, the institutions of *laïcité* in Senegal are controlled and applied largely by the executive branch. Since President Senghor's triumph over Prime Minister Mamadou Dia in 1962, Senegalese political institutions have strongly favored the executive over the legislative and judiciary. Because of this imbalance in power, decisions regarding religion–state relations are closely linked to the current president's political calculations and less strictly codified through rigid jurisprudential decisions. As presidential interests and ideologies have shifted over time, so has the application of *laïcité*.

In sum, Senegal's institutional relationship between religion and state demonstrates the three core dimensions of benevolent secularism: differentiation, cooperation, and principled distance (see table 4.1). This configuration maintains the differentiation between religion and state while actively promoting a high level of political engagement on the part of major religious institutions. These three features emerged at the critical juncture of independence and, as analyzed in chapter 5, endure to this day. Although they drew on institutions developed under French colonial rule, they stood apart in important ways. After a period of indeterminacy, the rule of President Senghor firmly established these institutional rules in both constitutional law and the practice of everyday politics. As in Ireland, principled distance is not always perfectly realized in Senegal. Among the Sufi *tariqa*s, it has long been a source of contestation, and the traditional African religions cannot be seen as equal partners in this process. Nevertheless, *laïcité* in Senegal on the whole took a benevolent form, quite distinct from its French namesake.

TABLE 4.1. ASSESSING BENEVOLENT SECULARISM IN SENEGAL

Indicator	Evidence
Differentiation	
Disestablishment	Article 1.1, Constitution of Senegal: "The Republic of Senegal is *laïque*."
Religious Freedom	Article 19, Constitution of Senegal: "Liberty of conscience, profession, and practice of faith."
Religion–State Cooperation	
Material Support	State bursaries to attend religious schools
Policy Consultation	State survey of religious elites in development of the Code de la famille
Principled Distance	
Impartial Access to Public Support	Funding of hajj for Muslim majority and of Holy Land pilgrimage for Catholic minority
Provide Religious Exemptions	Article 19.2, Constitution of Senegal: "Religious institutions regulate their affairs in an autonomous manner."

INSTITUTIONAL EFFECTS ON ACTOR PREFERENCES

Senegal's transition from colonial rule to independence presented a critical juncture, a window of institutional indeterminacy during which the current regime of *laïcité* emerged. There was a wide diversity of preferences regarding the place of religion in an independent state, and elites actively pursued these preferences as the end of colonial rule approached. Political factions jockeyed for position in the coastal urban centers and had every incentive to seek the favor of Sufi brotherhood elites. Some Muslim leaders sensed an opportunity to bring Islamic doctrine into state law because the departure of colonial authorities would allow the Muslim majority to unite political and religious authority in a way not possible under French rule. A group of clerics united across the Sufi brotherhoods to demand some kind of formal constitutional establishment of religion, including reserved legislative seats for the Muslim community. And yet out of this period of flux the twin tolerations emerged rather than either extreme of the secularism trap. What explains this outcome?

In short, this institutional configuration of *laïcité* secured the twin tolerations because it affected the preferences within the key blocs bargaining over the relationship between religion and state. Institutional structure thus encouraged a diverse coalition of support, notably Sufi Muslim leadership, state political elites, and the Catholic minority. This section traces the diverse ways in which institutions shaped preferences within these groups and tests the hypothesized institutional effects within each coalition bloc set out in chapter 1.

Benevolent secularism shapes preferences of a religious majority by empowering pious secularists and diminishing the appeal of religious integralism, or the position that the majority religion should be formally established in state law. Muslim elites advocating either pious secularism or religious integralism had actively contended with one another under colonial rule throughout the late nineteenth and early twentieth centuries. Advocates of an Islamic state waged several jihads against local and colonial rivals, whereas "among quietist ulemas who specialized in teaching, the access and control of political power has never been a central preoccupation."[25] With independence, calls for integralism and pious secularism coexisted and contended with one another among Senegal's Muslim elite.

Pious secularists in Senegal came to predominate among the Muslim majority in response to Senghor's structure of benevolent secularism. Pious secularism drew on Senegalese Sufi history, exemplified by Mouride founder Amadou Bamba, whose dedication to peaceful negotiation with state authorities continued to exercise tremendous influence even among non-Mouride *tariqas*.[26] As Robert Fatton argues, "[The *marabouts*'] legitimacy as spiritual and moral patrons of the peasant *taalibe* relies on their capacity to be perceived as the sacred symbol of protection from and opposition to the state."[27] On a more material level, the cooperative dimension of benevolent secularism benefited not only the *marabouts* but also their broader circles of followers, who were installed as clerks, bureaucrats, and interpreters for the administration. Institutionalized cooperation augmented the material strength of pious secularists—for instance, solidifying their control of agricultural holdings in the rural interior—while differentiation preserved the independence of brotherhood elites exemplified by Amadou Bamba. Religious integralism held little appeal for these pious secularists, who were concerned with preserving both the purity of the religious community and its autonomy from state coercion.

The predominance of pious secularists was accompanied by the failure of advocates of religious integralism. The preference for an Islamic state was alive and well as Senegal moved to independence but lost ground as the benevolent structure of *laïcité* emerged. The most prominent Muslim calls for an alternative to pious secularism came from the Conseil supérieur des chefs religieux and the Parti de la solidarité sénégalaise (PSS). Disaffected Mouride and Tidjann leaders founded the Conseil supérieur in 1958 to push for a more explicit Islamic identity in the postcolonial state. Its charter declared its intention to "maintain the dogmas of Islam in their true sense" and "to secure acceptance for any constitution which conforms to the interests of Islam."[28] The organization also demanded that Senghor set aside for Muslims half of the seats in the proposed national assembly, to be selected by the Conseil supérieur. Cheikh Tiadianne Sy, a leader of the Conseil supérieur, would go on to found the PSS, a political party to serve as the "champion[] of Islam" against the "Catholic menace."[29] In addition to the Conseil supérieur, which still drew largely on clerics from within the major Sufi *tariqa*s, an Islamic reformist movement began to gather steam in Senegal in the 1950s under the leadership of Cheikh Touré. His party, the Union culturelle musulmane (UCM), was founded in 1953 to revitalize both the public square and the faith community. As Roman Loimeier points out, other reformist groups had previously existed, but the UCM "was not only critical of the French colonial administration but also attacked the Senegalese Sufi orders, in particular *marabouts* who cooperated closely with the colonial administration."[30] The UCM challenged the Sufi orders' pious secularism and rejected the kind of material cooperation and pious withdrawal that characterized mainstream Sufi practice.

These movements ultimately lost out to pious secularists within the Muslim community. Pious secularists carried the debate because of the benevolent structure of *laïcité*, in particular its combination of differentiation and cooperation.[31] Attempts to resist pious secularism foundered primarily because the leading Sufi elites were pleased with the benevolent secular bargain and realized that their own personal authority would be undermined by critics of this institutional arrangement. The *khalife*s of the major Sufi orders had little interest in becoming an official part of the state bureaucracy and saw differentiation as important to maintaining their institutional autonomy. With Senghor's skillful consolidation of support from the diverse Sufi *tariqa*s, the Conseil supérieur disbanded without success in opposing a secular constitution. The PSS found almost no electoral support in 1959 and thus disbanded. Even the UCM was persuaded to reduce its strongest calls for integralism in exchange for inclusion in the cooperative dimension of Senegalese *laïcité*. The structure of political institutions thus had an impact on even actors advocating integralism as some changed their preferences and accepted participation in state institutions and others held fast to integralism but found little popular support. Reformist movements in the tradition of these bodies continued on, but as the critical juncture of secular emergence drew to a close, pious secularism held sway among the most prominent Sufi clerics.

Benevolent secularism had a distinct institutional effect among elites who wielded secular state power. These political elites were centered on the Quatre communes and by the independence period had more than a century of electoral experience, with representation in the National Assembly from 1848 and robust French citizenship rights, particularly after the Blaise Diagne laws of 1916.[32] In general, institutions of benevolent secularism should undercut more anticlerical voices among political elites and strengthen the hand of those seeking a mutually agreed accommodation with religious elites. It is noteworthy that full-throated anticlericalism was a rarity among political elites at Senegal's independence. Nevertheless, leading state elites such as Blaise Diagne and Lamine Guèye were Freemasons, and there were differences within this bloc over the place of religion in the independent Senegalese republic. The leading political powers of this period—Senghor, Dia, and Guèye—exemplified this diversity and the contestation between state actors during this period.

President Léopold Sédar Senghor best represented accommodationist preferences among state elites in Senegal at independence. Senghor, a Catholic, understood the effect that the institutional relationship between religion and state could have on his own political authority. Although a state official, Senghor was not anticlerical. He developed a serious interest in the writings of Jesuit anthropologist Pierre Teilhard de Chardin, finding there the philosophical grounding of his own "faithful socialism," which prompted him to write his "hommage à Pierre Teilhard de Chardin" in 1963.[33] In Senghor's writings about Teilhard and on the crucial role of religion in achieving socialist goals in Africa, one can hear the themes of cooperation and principled distance that would mesh well with benevolent secularism in Senegal.[34] He had a clear preference not only for differentiation but also for the active partnership between religious and state bodies in the pursuit of development and national independence. His preference for accommodation with religion rather than for the submission of religious actors to state authority shows in his speeches and writings throughout the independence period. As he put it before the National Assembly in 1951, "[Our party] fraternally united men from the land, landowners, workers from Dakar, Muslims and Catholics."[35]

Senghor's preference for accommodation was not the only perspective on religion–state relations among political elites in Senegal during the period of secular emergence, however. While robust anticlericalism was already rather weak among political elites in Senegal (at least as a serious political proposal), Senghor's major rivals demonstrated less-accommodationist preferences in relation to existing Sufi organizations. Lamine Guèye, Freemason and veteran politician whose main strength rested on French citizens in the Quatre communes, advocated "a rather rigid separation between the state and the 'mosque'" that differed from Senghor's pursuit of accommodation.[36] Guèye's core appeal with

French-educated elites in the coastal communes rested on tying Senegal's political development to French republican principles, not in altering those principles to accommodate a wider role for Senegal's religious leaders. As he remarked in a famous address in 1946, "We will be able to do everything through France, everything with the Republic, never anything without France!"[37] This was not necessarily anticlericalism, but it was a preference for a less-expansive role for religion in republican public life. Prime Minister Mamadou Dia's preference was more complex; he sought less accommodation with existing Sufi elites but favored using state resources to support Muslim reformers who rivaled traditional Sufi organizations. Religion could cooperate with state in some instances, but only after extensive state intervention to transform the nature of religious leadership. Thus, Dia advocated less-robust differentiation of religion and state because the state would become actively involved in training and professionalization of a religious bureaucracy. Neither Dia nor Guèye had preferences for a full-fledged anticlericalism that would drive religion from public life, but the system each proposed differed from Senghor's preferred structure of *laïcité*.

The eventual rivalries among these leaders were in part decided by the effects of the political institutions that each advocated. Dia and Senghor, initially in alliance, won support from *marabouts* attracted to their more expansive preference for cooperation. Guèye spoke for a more restricted slice of the electorate, and as voting expanded into rural areas, he struggled to appeal to more pious, rural Senegalese. As Senghor noted with evident satisfaction, "[My party] was received with favor by the greatest *marabouts* of Senegal; our opponents were politely led away."[38] Later, when the Dia–Senghor alliance gave way to rivalry, it was Senghor's more robust preference for differentiation and deference to existing Sufi elites that sealed his political victory. Although Dia was a Muslim and Senghor a Catholic, Senghor advocated the more benevolent relationship with existing Sufi elites and thus retained the loyalty of key Sufi leaders, especially those in the Mouride brotherhood. The structure of benevolent secularism ultimately played an important role in accounting for Senghor's triumph over his one-time ally. Dia's institutional proposal, with more limited cooperation and weaker differentiation, lost out among political elites because it risked resistance from the leading Sufi clerics. Loimeier describes in useful detail the institutional effect within the elite:

> Dia's policy of structural reform soon provoked opposition, in particular from the ranks of the powerful Sufi brotherhoods who were afraid that Dia's reforms would infringe upon their sinecures. Marabouts of both the Mourides and Tidjanns resented the idea of a Supreme Islamic council, fearing for their autonomy. Also, they felt threatened by Dia's efforts to set up farmers'

cooperatives, a process which reached its decisive stage in 1962: in that year collective fields were formed out of the alarbar-fields that were traditionally cultivated by farmers for the marabouts. . . . Furthermore, the Dia administration had reduced funds and favours for the marabouts and introduced a strategy of granting credits only for well-defined projects. This change of financial policy touched the relationship between government and marabouts at its very heart: the exchange of services between both parties came to an end and the government set about extending its control over hitherto uncontrolled territories.[39]

In the end, benevolent secular institutions affected the balance of power within the state elite bloc. After the rivalries between Guèye, Dia, and Senghor were settled, "[Senghor] also managed to incorporate much of Guèye's civil service support into his own following."[40] Diversity among these political elites set the stage for conflict, and the configuration of benevolent secularism helped to settle this dispute in favor of Senghor and his allies.

The final within-group effect of benevolent secularism in Senegal took place among the Roman Catholic minority. The hypothesized institutional effect within minorities is to promote those with a preference for engaging in public partnerships as opposed to those who prefer to retreat into defensive isolation from public life. Although minorities may have a constrained set of options during critical junctures, diverse strategies are still open to them. Senegal's Catholic minority, for instance, could have withdrawn from public life, resisted progress to more robust democracy, or even pursued emigration to France. The design of benevolent secularism, particularly its combination of cooperation and principled distance, encouraged Catholic elites to adopt a posture of engagement rather than withdrawal. Cooperation with state institutions brought benefits to the Catholic Church—for instance, through the use of educational stipends by Muslim students to attend Catholic schools. In a pastoral directive of 1964, the Catholic bishops set out regulations for the religious instruction of Muslim students who attended Catholic schools, pointing out how important it was that "all students receive a religious formation."[41]

Furthermore, the evenhandedness of principled distance provided Catholics with powerful symbolic recognition of their place in public life. President Senghor argued in 1960 that "fruitful cooperation among Muslims and Catholics" would be essential to addressing the challenges of social development after independence,[42] which clearly implied that cooperation would improve not only social development but also the Catholic community's security. Interfaith dialogue efforts gained pace as independence approached, and a joint Muslim–Catholic communiqué from the hierarchy and Sufi leaders spoke out on the importance of marriage in 1961.[43] When Hyacinthe Thiandoum was installed as archbishop of Dakar in 1962, Tidjann leader El Hajj Seydou Nourou Tall, President Senghor, and the head of the Senegalese army joined in the celebrations.[44] The combination of differentiation, cooperation, and principled distance engaged Catholic elites in public life and brought some reassurance that involving religion in politics need not threaten their basic rights.

Tracing debates within the relevant coalition blocs during the independence period highlights relevant actors' agency in advocating for their preferences during this period of institutional uncertainty as well as the impact of the dimensions of benevolent secularism on these internal debates. In different ways, the dimensions of differentiation, cooperation, and principled distance secured the twin tolerations by shaping the preferences held by Sufi clerics, political elites, and the Catholic minority. Table 4.2 summarizes these effects and highlights exemplary evidence of each. Within each group, benevolent secularism promoted elites who would support the twin tolerations rather than fall into either half of the secularism trap. Because of these within-group effects, Sufi clerics, political elites, and Catholic leaders could unite in a coalition that secured the state's toleration for religious associations and religious communities' toleration for the autonomous functioning of the state. This coalition remained diverse, and the tensions within each bloc did not simply disappear after the critical juncture. Nevertheless, institutions of secularism emerged, with lasting consequences for Senegalese political development.

Although there is evidence of these institutional effects during the independence period, it is important to note that debates within each bloc about the place of religion in Senegalese public life originated in earlier decades of French colonial rule. At that time, Muslim elites ranged from those who waged jihad to establish an Islamic state and others who sought coexistence with the colonial power. Some colonial administrators were willing to collaborate

TABLE 4.2. PREFERENCE EFFECTS OF BENEVOLENT SECULARISM IN SENEGAL

Coalition Partner	Hypothesized Within-Group Effect	Evidence in Senegal
Religious Majority	Empower pious secularists	Sufi disinterest in Conseil supérieur
Secular Elites	Weaken anticlericals and empower accommodation	Senghor victory over Guèye and Dia
Religious Minorities	Promote engaged minorities	Catholic–Muslim statement on marriage

with Sufi leaders, whereas others were more hostile to Muslim authorities. An indigenous political elite sought out and received representation in the French legislature, which included exposure to the more fervent anticlericalism of continental politics. Some Catholics sought to use state power to further conversions, whereas others engaged in partnerships with Muslim elites. By the interwar period, accommodationist French administrators, pious secularists among Sufi elites, and Catholic elites had formed a coalition that bore some resemblance to that postindependence coalition that secured the twin tolerations. It is fair to say that institutional conditions under French administration in the first half of the twentieth century played a part in influencing the preferences held by Muslim, Catholic, and secular elites even before the independence-era critical juncture.

However, this earlier influence does not diminish the independent impact of Senghor's institutions of *laïcité* on these preferences during the independence era. The departure of the French colonial administration threw into doubt the mutual commitment of state, Muslim, and Catholic elites to the twin tolerations. A potential cycle of suspicion and lack of credible commitments in a context of broader regime change can provide precisely the setting in which religion and political participation have proven so combustible in other settings. Senegal's political elites had preferences quite distinct from those of French colonial administrators and, as Smith points out, were in many ways "more Jacobin and secular than [the] colonial predecessor."[45] With power in the hands of local officials, some in the Muslim elite mobilized with new vigor for the legal establishment of an Islamic state. And without the formal protection by French rule, the Catholic minority faced new questions about its place in local public life. In each bloc, independence posed new challenges to elites and called into question which actors would win out in internal contestation about the place of religion in democratic life. Institutions of benevolent secularism proved central in shaping this contestation in the early years of independence.

ALTERNATIVE EXPLANATIONS OF *LAÏCITÉ*'S EMERGENCE

According to leading alternative explanations, Senegal's critical juncture of secular emergence was a least likely case for the twin tolerations. Theories of secularization, rational competition, and religious moderation would see the risk that the secularism trap will spring in a largely homogenous, underdeveloped, religiously orthodox country as it opens competitive politics.

A first alternative, secularization theory, sees the twin tolerations as a product of the broader process of religious disenchantment that accompanies economic and political modernization. In this framework, the twin tolerations emerge as a part of the decline of religious institutions and individual belief that is intricately linked to increased material security. Senegal's record during the independence period does not square with this theory's clearest predictions. It was an extremely economically underdeveloped country at independence. Individual religiosity was by all accounts extremely high at the time, as it remains today, according to public opinion evidence from the contemporary period (see chapter 5). It is true that some more "modernized" urban elites tended to be vocal advocates of *laïcité* in the late colonial period, but there is little evidence that the poorest, rural parts of the country served as hotbeds of resistance to the twin tolerations. Indeed, resistance from groups such as the Conseil supérieur grew from the rather educated, urbanized populations with more exposure to formalized Islamic education.

The empirical record of secular emergence in Senegal suggests a more complicated relationship between development and the twin tolerations. The Sufi orders, headquartered in less-developed, rural areas of the country, were actually quite content to support the twin tolerations so long as benevolent secularism worked to their benefit. The impulse to break down the twin tolerations actually came from communities more exposed to economic development, urbanization, and formal education. Moreover, the low level of development in Senegal at independence meant that traditional Sufi orders were widely popular and faced limited competition from Muslim challengers. If the Sufi orders were *less* influential at independence because of a higher level of economic development, there is little evidence that the twin tolerations would have been a more likely outcome. This suggests that the process of development may be as threatening to the twin tolerations as the presence of underdevelopment.

In contrast to secularization theory, rational choice theorists might contend that Senegal was not such an unlikely case for the twin tolerations after all. In this framework, the twin tolerations were a result of purely material competition among relevant actors during the critical juncture. Although Senegal appears to be homogenously Muslim, a material-interest-driven approach could contend that *laïcité* owes its existence to competition among Sufi orders for resources and membership, which urban elites easily exploited to secure their own power within the fledgling state. Rationalist accounts of religious liberty in the United States have emphasized how similar dynamics of religious pluralism raised the costs of any kind of established religion and thus increased the likelihood of state secularism.[46] In Senegal, secularism is a kind of hurting stalemate among religious and political factions and frequently a second preference (at best) among the religious groups that accept its emergence. To borrow from Stathis Kalyvas's focus on institutional structure, the hierarchical authority patterns of Sufi Islam facilitated the benevolent secular outcome because political elites could trust that the highest levels of Sufi elites spoke authoritatively on behalf of their *taalibes*.[47] Competition between groups and hierarchical coherence within them resulted in the twin tolerations.

There is little doubt that Sufi Islam's diversity and authority structures were a component of the emergence of secular benevolence in postcolonial Senegal. Senghor exploited rivalry among the Tidjanns and Mourides, and the fairly centralized authority of the brotherhoods, in particular the Mourides, did facilitate negotiations with state elites. But the rationalist argument is incomplete in a few crucial ways. First, as José Casanova has pointed out regarding the United States, there is no reason why internal diversity needs to eliminate the possibility of a general establishment for the majority religious community in a new state.[48] A kind of nonpreferential Protestant establishment was on the table in the United States, and rationalist analysis does not rule out a similar Muslim establishment not tied to any one *tariqa*. Second, although this rationalist argument gives a crisp account of formal disestablishment of religion, it says less about other dimensions of benevolent secularism. Most obviously, it is difficult on purely material grounds to understand the combination of cooperation and principled distance as well as why religious groups worked together as partners in cooperation with state authorities in policy areas such as education and family policy. Finally, by treating preferences as material, rational choice accounts miss out on the diversity *within* the coalition blocs over how to institutionalize the religion–state relationship. Multivocality was not simply a distinct material calculation but rather a reflection of diverse normative approaches to the appropriate relationship between religion and public life. Rationalist arguments make an important contribution to understanding secular emergence in Senegal, but they underspecify the role of institutions in shaping actor preferences and overestimate the intensity of competition among religious communities.

The final alternative, centered on religious moderation, would be unlikely to predict that the twin tolerations would emerge from Senegal's critical juncture. In the moderation framework, secularism results from religious actors adopting liberal political theologies and accepting their own place in the private realm in deference to state authority. This argument is difficult to square with the empirical record in Senegal mostly because it underestimates the orthodox theological grounds on which Senegal's religious communities came to prefer the emergence of the twin tolerations. Pious secularism won out with various Sufi leaders in large part because the design of benevolent secularism served their traditional material and spiritual purposes. The Mouride leadership in particular became a defender of *laïcité* without adopting liberal political theology. A secular state provided a continued foil to clerics who had grown accustomed to contrasting their own spiritual legitimacy with state bureaucrats' less-impressive authority while simultaneously promoting their visibility over other, noncooperative Muslim leaders. Liberal theology is not necessary to accept the terms of that bargain.

To be clear, advocates of religious moderation are right to point to religious actors' preferences as more than material and subject to change over time. However, the period of secular emergence in Senegal highlights the fact that "moderation" is an unhelpful standard by which to judge religious elites' theological positions and that these theological preferences can themselves be shaped by the structure of political institutions.

In sum, leading alternatives struggle to give a full account of the twin tolerations' emergence at independence in Senegal. The rationalist account is most helpful in highlighting the impact of Sufi pluralism on institutional outcomes, but it underspecifies those outcomes while overstating the intensity of competition among religious factions. Secularization and religious moderation theories underestimate the support of traditional religious elites for the twin tolerations. Each of these alternatives struggles in part because it overlooks the role of institutional structure in shaping actors' preferences about the place of religion in public life.

HINTS OF INSTABILITY: COOPERATION AND THE CODE DE LA FAMILLE

Although Senegal adopted benevolent secularism with support from a broad coalition after independence, serious tensions were built into this alliance. The extent of cooperation between state and religious institutions in the public square became particularly controversial as political elites drafted a unified civil code, in particular the parts related to family law. The debate about the Code de la famille highlights tensions between dimensions of benevolent secularism over the limits of public religion and what the state owes to its religious communities. This debate arose during the period of secular emergence, in the early 1960s, but was so controversial that it was tabled until after the critical juncture. It provides a useful bridge, then, between the brief window of institutional flux and the longer-term processes of evolution that are the focus of chapter 5.

The consultations related to the Code de la famille stretched over a decade, with the code finally passing into law in 1972. During this period, customary law still governed a range of personal matters, especially in rural areas. The Senghor–Dia power struggle interrupted the consultations over generating a unified civil code of family law, but after Senghor's *marabout*-aided victory, he continued the push for comprehensive reform. As it became clear that the code would allow very little space for sharia rulings, various Muslim leaders began to signal their displeasure with the law's development. In 1970, many of the original supporters of the Conseil supérieur des chefs religieux channeled this resistance into a new organization with a slightly different name, the Conseil supérieur islamique du Sénégal. This group presented a series of lengthy documents to the government outlining the provisions of sharia law that would be violated by the proposed code and in a letter in 1971 insisted that "[Islam] incorporates obligatory and immutable prescriptions that nothing can change for whatever reason."[49] These objections united Mouride and Tidjann leaders, itself no small feat. Yet Senghor's government insisted on moving ahead with the civil code.

The crisis that accompanied the Family Code clarifies tensions between two of the dimensions of benevolent secularism: differentiation of religion and state as well as cooperation between the two in the public square. On the one hand, the urban, French-speaking bureaucratic elite saw the family law as a key step in differentiating state law from religious and tribal custom. Customary law regarding family relations still predominated in much of the country, but it was unacceptable to modernizers in the political elite, in particular to advocates of women's rights. Ministry of Justice records related to the implementation of the code even insist that its provisions outlaw practices "without prescription in Islam *or* the Gospel."[50] Any formal state institutionalization of Islamic laws would violate this understanding of the principles of *laïcité*.

However, the *tariqas* objected with arguments that were also rooted in the structure of benevolent secularism. Pious secularists among the Sufi leadership supported *laïcité* so long as it respected the religious community's autonomy and promoted the cooperation of religion and state. By this standard, the code was a direct assault on a sphere that should be left to the religious community, family relations, and was a failure in the policy consultations that should unite religious and state actors. This view was, at least in theory, compatible with a kind of principled distance with minorities. A prominent group of Muslim critics has argued even recently that principled distance and cooperation among religions should apply in the realm of family law just as they do in pilgrimage funding, with "Muslims submitt[ing] to sharia, and Christians and non-Muslims to their own personal laws."[51]

On these grounds, brotherhood leaders roundly criticized the law and resisted its implementation. The code does in fact allow use of Muslim law for inheritance decisions in "exceptional cases," and over time these exceptional cases have become the norm. A policy review by Amsatou Sow Sidibé found roughly 90 percent of inheritance cases in Dakar were in fact decided by recourse to the Muslim legal exception.[52] Moreover, outside of the coastal cities, Muslim leaders have rendered the law nearly unenforceable in large areas. Mouride *khalife general* Abdou Lahatte Mbacké simply declared by fiat that the law would not apply in the holy city of Touba. As Keba Mbaye, the president of the Supreme Court, admitted with understatement in 1977, "The family code is not rigidly applied in our countryside."[53]

The Code de la famille debate shows the tensions that can coexist even once a coalition forms in support of the twin tolerations. Senghor seems to have made a wise decision to delay the code's promulgation because it could have had a more explosive impact in the tensest years of secular emergence. Its announcement in 1972, after a decade of religion–state cooperation, brought protest but no general breakdown in benevolent secularism. Diverse members of the coalition instead exercised their agency by contesting the policy within institutional boundaries. This contestation within institutional bounds is a characteristic of the secular evolution discussed in chapter 5. Opposition to the code is a regular feature of Muslim reformist movements as they try to build countercoalitions that succeed where the Conseil supérieur failed. The weak enforcement of the code motivates civil rights organizations, in particular those working for women's rights, and sharpens divides among religious and secular advocacy groups. Although the broader patterns of religious-secular cooperation have stabilized benevolent secularism, the ongoing clashes over the Code de la famille show the significant divides that coexist among blocs that support benevolent secular institutions.

Laïcité in Senegal, in contrast to its namesake in France, bears the dimensions of benevolent secularism: differentiation, cooperation, and principled distance. This chapter cataloged those dimensions in constitutional provisions, state policies, and less-formal patterns of elite behavior. It then traced the impact that this institutional structure had on the preferences within each of the three blocs that bargained over the relationship between religion and politics: the Sufi brotherhoods, the secular elites, and the Catholic minority. The configuration of benevolent secularism empowered elites within each of these blocs who came together to secure the twin tolerations during the critical juncture of secular emergence. Institutional structure increased the likelihood of the twin tolerations despite the fact that several leading alternative explanations of religion and democratic life would have pointed to the secularism trap as a likely outcome of this critical juncture.

Although the relationship between religion and democracy tends to inspire pride in Senegal, significant questions about the durability of benevolent secularism were left unanswered during the process of secular emergence. The contentious Code de la famille debate demonstrated the differences that existed even among the actors who supported benevolent secularism in Senegal. Senghor's decision to delay the final version of the code until after the critical juncture of secular emergence may have helped stabilize the twin tolerations initially, but it also laid the groundwork for future contention over the appropriate understanding of *laïcité bien comprise*.

5. Secular Evolution in Senegal

SOPI AND INSTITUTIONAL CHANGE

In 2000, after decades in which Senegal slowly expanded openness to political opposition, Abdoulaye Wade won election as Senegal's first president from outside of Senghor's Parti socialist (PS). Wade's Sopi coalition (using the Wolof term for "change") unseated incumbent President Abdou Diouf and ushered in a new level of democratic consolidation in Senegal. As power passed peacefully from the PS to Wade's Parti démocratique sénégalais (PDS), longtime opposition leaders gained control of the levers of state power. President Wade quickly set about instituting some constitutional reforms, building on those that had been enacted as part of political opening over the course of twenty years. Although political reforms such as changes to the presidential term received most attention, one less-electoral innovation sparked sharp debate: a draft constitution that removed language regarding the *laïque* nature of the Senegalese state. So began a tumultuous challenge to *laïcité*'s stability.

Wade's rise to power combined with broader changes to Senegal's religious landscape to call the endurance of *laïcité* into question. Wade's Mouride Sufi brotherhood had grown in clout since independence, while movements calling for the merger of Islam and state had grown under the influence of some Arab-educated Senegalese leaders. Wade and other politicians seemed willing to weaken *laïcité* if it would bring success at the ballot box. All three dimensions of benevolent secularism came into question: the stability of religion–state differentiation, the extent of religion–state cooperation, and the robustness of the state's principled distance among the diverse religious communities. This tumult peaked in 2009, when Catholic youth took to the streets of Dakar to protest remarks President Wade had made that offended many in the Catholic minority.

And yet the bid to break down *laïcité* and replace it with an alternative relationship between religion and state fell short. In spite of Wade's draft constitution, *laïcité* remains in Article 1, as do the other constitutional essentials described in chapter 4. Although Wade tried to "inaugurate a new paradigm in brotherhood–state relations,"[1] his eventual defeat in the 2012 election was in part a result of resistance to his manipulation. In spite of an environment that seemed ripe for the breakdown and replacement of *laïcité*, Wade's term in office was a period of secular evolution. *Laïcité* evolved in response to challenges, while maintaining the basic features of differentiation, cooperation, and principled distance that characterize benevolent secularism. How did benevolent secularism endure this turbulent period?

In this chapter, I argue that the mechanisms tied to institutional structure set out in the theoretical framework described in chapter 1 were responsible for this pattern of institutional change: strong interfaith relations and minimal religious-secular divisions. Wade's two terms in office, stretching from 2000 to 2012, provide empirical tests of the hypothesized coalition alliances and their effects on institutional evolution. This chapter traces institutional change during that period and ties those changes to interfaith and religious-secular relations, testing the theory's implications in both interviews of elites and public opinion research. On a comparative scale, the preservation of *laïcité* in Senegal during the past two decades is important evidence that even the revival of political Islam on a global scale need not undermine existing accommodations between Muslim leaders, minorities, and secular institutions. In fact, in challenging times, Senegal's traditional Muslim elites were among the key players in stabilizing benevolent secularism. More assertive forms of secularism would likely have undercut the public religious partnerships that proved so central in preserving democracy.

First, I document the changes to Senegal's religious and political landscape that seemed to constitute such a challenge to benevolent secularism. Second, I catalog the areas in which benevolent secularism was contested and the institutional outcomes of these challenges across the three core dimensions: differentiation, cooperation, and principled distance. Third, I trace evidence that this pattern of evolution, rather than institutional breakdown, is a result of the interfaith and religious-secular coalition ties set out in the theoretical framework of chapter 1. The period leading up to the presidential election of 2012 provides particularly vivid evidence of these coalition effects. Fourth, I turn to public opinion data to assess whether these elite-focused coalition alliances exist among the general population. Throughout the chapter, I make the case that benevolent secularism endures in Senegal because of the coalition alliances that are a result of the institutional structure of the religion–state relationship put in place at Senegalese independence.

SETTING THE STAGE FOR INSTITUTIONAL CHANGE: POLITICAL AND RELIGIOUS OPENING

The challenge to *laïcité* in Senegal arose from a period of significant change among political and religious elites. Beginning around 2000, leadership among the core coalition of state bureaucrats, Sufi leaders, and the Catholic minority shifted. This period of instability made the time ripe for institutional change and set the stage for the sharp controversies of the Wade administration. Changing leadership posed a trial for *laïcité* as actors tested the boundaries of seemingly settled state institutions. It is important to note that not all of these coalition changes undermined benevolent secularism; in fact, several played a part in preserving secular democracy from challengers.

Although Senegal remains a poor country by global standards, it has developed substantially since independence in 1960. The country's two major cities, Dakar and Touba, have swelled as long-entrenched rural agricultural lifestyles have given way to a more urbanized, light-industrial economy. Two and a half million Senegalese now call the Dakar metro area home, and Touba's population is approximately one million. And yet urbanization has not fueled religious decline. Pew Research Group polling shows that 98 percent of Senegalese think religion is "very important" and that 89 percent pray daily.[2] Afrobarometer survey research shows similarly high levels of religiosity and no variation between urban and rural areas, with 96 percent of urban residents and 95.7 percent of rural residents responding that religion is very important.[3] Assane Diagne of Catholic Relief Services observed to me that urbanization hasn't taken away religion's influence but rather "reorganized religious authority," and Abdoul Aziz Kébé quipped that "the city is not the city anymore."[4] Even among the elite NGO sector, there is little sense that religion is of declining importance. The Committee for Ethics of the Conseil des ONG d'appui au développement (CONGAD, Council of NGOs Supporting Development), an NGO umbrella organization discussed at length later, is chaired by both an imam and a priest. Boubacar Seck, CONGAD's director, spoke at length about how assumptions linking development to decline of individual religiosity simply do not mesh with Senegal's social reality.[5] At the institutional level, Mouride scholar Khadim Mbacké points out that various industrial initiatives take place under Mouride auspices, including electronics manufacturing and international commerce through Mouride branches outside of Senegal.[6] Thus, Senegal's economic development has contributed to broader processes of leadership pluralization rather than to the reduction of religion's public importance.

The Sopi election in 2000 demonstrated the well-noted pluralization of Senegal's elite political bloc.[7] This demonstration was in many ways the culmination of a slow political opening that had begun with Senghor's opening to opposition parties and had developed with the electoral reforms of Senghor's successor, Abdou Diouf, through the 1980s and 1990s. Whereas President Senghor strictly controlled the number and nature of opposition parties during his rule in the 1960s and 1970s, more than a dozen parties contested the presidential election in 2012, with even more parties at the local level.[8] This broad political fragmentation is one reason the run-up to the executive election was so fluid, with regular jockeying among and within political coalitions and questions posed until quite late in the game regarding the cohesion of the political opposition. Partisan fragmentation seemed to set the stage for a weakening of *laïcité*, not by empowering anticlericals but rather by encouraging candidates to jockey for the favor of religious institutions.

Important changes within the state elite coalition block also extended to civil society, in particular the growth of good-governance organizations and their relationship to *laïcité*. In addition to traditional advocates among the women's movement such as the Association des juristes sénégalaises, civil society organizations related to governance became closely tied to debates over *laïcité*. CONGAD and several organizations associated with the umbrella Assises nationales movement made tackling corruption and building quality governance among their top priorities. These actors engaged *laïcité* as an aspect of good governance, in particular framing the maintenance of *laïcité* as a matter of "transparency" and thus necessary to maintain as a part of a package of good-governance reforms such as decentralization and fiscal accountability. As Boubacar Seck put it to me, the faith community has a special responsibility to advocate transparency in *laïcité* because "without good governance no real development can take place."[9] These calls for transparency were not anticlerical per se, but they did challenge the undocumented aspects of religion–state cooperation. Tax policy in Touba, for instance, remains a realm largely beyond state control, and Beck's detailing of the tax revolt among Touba merchants in 1997 captures just how much state–religion relations are implicated in good-governance efforts.[10] Advocates are convinced that modern governance demands such reforms, but this disciplining comes with implications for the kind of cooperation that takes place between religion and state.

If political pluralization broadened the state actors interested in *laïcité*, shifts in Senegal's religious landscape were just as important in setting the stage for institutional change. Pluralization weakened the predominance of pious secularists among the Muslim majority and thus posed a particular challenge to the coalition supporting *laïcité*. The most obvious force moving change among the Sufi brotherhoods has been the tide of time: generational succession of Sufi leaders has complicated authority in the brotherhoods. Senegal's Sufi orders have followed a general dynastic succession pattern, with the sons of founding leaders succeeding the initial founder and other first-generation heirs. Succession decisions became more complex near the turn of the millennium. As multiple generations passed, particularly within the Tidjann and Mouride communities, the number of direct descendants grew, and *petits-fils* (grandsons) jockeyed for internal influence in various ways.[11] To build their public visibility, several of these *marabouts politiques* became involved in party politics, moving away from the distance from politics that the pious secularists had embraced. The most notable of the *marabouts politiques* is Kara Mbacké, founder of the PVD. The stresses posed by generational change are a regular feature of Sufi authority and will continue to challenge the Sufi cohesion that facilitated religion–state cooperation in the past.

Further weakening of pious secularism took place through the growth of "reformist" Muslim groups beginning in the 1980s. These groups are a diverse lot, but they generally are associations that stand at some distance from the official Sufi brotherhoods, frequently because of their leaders' Arab theological training. The first major reformist movement, mentioned in chapter 4, was the UCM of Cheikh Touré. Today Islamic associations have proliferated widely, from broad movements such as the Jamaat Ibadou Rahman to student associations at the Université Cheikh Anta Diop de Dakar and Islamic women's groups. These groups frequently criticize the syncretic aspects of Sufi practice and in their bolder moments have even called for the end of the *marabout–taalibe* relationship that grounds brotherhood influence. The most vocal reformists have explicitly challenged the secularity of state institutions, notably the Code de la famille. The Comité islamique pour la réforme du Code de la famille au Sénégal (CIRCOFS) is the most visible example of an explicitly revisionist movement working against the differentiation of religious and state institutions.

Forces such as urbanization further pluralized Muslim leadership in the lead-up to Wade's election.[12] Although urbanized actors are not necessarily opposed to *laïcité*, they do pose a challenge to the authority of the pious secularists atop the Sufi brotherhoods. Abdoul Aziz Kébé, a leading Tidjann scholar, argues that Sufi activists in urban centers are often more politically savvy than their superiors in the rural centers, which grants them substantial leeway in having an impact on media and political cycles.[13] As the peanut economy of the 1970s weakened over time, Mouride economic power rested more on the urban markets of Touba and Dakar and even on transnational economic networks stretching from other parts of West Africa to New York and Paris. Institutions known as *dahiras*, designed to ease the brotherhood members' adjustment to the city, have proliferated. The *dahiras* maintain links to the spiritual hubs but operate with a large degree of autonomy in day-to-day affairs. One particularly important Mouride *dahira*, Matlaboul Fawzayni, was responsible for building a major hospital in Touba, an undertaking so complex that state medical administrators eventually had to be charged with the administration of the hospital.[14] Cheikh Guèye's account of a cement-procurement conflict between the *khalife* and a group of Mouride businessmen in 1995 highlights these tensions. In "refusing to yield to [the *khalife's*] orders," these commercial elites "underlined the importance of groups of businessmen who ferociously defend their own interests, sometimes even in opposing the *khalife* and the *marabouts*."[15] On the whole, the highest-ranking Sufi elites retain unique social influence but face new figures who represent Islam in public life.

Although the Senegalese Catholic community remains less than 10 percent of the general population, authority within the community also pluralized in the lead-up to Wade's election. Cardinal Théodore Adrien Sarr, archbishop of Dakar, without a doubt remained the most important Catholic leader of the Senegalese community during Wade's administration. When Catholic youth took to the streets for protests in December 2009, for instance, it was Sarr's leadership that calmed the crisis. Nevertheless, lay Catholic organizations exercise a high degree of autonomy in public debates. As Father Léon Diouf writes, "A church cannot call itself local without the laity."[16] The bishops' pastoral letter after the Sopi election in 2000 called on the laity to "engage actively in politics noted for its charity" in the construction of the common good.[17] Business associations and youth groups such as the Scouts have long been important social networks, but a group of more politically active Catholic associations has proliferated since independence. These groups play a more active role in day-to-day civic life than does the official hierarchy. Notable lay organizations include Coordination des etudiants catholiques du Sénégal; the Union des femmes catholiques du Sénégal; a range of important Catholic social service and development agencies, in particular Caritas Sénégal; and Catholic media sources such as Horizons africains.

Présence chrétienne was one particularly important lay-led public voice for Catholicism in the public square during this period. The movement was founded in 1992 in response to John Paul II's visit to Senegal that year and calls for lay leadership to reinvigorate public life. It has offices in each diocese around Senegal to coordinate both national and local initiatives. In contrast to the hierarchy's distance from politics, Présence chrétienne president Théodore Ndok Ndiaye can speak more assertively in media and public debates. Présence chrétienne does not operate at cross-purposes to the official hierarchy but is more willing to enter into contentious public debates. Ndiaye remarked in conversation that Cardinal Sarr and other senior clerics tend to be hesitant about some of the more contentious public events, especially any seen to touch on electoral politics, but are generally supportive of lay-led projects as they develop.[18] Catholic associations worked to contain youth unrest after Wade's disparaging remarks in December 2009 and ultimately played a part in convincing Cardinal Sarr to address the issue publicly.

This broad pattern of pluralization among political elites and Muslim and Catholic communities upset the fairly placid bargain that had secured *laïcité* since the colonial period. It presented an opportunity for challengers to advance an institutional alternative to benevolent secularism, particularly by breaking down differentiation and principled distance to favor particular religious communities. Even where pluralization did not directly threaten the coalition blocs described in chapter 4, it complicated patterns of authority and thus provided an environment conducive to *laïcité*'s breakdown and replacement. Maintaining the religion–state relationship simply became more complicated than in the days of the "Dakar–Touba hotline" between Senghor and Mouride leaders.

TRACKING INSTITUTIONAL CHANGE IN SENEGALESE *LAÏCITÉ*

In this fluid environment, with significant changes in political and religious leadership, there was ample opportunity to push the boundaries of *laïcité* in Senegal. Would this result in the breakdown of *laïcité* or its more gradual evolution within the boundaries set out during the Senghor era? Evidence in this section demonstrates that *laïcité* in Senegal survived the challenges of the past decade in its benevolent form. The most dramatic attempts to break down differentiation and principled distance came to naught. With that said, there has been meaningful evolution on the dimensions of differentiation and cooperation as both education policy and party politics have expanded the role for religion in democratic life. Table 5.1 summarizes the changes documented in this section as well as the role of coalition ties in shaping secular evolution.

DIFFERENTIATION: WADE'S CONSTITUTION AND RELIGIOUS PARTY POLITICS

From Wade's earliest days in office, many worried that the differentiation between religious and state institutions could disintegrate. An initial draft of constitutional revisions made no reference to the *laïque* nature of the state, which would have marked a fundamental shift in the secularity of state institutions.

TABLE 5.1. SUMMARY OF SECULAR EVOLUTION IN SENEGAL

Area of Change	Institutional Challenge	Coalition Influence
1. Differentiation of Constitution	Removal of *laïcité* from draft constitution	Religious-secular partnership through Assises nationales
2. Principled Distance Among Brotherhoods and Catholic Minority	Wade administration favoritism and remarks offensive to Catholics	Interfaith condemnation of anti-Catholic remarks; Macky Sall pledge of equal distance
3. Religion and Public Education	Expansion of cooperation through optional religious instruction	Interfaith consent; religious involvement in curriculum development

In a powerful symbolic act, Wade's first trip after the election was to the *khalife* of the Mouride order, where in front of the camera for state television he prostrated himself as a disciple. The image of the head of the secular state submitting in public to a religious authority shook many and seemed to mark a basic weakening of the differentiation of religious and state institutions. This type of manipulation encouraged revisionist mobilization by Muslim leaders still resistant to the Code de la famille of 1972.[19] These individuals drew together under CIRCOFS to demand repeal of the civil Family Code and its replacement with an alternative grounded in sharia law. Although officially removing *laïcité* from the Constitution was not on this group's primary agenda, its proposed ends would have been quite similar: weakening the differentiation between religious and state institutions as well as undercutting the state's ability to formulate and implement policy autonomously from religious veto.[20]

Yet in spite of President Wade's initial draft constitution, differentiation endures in Senegal. Wade's constitution eventually reinserted the word *laïque*, and in spite of involvement from across the major brotherhoods CIRCOFS was ultimately unable to convince Wade to reconsider family law reform. For all of the developments of the post-Senghor era, the CIRCOFS campaign ran into an obstacle nearly identical to the one that the Conseil supérieur had faced in the early 1970s. Religious liberty, guaranteed regardless of religious affiliation, remained a cornerstone of Senegalese religion–state relations. Smaller communities of Protestants and Baha'i have also enjoyed religious freedom, even if social tensions occasionally flare around the religious practices of small minorities. During the Wade years, state officials remained active promoters of interfaith dialogue, with Wade's foreign minister Mandické Niang traveling to the Vatican to meet with the Pontifical Council for Interreligious Dialogue[21] and President Wade extolling the "extraordinary spectacle" of the Imams et oulémas du Sénégal meeting in dialogue with Catholic authorities.[22]

If core indicators of differentiation such as constitutional wording and religious liberty have endured, there has been significant evolution in the differentiation of religion from party politics. During Senghor's era, religious parties were forbidden, and the Sufi elites interacted with elections by issuing explicit endorsements, known as the *ndigël*.[23] This pattern, which rested on the fairly clear differentiation of political elites and religious leadership, came to a close, leading to Wade's election.[24] Interviews with both Mouride and Tidjann leaders indicate that the *ndigël* was unlikely to return. Abdoul Aziz Kébé argued that the "parental *ndigël*," treating voters as children to be instructed, was simply not acceptable to many in modern Senegal, particularly in better-educated urban communities.[25]

The end of the *ndigël* among the highest-level clerics has led to a blurring of the differentiation between religious movements and political parties through vibrant religious politicking among lower-level *marabouts*. As Guèye puts it, "The neutrality of the *khalife* in the end favors the fragmentation of the social body of the Mourides in relation with the state."[26] The Constitution still bans parties based on religious identity, but this ban is essentially unenforceable. In a country where religious elites and their allies have such social influence, how can one isolate what exactly a religious political party is in practice? Serigne Kara Mbacké of the PVD is the most prominent example of the *marabouts politiques*. Kara is a Mouride elite, a grandson of Amadou Bamba Mbacké, although not at the highest levels of the Mouride hierarchy. He is careful to repeat his respect for the secular nature of the state, and the PVD does not have religious tests for membership. Another party, the Front pour le socialisme et la démocratie/ Benno Jubël (FSD/BJ), was founded by the *marabout* Cheikh Abdoulaye Dièye and is led by his son Cheikh Bamba Dièye. In addition to formal parties, various Mbackés and other young *marabouts* have risen through the party lists, both as allies of Wade's PDS and as founders of their own parties, such as Abdou Samath Mbacké's Mouvement africain pour la rénovation sociale. The impact of such parties is not clearly against the principles of *laïcité*, although it does mark a less-clear differentiation between state and religious actors.

PRINCIPLED DISTANCE: MOURIDE FAVORITISM AND CATHOLIC PROTECTION

President Wade's bid to break down principled distance was more threatening to *laïcité* in Senegal than his tinkering with differentiation. As defined in chapter 1, principled distance requires the state authorities' even-handedness in dealings with all religious communities. As Rajeev Bhargava puts it, the state "must intend to help or hinder all relevant groups to an equal degree."[27] In favoring his own Mouride Sufi brotherhood, Wade broke down the state's principled distance among religious institutions for his own electoral gain, bidding to make a substantial shift in state policy and offering a direct threat to institutions of benevolent secularism. The challenges to principled distance showed through in areas such as political appointments, the sharing of funds, and the symbolic even-handedness in treatment of religious communities. Although less formalized than the changes to constitutional language of differentiation, this change still posed a serious bid to replace this dimension of benevolent secularism.

Wade challenged principled distance primarily by favoring his own Mouride brotherhood over other religious communities. At the same time as he prostrated himself before the Mouride *khalife*, he announced major infrastructural support to the Mouride capital of Touba through an airport/heliport complex. The political ranks of Wade's PDS featured a number of Mouride elites, notably Mandické Niang, Wade's foreign minister and former head of Rassemblement des Mourides, a Mouride lobbying association. Wade appointed another fellow Mouride, Mamadou Bamba Ndiaye, as the first minister to oversee religious affairs. The Mouride favoritism culminated in Wade's directive in 2011 that ministers consult Mouride leadership before forming state policy. As he put it, "All ministers in government, regardless of their brotherhood or religion, should go before the Mouride *khalife general* to solicit his prayers each time that they undertake an important mission of the state."[28] Muslims I interviewed regularly pointed to this kind of politicization of Wade's Mouride discipleship as a complaint against his administration. A senior civil society official pointed out to me that this politicization raised the stakes of competition among the Sufi brotherhoods, and although social unrest still seemed unlikely, the sense of equal distance among the religious was far less robust than before.

Weakening principled distance also showed through in the state's relationship with the Catholic minority. Although Wade's wife is a Catholic, his terms in office featured unprecedented tension between state and Catholic actors. Théodore Ndiaye of Présence chrétienne questioned the relative lack of Catholic representation among the Wade executive and legislative branches. "One lone minister, from a total of almost forty in the government; three or four deputies from a total of a hundred and fifty in Parliament, is this normal or comprehensible in a country like Senegal, the country of Senghor and Abdou Diouf? A land exceptional for its democratic advances, its tolerance, its dialogue!"[29] Catholic elites complained of regular discrimination in local land allocation for religious sites.[30] Jean-Paul Dias, a prominent opposition politician and Catholic, was arrested shortly after Good Friday services at Dakar's Cathédrale du souvenir africain.[31] These tensions came to a head around Christmas 2009. President Wade, defending a controversial public statue, commented that

Christians pray to Jesus, "who is not a real God. Everyone knows this, but no one says anything against it."[32] His remarks stirred street protests from Catholic youth and provided the most dramatic example of the deterioration of principled distance under his watch.

Although principled distance came under real threat during Wade's administration, it, like differentiation, survived more or less intact, but only because of sustained resistance from actors opposed to the breakdown of benevolent secularism. As discussed later in this chapter, Wade lost his controversial reelection campaign in 2012, and his successor, Macky Sall, has made a point of reasserting the state's principled distance among the religious communities. In the run-up to his final showdown with Wade, Sall publicly insisted, "There are no special laws for some *marabouts*. I say this clearly: we are in a secular, democratic republic, where religious liberty is guaranteed for all religions, for all brotherhoods."[33]

COOPERATION: EDUCATION POLICY AND DEVELOPMENT EFFORTS

The cooperative dimension of benevolent secularism also saw controversy during Wade's administration. Here, however, changes have remained within the institutional bounds of benevolent secularism, even if they did expand the scope of that cooperation. Evolution is particularly apparent in education policy. As pointed out in chapter 4, the most formal religious schools have long enjoyed state support in the form of bursaries granted to students who cannot afford to attend. In 2002, however, the state substantially widened the provision of religious education in two ways. First, religious education entered the public schools (*écoles de la république*), not just the private schools supported with state stipends. Students in public schools may elect to receive formal religious education, and provision is to be made for both Christian and Muslim options to be available to students, including up to four hours a week of religious instruction. Second, a range of students in Quranic schools known as *daaras* are to be considered as officially enrolled in schools, which is important because roughly 800,000 students fall into this sector and were previously considered nonenrolled by international development standards.[34] Taken together, these reforms reflect substantial concessions by the state to the general population's religious sensibilities.[35] Advocates hope that incorporation of the *daaras* will lead to higher standards and may in fact help reduce the number of young children who wind up in organized begging squads around Senegal's cities.

Although these reforms are compatible with benevolent secularism, they do indicate evolution to more extensive cooperation between religion and state.

Incorporating this group into state classrooms is a change, but there is no full-scale breakdown of religious differentiation from state institutions. Religious instruction remains optional and available in different forms. Abdoul Aziz Kébé pointed out that the curricular development takes place under the control of a state commission, although religious leaders associated with various *tariqas* have some input into the drafting process.[36] President Wade explicitly argued before the National Association of Imams and Ulemas that these policies place the state "at equal distance from Islam and Christianity."[37] These reforms were in part designed to draw support from Arab-educated Muslims, who also tend to populate Muslim reformist organizations. As Mamadou Bamba Ndiaye, Wade's spokesman on religious affairs, put it, "Many of [these Arab-educated Muslims] are unemployed . . . there are not Islamic tribunals, so some are now engaged in teaching."[38]

In many other ways, cooperation between religion and state continues unchanged since the period of secular emergence. The state continues to fund the hajj with cooperation from the various brotherhoods, and Catholic pilgrims to the Vatican and Holy Land enjoy similar support. President Wade created the General Commission for Pilgrimage to Islamic Holy Sites in 2009 to improve coordination of the hajj trip.[39] Guèye points out that the kinds of material support given to religious communities have also diversified and now include visa support for international travel, customs exemptions for brotherhood-tied businesses, and the use of heavy equipment for construction of religious facilities and residential compounds.[40]

Cooperation continues in policy development as well, with many consultations centered on development policy. Collaboration on antiexcision (i.e., anti–female genital mutilation) advocacy produced an extensive religious refutation of the practice, authored by Abdoul Aziz Kébé. In collaboration with the Ministry of Family, Social Development, and National Solidarity, Kébé produced a report on the relationship between gender, equality, and development in Islam, arguing for "the necessity of encouraging the participation of women in development promotion at all levels [political, social, and personal]."[41] Similar collaboration is ongoing regarding AIDS prevention and treatment. Paul Sanga, director of SIDA Service, a Catholic agency dedicated to this issue, spoke to me at length about cooperation between state, Catholic, and Muslim officials in halting the spread of the virus. Religious groups have participated in state policy development regarding HIV/AIDS through formal policy partnerships and informal consultations.[42] A joint Catholic–Muslim handbook on prevention stressed the religious roots of prevention. These stories of AIDS prevention and excision reduction are illustrative not only of the very interesting relationship between faith groups and development but also of the continued cooperation between state and religion in policy consultations. Development work spans a vast array of projects, such as efforts by women's groups on microfinance and the security of the food supply.[43]

As I argue in chapter 1, significant evolution can occur without the breakdown and replacement of benevolent secularism. Senegal's continued religious vitality and the increasing competitiveness of the religious and political landscapes have undoubtedly resulted in the evolution of *laïcité*. This evolution is particularly visible in two areas: party politics and education reform. However, these changes have not broken down the basic stability of benevolent secularism. This institutional outcome raises a crucial question: Why, given conditions favorable to change and a political leader willing to upset institutional boundaries, did *laïcité* in Senegal evolve but resist fundamental change? The answer to this question rests on the coalition alliances encouraged by the design of benevolent secularism.

EXPLAINING *LAÏCITÉ*'S ENDURANCE: COALITION TIES AND THE ELECTION OF 2012

With an opportunistic political leader, a fluid religious landscape, and a revival of religious integralism, why has *laïcité* proven so durable in Senegal? The framework set out in chapter 1 emphasizes the role of elite coalition ties, across faiths and religious-secular boundaries, in explaining secular evolution. Evidence links such elite ties to the endurance of benevolent secularism during Wade's tumultuous rule, particularly in the months leading up to his defeat in the election of 2012. These coalition effects depended largely on the continued dominance of pious secularists among the highest levels of Sufi leadership, particularly within the Mouride brotherhood. Even in this group, which Wade targeted for favoritism, religious elites favored maintaining benevolent secularism rather than pushing for a greater integration of Islam and the state.

In this section, I trace the role of coalition alliances in preserving *laïcité* under Wade's administration, with particular attention to debates about differentiation and principled distance. The analysis opens with responses early in the Wade administration, before moving to an extended consideration of the election in 2012, a climax of this contentious period.

COALITION ALLIANCES DEFENDING *LAÏCITÉ*

Although Wade attempted to mobilize parts of the religious community as allies in weakening *laïcité*, a robust set of religious-secular alliances undercut these efforts. This coalition resistance took shape quickly in response to Wade's *laïcité*-free draft constitution. "An immediate explosion of public controversy and debate" greeted the draft constitution,[44] which lacked the word *laïque*, and interview subjects regularly discussed the disclosure of the draft as a touchstone event nearly a decade after its circulation. Attempts to sacralize family law also met with resistance when the Collectif pour la défense de la laïcité et de l'unité nationale au Sénégal argued that the CIRCOFS campaign "regularly put the state's secularity in question."[45] Bamba Ndiaye, Wade's spokesman on religious affairs, implicitly acknowledged this kind of pushback when he quipped in a press interview: "It is because I am Mouride that I have to be objective."[46] These religious-secular alliances rest on broader patterns of cooperation encouraged by the structure of benevolent secularism. Cooperation in the policy realm—for instance, in fighting AIDS and encouraging literacy—has built alliances among Muslim leaders, political elites, and Catholic officials, in the process minimizing divides among religious elites and secular NGOs.

The importance of religious-secular ties was particularly apparent in the work of the Assises nationales du Sénégal—a broad coalition of civil society, opposition politicians, intellectuals, and faith leaders—to call for good governance and the preservation of Senegalese secularism. Far from being an anticlerical coalition, the Assises has the Committee on Social Questions, Values, Ethics, and Solidarity, which consulted widely with Catholic and Muslim leaders. The major initiative of the Assises was its *Chartre de gouvernance démocratique*, a comprehensive plan to improve governance in Senegal. It is remarkable that amid its discussion of budgetary decentralization and clean elections, the *Chartre* gives pride of place to robust defense of *laïcité*. It "reaffirms the neutrality of the State in confessional affairs and its equidistance in relation to religious bodies." It goes on to "agree that the State has the responsibility to assist all religious institutions in a transparent manner, without any discrimination, in conditions determined by law and in strict order to preserve social peace and guarantee national unity."[47] It also explicitly affirms support for liberty of individual conscience and the dual autonomy of state from religious and religious from state affairs. This language is structured as a clear refutation of attempts to break down differentiation and principled distance under the Wade administration. Endorsers of the *Chartre* were genuinely concerned that the increasingly close proximity between the state and Mouride brotherhood not only was outside the bounds of *laïcité* but also posed a threat to national unity given Senegal's diverse religious landscape.

In addition to these religious-secular partnerships, strong interfaith relations played a part in preserving *laïcité* during this period. Abbé Jacques Seck, a longtime leader in interfaith dialogue for the Archdiocese of Dakar, spoke at length about both formal and informal dialogue efforts that lend stability to *laïcité*. Abbé Seck pointed out that a range of younger seminary students are doing research on Islamic doctrine and practice, which will better prepare the ground for future dialogue efforts.[48] Leaders of the Muslim community who participate in such dialogue have been public voices in rejecting any attempt to sow religious division or any failure to demonstrate respect to their longtime dialogue partners. Even a son of Ahmed Khalifa Niass, a reformist once called the "ayatollah of Kaolack," was educated at the cathedral school in Dakar, as Muslim elites have been for generations.[49]

The interfaith response to the weakening of principled distance became clear in response to Wade's remarks regarding Catholic spirituality around Christmas 2009. One group of imams insisted, "The remarks made by President Wade have no Islamic foundation. . . . We recall that our country has always lived in religious harmony, and firmly condemn the harshness, since his ascension to power, of President Wade to the church."[50] Assane Diagne, a senior staff member at Catholic Relief Services, pointed out that in many ways Muslim allies were more free to speak out than the Catholic authorities themselves.[51] Cardinal Sarr eventually responded as well, condemning Wade's remarks and singing the praises of the "exemplary relations between Christians and Muslims" throughout Senegal's history.[52]

These coalition ties operated so effectively in part because of the continued strength of pious secularists within the highest ranks of Sufi leadership. Senior *marabouts* demonstrated little desire to play a revisionist role because benevolent secularism suits both their material and their normative interests. As corruption scandals dogged officials in Wade's administration, there was little incentive for the Mouride *khalife* to latch his religious legitimacy to party politicians. Pious dissatisfaction with Wade's administration initially came to the surface in an unusual area of contention: monument construction. Commissioned by Wade, the gargantuan *Monument de la renaissance africaine* on the outskirts of Dakar came under fire from several imams for its scantily clad male and female figures, which one called "a pagan monument hanging over Dakar."[53] Other clerics criticized the price tag (more than U.S.$25 million) and Wade's decision to personally pocket more than a third of the revenue generated from the monument. The monument controversy was just one prominent example of a broader trend: pious members of the Muslim elite continued to desire some distance between religion and state to avoid tainting the faith community with the muck of daily politics.

Although religious-secular and interfaith allies resisted the breakdown of differentiation and principled distance, they also demonstrated a willingness to support the evolution of benevolent secularism within historical boundaries.

Evolution in religion's role in education, for instance, did not raise strong resistance from either secular NGOs or the Catholic minority. Abbé Alphonse Seck, a senior official in the Archdiocese of Dakar, acknowledged that some bishops were initially hesitant about the proposed reforms, but their concerns were addressed over time, and they felt little need to mount opposition.[54] Introduction of optional religious education in state schools was meant to appeal to some in the secular development community. Universal primary education is one of the Millennium Development Goals. Political elites justified religious education by arguing that it will broaden enrollment. In 2007, an estimated 365,000 students took advantage of these services, representing a substantial share of the roughly one million elementary students in the state schools.[55] Likewise, the move to increase oversight of some Islamic education may be a more pragmatic path to progress than simply wishing that informal education would disappear.

Evolution in the area of party politics also did not spark significant resistance. Although the cropping up of religion in election campaigns makes some anxious, even the religiously inflected partisan mobilization by groups such as the PVD has not raised an outcry from *laïcité*'s defenders. Abbé Alphonse Seck spoke at length to me about community mediations that Kara Mbacké has taken part in with him and other Catholic leaders.[56] The FSD/BJ party actually enjoys support from many members of reform-minded NGOs. Fatou Kiné Camara, a lawyer, professor, and women's rights activist, was critical of several features of *laïcité* in Senegal but spoke favorably of Cheikh Bamba Dièye, notwithstanding his party's religious roots.[57] As in the area of religious education, institutions evolved to expand the participation of religious political parties in part because the coalition allies who defend *laïcité* recognize that this evolution is within the general boundaries set out by benevolent secularism.

A diverse body of evidence from the Wade administration confirms the hypothesis that coalition alliances across the religious-secular divide and among interfaith groups played a central role in driving institutional evolution rather than *laïcité*'s breakdown and replacement with an alternative form of religion–state relations. When differentiation and principled distance came under direct challenge, these groups joined together to resist the bid for change. In areas where evolution stayed within the bounds of benevolent secularism, such as optional religious education and religious political parties, coalition allies acquiesced and in some cases encouraged institutional change. These alliances exist because of the effects of benevolent secularism within the distinct coalition blocs during earlier periods of secular emergence. This dynamic explains the path-dependent nature of benevolent secularism: institutions alter preferences, which encourages coalition alliances that then protect those institutions from challengers over time.

LAÏCITÉ, COALITION TIES, AND THE ELECTION OF 2012

The controversy over the Wade administration's challenge to Senegalese secularism came to a head around the presidential election of 2012. Wade stood for a constitutionally dubious third term in office and was widely rumored to have designs on passing executive power to his son, Karim, after the election. Political tensions ran high as the elections approached, and once again Wade's personal interests led him to weaken the robustness of principled distance between the state and Senegal's religious communities. In this charged environment, the election was in part a referendum not only on Wade's personal leadership but also on the stability of the postindependence institutions of *laïcité*. Wade's ultimate defeat at the hands of Macky Sall in a run-off election was owing in part to the coalition alliances encouraged by the institutional structure of benevolent secularism. Catholic election monitors, secular NGO leaders, and even members of the Sufi brotherhoods Wade had targeted for manipulation acted to stabilize *laïcité* during this tumultuous period.

Groups such as the Assises nationales continued organizing to defend *laïcité* in the run-up to the vote. Serious public protests amid fears of electoral manipulation shook Senegalese politics. The M23 Movement, rooted in calls such as "Touche pas a ma constitution!" (Don't touch my constitution!) and "Y'en a marre" (Fed up), brought Senegalese youth, especially urban youth, to the streets to voice frustration at Wade's quest for another term in office, his attempts to change electoral rules in his favor, and his rumored desire to pass his rule to Karim. Street violence between protesters and security forces escalated over the second half of 2011 as elections approached in February 2012. These tensions extended into the relationship between religion and state. Wade did not hesitate to use his Mouride identity in a quest for support, insisting in mid-February, "I know that [Mouride support] brought me to power," and newspaper accounts speculated about huge cash payments offered to Mouride elites in exchange for an explicit election endorsement, or *ndigël*.[58] M23 activists rallied against Wade during a February visit to the seat of Tidjann power in Tivaouane, providing a visible signal to Sufi elites that their close alliance with the Wade administration would risk alienating segments of the youth.[59] In one of the campaign's most dramatic confrontations, protests in central Dakar resulted in security forces launching tear gas into the Mosquée El Hadj Malick Sy, a place of worship affiliated with the Tidjann order. Senior Tidjann officials were outraged by the "lightness" with which administration officials initially treated the matter, and they demanded resignations from cabinet officials.[60] In the protestors' view, this incident marked the culmination of the breakdown of principled distance under Wade's rule, the "profanation not only of a sacred place, but of an entire community."[61]

As Senegal grappled with such unrest and religious tension in the run-up to elections, interfaith alliances strengthened through decades of benevolent secularism played an important part in both undercutting Wade's manipulations and maintaining social order. Although more aggressive forms of secularism may have ruled out such public religious engagement, interfaith promotion of clean elections provided another way for coalition allies to push back on manipulation of *laïcité* in the election. Religious allies had played this role in the past, with the Catholic Church exhorting "transparent, peaceful and democratic elections" even in 1998, before Wade's victory.[62] Cardinal Sarr and Tidjan *khalife* Abdoul Aziz Sy al-Ibn built on this pattern as the contentious election of 2007 approached, jointly endorsing a "pacte republicain" that called for responsible governance.[63] As the election of 2012 neared, Catholic, Muslim, and civil society allies expanded these efforts. Présence chrétienne, Muslim partners, and NGOs such as Forum civil launched a series of fora, the Mardis de Brottier, designed to lay the groundwork for free and fair elections. As early as May 2011, a group of prominent imams joined with Cardinal Sarr to present a united front in favor of peaceful, transparent elections and continued these meetings as elections approached.[64] Calls for calm united Mouride, Tidjann, and Catholic elites in early 2012 as the first round of elections approached, and protests grew in intensity. Interfaith partners in defense of *laïcité* continued this role on election day itself, when Macky Sall bested Wade. Catholic associations monitored elections, playing a part in ensuring that Wade's allies could not tamper with results in the decisive second round of voting.[65]

As was the case throughout Wade's terms in office, the strength of pious secularism among Mouride elites was of crucial importance in the closing days of the election campaign. Rumors swirled that Wade's allies were showing up in Touba, the Mouride capital, with huge sums of cash on hand, seeking religious endorsement.[66] But the Mouride *khalife* distanced himself from such attempts. As a senior Mouride *marabout* put it in 2010, "There are too many temptations [in politics], too many unfulfilled promises. . . . [W]e are not in the republic of God."[67] Even as Wade scrambled for his political life and sought support from religious allies, the Mouride *khalife* made a point of isolating himself in a retreat rather than getting involved in electoral politicking.[68] Wade eventually secured a last meeting but no active endorsement. This indicator of pious secularism bore out Abdoul Aziz Kébé's prediction to me two years earlier: "The parental *ndigël* will not return; . . . manipulation of *laïcité* is driven by political opportunists, not by the brotherhoods."[69] As one commentator captured the mood, "It is necessary that [the *khalife*] guard his dignity."[70]

Perhaps the surest indicator of the strength of both interfaith ties and Mouride pious secularism was the behavior of Macky Sall, Wade's former ally and eventual rival, in the closing days of the campaign. While Wade played to his Mouride base, Sall mounted a full-throated defense of the dimensions of benevolent secularism in interviews and public appearances. When asked whether he feared that religious endorsements might undermine his campaign, Sall responded, "No *ndigël* will arise . . . no *marabout* will give a *ndigël* in this country."[71] Rather than seek endorsement, Sall made the rounds of various Sufi brotherhoods to seek only "prayers that social peace return to Senegal."[72] And in a remarkable affirmation of differentiation and principled distance just days before the electoral runoff, Sall insisted, "The *marabouts* are citizens. They live under the law like everyone. . . . There will not be special laws for *marabouts*. I say this clearly. We are a democratic and *laïque* republic. The freedom of religion will be guaranteed for all religions and brotherhoods."[73] He expressed similar sentiments in another interview shortly thereafter:

> Certainly, religious leaders play a very important role in Senegal—socially. In the private domain of religion, a *marabout* can have authority over the president, but not in public life. . . . It is very dangerous in Senegal for a man of politics, seeking the highest office, to manipulate the religious vote. . . . It is not for me to stigmatize Christians in their churches or to create confusion between the Sufi brotherhoods. Also, I refuse to enter into an artificial debate over whether the Tidjann or Mouride vote will favor me, which risks creating religious divisions that do not exist in Senegal.[74]

After months of protests and speculation about religious influence on the election, opposition cohesion held in the decisive second round vote, and Macky Sall was elected with a convincing 65 percent of the popular vote. Power again changed hands between political parties in this vibrant, if imperfect, democracy. And, most importantly to this study, in the face of the greatest challenge to *laïcité* since the early days of Senghor's rule, Senegal's elites united to defend benevolent secularism. The remarkable events in the weeks and months before the election should not obscure the fact that the alliances between Muslim, Catholic, and secular elites in Senegal were neither accidental nor unprecedented. They were instead a direct result of the three dimensions of benevolent secularism institutionalized at independence, in particular the combination of cooperation and principled distance that engages religious communities in public life, builds relationships of trust and shared interests between diverse elites, and provides generations of elites in religion, state, and civil society with shared experiences and channels of communication that facilitate united responses when challenges to *laïcité* emerge. Relationships forged in earlier periods of crafting education policy, cooperating in the fight against AIDS, and calling for good governance reforms bore fruit in the election season of 2012 and account for the evolution, rather than the breakdown, of *laïcité* in Senegal.

RELIGION–STATE CONSENSUS IN PUBLIC OPINION

The elite-based evidence discussed in the preceding section highlights the importance of cooperation across faith boundaries, particularly involving members of the Mouride brotherhood, in the evolution of benevolent secularism in Senegal. Coalition partners stabilized benevolent secularism during a turbulent political period. The predominance of pious secularism within the Mouride brotherhood was especially important, as elites showed limited interest in breaking down *laïcité* even though President Wade tried to favor them in this process. This predominance of pious secularism among Mouride elites begs a question: How does opinion among the Mourides compare to that of the Senegalese population as a whole? Is there evidence in public opinion of consensus both within the Muslim community and between Muslims and Christians on the place of religion in politics? Survey research from the Pew Research Group allows a test of these hypothesized shared views in the general population. Pew conducted a general population survey in Senegal in 2007 as part of its study *Islam and Christianity in Sub-Saharan Africa*.[75] It is helpful that this survey was taken well after Wade assumed the presidency because the relevant religious blocs had time to respond to the challenges to *laïcité*.[76]

The evidence from elite groups documented in the previous section yields two hypotheses about attitudes to religion–state relations in public opinion data. First, one would hypothesize that affiliates of the Mouride brotherhood are as supportive of *laïcité* as other Muslims because of the strength of pious secularism in Mouride political culture. Second, the hypothesized strong interfaith relations should result in general consensus among faith groups about the place of religion in democratic life. There should be limited differences between Catholics and Muslims over questions of *laïcité*.

To test these hypotheses, I analyze several questions related to the religion–state relationship in Senegal. Two questions regarding attitudes to sharia law and attitudes to religious leaders' involvement in politics capture support for differentiation of religious and state institutions. One question relates to the dimension of principled distance: willingness to support a candidate who follows another religion. These questions are detailed in table 5.2. As is the case in the ISSP data from Ireland and the Philippines, Pew asks little about the cooperative dimension of benevolent secularism that is so prominent in Senegal. All

TABLE 5.2. SECULARISM AND PUBLIC OPINION
IN SENEGAL: QUESTION WORDING

Variable	Question Wording	Source/Country	Coding
Differentiation			
1. Sharia Law	Do you favor or oppose the following? Making sharia, or Islamic law, the official law of the land in our country.	Pew: Senegal	0 (Favor) 1 (Oppose)
2. Religious Leaders Speak Out on Politics	In your opinion, should religious leaders keep out of political matters, or should they express their views on political questions?	Pew: Senegal	0 (Should express views) 1 (Should keep out of politics)
Principled Distance			
3. Vote Religious Minority	Would it be OK with you if the political leaders of our country have a different religion than yours, or do you want only political leaders who share your religion?	Pew: Senegal	0 (Want only political leaders who share your religion) 1 (OK if political leaders have a different religion)

Source: Pew Forum on Religion and Public Life, *Tolerance and Tension: Islam and Christianity in Sub-Saharan Africa* (Washington, D.C.: Pew Research Group, 2007).

variables are coded so that a positive coefficient corresponds to stronger support for the dimension of benevolent secularism captured by the question. Although the questions are imperfect measures of support for the diverse dimensions of benevolent secularism, comparison across religious traditions within Senegal provides some leverage in assessing relative unity or division on questions of religion in public life.

The coalition hypotheses relate to differences both between religious traditions and between Sufi brotherhoods, so the primary effects of interest are the differences between the Mourides, other Muslims, and the Catholic minority. The Pew data track Sufi brotherhood membership, so I first compare the

Mourides to other Muslims and then to the Catholic minority. In the multivariate models, non-Mouride Muslims serve as the referent category, so coefficients for Mourides and Catholics should be interpreted as effects relative to that baseline. In the multivariate analysis, for each dependent variable I report two models: one with simple religious identification and a slightly more complex model where I control for several demographic factors that could impact attitudes to religion and democracy.

Overall results in table 5.3 show, in the aggregate, stronger support for values of principled distance than for questions related to differentiation of religion from politics. The Muslim sample is relatively split both on the establishment of sharia as the law of the land and on the presence of religious leaders in politics. In these topline results, Catholics appear on the whole modestly more supportive of differentiation and, perhaps unsurprisingly given their minority status, more willing to vote for a political leader from a different religious tradition. More interestingly, the topline results indicate stronger support for differentiation and principled distance among Mouride Muslims than among the Muslim population as a whole. Mourides especially stand out in comparison with members of the Tidjann brotherhood on questions related to differentiation, where they are eight points less supportive of following sharia law as state law and nine points more supportive of keeping religious leaders out of politics. This compelling initial evidence confirms the expectation that pious secularism is especially dominant in the political culture of Mouridism.

Basic multivariate modeling through logistic regression tests the statistical significance of these differences and introduces a few statistical controls for

TABLE 5.3. SENEGAL TOPLINE RESULTS BY RELIGIOUS TRADITION

	Support for Sharia as Law of Land (%)	Support for Keeping Religious Leaders Out of Politics (%)	Willing to Support Political Leader Who Has a Different Religion (%)
Total		51	70
All Muslims	56	51	69
Mouride Muslims	52	55	72
Tidjann Muslims	60	46	66
Other Muslims	55	58	73
Roman Catholics	N/A	57	78

Source: Pew Research Group, *Tolerance and Tension*.

demographics and socioeconomic status. The results in table 5.4, both in the simple affiliation models and with demographic controls, are consistent with the two coalition hypotheses: (1) members of the Mouride brotherhood are as supportive of benevolent secularism as the rest of the Muslim community, and (2) there are minimal interfaith divides on questions of the relationship between religion and politics. In two of the six models, the Mourides are significantly *more* supportive of the dimension of benevolent secularism than other Muslims, and even in the models where the result is not statistically significant, the direction of the effect is consistently in the positive direction. The only other control variable that is so consistently important is education, which is also associated with support for benevolent secularism. The general lack of interfaith divides stands out as well. Catholics are significantly different than their Muslim compatriots in only one model (without controls), and that effect is eliminated

TABLE 5.4. TESTING BENEVOLENT SECULAR CONSENSUS IN SENEGAL

	Differentiation				*Principled Distance*	
	Sharia as Law of Land?		Religious Leaders Speak Out on Politics		Support Political Leader of Other Religion	
	Model 1	Model 2	Model 3	Model 4	Model 5	Model 6
Mourides	0.248*	0.212	0.220	0.237*	0.242	0.224
	[0.148]	[0.152]	[0.147]	[0.148]	[0.163]	[0.165]
Catholics			0.213	0.182	0.382**	0.255
			[0.222]	[0.232]	[0.265]	[0.281]
Sex		0.104		−0.0412		0.360**
		[0.148]		[0.135]		[0.149]
Age		−0.141		−0.0574		0.157
		[0.0281]		[0.0257]		[0.0284]
Education		0.717***		0.0975		0.764***
		[0.105]		[0.0940]		[0.108]
N	870	857	990	977	942	935

Note: All coefficients standardized (*** $p < 0.01$, ** $p < 0.05$, * $p < 0.1$). Logit Models with robust standard errors in brackets.
Source: Pew Research Group, *Tolerance and Tension*.

when education is included in the models. Taken together, these results are consistent with the elite consensus set out earlier. The Mouride community is actually modestly more supportive of differentiation than other Senegalese Muslims and so proved resistant to Wade's efforts to break down differentiation. And interfaith opinion on these matters is fairly consistent, which corresponds with the strong interfaith elite pushback against the breakdown of *laïcité*.

It is reasonable to ask whether there is some relationship between interfaith relations and the apparent strength of pious secularism among Senegal's Mourides. At the elite level, the same actors who are most active in Senegal's dialogue *islamo-chrétien* frequently invoke themes of pious secularism. There is some evidence that this trend among elites has a mirror in the general population. Mourides are more likely than other Muslims to be tied to the Catholic minority through interfaith dialogue and related events. Table 5.5 shows that the rate of participation in interfaith dialogues is much higher among Mourides than among other Muslims in Senegal. This is a particularly interesting finding because, of course, the institutional structure of benevolent secularism is explicitly intended to increase collaboration between faith communities and the state. In the absence of such cooperative engagement, Senegal's Sufi brotherhoods may be less dedicated to the pious secularism that has proven essential to preserving the twin tolerations in the past decade.

The strong support for pious secularism among Mourides in the Pew data increases our confidence that benevolent secularism shapes coalition politics not only at the elite level but also among the general population. The basic terms of *laïcité* in Senegal garner broad popular support, even from the community that is generally perceived as most politically cohesive. This broad support suggests that President Wade misread the likely outcomes of his attempt to break down aspects of *laïcité*. Even if some in the Mouride leadership would have

TABLE 5.5. RELIGIOUS TRADITIONS AND INTERFAITH ENGAGEMENT IN SENEGAL

	Do You Ever Participate in Interfaith Religious Groups?	
	Yes (%)	No (%)
Mouride Muslims	30	70
Other Muslims	18.40	81.60
Roman Catholics	42	58

Source: Pew Research Group, *Tolerance and Tension*.

been inclined to play along with him, they would have been pushing against the grain of popular opinion within the movement.

The combination of President Wade's election and changes to the religious landscape in Senegal in 2000 presented a challenge to *laïcité* unseen since the critical juncture during which benevolent secularism emerged. Coalition alliances across the religious-secular divide and among interfaith groups ensured that this period would be one of secular evolution that preserved the dimensions of benevolent secularism. Although that evolution brought about an increased presence of religious political parties and greater cooperation between religion and state in the provision of religious education, these changes were broadly compatible with benevolent secularism. The three core dimensions of benevolent secularism—differentiation, cooperation, and principled distance—endured this turbulent period. With President Macky Sall's electoral defeat of Wade in 2012, the immediate task of preserving benevolent secularism seemed complete.

Although Wade's administration has come to a close, patterns of demographic change and tensions built into the structure of benevolent secularism are likely to provide future periods of institutional change. These enduring tensions within *laïcité* stretch back to the Code de la famille debates and are especially visible in debates about the extent of religious autonomy from state control. Perceived violations of religious autonomy have been one issue that united the rather fractious Sufi brotherhoods and could play a role in provoking a more traditional secular-religious divide in the future. The autonomy of religious institutions has always been a special concern of *laïcité*, starting with the constitutional language in Article 19, which declares that "religious communities have the right to develop without obstacles" and "to regulate their affairs in an autonomous manner." The extent of "their affairs" is a key driver of contention, with Muslim reformists arguing that it should include legal standing over marriage, for instance, but with governance organizations claiming that the communal autonomy of brotherhood life increasingly undermines effective state development. Guèye points out that the original "land concessions" granted by the colonial regime and affirmed after independence "[do] not mean extraterritoriality" in law but have consistently been interpreted as such by the brotherhoods.[77] Fatou Kiné Camara observed that although such debates started over the Code de la famille, they now extend as well to state regulation of informal religious schools, where the rhetoric of *laïcité* is used to justify *nonintervention* on the part of political elites.[78] These debates are important for benevolent secularism more broadly. To what extent should religious groups receive exemptions from general state regulations? How do states resolve tensions between the dimensions of benevolent secularism, especially differentiation and cooperation? Recent history in Senegal suggests that these questions will be answered differently in different cases, depending on decisions within and between the coalition blocs supporting benevolent secularism.

A second, somewhat embryonic, source of future change has been an increase in religious diversity through international population flows. Modern migration has brought new actors to Senegal's religious landscape: Protestants, largely from other West African countries. These migrants, some fleeing political violence in places such as Côte d'Ivoire and others simply attracted to Dakar's active markets, are still quite small in size but have already been the source of some discontent at the local level. In the summer of 2010, a confrontation took place between Muslim youth and a Protestant community in the suburb of Pikine Tally Bou Bess that attracted national media attention. Local residents complained about the noise from the evangelical services and demanded the community's closure. A similar protest through the legal system in another residential area of Dakar, SICAP Liberté 5, took place earlier in 2010. In conversations about these incidents, complaints about the noise of such churches were coupled with the sense that the services were foreign religious traditions, not Senegalese. Abbé Alphonse Seck pointed out that because some of these communities consist of refugees, they are in a particularly vulnerable social position and do not have the opportunity for the daily informal interreligious dialogues that characterize the Muslim–Catholic relationship in Senegal.[79]

The institutional question regarding new diversity is how the concept of principled distance among religious traditions will survive if significant non-Muslim or Catholic communities arrive in Senegal. To put it bluntly, will the state fund pilgrimages to Azusa Street if a Charismatic Christian community takes off, or will it explicitly choose to fund only those religious traditions that have enjoyed cooperative relationship with the state since independence? The focus of this argument on interreligious ties suggests that the status of relations between Sufis, Catholics, and new minorities should be central in explaining future outcomes.

Although the general theoretical model proposed in chapter 1 holds up well in the period of recent institutional evolution in Senegal, two ambiguities in the model are important to acknowledge. First, one can certainly speak of a bloc of state and civil society elites in Senegal, but it is not accurate to say that this bloc represents a group personally devoted to atheism or nonbelief. The framework hypothesizes that benevolent secularism helps to undercut anticlericalism among political elites and in the process to reduce the religious-secular divide over time. However, the challenge from political elites in Senegal in the contemporary period was not a resurgence of anticlericalism, as in Ireland, but rather a willingness to advance sectarian politics if it brought electoral benefits. Although one can imagine a breakdown of the alliance between the

Sufi brotherhoods and civil society organizations such as the Assises nationales, it would not be quite accurate to call this breakdown a religious-secular divide.

Second, although the hypothesized *inter*group alliance patterns did drive the evolution of secularism during President Wade's terms in office, the *within*-group dynamics were also crucial. This was most apparent in the Mouride community, where the continued predominance of pious secularism undercut Wade's attempts to break down differentiation and principled distance. This challenge was not an intergroup effect (although such an effect existed simultaneously) but rather a continuation of the within-group effect of institutional structure traced during the independence period. The framework roughly schematizes that within-group effects *of* institutions take place at critical junctures and intergroup effects *on* institutions occur during periods of secular evolution, but there are likely direct within-group effects *on* institutions as well during the secular evolution process.

With these limitations in mind, the endurance of *laïcité* demonstrates the ways in which coalition actors exercise agency to preserve the institutional relationship between religion and state when *laïcité* faces institutional breakdown. These actors' preferences have been themselves shaped by the structure of benevolent secularism, which makes sense of the path-dependent nature of *laïcité* in Senegal.

6. Secular Emergence in the Philippines

BEYOND THE MALOLOS STALEMATE

With preachers contesting elected office, chapels in state buildings, and a state system of sharia courts, it may come as a surprise that Article 2.6 of the Constitution of the Republic of the Philippines (1987) states, "The separation of Church and State shall be inviolable." The phrase "separation of Church and State" does not appear even in the U.S. Constitution, which exercised so much influence in the Philippines, and yet it features prominently among the Declaration of Principles that opens that Philippine governing document. Although several rounds of constitutional revision have taken place since Spanish colonialism ended in 1898, the twin tolerations have generally coexisted with religious mobilization in this devout democracy. How did the Philippines, with its overwhelming Catholic majority and history of clerical control of state institutions, secure the twin tolerations at the critical juncture of independence?

The crucial juncture in the institutional development of the Philippines was the period around the Constitutional Convention of 1934 and the Commonwealth Constitution of 1935. The Commonwealth Constitution did not result in full independence (which did not arrive until after the disastrous Japanese occupation during World War II), but it set out the major features of the institutional relationship between religion and state that endured long after full independence in 1946. This juncture followed three centuries of Spanish colonial rule, from the sixteenth century to 1898 and over three decades of direct U.S. colonial administration (1898–1935). The Spanish had legally established Catholicism as a state religion, and American colonial authorities in turn imposed strict separation of religion and state on their arrival in 1898. At the Constitutional Convention of 1934, in preparation for the Americans' withdrawal, Filipino elites took up the task of configuring the relationship between religion and state for themselves. They had begun this process at the Malolos Congress of 1898 but deadlocked on the question of the place of religion in an independent Philippine republic. The Malolos Constitution was never fully implemented due to America's assumption of power, and thus Filipino actors did not resolve their stalemate over religion and democracy at this time. Would the twin tolerations emerge? Or would the secularism trap spring, either because Catholic authorities demanded formal establishment or because anticlerical political elites turned the state's coercive power on religious institutions? Any accommodation would need to account not only for the Catholic majority but also for prominent Muslim and Protestant communities. In 1934, the Constitutional Convention's deliberations provided the moment of institutional uncertainty in which Filipino elites took up these questions.

This chapter argues that institutional structure of benevolent secularism was integral in the emergence of the twin tolerations in the Philippines during this period. The hostile relationship between religion and state imposed during the early years of American rule gave way to what the Philippine Supreme Court later termed "benevolent neutrality," an institutional relationship characterized by the three dimensions of benevolent secularism: differentiation, cooperation, and principled distance.[1] Philippine institutions moved beyond the colonial dichotomy between Spanish religious establishment and American strict separation. Cooperation between religion and state, particularly in the realm of education and family policy, shaped the preferences of relevant coalition actors: elites in the Catholic hierarchy, state politicians, and minority religious communities. As anticlericalism faded among political elites and Filipino Catholic leadership became less dominated by Spanish prelates, the coalition supporting a benevolent form of state secularism took shape.

The emergence of the twin tolerations in the Philippines is of broad comparative importance because of the undeniable fusion of religion and state institutions under Spanish colonial rule. Ahmet Kuru has convincingly argued that the legacy of such an ancien régime comes with lasting implications for religious politics and helps account for the assertive forms of *laïcité* in places such as France and Turkey. In those cases, even decades after the fall of religiously legitimated authoritarian regimes, sharp conflicts between religious and secular elites endure in public life.[2] The emergence of the twin tolerations in the Philippines between 1898 and 1935 is especially important because it provides evidence of the process by which the legacies of an ancien régime gave way to new patterns of elite confidence building and mutual accommodation. Given the centuries of collaboration between Catholic clerics and Spanish colonial rule, how did the Philippines avoid anticlerical nationalism as it moved to independence? Answering this question is of importance not just to understanding the Philippines case but more broadly to understanding how societies can hope to overcome the damaging legacies of mixing religious legitimacy and authoritarian rule.

This chapter opens with a brief overview of the Filipino religious landscape. Then I document the formal institutions of religion–state relations that emerged at the critical juncture of the Philippine Commonwealth in the three dimensions of benevolent secularism: differentiation, cooperation, and principled distance. Next I provide evidence that this institutional configuration altered the preferences of the main blocs contesting the relationship between religion and democracy: political elites, the Catholic Church, and religious minorities. Debates within these blocs changed in response to the benevolence of secularism considered at the Constitutional Convention of 1934. Empirical evidence contrasts elite preferences in 1934 with those revealed around the Malolos Congress of 1898. After examining alternative explanations of secular emergence in the Philippines, the chapter ends with a debate on the extent of religious education in public schools that occurred shortly after the Commonwealth Constitution's adoption. This debate revealed lingering tensions among the coalition blocs in the Philippines.

THE RELIGIOUS LANDSCAPE OF THE PHILIPPINES

It is often (erroneously) noted that the Philippines is "Asia's only Christian nation," but this characterization only begins to describe the diversity both within and between religious traditions. At a basic level, the Philippines is not only Christian but also overwhelmingly Roman Catholic. Survey research carried out by the ISSP in conjunction with the Social Weather Stations research firm has found in each of its three waves since 1990 that Catholics make up more than 80 percent of the population.[3] In contrast to many of the majority Roman Catholic countries in Latin America, there has been no mass exodus from Catholicism to Protestant denominations; only 5 percent of the population report a shift away from Catholicism in the most recent wave of ISSP data. The presence of Catholicism is inextricably linked to the Spanish colonial rule that entrenched itself from the sixteenth century until the lopsided Spanish-American War at the close of the nineteenth century. The first Augustinian missionaries arrived with Spanish explorers in 1565, and they would go on to systematically evangelize the islands.[4] Catholic bishops were closely tied to the colonial center during both Spanish and American rule.

Although the archbishop of Manila and other elites of the Catholic Bishops' Conference of the Philippines (CBCP) are the unquestioned leaders of the Catholic Church in the Philippines, the religious orders and Charismatic movements are also central to understanding the past and future of Philippine secularism. Religious orders of various kinds—in particular Dominicans, Augustinians, Franciscans, and Recollects—evangelized the islands and received substantial landholdings from the Spanish administration for their cooperation. This collaboration fueled nationalist antifriar sentiment, notably in the character of Padre Damaso in José Rizal's classic nationalist novel *Noli me tángere* (Touch me not). Although such antifriar sentiment has faded, the orders remain important political actors. The elite Catholic universities of the Philippines are often run by religious orders, in particular the Jesuits at Ateneo de Manila University and the Christian Brothers at De La Salle University. The importance of orders shows through in civil society as well, where the Association of Major Religious Superiors of the Philippines, a collective of male and female religious leadership, enters the political realm more assertively than the official Catholic hierarchy headed by the CBCP. A second subgroup, more relevant to the secular evolution described in chapter 7 than to the period of secular emergence, is the ranks of Charismatic Catholicism in the Philippines. Major Charismatic associations such as El Shaddai and Couples for Christ claim millions of members and have built substantial media and grassroots organizing networks throughout the country.[5] The lay leadership of these organizations facilitates political action, notably the electoral candidacies of some Charismatic Catholic leaders, which are a significant feature of current church–state relations.

Although the Catholic community was the numerical center of Christian life as the Philippines moved to independence, significant Protestant communities have played an important role since the early American colonial period. Non–Roman Catholic Christians make up approximately 7.5 percent of the population according to the most recent round of ISSP surveys from 2008, a significant minority in a country of nearly 100 million people.[6] This group is itself quite diverse. Churches affiliated with the National Council of Churches of the Philippines generally correspond to denominations considered mainline Protestant in the United States, such as the Episcopal Church of the Philippines and the United Church of Christ in the Philippines. During the U.S. colonial era, Protestant American missionaries divided the Philippines among themselves, much as the Catholic religious orders had done centuries before, and this historical division is reflected in the spread of National Council churches today. More recently, evangelical Christian churches have organized under the Philippine Council of Evangelical Churches. In addition to these denominations, two distinct Filipino Christian communities claim substantial membership and were active in the independence period. The Philippine Independent Church, also known as the Aglipayan Church, is a nationalized form of the Catholic Church that formed during the anticlerical periods of the revolution against Spanish rule. Property controversies involving the Aglipayan Church played an important role at the juncture of secular emergence. The final major non-Catholic Christian community is the Iglesia ni Cristo (INC), which represents 3.6 percent of the population according to the ISSP survey.[7] The INC has a particular reputation for political cohesion and engaging in bloc voting come election season.

Although the Philippines is an overwhelmingly Christian country, it has a long-established Muslim minority that played a unique role in politics of religion in the independence period. Muslim Filipinos are a minority overall but a majority in particular parts of the country, and they have a distinct historical relationship to locales of both colonial and national power. Today Muslims make up approximately 5 percent of the general population, but because of political instability in some Muslim-majority areas this number is likely underestimated. The Muslim community has historically been concentrated in parts of Mindanao, a legacy of Muslim missionaries who arrived in the southern Philippines as early as the thirteenth century. The sultanates of Sulu and Maguindanao reigned over portions of the southern Philippines through the Spanish colonial period and experienced unique concessions and coercion even during American colonial administration. Today the Muslim population makes up a majority in portions of Mindanao and has also spread throughout the major cities of the Philippines, such as Manila and Cebu. Institutional Islam in the Philippines, as is typical in Sunni Muslim communities, is less hierarchically organized than the Catholic community. Networks of the ulema have formed in recent years, and they engage in a range of public advocacy. Notable Muslim groups include the National Ulama Conference of the Philippines and the Philippine Center for Islam and Democracy, a leading civil society organization that builds networks of Muslim leaders. The jurists associated with the state Sharia District Courts form another important elite network that affects religion–state relations.

This brief overview gives of a sense of the diversity within the Philippine religious landscape. Although the Catholic Church predominates and has done so since the independence period, religious minorities of various stripes were crucial coalition actors both in the period of institutional flux around the Constitutional Convention of 1934 and in later secular evolution.

ASSESSING BENEVOLENT SECULARISM IN THE PHILIPPINES

In contrast to the formal establishment of Catholicism in the Spanish colonial period and the assertive separation of religion and state under early American colonial rule, by the time of deliberations about the Commonwealth Constitution the religion–state relationship in the Philippines featured the three dimensions of benevolent secularism. The Commonwealth Constitution bore a heavy imprint of the formal language of the U.S. Constitution, but it would be inaccurate to categorize the Philippine religion–state relationship as an institutional copy of the U.S. relationship in Southeast Asia. Whereas American jurisprudence on religion and state places heavy emphasis on "strict neutrality," the Supreme Court of the Philippines points out in its extensive *Estrada v. Escritor* (455 Phil. 411 [2003]) decision that "[Philippine] constitutional history and interpretation mandate benevolent neutrality" (at 572). What the Philippine Supreme Court called benevolent neutrality is an institutional sibling of Irish and Senegalese secularism. It possesses the three dimensions of benevolent secularism: differentiation, cooperation between religion and state, and principled distance among all religious communities. This type clearly varies from the assertive secularism of France as well as the passive secularism of the United States. Cooperation in the Philippines at the critical juncture of secular emergence was rather less extensive than in Ireland and Senegal, with more emphasis on differentiation of religious and state institutions. Overall, however, the three dimensions stand out in significant ways, from constitutional language to relevant legislation and its implementation.

The basic differentiation of religion and state institutions in the Philippines rests on constitutional language regarding both establishment and free exercise. Article 3.1.7 of the Constitution of 1935 declared, "No law shall be made respecting an establishment of religion," but the Constitution of 1987 put it even more bluntly: "The separation of Church and State shall be inviolable." The earlier document spells out in Article 6.13.3 the differentiation of institutions in some detail as related to state funding: "No public money or property shall ever be appropriated, applied, or used, directly or indirectly, for the use, benefit, or support of any sect, church, denomination, sectarian institution, or system of religion." Although this type of language needed interpretation in the process of policy formation, it set a clear baseline of institutional differentiation. A return to formal establishment of Catholicism was off the table, as were the multiple religious establishments seen in several European cases. As in Senegal, the differentiation of religion and state institutions came with implications for religion's role in elections. The Administrative Code excluded "ecclesiastics" from election or appointment to a municipal office.[8] Later constitutional revisions would build on this prohibition in forbidding the registration of "religious denominations and sects" as political parties.

Article 3.1.7 of the Constitution of 1935 goes on to protect religious liberty for all, prohibiting laws that "prohibit the free exercise [of religion]." It then forbids religious tests for public office and "forever allows" the "enjoyment of religious profession and worship." Leaving aside whether this article grants adequate protection to *unenjoyable* religious worship, it is clear that the protections of free exercise are robust. Article 3.1.7 specifically states that this protection is not limited to certain traditions; the state must protect religious liberty "without discrimination or preference." The ordinance appended to this constitution reiterates the point: "Absolute toleration of religious sentiment shall be secured and no inhabitant or religious organization shall be molested in person or property on account of religious belief or mode or worship." Although the preamble of this constitution does "implore the aid of Divine Providence," this general statement is not limited to any religious community or communities.

These clauses set out the differentiation of religion and state in the Philippines; however, the other dimensions of benevolent secularism, cooperation, and principled distance feature as well in Philippine institutions of the late colonial period. As in both Ireland and Senegal, cooperation between religion and state existed in the educational realm. The Spanish colonial regime conducted education through religious schools, so structuring the place of religion in the new state schools was a flashpoint around the convention in 1934. Article 13.5 of the Constitution of 1935 established free primary public education and specified that all educational institutions would be "subject to regulation by the State." Religion and state schools would be differentiated. However, there would also be cooperation between religion and state in this area. The Constitution required public schools to "develop moral character" among students. Moreover, it allowed "optional religious instruction" in public schools, with the cost not born by the state. The cooperative nature of benevolent neutrality comes through in an account from the period describing optional religious instruction as "a profession as a people of our faith in God . . . that we give due importance to religion without making its teaching compulsory."[9] Vice President Sergio Osmeña argued at the time that "[optional religious instruction] was the maximum concession that a state which recognizes the principle of religious freedom and the separation of church and state could possibly give in interest of tolerance and good will."[10] Decades later Father Jaoquin Bernas, S.J., a noted constitutional lawyer and commissioner to the Constitutional Commission of 1986, pointed out in his commentary on the Constitution that, "in effect, this provision creates an explicit exception to the non-establishment clause . . . it will not be made to depend on the school administrator's interpretation of separation of church and state."[11]

In addition to cooperation in the area of religious education, other areas of material support for religion exist in the Philippines. The Constitutional Convention of 1934 did not leave such cooperation open to interpretation but instead placed several provisions directly into the text. The most obvious example is Article 6.14.3: "Cemeteries, churches, and parsonages or convents appurtenant thereto, and all lands, buildings, and improvements used exclusively for religious, charitable, or educational purposes shall be exempt from taxation." Article 6.13.3 also allowed state-funded religious officials "when such priest, preacher, minister, or dignitary is assigned to the armed forces or to any penal institution, orphanage or leprosarium." The most important Supreme Court decision during the period of secular emergence came in 1937, shortly after the adoption of the Constitution in 1935. In the case *Aglipay v. Ruiz* (64 Phil 201 [1937]), the Court ruled that state stamps commemorating the Thirty-Third International Eucharistic Congress of the Catholic Church were constitutionally permissible in spite of objections that they violated the new constitution's Establishment Clause. The majority opinion captures the cooperative nature of secular institutions: "Religious freedom, however, as a constitutional mandate is not an inhibition of profound reverence for religion. . . . [T]he elevating influence of religion in human society is recognized here as elsewhere" (at 206). This recognition of religion's "elevating influence" indicates the mutual support between religion and state that characterizes the cooperative dimension of benevolent secularism.

Finally, cooperation showed through in a more limited way at this juncture in elements of policy formulation. Articles 132 and 133 of the Revised Penal Code of 1930, for example, established the category "Crimes Against Religious Worship," explicitly forbidding interruption of religious worship and offense of religious feelings. Religious-state policy consultations in this period extended into a broad spectrum of areas. The Federation of Free Workers and the Federation of Free Farmers, groups founded by the Catholic Church, worked to shape state policy on labor and agriculture.[12]

Although cooperation between religion and state did emerge around the Commonwealth Constitution, it is important to acknowledge that this cooperation was less extensive than in the other two cases considered in this volume. The kind of religion–state partnership over primary schooling in Ireland, for example, would have been unacceptable to secular Filipino political elites. Likewise, the extensive material transfers to the Sufi brotherhoods in Senegal have no analogue in the Philippines under American colonialism. To give another example, in spite of the Catholic hierarchy's clear interest in promoting marriage, the Constitution of 1935 did not outlaw divorce, which remained legal until after World War II. If differentiation and cooperation are in some tension, this constitution tended more to differentiation. This tendency came with implications for the impact of political institutions on coalition actors' preferences: the Catholic elites were less content to accept the benevolent secular bargain and pushed its boundaries nearly from the time that the Constitution of 1935 was adopted.

The final dimension of benevolent secularism, the state's principled distance from all religious communities, was also featured in the Constitution of 1935 and in the institutions that grew from it. Although the issue of optional religious education was a priority for Catholic authorities, there was no religious limitation on who could pursue such education. Delegates to the Constitutional Convention of 1934 included Protestant and Muslim citizens, a pattern that would repeat itself in later periods of constitutional revision. Protestant chaplains were commissioned along with Catholics for Philippine prisons and military posts. Manuel Quezon, the first president of the Philippine Commonwealth, summed up this impartiality as it related to the powers of his office: "As an individual, I worship my God in accordance with my own religious belief. But as the head of the State I can have no more to do with the Catholic than I can with a Protestant denomination, the Aglipayan, the Mohammedan, or any other religious organization or sect in the Philippines."[13] In *Aglipay v. Ruiz*, the Supreme Court's decision to permit religiously motivated stamps, the Court noted that such cooperation is permissible only because such "general concessions [to religion] . . . are indiscriminately accorded" to religious communities in the commonwealth (at 206).

The state's principle distance among religious communities is also indicated in the exemptions and religious accommodations to civil law made during this period. Catholic priests were protected from breaking the seal of the confessional in state courts.[14] Members of the INC, a Christian church that forbids union membership, were exempted from closed-shop union agreements.[15] The more recent *Estrada v. Escritor* case shows that this pattern endures today. In this case, a Jehovah's Witness who lost a government job because of a marital arrangement that was alleged to violate the law won the case because the arrangement was in keeping with practices of the faith tradition, and the Court held that "accommodation of [alternative] morality based on religion" was central to the functioning of benevolent neutrality in a pluralistic society (at 589).

The most important indicator of exemptions related to principled distance came in the treatment of Muslim personal law. The Muslim minority in the Philippines received significant autonomy in legal recognition of its customs related to marriage and divorce. From the early years of American colonial rule, areas of Mindanao were a distinct juridical category, administered directly by the U.S. military and granted unique guarantees of noninterference in religious matters. As Peter Gowing explains, "The American government scrupulously avoided any interference with the freedom of the Moros to worship and practice their religious customs."[16] In spite of fears that administration by non-Muslim Filipinos would end these accommodations, the Commonwealth Constitution continued this pattern. In implementing this constitutional language after World War II, the New Civil Code of 1950 recognized that "marriages between Mohammedans or pagans who live in the non-Christian provinces may be performed in accordance with their customs, rites or practices. No marriage license of formal requisites shall be necessary," and Republic Act 394 of 1948 recognized Islamic divorces.[17] Later, this provision from the period of secular emergence carried forward to the Code of Muslim Personal Laws enacted by President Ferdinand Marcos in 1973 to signal to Muslims that "the government protects their religion and their rights, that they are treated equally with the rest of the population, and that they are an integral part of the Filipino nation."[18] Today, the state funds sharia courts as well as the professional sharia jurists who staff them. This legal standing for religious tribunals is difficult to imagine under the configuration of American secularism. It thus provides an especially useful insight into the ways in which religion–state relations in the Philippines have resembled benevolent secularism rather than strict adherence to the more separationist American model.

The granting of unique accommodations to Muslims in civil law certainly did not eliminate the challenges of representing Muslim interests in national-level Philippine politics. As Michael Mastura, a Muslim participant in the Constitutional Convention of 1971, memorably summarizes, "Even more traumatic than the prospects of physical extermination is the fear of being totally submerged in a Christian-based national Filipino identity."[19] Without diminishing the importance of these challenges, it remains true that the Philippine state has extended unique religious accommodations to Muslims from the commonwealth period to the present day. The ongoing debates regarding the devolution of political authority to portions of Mindanao are the latest stage in the long process of determining the precise accommodation between state law and the Muslim minority.

The institutional relationship between religion and state in the commonwealth period was about far more than the simple differentiation of religion and state through the Free Exercise and Establishment Clauses of the Constitution of 1935. It also demonstrated the dimensions of cooperation and principled distance that characterize benevolent secularism. Table 6.1 summarizes some of the evidence of these dimensions at or around the Commonwealth Constitution's adoption. Although more than one conversation I had in Manila involved a smile before someone said, "Of course, the Philippines is not really a secular country," the reality is that differentiation, cooperation, and principled distance

TABLE 6.1. ASSESSING BENEVOLENT
SECULARISM IN THE PHILIPPINES

Indicator	Evidence
Differentiation	
Disestablishment	Article 3.1, Commonwealth Constitution: "No law shall be made respecting an establishment of religion."
Religious Freedom	Article 3.7, Commonwealth Constitution, "forever allows . . . enjoyment of religious profession and worship."
Religion–State Cooperation	
Material Support	Optional religious instruction in post-1935 public schools
Policy Consultation	Impact of religious groups on labor and agricultural policy
Principled Distance	
Impartial Access to Public Support	Recognition of Muslim personal law
Provide Religious Exemptions	Exemption of INC from unionization requirements

have since the commonwealth period combined to make benevolent secularism a part of governance in that country. At the critical juncture provided by the Constitutional Convention of 1934, these institutions played a crucial role in securing the twin tolerations between religion and democracy by shaping the preferences of actors debating the place for religion in independent Philippine democracy.

INSTITUTIONAL STRUCTURE AND COALITION PREFERENCES

Benevolent secularism played such an important part in the emergence of the twin tolerations in the Philippines because it affected debates within the relevant coalition blocs regarding the relationship between religion and democratic politics. The general theoretical framework in chapter 1 sets out empirical expectations for the effects of benevolent secularism on actor preferences during critical junctures: empowering pious secularists within the religious majority, undercutting anticlericalism among political elites, and drawing minority communities into public partnerships. Tracing the effects of benevolent secularism in the juncture around the Commonwealth Constitution provides an opportunity to test these hypothesized effects in the Philippines.

Throughout this section, I trace the institutional effects of benevolent secularism within these coalition blocs primarily by contrasting elite preferences during the Constitutional Convention in 1934 with the deliberations during the Malolos Congress in 1898. Although occurring only thirty-six years earlier, the Malolos debates took place within a very different institutional context: the breakdown of the Spanish fusion of state and Catholic institutions.[20] By the late Spanish era, friar-landlords had become entrenched in the colonial system, "convinced that only under Spanish rule could Philippine Christianity survive, and that liberal reforms demanded by educated Filipinos could only be a source of irreligion."[21] Gowing calls the church–state debates at Malolos "the most exciting and dramatic of the convention," in large part because they were so divisive and ultimately inconclusive.[22] Contrasting attitudes within each coalition bloc in the wake of the Malolos deadlock with those at the Constitutional Convention in 1934 demonstrates the substantial effect of institutional variation on these internal debates. Catholic, secular, and Muslim elites deliberated in very different institutional environments during these two conventions.

At the Malolos Congress, convened after centuries of fusion of church and state under Spanish colonial rule, anticlericalism predominated among Filipino political elites. Republican currents from Europe influenced Filipino nationalists in the late nineteenth century, and calls for official disestablishment of the church and confiscation of the friars' landholdings were far from benevolent. The secular nationalist elite may not have been as militantly anticlerical as their counterparts in Spain, but they clearly saw disestablishment of the Catholic Church as part and parcel of the process of independence and social development. The eventual leaders of the revolution—such as José Rizal, Marcelo del Pilar, and Andrés Bonifacio—were staunchly opposed to the friars' political power, and several were active Masons. Del Pilar wrote to Rizal in 1889 to argue that "the faith of the Filipino will fade away completely" once the friars' political power was broken.[23] At the Malolos Congress, Apolinario Mabini, a Mason and important adviser to revolutionary leader Emilio Aguinaldo, pushed for language that would officially disestablish the Catholic Church and allow religious pluralism.[24] When American colonizers consolidated their administration of the islands, they insisted that the separation of church and state be "real, entire and absolute," an outcome welcomed by the anticlericals and enshrined in the Organic Act of 1902, which ruled in place of a constitution.[25] This imposed disestablishment was coupled with guarantees of religious liberty, in part to satisfy American Protestant missionary organizations that clamored to enter a land "oppressed by a tyrannical priesthood."[26] It is difficult to imagine the emergence of state toleration for religious involvement in public life in the midst of such anticlericalism.

However, by the Constitutional Convention in 1934 anticlericalism had faded among Filipino secular elites in response to the effects of benevolent secularism. Evidence of these changed preferences shows through in political elites' statements regarding the place of religion in Philippine public life. Commonwealth president Manuel Quezon was a Mason and as late as 1917 had declared the Catholic Church "the sworn enemy of democracy [in the Philippines]."[27] However, he recanted his Masonic allegiance in 1930 upon rejoining the Catholic Church. Whatever Quezon's motivations, his actions reveal the changed preferences of the secularist bloc in the Philippines by the early 1930s.[28] This change among political elites took place as the nature of secularism in the Philippines became more benevolent in nature. By the time deliberations on the Constitution were taking place in 1934, the basic differentiation of religion and state was largely uncontested, and so at the convention the state elite bloc demonstrated different preferences than it had at Malolos. Even those speaking against religious influence in education, such as Delegate Leoncio Esliza, would oppose such instruction not as an antireligion measure but to prevent "the keen eye of jealousy" from emerging among the Christian churches.[29] After the Constitution had fixed the general boundaries of benevolent secularism, President Quezon, the former Mason, would justify those institutions in reference to the good they did *for religion*: "[It is necessary] to protect any religion from any attempt on the part of the civil authorities to meddle or control the affairs that pertain to the Church."[30] The unvarnished anticlericalism of the revolutionary period was a thing of the past.

At the Malolos Congress and in the early years of American colonialism, pious secularists did not hold sway within the Catholic Church. The fall of Spanish colonialism and arrival of American administrators had thrown the Catholic Church in the Philippines into a state of disarray. Although some provision for a local clergy had been made in the early eighteenth century due to infighting between state authorities and the religious orders, these native priests were often poorly trained and seen as unfit for duty. Archbishop Sancho lamented in 1779 that his own local priests were reported as "wine-bibbers," "robbers," and "galley boatswains."[31] After the flight of their Spanish leaders, native Filipino clergy who remained were "defensive and alienated from the mainstream of society," in an environment where "survival was the only concern that could be realistically expected of a Church."[32] Catholic Church advocates at Malolos embraced the end to colonial rule, but they saw independence and state secularism as unrelated matters. Felipe Calderón, an author of the draft constitution, called for official Catholic establishment. Mabini and his allies' insistence on constitutional disestablishment stoked fears that liberal elites would not only end the friar-backed colonial system but also uproot the perceived Catholic character of the Filipino nation. The early, assertive treatment of religion by American colonial administrators did not help the pious secularists' cause. Catholic officials regularly complained that American administrators favored Protestants and anticlerical Masons in hiring and textbook selection at public schools.[33] With President William McKinley's religious allies claiming God had directed America to "Christianize" the Philippines, insecurity among Catholics was understandable.[34]

By the Constitutional Convention of 1934, however, the pious secularist position predominated within the Catholic community. Convention deliberations opened with an invocation from Bishop Alfredo Verzosa, who went on at some length to ask "omnipotent and omnipresent God" to look down on the assembly's deliberations.[35] Notes from the convention point to the "genuine satisfaction" among delegates at having moved beyond the "union of church and state under the Spanish regime" and report that two attempts to make religious education obligatory were "overwhelmingly defeated."[36] This effect within the Catholic leadership was owing to the configuration of benevolent secularism set in place in the years before the convention, in particular the expansion of religion–state cooperation. This dimension of benevolent secularism was particularly important to Catholic elites as both a source of their institutional strength and a signal that differentiation need not violate religious freedom. Evidence suggests this process began with institutional changes in the years immediately before the convention, as the Taft administration "made all concessions possible within the framework of the constitutional provision for separation of church and state."[37] The cooperative relationship between religion and state could be seen in the educational realm, where state and religious leaders combined to recruit Catholic teachers for Philippine schools.[38] As voting rights broadened electoral participation, the church could advocate its interests through democratic means, and Masons seemed less threatening than at the time of the Malolos Congress. Without the more cooperative turn in the religion–state relationship, pious secularists would not have come to such influence, and the stalemate over religious establishment that took place at Malolos could have easily played itself out again in 1934.

Benevolent secularism had a more varied impact on the preferences of different religious minorities in the Philippines. Among Muslims, the 1898–1934 period did indeed witness the anticipated transition from defensive isolation to more public engagement. The early years of American colonial rule saw a clear preference among Muslim elites for defensive withdrawal from political life elsewhere in the Philippines. There was no particular cooperation with state institutions. American authorities instead distinguished between the "regular provinces" and the "special provinces," such as Muslim areas, which were largely excluded from state administration.[39] Muslim elites protested outside rule in a continuation of centuries of resistance to Spanish administration. There is evidence that by the Constitutional Convention in 1934, however, more cooperative state outreach to Muslim leaders had engaged a new generation of Moro elites in public life and undercut advocates of defensive isolation. At the convention, Muslim delegates supported the extension of cooperation and principled distance, especially in areas of personal law. If anything, the Muslim minority wanted secularism to become more benevolent and continued to lobby for more substantial religious accommodations. As Patricio Abinales puts it, "Among the Muslims, growing appreciation of a new political game with Manila and the Filipinos as the centers of power steadily displaced suspicion toward Filipinization. Muslim leaders would take advantage of Quezon's offer to join colonial politics, and many began to declare themselves 'spokesmen for the Moros' to get seats in the National Assembly. . . . As participation in the Filipinized state deepened, so, too, did their integration."[40] Expanding cooperation and principled distance served to empower Muslims like those who joined in the deliberations rather than separatists arguing for confrontation with the Philippine state.

Institutional effects, however, were less clear-cut among minority Christian communities. In general, at the end of Spanish rule these groups showed a preference not for defensive withdrawal from public life but rather for the use of state power to drive the Catholic majority from public influence. The early years of the American colonial period saw a fragmenting of the non-Catholic Christian community into three major groups: the Aglipayan Independent Church, the INC, and those tied to American Protestant denominations.[41] Around the Malolos Congress and the early years of American colonial rule, these non-Catholic Christian denominations generally supported a strict separation of religion from public life, and the Protestant who was selected to head the public-school system early in colonial rule, George Anderson, "pursued a policy hostile to Catholic sensibilities."[42] The Aglipayan Church was especially notable because it emerged from a break with the Catholic Church and initiated a range of property-ownership disputes over Catholic land.[43] Communities of American Protestant missionaries hoped that American colonial power would break the Catholic monopoly on Philippine Christianity, and leaders such as Aglipay actively attempted to shape state institutions that would further this process.

There is limited evidence that as secularism became more benevolent around the convention in 1934, these non-Catholic Christians became more engaged in public life. Although the features of cooperation and principled distance drew the Muslim minority into public partnerships with state and Catholic elites, the Aglipayan Church continued to resist benevolent secularism in favor of much stricter separation of religion and state. Delegate Servando Castro, himself a minister in the Aglipayan Church, spoke out against the optional provision of religious education in public schools. He argued that home study, rather than religious courses in public schools, could produce "a good Christian and a virtuous man."[44] In the same spirit skeptical of any cooperation between religion and state, the Aglipayan leadership filed suit to prevent the state from issuing stamps commemorating the International Eucharistic Congress of the Catholic Church in 1935. Over time, Protestants of different types would come to cooperate with Catholics in public life, but in the debates around the Commonwealth Constitution there was only limited support for such ecumenical cooperation.

In sum, in the course of three decades, preferences among the key coalition blocs shifted in response to the shifting institutional configuration between religion and state. Table 6.2 summarizes these effects. Catholic elites no longer advocated the fusion of church and state experienced under Spanish rule and instead demonstrated the pious secularist preference for differentiation combined with cooperation. This shift in attitude is all the more striking in light of two facts. First, the Spanish colonial administration represented precisely the kind of ancien régime that should have left enduring divisions between religious and secular elites in public life, as in French or Turkish politics. And second, the reforms of Vatican II that supposedly made Catholicism safe for democracy were several decades in the future. In the 1930s, political elites generally left behind the harshest Masonic anticlericalism in favor of accepting religion, even Catholicism, as a partner in democratic life. Preferences among religious

TABLE 6.2. PREFERENCE EFFECTS OF BENEVOLENT SECULARISM IN THE PHILIPPINES

Coalition Partner	Hypothesized Within-Group Effect	Evidence in Philippines
Religious Majority	Empower pious secularists	Catholic bishops' participation in the Constitutional Convention of 1934
Secular Elites	Weaken anticlericals and empower accommodation	President Quezon's break with Masonry
Religious Minorities	Promote engaged minorities	Muslim engagement in convention deliberations

minorities were more diverse. Some, such as the Muslim minority, responded to increased principled distance and cooperation by engaging in public life. Others, such as the Aglipayans, remained staunchly resistant to the cooperative dimension of benevolent secularism. Although these findings of institutional effects are less unanimous than in Ireland and Senegal, they point to the same general conclusion: the structure of benevolent secularism affected debates within coalition blocs and in turn secured the twin tolerations during a period of great uncertainty in the religious politics of democracy in the Philippines.

ALTERNATIVE EXPLANATIONS OF BENEVOLENT NEUTRALITY'S EMERGENCE

The emergence of the twin tolerations in the Philippines around the critical juncture of the Constitutional Convention in 1934 challenges leading alternative explanations of the twin tolerations. Although each places attention on a force contributing to the convention's deliberations, weaknesses in each highlight the importance of incorporating institutional structure and actor preferences into the study of the religious politics of democracy.

Modernization theory's clearest prediction is that the twin tolerations depend on the weakening of traditional sources of religious authority through economic development. This basic sequence is of limited help in making sense of Philippine secularism. The secular *illustrados* did indeed come from more economically advanced classes, but they were not able to achieve the twin tolerations in the Philippines on their own. The twin tolerations emerged as a partnership, not the simple replacement of religious authority by state bureaucratic authority. This points to a broader weakness in modernization theory's treatment of the secular state. The theory sees secularism as fundamentally divorced from or contrary to the wishes of religious actors and the institutional relationship between religion and state as consisting mostly of differentiation between the two spheres. However, benevolent secularism in the Philippines eventually secured the support of most major religious actors and did so in large part through the other dimensions of cooperation and principled distance. It was only once the Catholic Church was unthreatened by the specter of anticlericalism and its own relative weakness that its leaders possessed the confidence to support the twin tolerations. A greater decline in the vitality of religious institutions would not have increased the likelihood of the twin tolerations.

Rational choice theories that are focused on competition between religious traditions make a distinct contribution in understanding the emergence of the twin tolerations in the Philippines, though they ultimately offer an unsatisfying explanation for the eventual consensus around the Commonwealth

Constitution. On the one hand, competition clearly did shape the politics of religion in the Philippines during this period, particularly in the years immediately surrounding the collapse of Spanish rule. Increased competition from the Aglipayans, the INC, and the American Protestant missionaries made Catholic elites more hostile to the state in the early decades of American colonialism. Religious diversity seemed a danger, and the promise of newfound pluralism made any secular institutions seem a threat to Catholic survival. The contentious debates over religion and politics at the Malolos Congress of 1898 seem quite in keeping with rationalist explanations. However, the patterns of contention as the Philippines moved into the Commonwealth Constitution debates fit less clearly with purely competition-based explanations. By most accounts, by the Commonwealth Constitution deliberations, religious competition was less severe, not more. The Catholic Church signed on to the benevolent secular bargain from a position of relative security in its majority status and could have chosen to use that more comfortable majority to exclude religious competitors. Catholics' enthusiasm for benevolent secularism makes sense only once elite preferences regarding the place of religion in public life, in particular the growth of pious secularism, are accounted for. To be sure, *some* diversity was an important condition for state secularism in the Philippines because it undercut hardline Catholic claims to formal control of state institutions. But the pious secularist preference for the twin tolerations, which institutions of benevolent secularism strengthened, did not simply rest on levels of competition.

Finally, advocates of the religious moderation thesis find some limited support in the Philippines. One could argue that the replacement of a Spanish-dominated Catholic hierarchy by an American-influenced native Catholic clergy, which clearly played a part in the constitutional debates of 1934, was an example of the presence of religious moderates as a necessary, if not sufficient, condition for the emergence of the twin tolerations in the context of religious mobilization. However, to call Filipino religious elites of the mid–twentieth century "moderate" points out the conceptual challenges facing the moderation thesis. In what way were religious elites "moderate" during the Commonwealth Convention deliberations? If "moderate" is defined as a normative acceptance of liberal political philosophy, it hardly applies to those Catholic authorities. Vatican II would be several decades in the future, and Catholic elites, in the context of a Catholic demographic majority, were still technically obliged to seek the union of church and state. Likewise, there is little evidence that the leaders of Protestant and Muslim minority communities would consider themselves "moderate" in their religious commitment. Moreover, the moderation thesis consistently overlooks the role of political institutions in affecting which normative positions, whether moderate or not, carry the day within religious communities. The institutional configuration of benevolent secularism played a central role in providing both Catholic and minority religious elites with orthodox religious justifications for supporting the twin tolerations.

Benevolent secularism emerged in the Philippines in spite of low to middling levels of economic development, limited religious pluralism, and the debatable moderation of religious elites. Each of these alternatives would have predicted, for its own reasons, that independence could set off the secularism trap: either the majority would seize control of state institutions, or anticlerical elites would respond to the threat of theocracy with coercion. Although each alternative theory sheds light on important forces shaping the place of religion in Philippine democracy, each falls short because it overlooks the role of institutional design in shaping the preferences of the coalition blocs that ultimately joined to secure the twin tolerations in this seemingly least likely case.

HINTS OF INSTABILITY: DIFFERENTIATION AND RELIGION IN PUBLIC SCHOOLS

With opening prayers from clerics and near unanimous support for its provisions regarding religion–state relations, the Constitutional Convention of 1934 proved a crucial period for cementing the twin tolerations between religion and democracy in the Philippines. However, as in Ireland and Senegal, significant differences existed among the coalition actors as to the appropriate balance between the three dimensions of benevolent secularism. The Catholic Church and to a lesser extent the Muslim minority would promote wider cooperation between religion and state, whereas secular political elites and Protestant minorities preferred stricter differentiation and worried that any expansion in cooperation would tend to break down the state's principled distance from the religious communities. These internal tensions came to view shortly after the Commonwealth Constitution's adoption around the issue of religious education in public schools. Could differentiation permit the presence of religion in secularized state public schools? If so, what specific shape would it take? At what point would cooperation between religion and state become the capitulation of state authority to religious influence?

Although the Commonwealth Constitution explicitly provided for optional religious instruction in public schools, Catholic elites pressed for more: the compulsory provision of religious instruction in public schools. "The policy of optional religious instruction never did satisfy the [Catholic] Church[,] which constantly agitated for a more vigorous implementation of religious instruction in the public schools."[45] Among the democratically elected members of the commonwealth's legislature, this Catholic position found a sympathetic hearing, and in 1938 the legislature passed a bill mandating religious education in public schools. President Quezon, determined that this bill would violate the recently passed Constitution, wrote, "Any attempt, directly or indirectly[,] to give to religious teaching in the school an importance lesser or greater than it is now accorded by law would be unconstitutional. . . . The intent and purpose [of the Constitution] is merely to tolerate the teaching of religion in the public schools and not to give it such prominence or encouragement."[46] He vetoed the bill, and the National Assembly dropped the matter for some time.

As with early periods of instability around the Code de la famille in Senegal and the Mother and Child Crisis in Ireland, the controversies around the scope of religious education in the Philippines indicated a tension among the dimensions of benevolent secularism. What extent of cooperation is compatible with the differentiation of religious and state institutions? Would expanding that cooperation inevitably lead to the breakdown of principled distance from religious communities, the capitulation to a religious majority's demands? And what constitutes acceptable influence on legislators by religious leaders when those elected officials must face democratic reelection by a devout population? Different answers to these questions coexisted among the partners of the coalition that secured the twin tolerations in the Philippines.

The controversy over compulsory religious education was especially important because it showed the tensions that could reemerge between political elites and the Catholic clerical leadership over the nature of religion–state relations. When the Catholic bishops released a (fairly mild) letter calling for reconsideration of the issue by legislators, the president shot back with themes that raised memories of the anticlericalism of the Malolos era: "If they want a showdown, they can have it. . . . We should not sacrifice our national life, our national harmony and unity on matters of religion, which we should not even discuss because it is unnecessary to do so."[47] If such sharp disagreements over the implementation of benevolent secularism arose within a few short years of the Commonwealth Constitution's adoption, it should come as no surprise that similar tensions would help drive secular evolution in the decades after the Philippines emerged from World War II as an independent democracy.

The early history of benevolent secularism in the Philippines is a striking example of the implications of institutional structure for the relationship between religion and democracy. Within a generation, benevolent secularism recast the coalition politics of religion and promoted a stable, if contested, form of secular democracy in the midst of extensive religious mobilization. An ancien régime faded away, replaced by a diverse coalition of Catholics, Muslims, and even Masons united in support of the twin tolerations. Pious secularists exercised more influence within the Catholic majority, anticlericalism faded among political elites, and at least some religious minorities engaged in the public partnerships encouraged by benevolent secularism. Although serious differences persisted within this coalition, the coalition played a central role in securing the twin tolerations during the period of secular emergence in the Philippines.

The general theoretical model of benevolent secularism during the period of secular emergence applies fairly well to the Philippines during the commonwealth period, but some limitations in that model also arise. First, the extent of cooperation was much less dramatic than in Ireland or Senegal during the relevant critical junctures in those cases. Although the three dimensions of benevolent secularism do exist in the historical record, differentiation is prioritized over cooperation during this critical period. This prioritization may explain a second weakness in the model's fit with the Philippine critical juncture: the mixed institutional effects on coalition bloc preferences. The Aglipayan minority, for instance, responded with hostility to the more benevolent turn in religion–state relations. One could make the case that pious secularism was also less entrenched among the Catholic majority and anticlericalism fairly close to the surface for many political elites. These relatively weak institutional effects actually map on well to the imperfectly realized nature of benevolent secularism in the Philippine Commonwealth. They may also demonstrate the residual effects of the Spanish ancien régime and the difficulty in resolving all of those tensions during the one juncture around the Constitutional Convention of 1934.

These weaknesses should not obscure the main conclusion that can be drawn from this period: the institutional structure of benevolent secularism played a central role in securing the twin tolerations in the Philippines by shaping the preferences of the actors who were contesting the place of religion in democratic life. After full independence in the wake of World War II, Philippine politics turned to issues of reconstruction and development that would ultimately call the stability of this institutional configuration into question.

7. Secular Evolution in the Philippines

PEOPLE POWER AND PLURALIZATION

In late February 2013, an eye-catching banner appeared on the facade of San Sebastian Cathedral in Bacolod City. With elections fast approaching, the banner declared certain candidates and parties Team Buhay (Team Life) and others Team Patay (Team Death). The banners were indicative of recent turmoil in the religion–state relationship in the Philippines caused by what is known as the Reproductive Health Law (RH Law). Political elites approved this legislative measure in spite of opposition from the CBCP, and the bishop of Bacolod, along with several other members of the Philippine hierarchy, promised to hold elected officials accountable. To quote one observer: "It [the banner] will not be taken down. And the bishop is prepared to go to jail if necessary to stand up for what he believes in."[1] The elections have since come and gone, and the empirical impact of religious endorsements for office was mixed. But the confrontation raised lingering questions about the stability of benevolent secularism in the contemporary Philippines.

The reproductive health (RH) controversy is just one of several challenges to confront benevolent secularism in the Philippines since the drafting of the Commonwealth Constitution. Establishing the Catholic Church as a state religion is no longer a relevant concern; even the bishops who campaigned against Team Patay acknowledge this point. But questions persist over the balance between differentiation, cooperation, and principled distance in benevolent secularism and how these institutional dimensions will change in response to a shifting religious landscape. This chapter begins with a concise look at the famous "People Power" Revolution of 1986 through a new lens: as an example of secular evolution. It then moves to three areas of institutional change in the past decade: (1) the RH Law; (2) the place of Islam in Philippine public life; and (3) the growth of religious political parties. In sum, evidence suggests that institutions of benevolent secularism can evolve in the face of contemporary challenges but that this evolution is most likely where elite ties remain robust. Those ties are strongest in areas encouraged by benevolent secularism; public roles for religious actors have contributed to secular stability in ways less likely had religions been more strictly privatized.

Since the restoration of democracy after the People Power Revolution, the primary source of stress on benevolent secularism has come from the pluralization of religious leadership in the Philippines. The impact of new religious pluralism is not limited to the Philippines. In Latin America, the historic dominance of the Catholic Church has faded in the face of competition from a range of Protestant movements. Population flows across Europe are introducing new religious actors into public life from Sweden to Spain. As globalization encourages migration around the world, secular institutions' ability to adapt to pluralization is a key question facing the relationship between religion and democracy. Pluralization has complicated the elite ties that stabilize benevolent secularism, adding new actors with distinct preferences over the future of religious politics.

In this chapter, I first take a novel look at the fall of the Marcos regime and the restoration of democracy at the Constitutional Commission of 1986 as an instance of secular evolution. Second, I turn to the more recent challenges to benevolent secularism driven by pluralization of Filipino religious leadership after the People Power Revolution, with particular attention to the RH Law controversy, and trace the role of elite alliances in shaping recent patterns of institutional change. Third, I turn to recent public opinion data to test the existence of shared coalition preferences in the general population.

PEOPLE POWER AS SECULAR EVOLUTION

The anticlerical-integralist tensions of the Malolos Congress of 1898 faded as the Philippines achieved full independence after the devastation of World War II. However, after roughly a quarter century of relative postindependence stability, a new challenge undermined benevolent secularism: Ferdinand Marcos's authoritarian rule from the declaration of martial law in 1972 until the

People Power Revolution of 1986. In the end, religious actors in general and Cardinal Jaime Sin of Manila in particular played a central role in calling the people to Epifanio de los Santos Avenue (EDSA) in 1986 and toppling the Marcos regime. The analysis in this section cannot do justice to the complex role of religion in the entire revolutionary period. It focuses on aspects of Marcos's rule that could be considered a challenge to benevolent secularism and on coalition responses to that bid for institutional change.

THE MARCOS REGIME AS THREAT TO BENEVOLENT SECULARISM

The Marcos regime, in addition to its broader challenge to democracy and civil rights, constituted a threat to benevolent secularism. As Marcos and his allies ramped up repression under martial law, the protection of religious liberty broke down, and patterns of cooperation between the regime and religious actors, including but not limited to the Catholic Church, came to an end. Marcos attempted to institute an alternative and nonbenevolent configuration of religion–state relations.

Marcos's breakdown of differentiation showed through in restrictions on religious liberty and coercion of religious actors. The state claimed unprecedented authority to define religious practice and in effect outlawed religious exercise that it deemed politically threatening. Catholic activists, especially from religious orders affiliated with the Association of Major Religious Superiors of the Philippines (AMRSP), were regular targets of Marcos's coercion.[2] The state expelled several religious ministers for political subversion in the early 1970s, shuttered church media outlets critical of martial law, and detained and tortured religious and lay activists who organized for peasant rights throughout the country.[3] The breakdown of differentiation and religious liberty was not simply a matter of Catholic activism; smaller Protestant churches, affiliated under the National Council of Churches of the Philippines (NCCP), bore significant state repression as well. By 1973, the NCCP had issued a letter calling for the lifting of martial law and the maintenance of human rights. Marcos and his allies responded in kind by raiding NCCP offices, detaining leadership figures, and expelling foreign missionaries such as Reverend Paul Wilson from the country.[4] Marcos's regime may never have gone as far as the El Salvadoran junta did in assassinating Archbishop Oscar Romero, but it clearly turned on parts of the religious community and in doing so broke down benevolent secularism's basic structure.

As repression grew through the late 1970s, religion–state cooperation began to erode. Policy consultation was an early feature of Marcos's rule, institutionalized through various channels, including the Church–Military Liaison Committee (CMLC). However, as early as 1977, Marcos felt compelled to assure Vatican officials "that the regime was not anticlerical," and tensions continued to rise through the 1980s. By 1983, Catholic leaders pulled out of the CMLC in protest of Marcos's treatment of "rebel priests." Defense Minister Juan Ponce Enrile could deny that the military was engaged "in an anticlerical campaign," but he and others surely knew that the mutual accommodation between religious and state actors was deteriorating rapidly.[5] Tensions built into 1986, even as Marcos attempted to reassure religious elites that friendly relations with the churches would always be maintained "in the spirit of freedom of religious enshrined in the Constitution."[6] Verbal gymnastics did little to obscure the institutional reality: Marcos's authoritarian regime was attempting to break down not only democracy and civil rights but also benevolent secularism.

COALITION ALLIANCES PRESERVING BENEVOLENT SECULARISM

Marcos and his allies' excesses provoked splits in the regime and the eventual triumph of the People Power Revolution of 1986. In the closing years of the Marcos regime, the decisive months of the People Power Revolution, and the deliberations of the Constitutional Commission of 1986, strong religious-secular and interfaith ties were central in responding to the potential breakdown in benevolent secularism.[7]

Groups such as the NCCP and the AMRSP had long-standing partnerships with advocates of human rights and the rural poor. The relatively small Protestant communities were nevertheless potent associates because they were "closely allied with sister churches in the United States and . . . members of the World Council of Churches,"[8] thus increasing their international visibility. As early as 1973, a group of more than one hundred pastors and priests signed a letter to Marcos requesting restoration of freedom of the press.[9] As persecution of religious leaders grew, Catholic and Protestant leaders came to mutual defense. Robert Youngblood explains how "the Catholic hierarchy . . . condemned the June 1974 raid on the NCCP and the deportation of Protestant missionaries, while activist Protestant ministers called the deportation in January 1976 of two Italian priests, Fathers Francis Alessi and Luigi Cocquino, for alleged subversion 'a palpable denial of justice.'"[10]

Later, alliances between the Catholic bishops and parts of the secular opposition strengthened and proved crucial in the People Power Revolution. As Rina Jimenez David, a leading voice in the women's movement, put it, "Our common enemy was martial law and the Marcos government. . . . [T]here wasn't any sharp division between [civil society] and the church."[11] Catholic officials worked with election observers under the National Citizens' Movement for Free Elections to document fraud in the snap election in 1986 that ultimately led to Marcos's fall. The climactic confrontation of the EDSA protests was itself a product of partnerships across elite blocs. Cardinal Sin called people into the streets to protect elements in the military that had broken with the regime and faced attack within Camp Aguinaldo. He particularly mentioned "our two, good friends," Defense Minister Juan Ponce Enrile and General Fidel Ramos, the officials within the Marcos regime whose defections helped seal its fall.[12] Sin's "friends" extended beyond Catholic boundaries; General Ramos, a crucial defector, was a Protestant.

After the revolution, religious-secular and interfaith elite ties extended to the Constitutional Commission of 1986. These ties were visible in representation to the commission itself. Commissioners such as Father Joaquin Bernas, S.J., Bishop Teodoro Bacani, and Sister Christine Tan were all well-known Catholic religious elites, and they were joined by a range of lay Catholics, including Maria Teresa Nieva, a leader of the Bishops-Businessmen's Conference; Jose Nolledo, a national president of the Holy Name Society; and Bernardo Villegas, a founding member of Opus Dei in the Philippines. Minorities also played an active part in debates regarding the place of religion in the Constitution. Reverend Cirilo Rigos and Reverend Gregorio Tingson, both Protestant clergymen, served on the commission, as did several Muslim representatives, including Ahmad Domocao Alonto. Another Muslim commissioner, Lugum Uka, gave an extended speech on the parallels between Muslim and Christian prayer before giving his hearty approval to the invocation of Almighty God in the Constitution's preamble.[13] More tangibly, at several points constitutional deliberations referenced "churches and religious bodies" in an attempt to capture the plurality of religious life in the Philippines.[14] When controversy could have arisen over religious education, commissioners pointed to evidence from the Catholic Educational Association of the Philippines and the Association of Christian Schools and Colleges to diffuse any tensions.[15]

In the commission's deliberations, these ties included discussion of equal protection for nonbelievers as well.[16] When the commissioners debated whether state schools should be constitutionally obligated to inculcate a love of God, the stage could have been set for a religious-secular deadlock much like the one that ended the Malolos constitutional debates in 1898. But several Catholic commissioners instead rose in defense of nonbelievers. As Commissioner José Laurel put it, "The majority of us are Christians, even Catholics like this humble servant. . . . [However,] even if one is an atheist, an agnostic, a disbeliever or a doubter, he is entitled to the protection under our Constitution."[17] As debate continued, Commissioner Blas Ople noted for the record that the commission should not be "misunderstood by the public as spurning God from the Education Article," and a round of applause broke out when the potential religious-secular showdown was ended amicably without even requiring a vote.[18]

BENEVOLENT SECULARISM RESTORED: THE CONSTITUTION OF 1987

In spite of the challenge posed by the Marcos regime, institutions of benevolent secularism endured martial law. The basic configuration of religion in democratic life broke with the alternative model put forward in the Marcos regime and returned to the general boundaries set out in the Commonwealth Constitution of 1935.

Differentiation between religion and state was enshrined in several places in the Constitution of 1987. Article 2.6 goes beyond the Commonwealth Constitution to state, "The separation of Church and State shall be inviolable," and Article 3.5 insists that "no law shall be made respecting an establishment of religion." At one point, Bishop Teodoro Bacani emphasized, "The question of the separation of Church and state is at no way at stake [in commission discussions]."[19] As commission records show, both clerical and lay members constantly returned to the theme of the mutual benefit that this separation brings to religion and state in the Philippines.

Differentiation combined with restored cooperation between religious and state institutions. Commissioner Hilario Davide, future chief justice of the Supreme Court, remarked during the commission's deliberations, "The new Constitution must be pro-God, pro-people, pro-Filipino."[20] According to future president Corazon Aquino, church–state separation was not a matter of coercion but instead a recognition that "good fences make good neighbors."[21] The cooperative dimension of benevolent secularism showed through in family policy. Article 2.12 explicitly protects "the life of the unborn from conception" and the "sanctity of family life" as the "basic autonomous social institution." As in 1934, cooperation is apparent in 1986 in commission debates related to religious instruction in public schools. Article 14.4 exempts religious schools from requirements of Filipino ownership in recognition of these schools' "tremendous contribution to the country" and to Filipino education, according to Commissioner Napoleón Rama.[22] Religious instruction may take place, at parents' option, within school hours and on school property. Commissioners also clarified that this instruction should defer to existing religious elites rather than undercut them; if any conflict were to arise about who should administer religious education, the ultimate decision would be made "by the church authority" rather than by any Department of Education officials.[23]

Principled distance returned as well, although, as in independence-era Ireland, questions arose about the unique influence of Catholic ideas related to the family. Whereas the Commonwealth Constitution of 1935 did not forbid divorce, the Family Code revision of 1987 and subsequent jurisprudence adopted sharper restrictions. Article 36 of the Family Code borrows explicitly from Roman Catholic canon law, Canon 1095, section 3, in declaring "void from the beginning" a marriage "contracted by any party who, at the time of the celebration, was psychologically incapacitated to comply with the essential marital obligations." Lest there be any doubt that this was the intent of the civil law's drafters, the Supreme Court of the Philippines pointed out in 1997, "It is clear that Article 36 was taken by the Family Code Revision Committee from Canon 1095" with the purpose of "harmoniz[ing] our civil laws with the religious faith of our people."[24] This language clearly privileges Catholic conceptions of marriage, but it is worth noting that the Code of Muslim Personal Laws provides exemptions for the Muslim minority, and the Supreme Court decision in *Estrada v. Escritor* (455 Phil. 411 [2003]) provided some protection for the claims of religious minorities to different standards in recognizing spousal relationships.

The revolution of 1986 is rightly considered a victory for democracy in the Philippines, but it also allowed the preservation of benevolent secularism. After benevolent secularism's weakening under martial law, the Constitutional Commission restored in 1986 each of the distinctive dimensions of benevolent secularism in the Constitution of 1987. The revolution was a victory not only for opponents of authoritarianism but also for elite actors advocating benevolent secularism.

PLURALIZATION AFTER PEOPLE POWER

Since the post-Marcos reestablishment of benevolent secularism, a new, subtler challenge has confronted Philippine institutions: significant pluralization of religious leadership in the Philippines. Important figures such as the cardinal of Manila jockey with lay-led Catholic movements, Muslim civil society organizations, and evangelical preachers for public influence.[25] Religious diversity is not itself new in the Philippines. Parts of Mindanao have been Muslim-majority for centuries, and various non-Catholic Christian denominations were important actors during the period of secular emergence analyzed in chapter 6. But in the past quarter century, the coalition elites that act to determine the nature of religion–state relations in the Philippines have diversified widely. In documenting the recent pluralization of religious authority in the Philippines, two trends bear noting. First, "religious" leadership is no longer the sole privilege of bishops. Lawyers, media tycoons, and local revival preachers all play a role alongside the traditional actors in the coalition politics of Philippine secularism. Second, these new religious leaders are a direct result of the growth of civil society since the end of the Marcos period and the restoration of benevolent secularism. The newly democratic Philippines expanded policy cooperation with religious leaders, and these leaders, frequently lay, have in turn become public voices of religious authority.

The first part of the Philippine secular collation, the Catholic majority, has seen significant changes since Cardinal Sin's central leadership during the People Power Revolution. On first glance, the Catholic Church in the Philippines may appear much as it did at the end of the Marcos regime. The archbishop of Manila, Cardinal Luis Antonio Tagle, remains a crucial public figure; the AMRSP takes leadership in progressive battles such as land reform; and the general public is more than 80 percent Roman Catholic. This surface continuity, however, misses out on substantial changes in both the leadership and structure of Philippine Catholicism in the past quarter century. Within existing church structures, the singular leadership provided by Cardinal Sin has not been replicated since his retirement in 2003. Outside of the hierarchy, the explosion of Catholic Charismatic communities has brought a new generation of lay leaders to positions of church leadership.

The most visible change since the end of the People Power Revolution was the departure of Cardinal Sin from the religious-political stage. Sin's leadership was central, first, in bringing a relatively peaceful end to Marcos's rule and then in stabilizing the fledgling democratic government of Cory Aquino. However, Sin's immediate replacement, Cardinal Gaudencio Rosales, was by most accounts less interested in the kind of political role that Sin came to exercise. The archbishopric of Manila saw its authority reduced by the creation of several newer dioceses in 2002 and 2003, including Novaliches, Parañaque, Cubao, Kalookan, and Pasig. As Antonio Moreno puts it, "Reducing the scope of the Archdiocese of Manila effectively minimized its influence and jurisdiction."[26] Without the unifying figure of Cardinal Sin, even "official" Catholic actors are increasingly divided within offices of the CBCP as well as among the religious orders that make up the AMRSP. Even among the Catholic bishops, authority has pluralized since People Power.

This diversity within the Philippine hierarchy has accompanied a proliferation of lay Catholic communities, especially through various Charismatic Catholic movements. In contrast to much of Latin America, the Charismatic movement in the Philippines has remained largely within the Catholic Church. The two most prominent Catholic Charismatic communities, El Shaddai and Couples for Christ, claim several million members each, and smaller communities such as Ligaya ng Panginoon have spread widely as well. Couples for Christ grew to such an extent that it fractured into several groups: Couples for Christ—International Council; Couples for Christ—Foundation for Family and Life; and Gawad Kalinga.[27] These movements, although internally diverse, share several important characteristics. They are lay led even while remaining within the Catholic fold, which has led to occasional tensions between their own leadership and that of the CBCP. They stress similar "gifts of the Spirit" as Pentecostal churches and "conduct their services in a very lively and emotional style, sharing the experience of miracles happening today."[28] They are also public movements, holding massive prayer rallies throughout the country and making several well-documented forays into political life. In short, although not competitors with the CBCP, these Catholic Charismatic communities further diversify the presence of Catholicism in Philippine politics.

Pluralization of Catholic leadership extends beyond the Charismatic movement as well. The Opus Dei movement, which has taken on global prominence in the past quarter century, has opened the University of Asia and the Pacific in the Metro Manila area, and prominent members such as Bernardo Villegas and Jesus Estanislao have served as governmental advisers and cabinet members.[29] If Opus Dei occupies a generally conservative place in the religious and political spectrum, other Catholic movements are more politically diverse. Basic Christian Communities/Basic Ecclesial Communities have played an important role in promoting lay involvement among poor Catholics, generally in progressive causes such as environmental protection, and the Bishops–Businessmen's Conference for Human Development serves as a centrist dialogue point between lay business elites and the CBCP. In each of these movements, lay leaders speak for Catholicism in the public square. Catholic authority has pluralized well beyond the bounds of the CBCP.

The most notable trend in non-Catholic Christianity in the Philippines since the fall of the Marcos regime is the growth of evangelical and Charismatic Protestant communities. While much of the Charismatic movement in the Philippines has remained within the Catholic fold, Charismatic and evangelical growth has also affected non-Catholic Christianity in the Philippines. Most importantly, this trend has empowered a generation of nondenominational preachers and their affiliates.[30] For example, Brother Grepor "Butch" Belgica, a prominent evangelical leader, has proud ties to American evangelical leaders such as Charles Colson, and his sermons draw heavily on themes such as "shaping godly leaders" and opposition to drugs and criminality.[31] Although evangelical communities remain small compared to the Catholic Church community, several leaders enjoy public influence. Among the most influential of these revivalist communities is Brother Eddie Villanueva's Jesus Is Lord Church, which claims 6 million members worldwide, and Pastor Apollo Quiboloy's

Kingdom of Jesus: The Name Above Every Name community, which claims 4 million members. These membership numbers are contested, but there is no doubt that these high-profile evangelists are a fundamentally new arrival on the Philippine religious landscape.

Although many of these religious communities are nondenominational, this new generation of religious leadership has institutionalized itself in civil society and media. These churches tend to join under the umbrella of the Philippine Council of Evangelical Churches (PCEC) rather than under the NCCP, whose members closely resemble mainline Protestant denominations in the United States. The PCEC adopts different priorities in Philippine public life than the NCCP. Whereas the NCCP churches are traditional allies of the Philippine Left in fights from land reform to human rights protection, PCEC members advance a distinct agenda, including prison ministry, environmental protection, and campaigns against substance abuse. As Christl Kessler and Jürgen Rüland put it, "[PCEC members'] main concern [is] winning souls among the poor and disadvantaged, rather than improving their worldly living conditions."[32] In addition to the PCEC, several Protestant pastors have built significant media empires to extend their reach beyond prayer rallies. Pastor Quiboloy's Kingdom Broadcasting Network/Sonshine Media Network International is one prominent example and extends its reach far beyond his movement's home in Davao City.

The Muslim community in the Philippines has also seen significant shifts in its leadership and structure in the post-Marcos era. Although the loose organizational structure of Sunni Islam is not a direct analogue to the Roman Catholic Church's hierarchy, several forces have united to produce more cohesive, publicly engaged Muslim leadership in the wake of People Power. First, coalitions such as the Ulama League of the Philippines and the National Ulama Conference of the Philippines have come to play a prominent role in organizing religious leadership in the Muslim community and engaging in structured dialogues in public life. The Philippine Center for Islam and Democracy, a civil society organization led by Amina Rasul, has played a central role in building such coalitions. Other groups of Muslim public elites are the explicit outcome of partnership with state institutions. The National Commission on Muslim Filipinos is an official body tasked with improving state relations with the Muslim community. The state-funded sharia court system has created a generation of lawyers, judges, and activists who exert public leadership in debates about religion and democracy, and the expansion of religious peace education in parts of Mindanao has created a cadre of Muslim educators steeped in benevolent secularism. Finally, interfaith dialogue groups such as the Bishops–Ulama Conference in Mindanao foreground Muslim, Catholic, and Protestant leaders who prioritize peace-building efforts.

Leadership within the "secularist" bloc in the Philippines has also diversified during this period. Although human rights and development organizations in civil society still provide important secular voices that affect religion–state relations, newer organizations organized around questions of women's rights, RH, and LGBT rights have taken on increasing importance. These organizations do not necessarily identify as anticlerical, but they do bring to the table new concerns about the impact of religion–state cooperation on public policy, especially policy related to controversial areas in family law. Important actors include the National Commission on the Role of Filipino Women, political parties such as the GABRIELA Women's Party, and the Family Planning Organization of the Philippines.

PLURALIZATION AND THE STABILITY OF BENEVOLENT SECULARISM

How has this pluralization of Filipino religious leadership affected the stability of benevolent secularism? The theoretical framework set out in chapter 1 does not have a deterministic hypothesis regarding the impact of pluralization on periods of institutional change. New pluralism in Ireland, for example, has not broken down benevolent secularism; institutions have evolved to include the Muslim minority. Pluralism's effect on secular evolution depends on its impact on the elite ties that stabilize benevolent secularism over time. Pluralism should lead to institutional evolution when new groups are grafted into the existing coalition alliances that promote evolution. However, if new actors are disengaged from these alliances or even undermine them, it should set the stage for more dramatic institutional change. Throughout this section, evidence documents links between the relative strength of religious-secular and interfaith coalition alliances, on the one hand, and patterns of recent institutional change in Philippine secularism, on the other.

In this section, I document changes that blend subtle secular evolution with more substantial changes in benevolent secularism. Although the basic dimensions of benevolent secularism are still observable in Philippine institutions, there is evidence that both patterns of partisan religious mobilization and ongoing sharp debates about the RH Law could set the stage for more extensive breakdowns in it. I document the changes in benevolent secularism in three particular areas: debate about the implementation of the RH Law; the institutional treatment of Muslim Filipinos; and the electoral participation of religious movements. After documenting institutional change, I tie those patterns of change to varying elite ties across religious-secular and interfaith boundaries. Table 7.1 summarizes some of this evidence across the three areas of institutional change considered.

TABLE 7.1. SUMMARY OF INSTITUTIONAL
CHANGE IN THE PHILIPPINES

Area of Change	Institutional Change	Coalition Ties
1. Reproductive Health Act of 2012	Mixed: no agreement on core questions related to contraception access, but compromise on issues of conscience protections and restrictions on abortion	Mixed: religious-secular tensions (for instance, Team Buhay/Patay banners), but elite cooperation through Ateneo de Manila University mediations
2. Accommodating Filipino Muslims	Evolution: accommodation through Bangasamoro peace process	Strong interfaith cooperation: for instance, through Bishops–Ulama Conference of Mindanao
3. Religion and Political Campaigns	Mixed: expansion of religious political parties and campaigns	Weaker interfaith ties with religious candidates and political parties

THE RH LAW: A MIXED OUTCOME

The most public challenge to benevolent secularism in the post-Marcos era is a result of debates about the RH Law. No issue in recent memory has so roiled the religion–state relationship in the Philippines as the legislation formally called Republic Act 10354, the Responsible Parenthood and Reproductive Health Act of 2012, or the RH Law. It spurred Carlos Celdran's protest that opened this book and called into question the future of policy cooperation among state and religious elites. Although benevolent secularism structures policy cooperation between religion and state around such controversies, in this case these consultations failed to resolve the core impasse between opponents and advocates of the legislation. With that said, evidence does indicate that cooperation yielded some significant alterations in the legislation that have stabilized the overall relationship between religion and state. As Sylvia Claudio, a leading voice in the women's movement in the Philippines, put it, "In a sense, it was a bill that everyone could live with."[33]

The RH Law was designed to affect an array of public-health issues, including increased access to some forms of birth control among the poorest Filipinos. President Benigno Aquino III and the bill's authors in Congress structured official dialogues with CBCP leaders on a number of occasions, and less-formal consultations took place through traditional actors such as the

Bishops–Businessmen's Conference and Ateneo de Manila University. The RH Law contains a range of provisions related to mobile health clinics and family health care that were considered relatively unobjectionable, but its requirements around contraceptive access and health education continued to provoke dissent from segments of the CBCP and allied organizations. Aquino finally pushed the legislation through the Congress in the closing months of 2012. After the crucial 113–104 vote in the House of Representatives, the RH bill moved forward and eventually received Aquino's signature to become law shortly before Christmas 2012.

Although consultation did not yield overall agreement, the eventual form of the RH Law does bear the imprint of benevolent secularism's dimensions: differentiation, cooperation, and principled distance. Differentiation shows through in the distinction between public and religious hospitals and public and private (religious) schools that appears in several places in the legislation. Cooperation also appears in spite of the contentious debates around the bill. The legislation calls for religious-state partnerships around natural family planning provisions and solicits "active participation" by "faith-based organizations, the religious sector and communities" in securing women's health and human development as well as in developing school curricula for reproductive education (Republic Act 10354, sec. 3[i]). Finally, the state's principled distance from all religious communities appears in more subtle but significant ways. The act recognizes the "religious convictions, ethics, [and] cultural beliefs" (sec. 2) that contribute to women's decisions. The use of the plural throughout that clause is no accident; drafters were quite conscious of the support for the RH Law among most other religious communities in the Philippines. Permitting religious schools to have a role in developing sex education materials was a key concession made to Catholic concerns about religious autonomy and reflects the principled distance between religious and state institutions that is at the core of benevolent secularism. And although the Supreme Court generally upheld the RH Law, it made conscience protections for religious individuals and institutions significantly more robust in its extensive decision on a pivotal case in 2014.[34]

The RH Law is still being implemented, so caution is necessary in analyzing its long-term impact on benevolent secularism. However, one can detect differentiation, cooperation, and principled distance at several points in its final version. It is far too dramatic to claim that the cooperative dimension of benevolent secularism has collapsed. Although the CBCP continues to have strong objections to portions of the RH Law, the three dimensions of benevolent secularism remain observable in the law's development and early implementation.

Because the RH Law's final form blends some features of institutional evolution and institutional breakdown, this episode of institutional change should correspond to mixed coalition alliances, both on interfaith grounds and across the religious-secular divide. On the one hand, there were weakened interfaith relations and increased divides between the Catholic bishops and secular activists on the core policy issue in question in this debate: expanded access to contraception. However, subtle cooperation across the religious-secular divide was responsible for elements in the legislation, such as religion–state cooperation in implementation and generous conscience protections that indicate benevolent secularism's enduring strength.

Although common interfaith partners were involved in the policy consultation that did occur on the RH Law, there was no interfaith consensus on the outcome of that process. The two major Protestant associations, the NCCP and the PCEC, endorsed the legislation. Bishop Efraim Tendero, then head of the PCEC, explicitly undercut Catholic pro-life arguments: "We believe that the RH Bill is pro-life. Life begins at fertilization, and the promotion of the use of artificial forms of fertilization does not take away life."[35] Although Reverend Rex Reyes, head of the NCCP, acknowledged the "heavy Catholic influence" on several areas of public law, he stressed to me, "We all have the right to speak up."[36] The pro–RH Law advocacy extended beyond Protestant churches; the Interfaith Partnership for the Promotion of Responsible Parenthood united Christian and Muslim voices in favor of the RH Law. These associations became allies of RH Law advocates, who routinely invoked the pluralistic nature of the Philippines to undercut Catholic arguments against the legislation. In an op-ed written shortly after the RH Law's passage, Senator Miriam Defensor Santiago, a sponsor of the bill, made precisely this point: "Apart from the Catholic Church, all other major religions in the Philippines support the RH Bill."[37] As Senator Risa Hontiveros, a leader of the Akbayan Party, put it, "Many of us are Catholic leaders, . . . but you have to vote for all Filipinos, whatever their religion may be or even if they have no religion."[38]

Religious-secular divides on this policy issue also contributed to the failure of the consultative pattern associated with benevolent secularism. When Carlos Celdran dressed up as José Rizal to protest Catholic lobbying on this issue, he was intentionally invoking the era of sharp religious-secular division leading to the Malolos Congress. At one point, the press quoted then CBCP president Bishop Nereo Odchimar as threatening the "proximate possibility" that President Benigno Aquino would be excommunicated as a result of his support for the bill.[39] Leaders of the CBCP's Episcopal Commission on Family and Life, such as Father Melvin Castro, did not yield in the consultative process, and many advocates of the RH Law were more than happy to tangle with the bishops over an issue where polling showed grassroots Catholic opposition to the bishops' position. RH advocates in fact included many Catholics, such as President Aquino, Senator Defensor Santiago, and several other prominent RH

Law sponsors. As columnist Conrado de Quiros put it, "This is not just a case of [a bishop] not speaking for [all bishops]; this is a case of him not speaking for the Church—the Church as defined by the entire community of the faithful."[40] David Balangue, a leading RH Law advocate within the business community, pointed to this internal division as crucial: "Even among the church groups, they're divided. . . . [T]he church has no stranglehold on Filipinos."[41] A group called Catholics for Reproductive Health explicitly advocated for the RH Law, and groups of professors from two of the leading Catholic universities in the Philippines, Ateneo de Manila University and De La Salle University, publicly supported the legislation. The highest university administrators expressed their opposition to the law but "encouraged discussions and respected the opinions of faculty members even while disagreeing with them."[42]

And yet it is crucial to recall that the RH Law's development demonstrated indicators of enduring benevolent secularism and that these indicators are themselves tied to operation of the hypothesized coalition alliances. Certain religious and secular advocates were indeed sharply divided, but others, operating largely out of the media spotlight, acted to preserve the dimensions of benevolent secularism in the legislation. As Meneleo Carlos Jr., cochairman of the Bishops–Businessmen's Conference, a crucial mediating body, put it, "I think we were realistic enough to realize that we couldn't just buck [the bill] . . . but we certainly wanted to guide it."[43] Father Joaquin Bernas, a commissioner on the Constitutional Commission of 1986, scolded "bishops at war" who would go after RH supporters in elections as "counter-productive to the formation of a kind of politics that is based on principles."[44] Father Eric Genilo, a Jesuit ethicist at the Loyola School of Theology, played an extensive role in trying to mediate a compromise between hard-line CBCP officials and RH Law supporters.[45] Genilo, Bernas, and Father John Carroll, all Jesuits tied to Ateneo University, wrote and spoke at length on changes that would make the RH legislation more acceptable to the Catholic tradition, particularly through provisions related to conscience exemptions for religious individuals and institutions and through robust language protecting human life. These mediating voices were motivated in part by the desire to craft laws that preserved interfaith legal protections in state law. As Genilo put it to me, "[The CBCP] does not speak for the Iglesia ni Cristo on this issue. The bill is national law. . . . [I]t should not only be a Catholic bill."[46] These attempts at religious-state cooperation secured real concessions in areas of conscience protection, religious education, the promotion of natural family planning, and continued restrictions on abortion—all of which are consistent with benevolent secularism. As Bernas wrote in the aftermath of the law's approval, with between-the-lines satisfaction, "I notice that the points that I would have considered constitutionally objectionable have been removed or nuanced."[47]

There is evidence that alliances across the religious-secular divide have reasserted their influence in the bill's aftermath. The archbishop of Manila, Cardinal Tagle, is reportedly "good personal friends" with President Aquino, and Aquino took time to attend a mass celebrating Tagle's elevation to the College of Cardinals in the weeks before the final RH bill votes.[48] Eleanor Dionisio argues that Tagle has ambitions for a public agenda well beyond the RH Law, including "economic inequality, political disenfranchisement, human rights violations and corruption."[49] Aquino signed the RH bill into law in a private rather than public ceremony, and Department of Health officials have reached out to religious leaders to discuss implementation of the various public-health programs contained in the final version of the act.[50] Many opponents of the RH Law, such as the Ang Kapatiran Party, are also among leaders of anticorruption initiatives that unite religious voices with many secular actors in civil society.[51] Although leaders of the CBCP still object to the law as bad policy, leading clerical voices have expressed the need to continue with other areas of policy cooperation between religion and state. In the words of CBCP president Archbishop Socrates Villegas, "'We cannot see eye-to-eye with our pro-RH brethren on this divisive issue, but we can work hand in hand for the good of the country."[52] As Bernardo Villegas, a founder of Opus Dei in the Philippines and a leading critic of the RH Law, summed up, "I don't think there will be long-lasting [conflict] because there is so much synergy. . . . [T]here are so many social issues in which the church and civil society have been collaborating."[53]

At the same time, there are forces on both sides of the religious-secular divide that are spoiling for further fights. The more profound challenge to benevolent secularism may come from strengthened anticlerical sentiment as a result of the RH controversy. It is no great exaggeration to say that the CBCP was the main actor responsible for delaying this legislation, perhaps by a decade, and a quick spin through opinion columns related to the RH Law shows real resentment at the CBCP's influence.[54] There are voices within both Catholic and secular blocs who remain skeptical that religion–state cooperation will recover from the RH controversy. As Archbishop Ramon Arguelles bluntly put it, "Government used everything—money, pressure, cheating—to pass the RH Law. And now they're pleading for reconciliation? I don't think so."[55]

In the end, any breakdown in consultation over the RH Law did result from divisions within blocs that frequently ally to defend benevolent secularism. These divisions are linked to the broad pluralization of political and religious actors in post-Marcos politics. As Father Genilo pointed out, "There are so many groups involved. . . . You get lost in the whole chaotic discussion. . . . You are one person among many."[56] However, because religious-secular alliances operated in subtle ways, the final bill was more benevolent in its respect for differentiation, cooperation, and principled distance. There is reason to think that the conciliation-minded elites on both sides of the religious-secular divide will eventually carry the day. If this is the case, Philippine benevolent secularism will have endured its most direct threat since the end of martial law in 1986.

ACCOMMODATION OF ISLAM

In contrast to the mixed outcome around the RH Law, the institutional place of Islam in the Philippines indicates a relatively smooth evolution within historical bounds. If anything, the principled distance between the Philippine state and its Islamic community has become more robust in recent years, with President Aquino, among other steps, declaring Eid al-Fitr a public holiday.[57] More substantively, a peace agreement involving parties to the armed conflict in Bangsamoro, sometimes known as Muslim Mindanao, includes significant cultural recognition for the Muslim minority and appears to mark new progress in ending that long-standing conflict. As former Jesuit provincial Father José Magadia summed up with good humor, "Muslims want to enjoy an equally unsecular state [as Christian Filipinos enjoy]."[58] A new generation of Muslim leaders, in particular those tied to the sharia courts system and the Mindanao peace process, has acted to strengthen benevolent secularism rather than to challenge it.

The Philippine Center for Islam and Democracy has been a focal point of much of this recent secular evolution. It has extended the range of issues on which the Muslim minority interacts with the Philippine state. This extension has included bringing Muslims into the policy consultation process characteristic of benevolent secularism, whether through work with the Parish Pastoral Council for Responsible Voting and the National Movement on Free Elections on religious monitoring of elections or through work with the Commission on Human Rights to improve human rights protections for Muslim citizens, particularly in areas outside of Muslim-majority Mindanao where they are often rather small, vulnerable minority communities.[59] In each of these programmatic areas, the center creates a new cadre of Muslim elites who are integrated into the pattern of benevolent secularism through interactions with both the Philippine state and various Christian elites.

Exemplary evidence of benevolent secularism's endurance exists in growing collaboration between the Department of Education and Muslim educators in madrasa education in areas with significant enough Muslim populations to sustain schools. This collaboration is in keeping with the generally cooperative relationship between religion and state in the area of education in the Philippines and the other cases of benevolent secularism. As Jeffrey Ayala Milligan points out, the Philippine constitutional language regarding moral formation "opens the door to a greater involvement of religion in education than is the case in the United States."[60] Manaros Boransing, then undersecretary of education for Mindanao affairs, and his colleagues in the Department of Education developed programs such as Project Madrasa Education and Arabic Language and Islamic Values Education (ALIVE) that emphasize Islamic components of education and seek to improve the quality of education available to Muslims both in Mindanao and in areas such as Metro Manila.[61] The Department of Education's involvement in madrasa education is one indicator that political institutions have evolved in the past decade to more closely typify principled distance.

Principled distance in treatment of the Muslim minority has also evolved in another area, although not without controversy: the sharia court system.[62] This system, established under Marcos through the Code of Muslim Personal Laws, continues to operate with a class of professional judges and lawyers trained in state institutions.[63] As a part of the recently signed peace agreement in Mindanao, a future Bangsamoro Basic Law may even extend provisions of sharia into certain aspects of business and contractual law. Although proponents of the sharia court system point to shortcomings, notably in vacant judgeships and the relatively limited geographic concentration of the courts themselves, there is little doubt that the system represents a significant accommodation to the Muslim minority in public affairs.[64]

In contrast to the RH Law, increasingly robust principled distance extended to the Muslim minority corresponds to strong interfaith and religious-secular partnerships. The growing public role of Islam in the past decade indicates that the pluralization of religious leadership need not undercut the strong interfaith relations that stabilize benevolent secularism in the Philippines. Diversification of the Muslim landscape has provided more points of contact with political elites, more opportunities for collaboration with Christian associations, and more solid footing for the benevolent secular nature of Philippine institutions. The Philippine Center for Islam and Democracy has played an important bridging role between secular institutions and the Muslim community, generating a generation of clerics and activists who are well connected to civil society organizations in the Philippines and abroad. These relationships lay the groundwork for further evolution to the Muslim minority—for instance, new areas of cooperation such as election monitoring and human rights protection.

Interfaith cooperation has likewise played an active role in fostering secular evolution by building partnerships around issues such as peace building in Mindanao. Cooperation with the Department of Education on peacemaking curricula, for instance, takes place with Catholic support and in the context of strong interfaith alliances through the Bishops–Ulama Conference of Mindanao. This type of interfaith partnership fosters cooperation with state institutions that in turn is explicitly designed to improve interfaith relations among the next generation of young Filipinos. As Senator Ralph Recto argued in the ALIVE program's early stages, "Madaris [madrasas] should be an institution that would promote the solid foundation of Islamic values and cultural traditions and foster better understanding among Christians and Muslims. They would serve as a beacon for the enlightenment of our people, illuminating our way towards religious harmony."[65] As of 2010, the Department of Education employed nearly 2,000 teachers in public elementary schools through the ALIVE program alone,[66] thus fostering a generation of Muslim educators in the Philippines who engage the Muslim minority in public life. Interfaith groups were partners in the negotiations leading to the landmark Bangsamoro peace agreement and remain active in building lasting peace in the wake of that agreement's signing. In a statement calling for "reconciled diversity" in the wake of the peace agreement, Catholic elites reaffirmed the willingness of "various Catholic institutions such as schools and universities, seminaries, peace centers, radio stations, etc." to work with state actors and Muslim partners in implementing the agreement.[67] The role of these interfaith ties in increasing the fairness with which the state and Muslim minority interact is strong evidence of the importance of coalition alliances in driving the evolution of secular institutions in the Philippines.

RELIGION ON THE CAMPAIGN TRAIL

Finally, although formal constitutional language from 1987 regarding differentiation and free-exercise protections remains unchanged, there has been significant weakening in the application of differentiation in one area: religion and party politics. These changes are quite similar to those in Senegal in the past two decades and reflect benevolent secularism's ambivalent stance to religious political parties. As in Senegal, explicitly religious political parties are restricted in the Philippines. Article 9.C.2.5 of the Constitution of 1987 forbids the registration of "religious denominations and sects" as political parties. Furthermore, "the religious sector" is expressly forbidden to run as part of the "party-list" section of the legislature.[68]

Yet in spite of these prohibitions the post–People Power era has seen significant expansion in the electoral presence of religious actors. The noted Catholic priest and social reformer "Among Ed" Panlilio ran for and won election as governor of Pampanga in 2007, although he knew he would be suspended from active ministry in keeping with Vatican directives and canon law. This trend extends to new leaders in the Catholic Charismatic community as well, most notably through Mike Villarde's El Shaddai movement, which was close to the administration of President "Erap" Estrada before his ouster and has since formed its own political party, the Buhay Party list. Brother Eddie Villanueva, founder of the Pentecostal Jesus Is Lord Church, has run multiple times for the presidency. As in Senegal, election agencies could, in theory, exclude religious parties from elections but have been hesitant to do so. Buhay, Ang Kapatiran, Bangon Pilipinas, Citizens' Battle Against Corruption, and Alagad are just a few of the parties linked by leadership and membership to particular religious leaders or communities. But most of these parties also have membership outside of their religious bases; Ang Kapatiran leaders described the party to me as "ecumenical" and even including Muslim members, inspired by Catholic social teachings, and extending to "universal principles" of justice.[69] Petitioners have asked the Commission on Elections to disqualify some of these party lists for their religious identity, but so far the commission has avoided confrontation. Perhaps most controversially, as noted at the beginning of this chapter, the elections in 2013 featured the explicit division of candidates into Team Buhay and Team Patay by some in the Philippine Catholic hierarchy. Here, clerics were not directly running for office but were clearly blurring the differentiation between their own religious authority and the credibility of various candidates and party lists. Taken as a whole, the presence of clerics as candidates, the growth of religiously grounded political parties, and the explicit endorsement of candidates by religious elites serve as indicators that differentiation between religion and state in the electoral realm is not what it used to be.

This change in the configuration of religion and democratic politics could pose a significant challenge to benevolent secularism both by breaking down the differentiation of religious and state institutions and by undercutting the state's principled distance from religious communities in the quest for votes. In the long term, it could also erode the dedication to pious secularism among the Catholic majority because some of these partisan voices advocate preferences regarding the religion–state relationship that sound much closer to religious integralism. Religious political parties need not doom the coalition alliances that have stabilized benevolent secularism since People Power, but they do provide a new source of institutional instability.

The weakening of differentiation through increased partisan behavior by religious elites is driven largely by newer actors outside of traditional religious-secular elite ties. The pluralization of Philippine religion, especially through some newer Charismatic Catholic and Protestant elites less dedicated to pious secularism, has fueled this trend. In an age of pluralized religious leadership, clerics and lay religious leaders can build their public visibility and perhaps receive material support from state officials by stepping into partisan politics. Although Catholic clerics generally resisted Among Ed's career path from clerical to political office, the more diverse crop of new religious elites in the Philippines has stepped more openly into the partisan ring. The Papanga

Christian Ministers Council endorsed and campaigned for Among Ed, and Charismatic clerics such as Pastor Apollo Quiboloy in Davao City offer coveted partisan endorsements in both local and national elections.[70] As Among Ed put to me, "I [was] endorsed by many interfaith groups. . . . [To them,] my being governor-priest was a big help. But some of my Catholic brother priests were not as happy. . . . [T]o these, I should not have even entered politics in the first place."[71] The wave of endorsements from certain parts of the Catholic hierarchy in the elections of 2013 can be similarly traced to increased religious-secular divisions related to the RH debate and actors largely outside of the CBCP. As Norman Cabrera, president of Ang Kapatiran Party, put it, "[Bishops] don't want to be seen at the forefront. . . . [Y]ou have to disturb [them]."[72] Initiatives such as Catholic Vote Philippines and the White Vote Campaign were explicitly rationalized as a response to the unique deterioration in religion–state relations around RH policy. But traditional religious elites such as CBCP leaders remained hesitant to explicitly back such efforts. As Bishop Broderick Pabillo, chairman of the CBCP's Committee on Public Affairs, said in conversation, "They are lay faithful; they have their own ideas, inspired by the church, . . . but [we] have to be shepherds for all, not only for [them]."[73]

Because the decreased differentiation between religion and state in electoral politics can be traced to weakened elite alliances, we should expect that more robust differentiation in this area would come not from anticlerical critiques of religious mobilization but instead from pious secularist religious elites who resist this type of politicized religion. Even before the elections in 2013, many Catholic leaders showed concern about growing religious partisan involvement. In the words of Father John Carroll, S.J., a leading political sociologist at Ateneo de Manila University, Catholic bishops "were quite uncomfortable with their newfound role," although they were convinced that Philippine democracy needed their involvement at key moments.[74] J. C. de los Reyes, a former presidential candidate of Ang Kapatiran, acknowledged some support from individual bishops, but he described the CBCP's more general attitude to electoral mobilization as "silence almost tantamount to resignation."[75] By most accounts, campaigns against Team Patay in the elections were of limited effect as politicians openly questioned the existence of a coherent "Catholic vote."[76] Catholic bishops now speak of "critical collaboration" with Philippine elected officials[77] and focus efforts on election monitoring through groups such as the Parish Pastoral Council for Responsible Voting. Among Ed's suspension from the ministry shows that pious secularists in the Catholic community prefer to keep electoral politics at arm's length. This preference shows through in some Protestant voices as well. Reverend Rex Reyes, executive director of the NCCP, worried that partisan mobilization would undermine the church's role as "an agent of reconciliation" and "a moral authority" in Philippine politics.[78] At the more evangelical end of the Protestant spectrum, Butch Belgica argued that electoral involvement has "gone to the extreme" and called for a focus on building the church from within rather than through elected office.[79] Some leaders of Couples for Christ, the million-plus member Catholic Charismatic movement, adopted a larger role in party politics in the closing months of the Estrada administration and the 2001 elections, only to see this public involvement contribute to a split that has now broken the movement into several parts.[80] The fracturing of Couples for Christ has clearly served to remind even devout elites of the benefits of differentiating state and religious institutions.

On the whole, the period since the People Power Revolution has seen the evolution of benevolent secularism in the face of a pluralized religious landscape. Significant change has occurred in areas where religious-secular and interfaith ties are least robust. Areas of most clear-cut institutional evolution, especially involving the Muslim minority, correspond to the observable operation of these coalition alliances in spite of pluralization, whereas those areas that show more evidence of weakening benevolent secularism, especially religious partisan campaigning, indicate strained elite ties traceable to religious pluralization.

BENEVOLENT SECULARISM, PLURALIZATION, AND PUBLIC OPINION

The elite-based evidence from the post–People Power era indicates that benevolent secularism endures in the Philippines because even new actors on the religious stage generally support the institutional combination of differentiation, cooperation, and principled distance through religious-secular partnerships and interfaith alliances. As in Ireland and Senegal, the elite patterns documented in the previous section correspond to a set of hypotheses about general public opinion. Did tensions between the Benigno Aquino administration and the CBCP indicate broader gaps between Catholic Filipinos and others on questions related to the dimensions of benevolent secularism? And is there evidence that new religious actors such as Charismatic Catholics are unique among the rest of the Catholic majority in attitudes to religious involvement in politics? The same survey research from the ISSP used in testing Irish attitudes gives the opportunity to test these coalition-based questions in the contemporary Philippines.

The theoretical framework in chapter 1 contends that the institutional structure of benevolent secularism should empower pious secularists within the Catholic community, thus cutting down on religious-secular divides and promoting strong interfaith relations over time. Among the general public, then, this framework generates a crisp hypothesis: Catholic Filipinos should be just as supportive of the dimensions of benevolent secularism as their fellow non-Catholic citizens. Even though this group is the numerical majority, its members should be no less supportive of differentiation, cooperation, and principled distance.

Among the Charismatic Catholic subset of the population, the elite evidence does not yield a single deductive hypothesis about opinion patterns. On the one hand, Charismatic Catholic elites remain closely tied to official Catholic bodies such as the CBCP and are not mobilized primarily to secure political goals. However, elite behavior from some Charismatic leaders does point to greater electoral activity and a greater openness to mobilizing members for particular candidates. It could be that this elite behavior would correspond to diminished public opinion support for the dimensions of benevolent secularism.

To test these hypotheses, I return to the ISSP survey utilized for Ireland. Question 1 in table 7.2 captures public attitudes to differentiation. The question asks about religious leaders' impact on election decisions, which is particularly fitting given the significant increase in religious campaigning documented in

TABLE 7.2. BENEVOLENT SECULARISM AND PUBLIC OPINION IN THE PHILIPPINES: QUESTION WORDING

Variable	Question Wording	Source/Country	Coding
Differentiation			
1. Religious Leaders Elections	How much do you agree or disagree with the following? Religious leaders should not try to influence how people vote in elections.	ISSP Religion III Module (Ireland; Philippines)	1 (Strongly Disagree) to 5 (Strongly Agree)
Principled Distance			
2. Equal Respect	How much do you agree or disagree with the following statement? We must respect all religions.	ISSP Religion III Module (Ireland; Philippines)	1 (Strongly Disagree) to 5 (Strongly Agree)

Source: International Social Survey Programme Research Group, *International Social Survey Programme (ISSP): Religion III* (Cologne, Germany: GESIS, 2008).

the previous section. Question 2 examines support for principled distance by asking whether all religions should be respected. This question gives some sense of respondent attitudes to religious pluralism. For both questions, a higher number on the ordinal scale corresponds to stronger support for that dimension of benevolent secularism. As in Ireland and Senegal, existing polling in the Philippines is particularly weak in assessing the cooperative dimension of benevolent secularism.

Unfortunately, the ISSP data, which provide useful dependent variables related to religion and politics, do not directly track participation in Charismatic Catholic movements. Nevertheless, the ISSP does ask respondents a question that can be used as a rough proxy for Catholic Charismatics: "Would you say that you have had a 'born-again' experience?" Christl Kessler's extensive research on Philippine Charismatics identifies the born-again experience as a key feature of Charismatic religiosity in the Philippines.[81] According to ISSP data, born-again Catholics make up approximately 25 percent of the total Catholic sample, which is larger than the roughly 15 percent Charismatic Catholic respondents that Kessler finds. Even though the Charismatic community is growing, and the ISSP data are about five years newer than Kessler's, it is likely that identifying "born-again Catholics" overstates the size of the Charismatic Catholic movement. This means that this identification strategy likely miscodes some non-Charismatics in the Charismatic camp and thus could underestimate potential differences between the two groups of Catholics.

Table 7.3 reports overall results for the two questions of interest, broken down by religious tradition. At the aggregate level, there is little support for involving religious leaders in voting decisions and widespread support for the idea that all religions should be respected. Turning to the results by religious tradition, there is little evidence that the Catholic majority is less supportive of either differentiation or principled distance than various religious minorities. The results by tradition show very little variation by religious tradition, and the one difference that does seem to be substantial, between Catholics and non-Catholic Christians on religious leaders and voting decisions, actually shows more robust support for differentiation among the Catholic majority. Within the Catholic community, there are minimal differences between born-again Catholics and the rest of the Catholics sampled. Even if the category "Born Again" is somewhat broader than the category "Charismatic Catholicism," there is little evidence in these topline results that Charismatics in the Catholic community have unique preferences regarding the place of religion in public life.

To test the strength of pious secularism among the Catholic majority in a more robust fashion, I report basic multivariate models in table 7.4 with and without major demographic controls. All models in table 7.4 use non-Catholic Christians as the excluded referent category, so the religious tradition

TABLE 7.3. PHILIPPINES TOPLINE RESULTS
BY RELIGIOUS TRADITION

	N	Support for Statement: "Religious Leaders Should Not Influence Voting" (%)	Agreement with Statement: "We Must Respect All Religions: (%)
Total	1,200	79.8	89.7
All Catholics	971	79.9	89.5
Born-Again Catholics	263	80.1	89.1
Non-Born-Again Catholics	708	79.9	89.6
Non-Catholic Christians	80	70.6	91.2
Muslims	65	80.8	92.3

Source: ISSP Research Group, *ISSP: Religion III.*

coefficients should be interpreted as differences with that group.[82] The theoretical expectations about the strength of Catholic pious secularism are confirmed; in fact, in attitudes to religion and elections, the Catholic majority is actually *more* supportive than other Christians of the value of differentiation that is at the core of benevolent secularism. With or without a handful of important demographic controls, Catholics are more supportive of keeping religious leaders out of elections than are non-Catholic Christians. This is also the case for those who identify in survey research as being from an "other" religious tradition, and Muslims are indistinct from non-Catholic Christians. These results lend strong support to the hypothesis that pious secularism is visible not only among Catholic elites but also in the Catholic general population. Efforts to treat religions unequally or to insert religious leaders into electoral campaigns are less likely to find support within the Catholic majority than outside of it. Pious secularism seems to have carried the day at the mass level.

If Filipino Catholics as a whole seem little different from minority religious communities, evidence from elites presented in the previous section raises the prospect that the rise of Charismatic Catholicism may be destabilizing benevolent secularism, especially in its impact on religion and partisan election campaigning. Are Charismatic Catholics less dedicated to benevolent secularism than others among the majority religion? Both bivariate and multivariate models of variation within the Catholic community find little support for the idea that born-again Catholics have significantly different preferences on the place of religion in democratic politics. These models are presented in

TABLE 7.4. TESTING BENEVOLENT SECULAR CONSENSUS IN THE PHILIPPINES

	Differentiation		Principled Distance	
	Religious Leaders' Impact on Vote		Respect for All Religions	
	Model 1	Model 2	Model 3	Model 4
Catholic	0.258*	0.270*	−0.0438	−0.0449
	[0.149]	[0.150]	[0.170]	[0.169]
Muslim	−0.0285	−0.0415	−0.0192	0.0264
	[0.176]	[0.181]	[0.214]	[0.222]
Non-Christian/	0.364*	0.356*	−0.0172	−0.0498
Non-Muslim	[0.186]	[0.186]	[0.229]	[0.231]
Sex		0.0509		−0.0709
		[0.0708]		[0.0796]
Age		0.00107		−0.000737
		[0.00233]		[0.00257]
Education		0.0264		0.0661***
		[0.0161]		[0.0175]
Urban/Rural		0.0651**		0.0108
		[0.0265]		[0.0285]
Religious		−0.0106		−0.0170
Attendance		[0.0258]		[0.0284]
N	1,196	1,188	1,198	1,190

Note: All coefficients standardized (*** $p < 0.01$, ** $p < 0.05$, * $p < 0.1$). Ordered Probit Models with robust standard errors in brackets. Non-Catholic Christians are the referent category.
Source: ISSP Research Group, ISSP: Religion III.

table 7.5. There is no statistically robust evidence that born-again Catholics are less supportive of the differentiation of religion and politics in elections. All coefficients are in the negative direction, but none approaches conventional levels of statistical significance. One would think that this trend helps to explain why Charismatic Catholic movements have been less than overwhelmingly successful in some of their electoral activity. At the very least, it shows that born-again

TABLE 7.5. THE BORN-AGAIN CATHOLIC DIFFERENCE?

	Differentiation		Principled Distance	
	Religious Leaders' Impact on Vote		Respect for All Religions	
	Model 1	Model 2	Model 3	Model 4
Born-Again Catholics	−0.0328 [0.0822]	−0.00283 [0.0835]	−0.126 [0.0913]	−0.128 [0.0926]
Sex		0.0747 [0.0797]		−0.0586 [0.0892]
Age		−0.000699 [0.00259]		−0.000981 [0.00285]
Education		0.0179 [0.0175]		0.0722*** [0.0199]
Urban/Rural		0.0517* [0.0289]		0.0235 [0.0318]
Religious Attendance		−0.0129 [0.0291]		−0.0401 [0.0315]
N	967	959	969	961

Note: All coefficients standardized (*** $p < 0.01$, ** $p < 0.05$, * $p < 0.1$). Ordered Probit Models with robust standard errors in brackets. Sample includes only Catholic respondents, who serve as the reference category for the born-again Catholic effect.
Source: ISSP Research Group, ISSP: Religion III.

Catholics are not necessarily a source of division in the coalition alliances that have driven secular evolution in the past quarter century.

In sum, the public opinion evidence indicates that pious secularism predominates among Filipino Catholics, and there is little evidence that the rise of Charismatic Catholicism is eroding coalition alliances in a way that will threaten benevolent secularism. As tested here, born-again Catholics' attitudes to the political role of religion are indistinguishable from the attitudes held by the rest of the Catholic majority. This suggests that the pluralism brought through the Charismatic revival need not undermine the configuration of religion and Philippine democracy that traces to the Commonwealth Constitution.

With that said, non-Catholic Christians do indeed demonstrate greater support for involving religious leaders in voting decisions, which indicates that continued pluralization *outside* of the Catholic majority may serve as an important source of future institutional change in the benevolent secularism of the Philippines.

Well after the Commonwealth Constitution of 1935, benevolent secularism still characterizes religion–state relations in the Philippines. The coalition between the Catholic Church, minority religions, and political elites that installed these institutions in 1934 endured the Marcos dictatorship to reaffirm the key tenets of benevolent secularism at the Constitutional Commission in 1986. But the sharp recent fight over the RH Law reveals lingering tensions in benevolent secularism. Although some political elites and Catholic officials worked behind the scenes to make the bill more accommodating to religious interests, it would be a mistake to overlook the real religious-secular divides that were not reconciled with the bill's signing. Only time will tell if these tensions dissipate as the bill is implemented through agencies such as the Department of Health or give rise to further fights over issues such as divorce policy. Agency matters in the wake of such disputes, and the structure of benevolent secularism does not determine the future of institutional change. The recent election of President Rodrigo "Rody" Duterte, who has a strained relationship with the CBCP, raises new questions about the future of these institutions.[83]

The model of secular evolution proposed in chapter 1 fits quite closely with the rise and fall of the Marcos regime and the restoration of benevolent secularism in its aftermath. Coalition alliances, especially those resting on strong interfaith relations and cooperation between secular civil society groups and the Catholic majority, played a central role initially in opposing the authoritarian regime and later in restoring benevolent secularism through the Constitutional Commission of 1986. Alliances, themselves encouraged by religion's role in public life, proved central in preserving institutions in the face of Marcos's bid to break down the twin tolerations.

The period after the People Power Revolution, especially the past several years, presents more difficulties for the model of institutional evolution primarily because the pluralization of religious leadership makes it more difficult to assess the status of religious-secular divides and interfaith relations. The RH Law controversy foregrounds this difficulty. On the one hand, it clearly did not represent a total breakdown in benevolent secularism. Catholic elites were consulted at several points in the process, and the eventual Supreme Court decision on the law made several accommodations for religious conscience that are characteristic of benevolent secularism. Institutions evolved in this challenging environment because of precisely the kinds of religious-secular partnerships fostered by benevolent secularism. On the other hand, it would be misleading to overlook the real tensions between religious and secular elites during this period. These tensions are in large part a result of the pluralization of leadership within both civil society and the Catholic majority. Given the pluralization of religious leadership in the Philippines and beyond, there are more opportunities and perhaps incentives for religious-secular tensions to emerge between alliance actors. The future of benevolent secularism in the Philippines will ultimately rest on how existing coalition alliances respond to the new, pluralized Philippine religious landscape.

Conclusion

THE FUTURE OF RELIGION AND SECULAR DEMOCRACY

The religious politics of Ireland, Senegal, and the Philippines provide diverse evidence of cases that have moved beyond the secularism trap. In environments that seemed primed for a breakdown between religion and democracy, leading religious actors have become defenders of the twin tolerations. The process of building such support was not always smooth, but today religious-secular and interfaith ties in these cases have generally worked to stabilize political institutions. Insofar as threats to the twin tolerations emerged, particularly in the Philippines and Senegal, they were from self-interested autocrats such as Ferdinand Marcos and Abdoulaye Wade, not from theocratic religious mobilization. The public role for religion encouraged by benevolent secularism did not remove contention over the relationship between religion and democracy, but instead encouraged elite ties that helped mediate such contentious episodes.

The structure of benevolent secularism helps explain why actors remained faithful to secularism in these cases. Evidence suggests that in each case institutional alternatives would have undercut democratic politics and even political stability. Official religious establishment would clearly have alienated minorities and threatened the twin tolerations, irrespective of the theoretical compatibility between establishment and liberal rights in places such as the United

Kingdom. This outcome likely comes as little surprise, particularly to readers shaped by liberalism's assumptions about religion in democratic politics. However, more assertive forms of institutional secularism could have proven similarly damaging to maintaining the twin tolerations. Removing religion from the Philippine public square, for instance, would have removed a major source of resistance to Marcos's authoritarian rule, and a more exclusive form of *laïcité* in Senegal could have provoked devastating urban–rural standoffs in the republic's early years of independence.

Benevolent secularism has mattered primarily because of the coalitions it encourages. The religious-secular divide and dangerous competition along interfaith lines are not natural occurrences, preprogrammed into the ideologies of contending religious rivals. Rather, the extent of such divisions is malleable, subject to changes in the institutional setting that democracy provides to religion. In contrast to theoretical assumptions that religion necessarily serves as a conversation stopper and thus is a dangerous addition to political debates, evidence in these cases suggests that in certain institutional environments public religion can build bridges among unlikely allies, in the process not only stabilizing democratic life but also pursuing causes as diverse as environmental protection and women's rights. These coalitional mechanisms suggest a significant reorientation by political scientists seeking to make sense of the "political ambivalence of religion."[1] We should pay more attention to bargaining between and within religious movements as well as to the institutional environments that affect these patterns of cooperation.

Among these coalition partners, pious secularists among the religious majority should receive special attention. It is remarkable the degree to which even apparently contending schools such as modernization theorists, rational choice analysts, and advocates of religious moderation share the assumption that orthodox religious majorities will prefer the fusion of religious and state power. This assumption simply cannot hold up to the empirical record. There are several reasons why pious secularism may take hold among religious majorities, ranging from ascetic political theology to hard experience with state co-optation of religious institutions. Too many liberal theorists seem to have forgotten just how badly religious institutions wanted to maintain differentiation for much of European history. The lesson is better remembered by religious elites in the field. Pious secularists can still complicate religion–state relations, especially in their claims to autonomy from state control, but their predominance fundamentally alters the dilemma posed by the secularism trap.

If scholarship in religion and politics should move beyond the most simplistic assumptions about the relationship between religion and democracy, where does this study suggest future insights might lie? First, the study's attention to changes in preferences within religious blocs and to the impact that these changes can have on partnerships between those blocs opens a broad area of research for comparative analysis. What conditions affect preferences among groups and how groups form partnerships or rivalries? Here, I advance a largely institutional theory, but a range of other theoretical options may motivate future study. International flows of populations and ideas played an important role in this study and may shape coalition alliances by changing the actors around a bargaining table. Pluralization of religious authority, particularly through the rise of lay-led social movements and civil society organizations, may facilitate alliance building but may also provoke more traditional religious elites to withdraw from historical partnerships. Certain issue areas related to gender and sexuality may be more likely to destabilize alliances, whereas others related to development or armed conflict may have different effects. These examples are just a few of the ways in which studying coalition alliances and shifts in preferences can animate future scholarship around religion and comparative politics.

This study also suggests moving research in religion and politics into the careful study of links between mass and elite opinion and behavior. Given the increasing wealth of comparative public-opinion data, there are more opportunities than ever to test individual-level theories about the impact of religion on political preferences. And researchers can track elite preferences through traditional fieldwork as well as through digital communications. However, tracking links between the two levels of analysis is more complex. It is easy enough to use polling work to evaluate how the mass public views religious elites but more challenging to demonstrate how that knowledge might affect the behavior of elites. Although the challenge is significant, the promise is also substantial. Public opinion might put a break on elite behavior, particularly if what this project calls "pious secularism" is actually more robust among the general public than among clerical elites. Linking mass and elite levels of analysis is another important stage in moving beyond the secularism trap, with its assumption that increased political participation from the general public threatens the twin tolerations between religion and democracy.

Taken as a whole, these findings suggest that religious actors regularly remain faithful to secularism, making commitments to play by the rules of the democratic game, even if doing so involves losing policy debates. And those commitments become more credible when made in the public square and reinforced by political institutions that minimize divides among coalition partners. As new challenges confront secular states over time, they are best served by such a diverse coalition, where both the religious and the secular as well as majorities and minorities have a stake in preserving existing institutions.

RECAPPING AND LOOKING FORWARD

In Ireland, Senegal, and the Philippines, political institutions have played a role in reconciling religious actors and democracy. Throughout this volume, I have argued that one variety of institutional relationship between religion and state, benevolent secularism, has proven particularly effective in securing the twin tolerations while avoiding the worst extremes of the secularism trap. Institutions matter in these cases and beyond because they shape the preferences within religious blocs and thus encourage the formulation of alliances that cross both boundaries between faith groups and the religious-secular divide. The preceding studies document that these institutional effects originate in critical junctures of regime formation and extend over time as coalition alliances form to undercut challenges. The stability of these alliances in turn helps explain the path-dependent nature of secularism; even during periods that seem ripe for institutional collapse, coalition allies stabilize existing institutions and encourage their gradual evolution to new social conditions. The combination of elite interviews and survey analysis shows that these alliances exist at various levels of analysis and raises the interesting question of how elite and mass dynamics combine to drive the religious politics of democracy.

The Irish case provided some of the strongest evidence of the responses of religious minorities to benevolent secularism at critical junctures. The correspondence between Éamon de Valera and the leaders of Methodist, Presbyterian, Church of Ireland, and Jewish communities clearly demonstrates the effect of benevolent secularism's dimensions of differentiation, cooperation, and principled distance in reassuring minority groups of their legal standing. Ireland also gives some warning that benevolent secularism is not without its vulnerabilities. Principled distance was imperfectly maintained early in independence, as the Mother and Child Crisis indicated. However, over time the interfaith and religious-secular alliances promoted by benevolent secularism helped make this important dimension more robust. These alliances have operated to stabilize benevolent secularism even in the face of the Catholic Church sex abuse scandals, the arrival of unprecedented religious diversity, and major changes in education policy.

If we look forward in Ireland, the theoretical framework set out in this project points to the importance of maintaining religious-secular partnerships in promoting future institutional stability. With the primary challenge to Irish benevolent secularism coming from the rapid increase in the religiously unaffiliated, the dynamics of religious-secular partnerships will come under new strain. There may be fewer young elites within religious institutions, and those who remain may be less willing to participate in partnerships with a broader secular culture. Likewise, as the secular bloc grows in Ireland, its leaders may become less patient with religious institutions and less interested in maintaining the religion–state cooperation that characterizes benevolent secularism. If religious-secular divides were to grow more pointed over time, we should expect corresponding periods of institutional instability and perhaps even the full breakdown of benevolent secularism in this case. If institutions fail, it seems more likely that this failure will be from religious-secular divisions than from interfaith tensions; to date, Ireland's newer faith communities have been fairly eager participants in the benevolent bargain.

The evidence in Senegal demonstrated the effect of benevolent institutions in shaping preferences among the highest-ranking Sufi brotherhoods. Even when Islamist reform movements such as the Conseil supérieur have attempted to break down *laïcité*, the Sufi leaders have shown ambivalent support because the combination of differentiation, cooperation, and principled distance has served their interests quite well over time. The response of a wide array of actors to the manipulations of the Wade administration was one of the most dramatic examples in this study of coalition alliances defending institutional stability. Umbrella coalitions such as the Assises nationales put *laïcité*'s protection on the political agenda and showed the diverse set of actors who have come to support benevolent secularism. Although this evidence is compelling, the major ambiguity in Senegal remains the extent to which certain aspects of *laïcité* are tolerated but not necessarily embraced by the Sufi brotherhoods. The Code de la famille puts this ambiguity in concrete terms. Sufi elites tolerated the legislation because it simply did not apply in their heartlands, and the state was in no position to impose it there by force.

A look forward in Senegal indicates that *laïcité*'s stability will continue to rest on the alliances that have defended it in the past decade. Any institutional breakdown, then, should be predated by observable tension in the coalition alliances between faith groups and across the religious-secular divide. As religious leadership fragments over generations and leaders compete more aggressively for followers, we may theoretically observe less-enthusiastic participation in interreligious dialogues. The intersection of religious authority with partisan politics may also strain these alliances. The greatest challenge to traditional coalition alliances may come from international currents, whether population flows of evangelical Christians, ideological influence from Arab-educated Muslim reformers, or more assertively secular activists in parts of civil society. To date, these forces have not undermined the coalition supporting benevolent secularism. However, should these forces weaken alliances over time, the next challenge from an actor like Wade may have more dramatic results.

The Philippines shows what a difference institutional design can make at constitutional negotiations. Whereas religious and secular actors deadlocked on the place of religion during the Malolos debates of 1898, the Commonwealth Constitution deliberations of 1934 were marked by general unanimity and cooperation. Although the legacies of Spanish colonial rule continued to stoke occasional tensions between religion and state, the religious-secular divide reduced in scope quite quickly. Understanding the Marcos regime as a violation of, among other things, the dimensions of benevolent secularism sheds new light on why interfaith partnerships played such a prominent role in the push to restore democracy. If the evidence from that period confirms several of the theoretical expectations at the core of this project, the more recent history of religion and democracy is more contentious. Religious-secular partners did receive real concessions in the RH Law negotiations, but the fact remains that the debate ended without consensus from the CBCP. The longer-term effects of this failure remain to be seen.

In the future, benevolent secularism in the Philippines will rest on how key religious and political actors choose to respond to the pluralization of religious authority. For example, will newer Muslim associations such as the National Ulama Council of the Philippines find strong allies in the Catholic bishops? Will the Charismatic movement's involvement in electoral politics draw more traditional religious authorities into partisan campaigning as well? The elections of 2013 showed not only undeniable partisan mobilization of religion but also resistance to this phenomenon from pious secularists worried that taking religion on the campaign trail threatens the moral credibility of the Philippine church. The election of President Rodrigo Duterte raises the likelihood of strained religion–state relations in the near future.

TENSIONS IN THE DIMENSIONS

Although benevolent secularism has played an important role in reconciling religion and democratic politics in these three cases, a tension is built into this institutional model: How much benevolence is too much? To pose the challenge in a more precise manner, at what point does the cooperative dimension of benevolent secularism come into tension with the differentiation of religious and state institutions or even with the principled distance between the state and all religious communities? Debates over mandatory religious education in the Philippines, the Mother and Child Crisis in Ireland, and the Code de la famille in Senegal centered on this tension.

Benevolent secularism's most unique claim may be that cooperation between religion and state need not threaten the principled distance between the state and various religious communities. There is no necessary trade-off between cooperation and principled distance. Schools in Ireland have reflected some denominational diversity since independence, for instance, and in the face of increased religious diversity have begun to expand patronage models, including multidenominational education. In many ways, debates over patronage reform in Ireland demonstrate the ability of cooperation and principled distance to coexist even in rapidly changing societies. The interfaith nature of policy consultations in contemporary Ireland shows a similar impulse. Principled distance is certainly difficult to maintain in any religiously dynamic society; minorities pose challenges to principled distance even in more passive secular states such as the United States and more aggressively secular models such as France. However, there is little theoretical or empirical reason to believe that the cooperative dimension of benevolent secularism makes principled distance *more* vulnerable to breakdown.

Whereas principled distance and cooperation may actually reinforce one another, there are distinct tensions between differentiation and cooperation. These tensions come to the surface most regularly in patterns of religious influence over policy formation. In each of the three controversies identified at the beginning of this section, elites within the religious majority advocated for policy positions that were not broadly shared by religious minorities and that seemed to blur the line between consultation and the establishment of religious positions in law. When does cooperation come at the cost of differentiation? To evaluate this balance, analysts can return to Alfred Stepan's conceptualization of the twin tolerations, in particular the toleration that the religious community owes to state institutions. As Stepan puts it, "Democratic institutions must be free, within the bounds of the constitution and human rights, to generate policies. Religious institutions should not have constitutionally privileged prerogatives that allow them to mandate public policy to democratically elected governments. At the same time . . . [religious communities and individuals] must be able to advance their values publicly in civil society . . . as long as their actions do not impinge negatively on the liberties of other citizens or violate democracy and the law."[2]

This standard allows for fairly extensive religious cooperation in the policy process, while setting out some guidelines for when cooperation may threaten differentiation. First, any constitutional privilege given to religious authorities over state law is a breakdown in differentiation; this is the problem with enshrining religious judges as ultimate arbiters of family law. A second guideline is subtler. To respect differentiation, religious involvement in public debates should not rest *solely* on exclusive doctrinal claims because these claims have the effect of impinging on other citizens' ability to engage in democratic deliberation. Doctrine can motivate religious actors, but if the limitation of public debates to certain faith traditions is to be avoided, actors should be able to advance arguments accessible beyond one religious community. In this regard, it is important that the CBCP made its case against the RH Law in terms of the negative social impact of contraceptives. Although advocates of the RH Law may strongly disagree with that argument, the fact that the CBCP made it in such terms did not exclude any religious or nonreligious actors from the policy debate. For cooperation to balance with differentiation, whether in policy consultation or in areas of material cooperation such as education, the effect of that cooperation should not be the impingement of other citizens' full participation in those same policy areas.

Focusing on the tensions among the dimensions of benevolent secularism returns this empirical argument to some of the debates within political theory regarding the place of religion in democratic politics. The cooperation between religion and state, especially in the formulation of policy, is likely to raise objections from certain liberals who see religion both as inherently opposed to the compromise required by democracy and as a uniquely dangerous source of social division. However, such cooperation recognizes what Jürgen Habermas has termed "an awareness of what is missing" from entirely secular public debates.[3] Involving religious communities in the public square can strengthen the solidarity and social cohesion needed for democratic politics. Religious leaders' working across faith lines to resist the Marcos dictatorship in the Philippines or to ensure electoral transparency in Senegal brings this theoretical point into empirical focus. The combination of cooperation with differentiation and principled distance moves beyond blunt assertions that religion is a conversation stopper and into the more fruitful debate about what conditions may actually strengthen or weaken democratic politics.

The functioning of benevolent secularism in the cases considered here should further calm liberal fears that religion talk will necessarily fuel interreligious tensions and impede the compromise necessary for democracy to function. In fact, it is precisely the benevolent nature of religion–state relations in these cases that results in the improved interfaith relations that stabilize secularism over time. Senegal provides strong evidence on this point. More religious debates in public life have not threatened interfaith harmony. Catholic and Muslim cooperation on AIDS prevention is just one example of the myriad of public issues that encourage religious collaboration and promote the sense of these faith groups' shared national responsibility. And, of course, when President Wade made disparaging remarks about Catholic ritual practice to deflect attention from his own political troubles, Muslim leaders, alongside Catholic clerics, spoke out against his manipulation. The prominent public role for religion, encouraged by *laïcité* in its Senegalese translation, is a major contributor to the *dialogue islamo-chrétien* that distinguishes Senegal's political life.

In sum, there are indeed tensions among the three dimensions of benevolent secularism, but they do not render the institutional model inoperable.

Cooperation and principled distance may actually reinforce one another, and although principled distance may break down in any setting, it is not clear that cooperation between religion and state makes this breakdown more likely to occur. The tension between differentiation and cooperation can become more direct, but some basic guidelines can help to distinguish forms of cooperation that threaten to break down the very differentiation of religion and state. Cooperation can take problematic forms, but the alliances that benevolent secularism encourages can play a role in maintaining the balance among these dimensions.

QUESTIONS RAISED: GETTING TO YES AND THE SOURCES OF PUBLIC OPINION

In addition to these tensions within the model of benevolent secularism, the argument explored in this book raises but cannot fully answer two important and related questions about the sources of elite bargaining. One concerns the conditions that may prevent benevolent secularism from emerging in the first place, and the second has to do with the links between elite bargaining and public opinion.

First, if benevolent secularism can serve the interests of political elites, religious majorities, and religious minorities, why does it sometimes fail to emerge? What conditions prevent this institutional configuration from garnering support from elites? This question is particularly important given the ongoing contentious debates about religion's place in a more democratic Arab world. Although a full discussion of this issue is beyond the scope of this volume, the three cases suggest that certain historical conditions may hamper the kind of bargaining that allows benevolent secularism to emerge in the first place. This failure is particularly likely in cases that have a legacy of mistrust and coercion between political elites and the majority religious community. In these kinds of ideologically polarized environments, extensive, preexisting divides may make the kind of coalition building at the heart of benevolent secularism unsustainable. The Arab Awakening highlights the challenges of overcoming divides. Whereas the religious-secular gap appears to have been managed (though not eliminated) in Tunisia by cooperation during years of exile, sharp suspicions among religious and secular actors in Egypt seem to be heightening the divide. The burden posed by such historical legacies hampers all institutions, of course, not simply those of benevolent secularism.

The Philippines provides the clearest look at why benevolence may not emerge and how this may change over time. Recall that at the Malolos Congress in 1898, as Spanish rule weakened but before American colonial authority consolidated, delegates deadlocked on the constitutional relationship between religion and state. Sharp divides between secular and religious actors prevented a bargain like benevolent secularism from emerging. Leading secular nationalists, a camp that included several Masons, had fresh memories of the role that the Catholic hierarchy had played in cementing Spanish colonial rule and found the very presence of an organized Catholic clergy threatening to the autonomy of the secular republic. Catholic elites, for their part, often assumed that Spanish anticlericalism would accompany republicanism in the Philippines and were terrified that independence would leave church properties vulnerable to expropriation and nationalization. This deadlock ended by the late American colonial period as both Catholic clerics and nationalist elites established patterns of cooperation that built mutual confidence and entrenched the benevolent secular coalition that endures to this day. The confidence building took several decades, but over time the sharp religious-secular divisions of Malolos gave way to the benevolent bargain of the Commonwealth Constitution. Future scholarship should focus on similar processes of confidence building and on the processes by which credible commitments emerge between once-polarized political actors.

My argument raises a second area for further research: the causal relationship between public opinion and institutional design. The one-off survey data presented in the chapters on secular evolution show a correlation between the elite consensus described in the case study chapters and patterns of opinion among the general public. But this correlation raises the more difficult question about what causal relationship connects cultural attitudes to elite alliances and ultimately to the configuration of religion and state. One response is that fairly stable cultural values contribute to the path dependence of benevolent secularism; culture drives an institutional outcome because elites face popular constraints on their bargaining. Another option is that culture largely follows elite cues and the institutional environment that structures politics. On this telling, public opinion will respond to changes in constitutional institutions, for instance. Sorting out the direction of causality requires attention to periods of institutional change and to patterns of public opinion over time. Scholars have multiple rounds of surveys from the ISSP, the World Values Survey, and Global Barometer surveys at their disposal, so there is more opportunity for this kind of important research.

It seems likely that the relationship between culture and institutional design can move in different directions at different points in time. For instance, if elites with high social legitimacy either advocate institutional change or respond to it with clear hostility, it is likely that these elite cues can shape opinion among followers. Something like this took place in the emergence of the Religious Right in the United States in the 1970s as elites condemned what they perceived to be antireligious shifts in American jurisprudence and in the process mobilized white evangelical voters into a core component of the Republican Party electorate. But public opinion almost certainly acts as a constraint on elites as well. In the Philippines, for instance, recent debates about the RH Law regularly referred to strong support even among practicing Catholics for access to state-funded contraceptives. Polling was a near constant refrain from advocates of the bill. The Catholic bishops were certainly aware that they did not speak for their flocks in opposing the RH Law, and this realization likely influenced some clerics' openness to pursuing more modest patterns of resistance to the bill.

Evidence from Ireland shows the role of public opinion in promoting pious secularism within Catholic elites. To put it bluntly, the divorce referenda in Ireland showed that the Catholic Church had not decisively won the political argument even within its own pews. The broader, comparative importance of this point lies in the role of popular religious attitudes in minimizing the chances of a breakdown of secularism. Religious elites in Ireland and elsewhere have an interest in shaping public policy, to be sure, but they also need to maintain spiritual credibility that can be undermined by their political adventurism. This is especially true if these political forays run against public preferences, as expressed either through public opinion polling or through policy referenda. The Irish experience suggests that many religious elites are aware of these dangers and that this awareness promoted the pious secularism of the Irish hierarchy throughout the 1970s and 1980s. Future research can probe the ways in which religious elites respond to the political preferences of their flocks, particularly when the laity and clerical elite have different policy priorities.

AMBIGUITIES IN THE MODEL

Although the model of benevolent secularism's institutional effects presented in this book helps make sense of its emergence and evolution in religion and democracy in the three cases described, there are several ambiguities in the model. A first ambiguity is the role of preindependence institutional structures in influencing the emergence of the twin tolerations during critical junctures. Although the institutional relationship between religion and state was thrown into flux by independence in each of these cases, the actors who contested those institutions had themselves come to positions of leadership under colonial institutions that regulated religion and politics. In Ireland, for instance, the coalition of state and religious elites who negotiated Irish secularism were in their own right affected by British colonial policy. The Catholic school system was the most obvious example of this influence; because of the British decision to fund denominational schools, the Catholic system at independence was pervasive, and a state educational sector would have had to be built from scratch. The presence of Church of Ireland elites was likewise an explicit legacy of the preferential treatment that this minority received throughout the colonial period. And the very language of nonendowment was owing to British governing guidelines that stretched back to the late nineteenth century. In Senegal, the debates occurring around 1960 took place in the wake of French collaboration with some Sufi clerics as early as the late nineteenth century through what historian David Robinson has called "paths of accommodation."[4]

The existence of colonial legacies does not in and of itself take away from the critical importance of junctures such as independence and constitution drafting. The coalitions that would come to support benevolent secularism in each of the cases described here simply did not exist under colonial rule in large part because colonial officials and appointments heavily influenced all coalition blocs. Political elites at the highest levels were members of the colonial hub, and even religious majority and minority actors were frequently tied to the colonial administration. The preference of each bloc of actors rested on interactions with the colonial state, a pattern of political life that fundamentally changed with independence. Independence thus did provide a moment of institutional uncertainty, and the configuration of religion and politics that emerged during that period had an independent impact on the preferences of the coalition blocs that would eventually unite in support of the twin tolerations. Colonial institutional legacies do suggest a further avenue for research into how such patterns compare to the patterns of the postindependence relationship between religion and state, but they do not indicate that debates at critical junctures were entirely endogenous to earlier colonial administrative decisions.

The mechanism through which institutions shape actor preferences is another area of ambiguity within the model of benevolent secularism that would benefit from further specification. Several mechanisms would be broadly compatible with the theoretical framework and empirical findings set out in this research. Although each requires further testing, they are consistent with both the theoretical expectations about benevolent secularism and the evidence gathered across the three country cases at the center of this book. First, benevolent secularism operates by constructing networks of experts, resembling what scholars of international relations have come to call "epistemic communities," that are dedicated to preserving the twin tolerations.[5] Preferences among coalition blocs become more similar over time because the relevant actors find themselves on the same state commissions, policy consultations, and dialogue boards. For example, the network of religious and secular experts around public health in Senegal means that such questions, rather than being simply a matter of technocratic policy formation, provide opportunities for further religion–state cooperation. Second, a set of learning mechanisms is implicit in this account, especially with respect to institutions' impact on cementing alliances over time. Relevant actors learn to deliberate over religious topics that liberal theory often assumes to be conversation stoppers, and hard-liners within religious and secular blocs perceive less-intense threats from rival coalition blocs. Even where disagreements exist, such as in Irish divorce policy, actors such as the Catholic bishops learn how to make arguments that acknowledge the differentiation of religion and state as well as the need to maintain principled distance. Third, benevolent secularism promotes contact across social divisions that could reshape cultural norms over time. Although Protestant–Catholic competition in the Philippines was sharp in the early years of American colonialism, the turn to benevolent secularism under the Philippine Commonwealth promoted more contact between elites from various Christian denominations. Over time, this elite-level social contact eased interfaith tensions and set the foundation for joint Catholic–Protestant resistance to the Marcos dictatorship.

A final ambiguity in the model of benevolent secularism arises from the pluralization of religious authority in the wake of globalization. At a broader level, the elite-based bargaining model described in chapter 1 is certainly more complicated in an era of religious Internet chat rooms, self-appointed street preachers, and campus-based atheist associations. This diversity brings methodological challenges as well. When we assess the strength of interfaith relations, for instance, or the extent of the religious-secular divide, it is increasingly unclear which actors speak authoritatively for dynamics at the elite level and what possible gaps there may be between elite discourse and attitudes among the general public.

An example from Ireland puts this challenge to the model in concrete terms. Muslims in Ireland are an internally diverse bunch, and documenting their relationship to the state and other faith groups is complicated by such pluralization. Cooperation between the state and the Muslim minority as well as interfaith dialogue tend to center on the Islamic Cultural Centre of Ireland, a well-financed Sunni community in South Dublin. However, the center is not the only voice in the Irish Muslim community. Mary Fitzgerald of the *Irish Times* received substantial attention for her reporting in 2011 on "disgruntled Muslims" who objected to the state's privileging of the Islamic Cultural Centre over other Muslim associations.[6] Abdel Zeroug, coordinator of the Arab Community Forum of Ireland, spoke at length to me of the ethnic and linguistic diversity within the Muslim community, and he clearly worries that treating Islam like a unified Protestant denomination risks missing signs of disaffection among parts of the community not represented by the Islamic Cultural Centre's Arab-speaking, Sunni leadership, backed by the Maktoum Foundation of Dubai.[7] How should the state maintain principled distance given the pluralized nature of Muslim leadership? And how should a researcher assess the strength of interfaith relations as a whole in this environment? To date, the core elite alliances in this model of benevolent secularism have held up in this diverse set of cases, but future pluralization within and between religious communities will bring further challenges both to the model's logic and to the research process used to assess its claims.

THE FUTURE OF BENEVOLENCE

Throughout this book, I make the case that benevolent secularism has played a unique and often overlooked role in getting beyond the false choice posed by the secularism trap. It is important to acknowledge that the critical junctures in each of these cases took place between fifty and one hundred years ago. Much has changed in debates about religion and democracy over that time, and it is likely that the future of benevolent secularism will be owing to forces that have only begun to shape secular evolution in these three cases.

First, whereas questions of formal religious establishment haunted constitutional conventions earlier in the twentieth century, today's debates about the nature of secularism are more likely to center on questions of conscience exemptions and religious autonomy. This development is substantial; rather than make claims to control state institutions, religious institutions increasingly find themselves playing defense against civil laws that infringe on areas once under religious control. This change in position is especially true in western Europe but has also come to the fore in the RH Law debates in the Philippines. As the bureaucratic reach of the state extends farther into areas of concern to religious institutions, this trend is likely to continue. Because the very nature of benevolent secularism is supposed to serve the interests of the religious community at large, there is ample ground for making exemption claims in benevolent secular states. Sufi orders in Senegal have claimed exemptions from various state economic policies, and Irish religious institutions are exempted from several discrimination laws in the interest of preserving their "religious ethos." Similar exemption debates have already cropped up in such areas as LGBT rights, reproductive medicine, and curriculum development.

However, although benevolent secular institutions generally accommodate such claims from both religious groups and individuals, these claims do raise serious questions about the ability to maintain benevolent secularism's principled distance in the future. What principled grounds, for instance, should decide whether Catholics' objections to funding abortions should be treated the same as Jehovah Witnesses' objections to blood transfusions? These kinds of questions involve state institutions in setting slippery distinctions between religions and cults or in arriving at a resolution simply in terms of material power: that is, those groups that mobilize lawyers get exemptions. Keeping some principle in "principled distance" will become even more challenging as claims to religious autonomy from state control grow in the face of the expansion of the bureaucratic state.

A second challenge to the future of benevolent secularism is the influence of international bodies on what have largely developed as national-level institutions. The most obvious source of international pressure comes from transnational judicial bodies such as the European Court of Human Rights, which issues increasingly binding rulings on member states' domestic law. To date, the court has shown a fairly wide margin of appreciation of local differences in the realm of religion–state relations, which reflects the wide variety of institutional relationships between religion and state even within Europe. But cases related to abortion access in Ireland and classroom crucifixes in Italy suggest that this margin of appreciation may be narrowing over time. Whatever one's views on the particular cases in question, these international dynamics certainly destabilize the coalition alliances that have stabilized benevolent secularism over time. Local elites can increasingly look to power sources beyond their borders to get a better bargain in institutional debates, and international actors can explicitly target "undesirable" local institutions for transformation.

The role of international flows in destabilizing benevolent secularism shows through clearly in the Philippines. The RH Law was an international as well as a domestic political event, closely covered by watchdog groups in the orbits of both women's rights and Catholic politics. These international influences empowered hard-liners on both sides of the debate, which had financial support from and linkages to powerful international bodies, and made it especially difficult for the CBCP to accept anything other than total surrender from the bill's advocates. In a counterfactual world in which international networks had little connectivity to domestic debates, the religious-secular alliances represented by groups such as the Bishops–Businessmen's Conference may have been able to secure more cooperation between the two sides. However, the current reality is that such international influences frequently represent strong constraints on the mutual accommodation that is at the heart of benevolent secularism. Religious-secular divides travel along with information and funding in today's globalized advocacy environment. Benevolent secularism, whether in the Philippines, Senegal, or Ireland, arose as a basically domestic institutional solution, sustained by domestic partnerships between faith groups and political elites. International dynamics threaten such accommodation.

It is important to note that destabilizing international influences can flow from any part of a secular coalition. More assertive secularists in Ireland have drawn strength from European networks promoting stricter versions of secularism. Muslim reformists in Senegal draw inspiration from sharia courts in several parts of the Muslim-majority world, in particular parts of the Arab Middle East. And Protestant minorities are leaving an imprint on secular debates in the Philippines. The optimist would note, of course, that international flows may also have a positive effect, with cases such as Senegal and Indonesia inspiring pious secularists in other parts of the Muslim world. Although this is certainly theoretically true, there is significant evidence that one primary impact of international flows has been to destabilize rather than to reinforce religious-secular alliances. This trend is likely to continue into the future and deserves careful attention from scholars of religion and democracy.

Although international influences will shape secular evolution, there is also evidence that local coalitions can respond to these challenges. The limited international influence on Senegalese secularism demonstrates this point. Many worry that international Islamist movements will destabilize support for *laïcité*, especially among younger generations, but religious leadership remains largely nationalized in Senegal. The Mourides proudly point out that they are the most indigenous of the major Sufi movements, and Amadou Bamba Mbacké is a hero of national resistance. Muslim elites who have left to study in Arab institutions throughout North Africa do exercise increasing influence in public debates, particularly among educated, urban communities; however, leading *arabisants* have become incorporated into the secular coalition. Several interview subjects remarked that national traditions of tolerance in local African religious practice remain more important than international Islamic influences. This nationalization of leadership comes with consequences for secular evolution. Debates that claim large-scale global attention, particularly regarding apostasy, have fairly limited traction in Senegal. Reformists may compare family law in Senegal to family law in Morocco or *laïcité* in Senegal to the very different institutions of the same name in France, but the story of secular evolution in Senegal remains highly nationalized. Given the inconsistent impact of international influences, future scholarship might highlight the conditions under which international actors do (or do not) shape domestic institutions of religion–state relations.

A final area likely to destabilize benevolent secularism is the growth of the religious "nones," particularly among younger Westerners. The "nones" as a group include both affirmed atheists and agnostics as well as those who simply do not identify with a particular religious tradition. They pose a challenge to benevolent secularism in two ways. First, many are resolutely nondenominational; they do not want to form a Church of the Nones to have equal access to education funding, for instance. Members of this group are not necessarily hostile to benevolent secularism, but they may be less likely to see the general social benefits that come from the cooperation between religion and state. More challenging is the smaller but growing community of explicitly anticlerical nonbelievers who see benevolent secularism as a prop for superstition and a source of discrimination against their views. Such groups are not entirely new on the political scene, but they do seem to have new levels of popular support and funding at their disposal. These groups push on religious-secular alliances, making it more difficult for both religious and secular actors to cooperate in the public sphere.

As the "none" demographic grows, at least within the West, benevolent secularism needs to evolve to incorporate at least some of its members into coalition alliances. This can be done first by showing increased sensitivity to maintaining a principled distance from nonbelievers as well. Perhaps nonbelievers do not want their own schools, but efforts such as Educate Together in Ireland show that benevolent secular states can take nonbeliever preferences seriously. Second, religious actors in benevolent secular states would be wise to present new areas for positive cooperation between religious and nonreligious actors in public life. Showing the benefits that stem from cooperation in areas as diverse as anticorruption drives and environmental advocacy may blunt the edge of the sharpest anticlerical portions of the unaffiliated community. At its most robust, benevolent secularism has always rested on this kind of positive cooperation rather than on a passive tolerance between religious and secular groups.

Benevolent secularism is no silver bullet for resolving tensions between democracy and religion, but there is good reason to think that it can play a central role in avoiding the secularism trap by bridging religious-secular divides and improving interfaith relations. This trap has long been an impediment to democratization, and the institutional structure of religion–state relations can prove decisive in avoiding its snare. The precise shape of secular benevolence may vary from case to case, but its basic mechanism of altering the coalition politics of secularism travels more broadly from Ireland, Senegal, and the Philippines to cases where the secularism trap still looms.

NOTES

INTRODUCTION

1. Alfred Stepan, "Religion, Democracy, and the 'Twin Tolerations,'" *Journal of Democracy* 11, no. 4 (2000): 37–57.

2. James Mahoney, "Path Dependence in Historical Sociology," *Theory and Society* 29, no. 4 (2000): 507–48; James Mahoney and Dietrich Rueschemeyer, *Comparative Historical Analysis in the Social Sciences* (Cambridge: Cambridge University Press, 2003); Paul Pierson, "Increasing Returns, Path Dependence, and the Study of Politics," *American Political Science Review* 94, no. 2 (2000): 251–67.

3. Gary J. Jacobsohn, *The Wheel of Law: India's Secularism in Comparative Constitutional Context* (Princeton: Princeton University Press, 2003); Jean Bauberot, "The Two Thresholds of Laicization," in *Secularism and Its Critics*, ed. Rajeev Bhargava (Oxford: Oxford University Press, 1998), 94–136.

4. Ahmet T. Kuru, *Secularism and State Policies Toward Religion: The United States, France, and Turkey* (Cambridge: Cambridge University Press, 2009).

5. See, for example, Ellen Lust, "Missing the Third Wave: Islam, Institutions, and Democracy in the Middle East," *Studies in Comparative International Development* 46 (2011): 163–90; Alfred Stepan, "Tunisia's Transition and the Twin Tolerations,"

Journal of Democracy 23, no. 2 (2012): 89–103; Jocelyne Cesari, *The Awakening of Muslim Democracy: Religion, Modernity, and the State* (New York: Cambridge University Press, 2014).

6. My use of the term *secularism* here and throughout the book refers to the institutional level of analysis, not to secularization of individual belief. My argument is concerned with state institutions captured through constitutional documents, state regulatory law, and bureaucratic practice, not with explaining individual religiosity. See José Casanova's book *Public Religions in the Modern World* (Chicago: University of Chicago Press, 1994) for an extended discussion on why it is essential to distinguish institutional and individual levels of analysis in the study of secularism. For a related discussion of my book's core theoretical framework, see David T. Buckley, "Beyond the Secularism Trap: Religion, Political Institutions, and Democratic Commitments," *Comparative Politics* 47, no. 4 (2015): 442–47.

7. Edward Djerejian, "The US and the Middle East in a Changing World," *U.S. Department of State Dispatch* 3, no. 23 (1992): 444.

8. Jillian Schwedler, *Faith in Moderation: Islamist Parties in Jordan and Yemen* (Cambridge: Cambridge University Press, 2006); J. A. Clark, "The Conditions of Islamist Moderation: Unpacking Cross-Ideological Cooperation in Jordan," *International Journal of Middle East Studies* 38, no. 4 (2006): 539–60; Michael D. Driessen, "Public Religion, Democracy, and Islam," *Comparative Politics* 44, no. 2 (2012): 171–89.

9. Vali Nasr, "The Rise of 'Muslim Democracy,'" *Journal of Democracy* 16, no. 2 (2005): 13–27. See also Nader Hashemi, *Islam, Secularism, and Liberal Democracy: Toward a Democratic Theory for Muslim Societies* (Oxford: Oxford University Press, 2009).

10. Alfred Stepan, "The Multiple Secularisms of Modern Democratic and Nondemocratic Regimes," in *Rethinking Secularism*, ed. Craig Calhoun, Mark Juergensmeyer, and Jonathan Van Antwerpen (Oxford: Oxford University Press, 2011), 114–39; Ahmet T. Kuru, "Passive and Assertive Secularism," *World Politics* 59, no. 3 (2007): 568–94; Michael Daniel Driessen, *Religion and Democratization: Framing Religious and Political Identities in Muslim and Catholic Societies* (New York: Oxford University Press, 2014).

11. Stepan, "Religion, Democracy, and the 'Twin Tolerations.'"

12. Peter L. Berger, *The Desecularization of the World: Resurgent Religion and World Politics* (Grand Rapids, Mich.: Eerdmans, 1999).

13. Rajeev Bhargava, *Secularism and Its Critics* (Delhi: Oxford University Press, 1998).

14. Monica Duffy Toft, "Getting Religion? The Puzzling Case of Islam and Civil War," *International Security* 31, no. 4 (2007): 97–131; Robert Hefner, "Rethinking Islam and Democracy," in *Rethinking Religion in World Affairs*, ed. Timothy Samuel

Shah, Alfred Stepan and Monica Duffy Toft (New York: Oxford University Press, 2012), 85–103.

15. For more on these attitudes, see Anna Grzymała-Busse, *Nations Under God: How Churches Use Moral Authority to Influence Policy* (Princeton: Princeton University Press, 2015), and David T. Buckley, "Demanding the Divine? Explaining Cross-National Support for Clerical Control of Politics," *Comparative Political Studies* 49, no. 3 (2016): 357–90.

1. BENEVOLENT SECULARISM

1. Daniel Lerner, *The Passing of Traditional Society: Modernizing the Middle East* (Glencoe, Ill.: Free Press, 1958), 151.

2. Peter L. Berger, *The Sacred Canopy: Elements of a Sociological Theory of Religion* (Garden City, N.Y.: Doubleday, 1967), 517.

3. Alfred Stepan, "The Multiple Secularisms of Modern Democratic and Nondemocratic Regimes," in *Rethinking Secularism*, ed. Craig Calhoun, Mark Juergensmeyer, and Jonathan Van Antwerpen (Oxford: Oxford University Press, 2011), 115; Robert Alan Dahl, *Polyarchy: Participation and Opposition* (New Haven: Yale University Press, 1971), 739; Arend Lijphart, *Patterns of Democracy: Government Forms and Performance in Thirty-Six Countries* (New Haven: Yale University Press, 999), 738.

4. Guillermo A. O'Donnell, Philippe C. Schmitter, and the Latin American Program of the Woodrow Wilson International Center for Scholars, *Transitions from Authoritarian Rule: Tentative Conclusions About Uncertain Democracies* (Baltimore: Johns Hopkins University Press, 1986), 740.

5. Seymour Martin Lipset, "Some Social Requisites of Democracy: Economic Development and Political Legitimacy," *American Political Science Review* 53, no. 1 (1959): 92.

6. Adam Przeworski, *Democracy and the Market: Political and Economic Reforms in Eastern Europe and Latin America* (Cambridge: Cambridge University Press, 1991), 93.

7. Stathis N. Kalyvas, "Commitment Problems in Emerging Democracies—the Case of Religious Parties," *Comparative Politics* 32, no. 4 (2000): 379.

8. John Waterbury, "Democracy Without Democrats? The Potential for Political Liberation in the Middle East," in *Democracy Without Democrats? The Renewal of Politics in the Muslim World*, ed. Ghassan Salame (London: Tauris, 1994), 39.

9. Daniel Philpott, "Explaining the Political Ambivalence of Religion," *American Political Science Review* 101, no. 3 (2007): 505.

10. Alfred Stepan, "Religion, Democracy, and the 'Twin Tolerations,'" *Journal of Democracy* 11, no. 4 (2000): 37–57.

11. Jeffrey Haynes, *Religion and Politics in Africa* (London: Zed Books, 1996).

1. BENEVOLENT SECULARISM

12. Ahmet T. Kuru, *Secularism and State Policies Toward Religion: The United States, France, and Turkey* (Cambridge: Cambridge University Press, 2009), 304.

13. Jillian Schwedler, *Faith in Moderation: Islamist Parties in Jordan and Yemen* (Cambridge. Cambridge University Press, 2006), 187; J. A. Clark, "The Conditions of Islamist Moderation: Unpacking Cross-Ideological Cooperation in Jordan," *International Journal of Middle East Studies* 38, no. 4 (2006): 539–60; Michael D. Driessen, "Public Religion, Democracy, and Islam," *Comparative Politics* 44, no. 2 (2012): 171–89.

14. James Mahoney and Kathleen Ann Thelen, *Explaining Institutional Change: Ambiguity, Agency, and Power* (Cambridge: Cambridge University Press, 2010), 312.

15. Richard Rorty, "Religion as Conversation-Stopper," *Common Knowledge* 3, no. 1 (1994): 1–6.

16. Jürgen Habermas and Ciaran Cronin, *An Awareness of What Is Missing: Faith and Reason in a Post-secular Age* (Cambridge: Polity Press, 2011), 569; Jeffrey Stout, "The Folly of Secularism," *Journal of the American Academy of Religion* 76, no. 3 (2008): 533–44; Emile Perreau-Saussine, *Catholicism and Democracy: An Essay in the History of Political Thought* (Princeton: Princeton University Press, 2012); Abdullahi Ahmed an-Na im, *Islam and the Secular State: Negotiating the Future of Shari a* (Cambridge, Mass.: Harvard University Press, 2008).

17. Stepan, "Religion, Democracy, and the 'Twin Tolerations,'" 39–40.

18. Mahoney and Thelen, *Explaining Institutional Change*; Jacob Hacker, "Privatizing Risk Without Privatizing the Welfare State: The Hidden Politics of Social Policy Retrenchment in the United States," *American Political Science Review* 98, no. 2 (2004): 243–60.

19. It is possible, of course, for states to implement a basically new configuration of religion–state relations; this kind of institutional breakdown and replacement is distinct from secular evolution. One example of this alternative outcome is Sweden's decision to disestablish its official church in 2000. At that point, Sweden moved from a kind of liberal religious establishment to a secular state structure. It replaced its institutional relationship between religion and state.

20. Berger, *Sacred Canopy*, 108.

21. Karl Deutsch, "Social Mobilization and Political Development," *American Political Science Review* 55, no. 3 (1961): 498.

22. Ibid.; Samuel P. Huntington, *Political Order in Changing Societies* (New Haven: Yale University Press, 1968).

23. David T. Buckley and Luis Felipe Mantilla, "God and Governance: Development, State Capacity, and the Regulation of Religion," *Journal for the Scientific Study of Religion* 52, no. 2 (2013): 328–48.

24. Anthony James Gill, *The Political Origins of Religious Liberty* (Cambridge: Cambridge University Press, 2008); see also Roger Finke and Rodney Stark, *The*

Churching of America, 1776–1990: Winners and Losers in Our Religious Economy (New Brunswick, N.J.: Rutgers University Press, 1992).

25. Kalyvas, "Commitment Problems," 379; see also Carolyn Warner and Manfred Wenner, "Religion and the Political Organization of Muslims in Europe," *Perspectives on Politics* 4, no. 3 (2006): 457–79.

26. For one example, see George Packer, "The Moderate Martyr," *New Yorker*, September 11, 2006. For a broader discussion of the perils that can emerge in identifying ideologically "safe" religious allies for state outreach, see Elizabeth Shakman Hurd, *Beyond Religious Freedom: The New Global Politics of Religion* (Princeton: Princeton University Press, 2015).

27. Adam Przeworski and John D. Sprague, *Paper Stones: A History of Electoral Socialism* (Chicago: University of Chicago Press, 1986).

28. For one extended empirical example, see Jeremy Menchik, *Islam and Democracy in Indonesia: Tolerance Without Liberalism* (New York: Cambridge University Press, 2015).

29. In *American Grace: How Religion Divides and Unites Us* (New York: Simon & Schuster, 2011), Robert D. Putnam and David E. Campbell provide an impressive overview of the emergence of the Religious Right as a move reactive to perceived liberalization of broader political culture.

30. Stepan, "Multiple Secularisms"; Kuru, *Secularism and State Policies Toward Religion*; Jonathan Fox, *A World Survey of Religion and the State* (New York: Cambridge University Press, 2008).

31. Rajeev Bhargava, *Secularism and Its Critics* (Delhi: Oxford University Press, 1998): 493–94.

32. Ahmet T. Kuru, "Passive and Assertive Secularism," *World Politics* 59, no. 3 (2007): 568–94.

33. Rajeev Bhargava, "The Distinctiveness of Indian Secularism," in *The Future of Secularism*, ed. T. N. Srinivasan (Oxford: Oxford University Press, 2007), 40.

34. Jocelyne Cesari, *The Awakening of Muslim Democracy: Religion, Modernity, and the State* (New York: Cambridge University Press, 2014).

35. Bhargava, "The Distinctiveness of Indian Secularism," 41.

36. Ibid., 42.

37. Religious exemptions are certainly not new; the recognition of conscientious objectors to military service is only one common and old example. However, as states and international bodies have become increasingly active in policy ranging from regulation of hiring practices to promotion of healthy diet, religious communities have become more engaged in seeking exemptions from generally applied laws.

38. Kuru, "Passive and Assertive Secularism," 571.

39. I thank José Casanova for this elegant formulation.

40. Stepan, "Religion, Democracy, and the 'Twin Tolerations.'"

41. When describing the preferences of actors on either side of the religious-secular divide, I use the language of "interests" for the sake of convenience. Interests should not be taken in strictly material terms, however. Religious and secular actors bring a blend of material and normative interests to debates over religion–state relations.

42. William Gerald McLoughlin, "Pietism and the American Character," *American Quarterly* 17, no. 2 (1965): 163. McLoughlin's definition is drawn from the classic treatment of pietist movements by German theologian Ernst Troeltsch. See Troeltsch's distinction between church and sect in Ernst Troeltsch and Olive Wyon, *The Social Teaching of the Christian Churches* (New York: Macmillan, 1931).

43. Charles Hirschkind, "Civic Virtue and Religious Reason: An Islamic Counterpublic," *Cultural Anthropology* 16, no. 1 (2001): 17; see also Saba Mahmood, *Politics of Piety: The Islamic Revival and the Feminist Subject* (Princeton: Princeton University Press, 2005).

44. David Martin, "Secularization and the Future of Christianity," *Journal of Contemporary Religion* 20, no. 2 (2005): 145–60.

45. Stathis N. Kalyvas, *The Rise of Christian Democracy in Europe* (Ithaca: Cornell University Press, 1996).

46. José Casanova, *Public Religions in the Modern World* (Chicago: University of Chicago Press, 1994).

47. I use the term *anticlericalism* throughout to mean coercive exclusion of existing religious elites from the public sphere. Because religious structures vary across religious traditions, these elites may not always be "clerics" in the Christian sense but share a status as leaders of existing religious social structures. Anticlerical sentiment is not simply antireligious; rather, it is more particularly geared against an existing set of religious elites or authority structures.

48. For the purposes of this analysis, explicitly atheistic associations are generally treated as a portion of secular civil society rather than as a minority religious community in large part because such associations frequently do not want to be identified as just another religious denomination. Insofar as they affect the religious politics of democracy, it is through the religious-secular divide rather than through interfaith relations.

49. Ellen Lust, "Missing the Third Wave: Islam, Institutions, and Democracy in the Middle East," *Studies in Comparative International Development* 46 (2011): 163–90; Lisa Blaydes and Drew Linzer, "Elite Competition, Religiosity, and Anti-Americanism in the Islamic World," *American Political Science Review* 106, no. 2 (2012): 225–44; Ates Altinordu, "The Politicization of Religion: Political Catholicism and Political Islam in Comparative Perspective," *Politics & Society* 38, no. 4 (2010): 517–51.

50. Jonathan Fox, *Political Secularism, Religion, and the State: A Time Series Analysis of Worldwide Data* (New York: Cambridge University Press, 2015).

51. This logic of case selection during secular emergence is distinct from both of John Stuart Mill's traditional methods of case-based comparative inference. Like his Method of Similarity, the cases share an outcome and an independent variable of

interest. However, unlike that method, they also share several potential alternative explanations, but with values on those alternatives that should predict a negative rather than positive outcome. Thus, it is most straightforward to think of these cases as least likely according to alternative theories but likely according to the institutional theory set out earlier in this chapter.

52. David Collier, "Understanding Process Tracing," *PS: Political Science and Politics* 44, no. 4 (2011): 823–30.

53. Alexander L. George and Andrew Bennett, *Case Studies and Theory Development in the Social Sciences* (Cambridge, Mass.: MIT Press, 2005), 179.

54. José Casanova, "Civil Society and Religion: Retrospective Reflections on Catholicism and Prospective Reflections on Islam," *Social Research* 68, no. 4 (2001): 1041–80.

55. It should be noted that although Sufi Muslim brotherhoods dominate Islamic life in Senegal, there is diversity within the Muslim community, and even the largest brotherhoods (the Tidjanns and Mourides) do not count the allegiance of a clear majority of Senegal's population. And there is internal diversity even within religious groups normally assumed to be "hierarchical," such as the Catholic Church. On demographic grounds, one would certainly think that Senegal would have been a candidate for the secularism trap's snare. For more detailed analysis of the religious landscape of modern Senegal, see Khadim Mbacké and John O. Hunwick, *Sufism and Religious Brotherhoods in Senegal* (Princeton: Markus Wiener, 2005).

2. SECULAR EMERGENCE IN IRELAND

1. John Charles McQuaid Papers, Archives of the Archdiocese of Dublin, AB8/A/V(47–61).

2. John Gibbons, "Ayatollah Would Have Seen McQuaid as Kindred Spirit," *Irish Times*, August 6, 2009.

3. For an extended consideration of the distinct features of and unresolved tensions within the Irish constitutional approach to religion–state relations, see Eoin Daly, *Religion, Law, and the Irish State: The Constitutional Framework in Context* (Dublin: Clarus Press, 2012).

4. Bill Kissane, *New Beginnings: Constitutionalism and Democracy in Modern Ireland* (Dublin: University College Dublin Press, 2011), 68.

5. For a much more comprehensive analysis of distinct periods in Irish constitutional development, see ibid.

6. As with many postcolonial holdings, Ireland achieved full independence only after a protracted period that included limited local devolution of power. The Irish Free State of 1922 had a constitution but retained a legal relationship with the British Crown. The Free State Constitution was finally replaced with the Constitution of 1937, which removed references to the monarchy. The term *independence period* used

throughout this chapter thus refers roughly to the stretch between 1922 and 1937 as Irish nationalists crafted the institutions of the Republic of Ireland.

7. Central Statistics Office of Ireland, *1936 Census of Ireland* (Dublin: Stationery Office, 1936).

8. International Social Survey Programme Research Group, *International Social Survey Programme (ISSP): Religion III* (Cologne, Germany: GESIS, 2008).

9. Tom Inglis, *Moral Monopoly: The Rise and Fall of the Catholic Church in Modern Ireland*, 2nd ed. (Dublin: University College Dublin Press, 1998).

10. See ibid., 39–64, for a more detailed overview of the institutional structure of Catholicism in Ireland.

11. Central Statistics Office of Ireland, *1936 Census of Ireland*; ISSP Research Group, *ISSP: Religion III*; Central Statistics Office of Ireland, *2006 Census of Ireland* (Dublin: Stationery Office, 2006).

12. Dermot Keogh, "The Constitutional Revolution: An Analysis of the Making of the Constitution," in *The Constitution of Ireland 1937–1987*, ed. Frank Litton (Dublin: Institute of Public Administration, 1988), 22.

13. Gerard W. Hogan, "De Valera, the Constitution, and the Historians," *Irish Jurist* 40 (2005): 291–320.

14. The details of Endowment Clause jurisprudence in Ireland are beyond the scope of this analysis, but Irish jurists have rejected a simple analogy to U.S. Establishment Clause jurisprudence. Justice Keane wrote in 1998, "The provisions of our Constitution are, however, so markedly different that, as *Costello P.* found, [U.S. Establishment Clause jurisprudence was] not of assistance in the construction of Article 44.2.2 of the Constitution" (*Campaign to Separate Church and State Ltd v. Minister for Education*, 3 IR 321 [Supreme Court of Ireland, 1998], at 361).

15. *Re Article 26 and the Employment Equality Bill 1996*, 2 IR 321 (Supreme Court of Ireland, 1997), at 354.

16. *Campaign to Separate Church and State Ltd v. Minister for Education*, at 363.

17. *Quinn's Supermarket v. Attorney General*, IR 1 (Supreme Court of Ireland, 1972). As in many democracies, the Irish courts have not given a clear definition of which religions merit legal protection. This general challenge is part of what Winnifred Fallers Sullivan has provocatively called the "impossibility of religious freedom" that confronts all secular democracies (*The Impossibility of Religious Freedom* [Princeton: Princeton University Press, 2005]).

18. This is not to say that religious liberty is never restricted outside of the law. In one notorious episode in 1931, Catholics in County Mayo prevented a Protestant librarian from assuming her post on the grounds that her literary choices would corrupt Catholic youth (John Henry Whyte, *Church and State in Modern Ireland, 1923–1979*, 2nd ed. [Dublin: Gill and Macmillan, 1980], 43–46). Anti-Semitism has likewise reared its ugly head in Ireland at times in the modern period, though it is owed more to popular prejudice than to any formal force of law (Dermot Keogh, *Jews*

in Twentieth-Century Ireland: Refugees, Anti-Semitism, and the Holocaust [Cork, Ireland: Cork University Press, 1998]). In law, basic religious liberty has on balance been protected from the independence period to the present day.

19. *Thomas A. Maguire v. Attorney-General and Very Rev. Canon Maguire*, 77 ILTR 139 (Supreme Court of Ireland, 1943).

20. Some forms of religion–state collaboration in social services had begun to take place under British colonial rule. The process of providing for Catholic institutions included training of priests at state cost in Maynooth in 1795 (Inglis, *Moral Monopoly*, 114–17) and Catholic education with state funding by the mid–nineteenth century (Donald H. Akenson, *The Irish Education Experiment: The National System of Education in the Nineteenth Century* [London: Routledge & Kegan Paul, 1970]). As Ruth Barrington points out, a similar phenomenon took place on a smaller scale in the realm of health care, where orders of women religious became heavily involved in state workhouses ("Catholic Influence on the Health Services 1830–2000," in *Religion and Politics in Ireland at the Turn of the Millennium*, ed. James Patrick Mackey and Enda McDonagh [Dublin: Columba Press, 2003], 152–65). Although these policies involved financial transfers, they were more a means of colonial control than an indication of anything approaching benevolent secularism.

21. The place of religious education in Irish law and jurisprudence deserves far more detailed attention than it can receive in this book. For substantial overviews, see J. Whyte, *Church and State*, a classic treatment of the subject, as well as Eoin Daly, "The Constitution and the Protestant Schools Cuts Controversy: Seeing the Wood for the Trees," *Irish Journal of Legal Studies* 1, no. 1 (2010): 84–107, and Gerard Whyte, "Religion and Education: The Irish Constitution," paper presented at "TCD/IHRC Conference on Religion and Education: A Human Rights Perspective," Dublin, November 27, 2010, for more recent perspectives.

22. Irish Department of Education and Skills, *Information on Areas for Possible Divesting of Patronage of Primary Schools* (Dublin: Central Printing Office, 2011).

23. G. Whyte, "Religion and Education."

24. J. Whyte, *Church and State*, 54–55.

25. Ibid., 51.

26. Article 43 quoted in ibid., 53.

27. Ibid., 62–95.

28. Gerard W. Hogan, "Law and Religion: Church–State Relations in Ireland from Independence to the Present-Day," *American Journal of Comparative Law* 35, no. 1 (1987): 52.

29. J. Whyte, *Church and State*, 41.

30. Constitutional Review Group, *Report of the Constitutional Review Group* (Dublin: Stationery Office, 1996).

31. The story of Ireland's relations with the Vatican during the independence period is fascinating, and Dermot Keogh's comprehensive research gives a terrific sense

of the delicate balance that De Valera struck (*Ireland and the Vatican: The Politics and Diplomacy of Church–State Relations, 1922–1960* [Cork: Cork University Press, 1995]).

32. In addition to these formal institutional links, the informal positive links between the Catholic Church and the Irish state in the 1930s were extensive. John Whyte's classic account of the church–state relationship in this period documents numerous forms of positive state support for religion, including the state assistance granted to the Eucharistic Congress of 1932, the regular role of clerics in blessing new state infrastructure projects, and extensive pilgrimages by Irish officials looking to build political careers (*Church and State*, 45–50).

33. *O'Shiel v. Minister for Education*, 2 IR 321 (High Court of Ireland, 1999), at 347.

34. Daly, "The Constitution and the Protestant Schools Cuts Controversy."

35. Quoted in Dermot Keogh and Andrew McCarthy, *The Making of the Irish Constitution 1937: Bunreacht Nna Héireann* (Douglas Village, Ireland: Mercier Press, 2007), 154.

36. The accounts of Protestant objections to de Valera's visit to the United States in 1921 are extremely enlightening in this regard. A mob in virulently anti-Catholic Birmingham, Alabama, proved particularly disruptive to the future Irish leader. For more general accounts, see "Protestants Plead for Irish Republic," *New York Times*, April 6, 1920, and John Bowman, "De Valera on Ulster, 1919–1920: What He Told America," *Irish Studies in International Affairs* 1, no. 1 (1979): 3–18.

37. Kissane, *New Beginnings*, 67.

38. Quoted in Keogh, "Constitutional Revolution," 83.

39. Draft copy of the Constitution of 1937, McQuaid Papers, Archives of the Archdiocese of Dublin.

40. For the most comprehensive account of the archival materials related to McQuaid's influence on de Valera and the drafting process, see Keogh and McCarthy, *Making of the Irish Constitution 1937*.

41. Father Cahill's frequent approving references to the Polish Constitution of 1921 are telling in this regard. There, too, formal establishment was eschewed in favor of enshrining Catholic social thought in various constitutional provisions.

42. J. Whyte, *Church and State*, 12–16.

43. Joseph P. Walshe, "Secretary's Report to Eamon de Valera on His Visit to Rome," *Documents in Irish Foreign Policy* 5, no. 43 (1937), http://www.difp.ie/docs/1937/Visit-to-Rome-_-Constitution/2189.htm (accessed June 16, 2016).

44. Quoted in Keogh, *Ireland and the Vatican*, 80.

45. Quoted Marcus Tanner, *Ireland's Holy Wars: The Struggle for a Nation's Soul, 1500–2000* (New Haven: Yale University Press, 2001), 321–22.

46. Quoted in ibid., 315.

47. Ibid., 320.

48. Quoted in Kenneth Milne, "The Protestant Churches in Independent Ireland," in *Religion and Politics in Ireland at the Turn of the Millennium*, ed. James Patrick Mackey and Enda McDonagh (Dublin: Columba Press, 2003), 66.

49. Quoted in Tanner, *Ireland's Holy Wars*, 284.

50. Ibid., 207.

51. Reverend Trevor Morrow, interviewed by David T. Buckley, Dublin, May 17, 2011. Morrow, a former moderator of the Presbyterian Church in Ireland, pointed out this important relationship between de Valera and Irwin in conversation. Although Irwin certainly did not exercise the influence of Catholic clerics such as McQuaid, it is telling that Protestant clerics were involved in the drafting of the religion provisions. When de Valera wrote that the recognition of the Protestant denominations would appease their leaders, he was speaking from more than simple conjecture.

52. Quoted in Keogh, "Constitutional Revolution," 38.

53. Keogh, *Jews in Twentieth Century Ireland*.

54. Keogh, *Ireland and the Vatican*, 11. The Irish Catholic bishops had a tense relationship with militant republicanism, in particular the brand practiced by the republicans who rejected the Irish Free State and launched internal armed conflict in 1922.

55. Quoted in Kyle Dwyer, "De Valera and the Church's Special Position," *Irish Examiner*, January 5, 2013.

56. William Butler Yeats, "Debate on Divorce Legislation Resumed," *Seanad Eireann Debates* 5 (June 11, 1925): 435.

57. Quoted in Dermot Keogh, "The Jesuits and the 1937 Constitution," *Studies* 78, no. 309 (1989): 83.

58. Keogh, *Ireland and the Vatican*, 93–94.

59. Keogh relates a telling story of the Labour Party amending its party constitution in 1938 at the behest of the Catholic bishops, who worried that it went a step too far toward socialism. He remarks, "It must have been the first time in the history of European socialism that a party of the left changed its Constitution at the behest of Catholic bishops" ("Constitutional Revolution," 7).

60. Anthony James Gill, *The Political Origins Religious Liberty* (Cambridge: Cambridge University Press, 2008), 45.

61. Ibid., 291.

62. In *Church and State*, John Whyte provides a meticulous account of the Mother and Child Crisis debates and their fallout. Anyone with an interest in how the Catholic hierarchy exercised political influence during this period should spend an afternoon with his research.

63. Quoted in J. Whyte, *Church and State*, 242.

64. Quoted in ibid., 269.

65. Ibid., 270.

66. Ibid., 297.

3. SECULAR EVOLUTION IN IRELAND

1. "Kenny Defends Attack on Vatican," *Irish Independent*, September 4, 2011.

2. Quoted in David Quinn, "Atheism a Stranger to Reason," *Irish Catholic*, June 29, 2011.

3. Reverend Diarmuid Martin, "Keeping the Show on the Road: Is This the Future of the Irish Catholic Church?" speech to the Cambridge Group for Irish Studies, Magdalene College, Cambridge, February 22, 2011.

4. Bill Kissane, "The Illusion of State Neutrality in a Secularising Ireland," *West European Politics* 26, no. 1 (2003): 92.

5. Central Statistics Office of Ireland, *2011 Census of Ireland* (Dublin: Stationery Office, 2011).

6. Michael Nugent, interviewed by David T. Buckley, Dublin, May 16, 2011.

7. Archbishop Cahal Daly, testimony, New Ireland Forum, "Public Session: Thursday, 9 February 1984," Dublin Castle, Official Publications Collection, Trinity College Dublin.

8. Reverend Diarmuid Martin, "The Relationship Between Church and State," speech to the Mater Dei Institute, March 15, 2011, http://www.dublindiocese.ie/index.php?option=com_content&task=view&id=2333&Itemid=372 (accessed April 10, 2013).

9. Sister Ethna Regan, interviewed by David Buckley, Mater Dei Institute, Dublin, May 12, 2011.

10. Linda Hogan, interviewed by David Buckley, Trinity College Dublin, Dublin, May 12, 2011.

11. Father Gerry O'Hanlon, interviewed by David Buckley, Jesuit Centre for Faith and Justice, Dublin, May 19, 2011.

12. Martin, "Relationship Between Church and State."

13. Central Statistics Office of Ireland, *2011 Census of Ireland*.

14. Quoted in John Henry Whyte, *Church and State in Modern Ireland, 1923–1979*, 2nd ed. (Dublin: Gill and Macmillan, 1980), 349.

15. Reverend Dr. Trevor Morrow, interviewed by David Buckley, Dublin, May 17, 2011.

16. However, Irish High Court justice Gerard Hogan, writing in a nonofficial capacity, points out that the earlier version of Article 44 actually had in fact limited judicial impact ("Law and Religion: Church–State Relations in Ireland from Independence to the Present-Day," *American Journal of Comparative Law* 35, no. 1 [1987]: 47–96). Even early pro-church judges such as Justice Duffy were hesitant to use Article 44 to grant particular privileges to the church.

17. Quoted in Whyte, *Church and State*, 406.

18. *Mary McGee v. Attorney General and the Revenue Commissioners*, IR 1 (Supreme Court of Ireland, 1974), at 318. Even Chief Justice William FitzGerald, who dissented from the majority decision, went out of his way to insist that "the issue to

be determined is not based, and was not argued, on any issue related to any particular religion" (at 300).

19. New Ireland Forum, *Report of the New Ireland Forum* (Dublin: Central Printing Office, 1983), 21.

20. Ibid., 27.

21. No issue better captures this development than divorce. Unlike contraception, divorce was a constitutional prohibition and thus required a popular referendum for any change. Two referenda, in 1986 and 1995, eventually settled the matter in favor of liberalized divorce laws. The divorce restrictions in the Constitution of 1937 were clear and, as Gerard Hogan points out, "drafted so widely as to bring [the Constitution] into potential conflict with the canon law of the Catholic Church," which allows for the dissolution of marriages in limited circumstances ("Law and Religion," 84). In spite of polling that indicated initial support for the divorce referendum of 1986, the referendum went down to broad defeat, and a decade later it passed by less than one percentage point. Clearly, popular sentiment was more resistant to change than the Supreme Court majority that decided *McGee*. Nevertheless, the outcome of this extended and contentious process was a liberalization of laws and the further strengthening of the principled distance between state institutions and various religious communities.

22. Quoted in John Cooney, "Gormley: It's Time Bishops Stopped Interfering," *Irish Independent*, June 18, 2010.

23. Some may point to ongoing abortion restrictions as an indication that secularism in Ireland still tilts to Catholic interests. To an extent, this is true; Catholic leaders in Ireland have resolutely opposed advocates of abortion provision in Ireland, as they have around the world. Linda Hogan, former member of the Irish Council for Bioethics, pointed out in a conversation with me that other areas at the intersection of science and religion likely to provoke the Catholic hierarchy, in particular reproductive assistance, are largely unlegislated (interview, May 12, 2011). However, chalking up enduring Catholic influence in these areas to some imperfection in Irish state secularism is off the mark. As Emily O'Reilly documents at length, the forces that have opposed abortion are primarily lay Catholic associations, not the official hierarchy (*Masterminds of the Right* [Dublin: Attic Press, 1992]). Moreover, Catholic leaders who have opposed abortion generally ground their arguments in natural law appeals to human dignity, which are not necessarily sectarian. Indeed, evangelical and Muslim communities have generally agreed with the Catholic position on abortion; as Linda Hogan puts it, "on values issues, these communities are happy to let Catholic groups do the lifting" (interview, May 12, 2011).

24. Kissane, "Illusion of State Neutrality," 88.

25. Ruairi Quinn, "Launch of Forum on Patronage and Pluralism in the Primary Sector," Department of Education and Skills, Dublin, April 19, 2011.

26. Reformers must balance various constitutional interests throughout this process. On the one hand, Article 42.3.1 forbids the state from "oblig[ing] parents in violation

of their conscience and lawful preference to send their children to schools established by the State, or to any particular type of school designated by the state." Article 42.4 goes on to guarantee free primary education "with due regard for the rights of parents, especially in the matter of religious and moral formation." This deference to parents' preferences is increasingly difficult to implement in pluralist Ireland. Moreover, the state does not have the option of simply removing itself from moral instruction, as is the case in the United States. Article 42.3.2 requires "children receive a certain minimum education, moral, intellectual, and social," and Article 44.2.4 requires that "state aid for schools shall not discriminate between schools under the management of different denominations."

27. There are basically two types of nondenominational primary schools. The first is controlled by a group called Educate Together, which promotes a multireligious curriculum. This type is discussed in some depth in this chapter. There are approximately sixty Educate Together primary schools, with 13,000 students, across Ireland (John Holohan, interviewed by David Buckley, Dublin, May 19, 2011). The second type is controlled by Vocational Educational Committees, which control a range of secondary schools but only a small handful of primary schools.

28. Eoin Daly, "Citizens Should Have Access to Non-sectarian Public Schools," *Irish Times*, May 26, 2011.

29. Eoin Daly, interviewed by David Buckley, Dublin, May 26, 2011.

30. Nugent interview, May 16, 2011.

31. John Coolahan, "Address for the Launch of the Forum on Patronage and Pluralism in the Primary Sector," Clock Tower, Department of Education and Skills, Dublin, April 19, 2011.

32. Holohan interview, May 19, 2011.

33. Katy Radford, *Health, Faith, and Equality* (Dublin: Irish School of Ecumenics, 2008).

34. Ali Selim, interviewed by David Buckley, Islamic Cultural Centre of Ireland, Dublin, May 23, 2011.

35. Oliver Scharbrodt, interviewed by David Buckley, Cork, Ireland, May 16, 2011. Although Islam has generally been incorporated within Irish secularism, with all of its typical benevolence, there have been limited areas of friction. For instance, An Garda Síochána, the Irish police association, has ruled that Sikh head coverings are not permitted according to its uniform code.

36. Kieran Flynn, "Understanding Islam in Ireland," *Islam and Christian–Muslim Relations* 17, no. 2 (2006): 223–38.

37. Claire Hogan, interviewed by David Buckley, Dublin, May 20, 2011.

38. Quoted in Flynn, "Understanding Islam," 230.

39. Selim interview, May 23, 2011.

40. Patricia McDonagh, "Muslim Anger at Opposition Calls for School Ban on Hijab," *Irish Independent*, June 2, 2008.

41. Archbishop Cahal Daly, testimony, New Ireland Forum, "Public Session: Thursday, 9 February 1984." Daly referenced Protestants in Northern Ireland, but the substance of his testimony applied much more broadly to ensuring equal protection for Protestants across the island of Ireland.

42. Coolahan, "Address for the Launch of the Forum on Patronage."

43. Andy Pollak, "President Opens Centre for Islam in Clonskeagh," *Irish Times*, November 15, 1996.

44. Ali Selim, "Urgent Need for Interfaith Dialogue Based on Mutual Trust," *Irish Times*, April 22, 2008.

45. Ciaran Byrne and Shane Doran, "Muslims Give Their Blessing: Vast Majority Very Happy Here, Says Poll," *Irish Independent*, December 19, 2006.

46. Selim interview, May 23, 2011.

47. Patsy McGarry, "The Changing Face of Faith," *Irish Times*, May 10, 2008.

48. Enda Kenny, "Remarks on Structured Dialogue," *Dáil Debate* 762, no. 3 (April 24, 2012): 308.

49. Quoted in Carl O'Brien, "Quinn Presses Orders Over Redress Shortfall," *Irish Times*, July 11, 2011. In informal communication with me, Ruairi Quinn expressed his interest in Catholic theological debates between thinkers such as Joseph Ratzinger (Pope Benedict XVI) and Hans Kung.

50. Brigid Reynolds, Sean Healy, and Conference of Religious of Ireland, *Social Partnership in a New Century* (Dublin: Conference of Religious of Ireland Justice Commission, 1999).

51. Bertie Ahern, "Speech by an Taoiseach, Mr. Bertie Ahern T.D., at the Inauguration of the Structured Dialogue with Churches, Faith Communities, and Non-confessional Bodies," Dublin Castle, February 26, 2007.

52. Bertie Ahern, "Address by an Taoiseach, Bertie Ahern T.D., at a Reception for Churches and Faith Communities in the Structured Dialogue," Dublin, April 22, 2008.

53. Although broader in focus than simple reform of primary-school patronage, the IHRC report was timed to shape the patronage debate. The IHRC is a semigovernmental agency tasked by the Human Rights Commission Act of 2000 with providing the Irish state with a report on the state's compliance on a range of international human rights documents. Although Minister Quinn was not bound by the IHRC recommendations, they certainly reflect a kind of consensus on the direction that pragmatic reform should take. The report's launch at the Dublin City Council attracted a large crowd and substantial media attention as a window into the likely shape of future education reform in Ireland.

54. The report's recommendations go on in some detail to describe how this denominational system might be brought in line with human rights standards, including reforms to curriculum elements that may violate the rights of nonbelievers, the expansion of Ombudsman bodies to oversee denominational school compliance, and

the relocation of religious instruction to the beginning or end of the day to facilitate students who wish to be exempt from this portion of the day (Irish Human Rights Commission [IHRC], *Religion and Education: A Human Rights Perspective* [Dublin: IHRC, 2011], 104–6).

55. Binchy played a leading role as a well-respected conservative spokesman during the contentious referenda debates of the 1980s and 1990s (O'Reilly, *Masterminds of the Right*). Even those who disagree with him on all issues spoke warmly of his intellect. Binchy's role as launcher of the IHRC report is perhaps the strongest, if most subtle, sign that patronage reform in Ireland is not likely to fundamentally overturn the existing benevolent relationship between religion and state there.

56. International Social Survey Programme Research Group, *International Social Survey Programme (ISSP): Religion III* (Cologne, Germany: GESIS, 2008).

57. *Fitzpatrick v. K*, IEHC 000 (High Court of Ireland, April 2008).

58. Gay and Lesbian Equality Network (GLEN), *Dail Debates on Civil Partnership* (Dublin: GLEN, 2010).

59. David Quinn, interview by David Buckley, Dublin, Ireland, May 25, 2011.

60. Section 37 of these acts states that "religious, educational or medical institutions" are not engaged in discrimination if they give "favourable treatment" or "take[] action which is reasonably necessary to prevent an employee or a prospective employee from undermining the religious ethos of that institution." In practice, these exemptions have been particularly important in hiring for religious schools. As Peter Mullan, communications director for the Irish National Teachers Organization, put it to me, "A lot of our members live in fear" that Catholic authorities may decide to release them from employment because of homosexuality (interviewed by David Buckley, Dublin, May 24, 2011).

4. SECULAR EMERGENCE IN SENEGAL

1. Ahmet T. Kuru, "Passive and Assertive Secularism," *World Politics* 59, no. 3 (2007): 568–94.

2. Alfred Stepan and Graeme B. Robertson, "Arab, Not Muslim, Exceptionalism," *Journal of Democracy* 15, no. 4 (2004): 140–46.

3. Khadim Mbacké and John O. Hunwick, *Sufism and Religious Brotherhoods in Senegal* (Princeton: Markus Wiener, 2005).

4. David Robinson, "French 'Islamic' Policy and Practice in Late Nineteenth-Century Senegal," *Journal of African History* 29 (1988): 415–35.

5. Ed Van Hoven, "The Nation Turbaned? The Construction of Nationalist Muslim Identities in Senegal," *Journal of Religion in Africa* 30, no. 2 (2000): 225–48.

6. Senegal is not the only case where French colonial religion–state policy did not bear a resemblance to *laïcité* in mainland France. As J. P. Daughton points out in his excellent study of religion in French colonial Indochina, Madagascar, and Polynesia,

even at the height of anticlericalism in mainland France colonial administrators frequently found a place for religious communities in public functions such as education and health care (*An Empire Divided: Religion, Republicanism, and the Making of French Colonialism, 1880–1914* [Oxford: Oxford University Press, 2006]). One French administrator in Senegal remarked that anticlerical *laïcité* would be counterproductive because the Muslim leaders and population "were happy to see that the whites had religious leaders of their own" (quoted in Elizabeth Foster, "An Ambiguous Monument: Dakar's Colonial Cathedral of the Souvenir Africain," *French Historical Studies* 32, no. 1 [2009]: 107).

7. Djibril Samb, *Comprendre la laïcité* (Dakar, Senegal: Nouvelles éditions africaines du Sénégal, 2005), 116; all translations are mine unless otherwise noted.

8. Quoted in Souleymane Bachir Diagne, "A Secular Age and the World of Islam," in *Tolerance, Democracy, and Sufis in Senegal*, ed. Mamadou Diouf (New York: Columbia University Press, 2013), 46.

9. Kuru, "Passive and Assertive Secularism."

10. Samb, *Comprendre la laïcité*, 126–27.

11. It is important to acknowledge that although Senegal did move steadily toward democracy after independence, there were still real constraints on political competition throughout Senghor's terms in office. The executive strictly limited political parties. The basic features of *laïcité* thus emerged during a period that was imperfectly democratic. See Leonardo Alfonso Villalón, "Negotiating Islam in the Era of Democracy: Senegal in Comparative Regional Perspective," in Diouf, *Tolerance, Democracy, and Sufis in Senegal*, 239–68.

12. Samb, *Comprendre la laïcité*, 115.

13. Roman Loimeier, "The Secular State and Islam in Senegal," in *Questioning the Secular State: The Worldwide Resurgence of Religion in Politics*, ed. David Westerlund (London: Hurst, 1996), 183–97.

14. Donal B. Cruise O'Brien, "Le contrat social sénégalais à l'épreuve," *Politique Africaine* 45 (2003): 9–20.

15. Donal B. Cruise O'Brien, *Symbolic Confrontations: Muslims Imagining the State in Africa* (New York: Palgrave Macmillan, 2003).

16. Loimeier "Secular State," 187–89.

17. Diagne, "A Secular Age and the World of Islam," 46.

18. Khadim Mbacké, interviewed by David Buckley, Dakar, Senegal, June 30, 2010.

19. Étienne Smith, "Religious and Cultural Pluralism in Senegal," in Diouf, *Tolerance, Democracy and Sufis in Senegal*, 147.

20. Joseph-Roger de Benoist, *Histoire de l'Église Catholique au Sénégal: Du milieu du Xve siècle à l'aube du troisième millénaire* (Dakar, Senegal: Karthala, 2008), 431.

21. It is important to note that the principled distance of Senegalese secularism is imperfectly realized. Fatou Kiné Camara argues that traditional African religions remain slighted by the secular state (interviewed by David Buckley, Dakar, Senegal,

June 23, 2010). Although Muslim and Catholic groups clearly are within the bounds of contemporary principled distance, it is less clear how smaller Christian or other religious communities fit within this lasting pattern.

22. These land concessions were in fact another preindependence legacy, indicating the strong path-dependent character of the religion–state relationship in Senegal. In 1928, the French granted land ownership over Touba's Grand Mosque and four hundred hectares around it to the family of the *khalife general*, and the brotherhood has built on this general pattern ever since to consolidate its influence (Cheikh Guèye, *Touba: La capitale des Mourides* [Dakar, Senegal: Karthala, 2002], 286).

23. Cruise O'Brien, *Symbolic Confrontations*, 35.

24. Souleymane Bachir Diagne, interviewed by David Buckley, New York, March 2010.

25. Cheikh Anta Babou, "The Senegalese 'Social Contract' Revisited," in Diouf, *Tolerance, Democracy, and Sufis in Senegal*, 126.

26. David Robinson, *Paths of Accommodation: Muslim Societies and French Colonial Authorities in Senegal and Mauritania, 1880–1920* (Athens: Ohio University Press, 2000).

27. Robert Fatton, "Clientelism and Patronage in Senegal," *African Studies Review* 29, no. 4 (1986): 66.

28. Quoted in Leonardo Villalón, *Islamic Society and State Power in Senegal: Disciples and Citizens in Fatick* (Cambridge: Cambridge University Press, 1995), 207–8.

29. Quoted in Christian Coulon, *Le marabout et le prince: Islam et pouvoir au Sénégal* (Paris: Pedone, 1981), 159.

30. Roman Loimeier, "Dialectics of Religion and Politics in Senegal," in *New Perspectives on Islam in Senegal*, ed. Mamadou Diouf and Mara Lieichtman (New York: Palgrave MacMillan, 2009), 241.

31. Senghor's personal skill should also be given at least some of the credit for this outcome. When the Conseil supérieur demanded reserved seats under its control, Senghor cleverly said that half of the seats would be too few for Muslims, given Senegal's general population, and proposed a larger number that would not be controlled by the Conseil (Mbacké and Hunwick, *Sufism and Religious Brotherhoods*, 108–9).

32. Alfred Stepan, "Stateness, Democracy, and Respect: Senegal in Comparative Perspective," in Diouf, *Tolerance, Democracy, and Sufis in Senegal*, 205–38.

33. Léopold Sédar Senghor, *Liberté* (Paris: Éditions du seuil, 1964).

34. Senghor argued that Christians and Muslims in Africa faced a similar opportunity for linking their religions with socialism. He even linked Teilhard's thought to that of "reforming Muslims" working during the same time period (Léopold Sédar Senghor, *Pierre Teilhard de Chardin et la politique africaine* [Paris: Éditions du seuil, 1962], 65).

35. Quoted in Irving Markovitz, "The Political Thought of Blaise Diagne and Lamine Guèye: Some Aspects of Social Structure and Ideology in Senegal," *Présence Africaine*, no. 72 (1969): 37.

36. Mamadou Diouf, "Introduction: The Public Role of the 'Good Muslim': Sufi Islam and the Administration of Pluralism," in Diouf, *Tolerance, Democracy, and Sufis in Senegal*, 16.

37. Quoted in Markovitz, "Political Thought of Blaise Diagne and Lamine Guèye," 34.

38. Quoted in ibid., 37.

39. Loimeier, "The Secular State," 186.

40. Markovitz, "Political Thought of Blaise Diagne and Lamine Guèye," 38.

41. Conference Episcopale du Sénégal, *Paroles d'eveques 1963–2000* (Dakar, Senegal: Imprimerie Saint-Paul, 2000), 30.

42. Quoted in Léon Diouf, *Église locale et crise africaine: Le Diocèse de Dakar* (Paris: Karthala, 2001), 80.

43. Ibid.

44. De Benoist, *Histoire de l'Église*, 420.

45. Smith, "Religious and Cultural Pluralism in Senegal," 159.

46. Anthony Gill, *The Political Origins of Religious Liberty* (Cambridge: Cambridge University Press, 2008).

47. Stathis N. Kalyvas, "Commitment Problems in Emerging Democracies: The Case of Religious Parties," *Comparative Politics* 32, no. 4 (2000): 379–98.

48. José Casanova, *Public Religions in the Modern World* (Chicago: University of Chicago Press, 1994).

49. Quoted in Villalón, *Islamic Society*, 228.

50. Fonds de la Code de la famille, Archives nationales du Sénégal, Dakar.

51. Maïmouna Gueye, "Code du statut personnel ou Code de la famille," *Le Soleil*, April 23, 2003.

52. Cited in Villalón, *Islamic Society*, 229.

53. Quoted in ibid.

5. SECULAR EVOLUTION IN SENEGAL

1. Cheikh Guèye, *Touba: La capitale des Mourides* (Dakar, Senegal: Karthala, 2002), 274; all translations are mine unless otherwise noted.

2. Pew Forum on Religion and Public Life, *Tolerance and Tension: Islam and Christianity in Sub-Saharan Africa* (Washington, D.C.: Pew Research Group, 2007).

3. Michael Bratton, E. Gyimah-Boadi, and Robert Mattes, *Afrobarometer Round 3: The Quality of Democracy and Governance in 18 African Countries, 2005–2006*, ICPSR 22981-v1 (Ann Arbor, Mich.: Inter-university Consortium for Political and Social Research, 2009).

4. Assane Diagne, interviewed by David Buckley, Dakar, Senegal, June 18, 2010; Abdoul Aziz Kébé, interviewed by David Buckley, Dakar, Senegal, June 29, 2010.

5. Boubacar Seck, interviewed by David Buckley, Dakar, Senegal, June 22, 2010.

6. Khadim Mbacké, interviewed by David Buckley, Dakar, Senegal, June 30, 2010.

7. Shaheen Mozaffar and Richard Vengroff, "A 'Whole System' Approach to the Choice of Electoral Rules in Democratizing Countries: Senegal in Comparative Perspective," *Electoral Studies* 21, no. 4 (2002): 601–16; Dennis Galvan, "Political Turnover and Social Change in Senegal," *Journal of Democracy* 12, no. 3 (2001): 51–63; L. J. Beck, "Reining in the Marabouts? Democratization and Local Governance in Senegal," *African Affairs* 100, no. 401 (2001): 601–21.

8. This pluralization was likely intended to fragment the opposition to Parti socialiste rule, although it may have in the end encouraged the internal Socialist splits that eased President Wade into power in the run-off election in 2000. Abdou Diouf enjoyed a slight plurality after the first round of elections in 2000 but received essentially the same share of the vote in the second round, whereas Wade gathered support from other major candidates, including Moustapha Niasse, a former Socialist minister who broke with Abdou Diouf before the election and helped to seal his eventual defeat.

9. Boubacar Seck interview, June 22, 2010.

10. Beck, "Reining in the Marabouts."

11. These kinds of succession struggles have clearly contributed to the fragmentation in the Tidjann community, and although the Mourides have thus far maintained a more coherent authority structure, internal dissension appears to be on the rise among them as well.

12. The growth of diverse Muslim religious media outlets, particularly in urban areas, is also tied to this broad process of pluralization. Roman Loimeier points out the wide array of radio and newspaper sources, in particular the widely respected newspaper *Wal Fadjri*, that are Muslim in nature but not directly controlled by the central leaders of any brotherhood ("Dialectics of Religion and Politics in Senegal," in *New Perspectives on Islam in Senegal*, ed. Mamadou Diouf and Mara Lieichtman [New York: Palgrave MacMillan, 2009], 237–56).

13. Kébé interview, June 29, 2010.

14. Ellen Foley and Cheikh Anta Babou, "Diaspora, Faith, and Science: Building a Mouride Hospital in Senegal," *African Affairs* 110 (2010): 75–95.

15. Guèye, *Touba*, 271.

16. Léon Diouf, *Église locale et crise africaine: Le Diocése de Dakar* (Paris: Karthala, 2001), 92.

17. Conference Episcopal du Sénégal, *Paroles d'eveques 1963–2000* (Dakar, Senegal: Imprimerie Saint-Paul, 2000), 241.

18. Théodore Ndok Ndiaye, interviewed by David Buckley, Dakar, Senegal, June 26, 2010.

19. Leonardo Alfonso Villalón, "From Argument to Negotiation: Constructing Democracy in African Muslim Contexts," *Comparative Politics* 42, no. 4 (2010): 375–93.

20. Marie Brossier, "Les débats sur le Droit de la famille au Sénégal," *Politique Africaine* 96 (2004): 78–98.

21. El Hadji Abdoulaye Thiam, "Visite de Mandické Niang au Vatican," *Le Soleil*, March 16, 2010.

22. Thiané Ndiaye, "Me Abdoulaye Wade lors la rencontre des Imams et oulémas du Sénégal," *Le Messager*, April 27, 2006.

23. The Mourides have a stricter *marabout*–disciple relationship by reputation, and an interesting survey by the Groupe d'etudes et de recherches constitutionnelles et politiques in 1999 indicates that Mourides are more likely to obey political advice from their *marabouts* than are Tidjann disciples (*Étude sur le comportement electoral dans les regions de Thies et Diourbel* [St. Louis, Senegal: Université Gaston Berger, 1999]).

24. Xavier Audrain, "Du 'ndiggël avorté' au Parti de la vérité," *Politique Africaine* 96 (2004): 99–118.

25. Kébé interview, June 29, 2010.

26. Guèye, *Touba*, 282.

27. Rajeev Bhargava, *Secularism and Its Critics* (Delhi: Oxford University Press, 1998), 504.

28. Quoted in Louis Seck, "Wade demande à ses ministres d'aller recueillir des prières à Touba avant chaque mission importante," *Le Populaire*, January 21, 2011.

29. G. Nesta Diop, "Avec un seul ministre et quatre députés: Les chrétiens du Sénégal crient leur frustration," *Wal Fadjri*, June 25, 2007.

30. Jean-Pierre Mane, "Les chrétiens 'zappes' dans la distribution des terres," *L'Observateur*, May 25, 2010.

31. "Le directeur de la Sûreté nationale: 'Jean-Paul Dias n'a pas été interpellé à l'intérieur de la cathédrale,'" Agence de presse sénégalaise, April 14, 2006.

32. Quoted in "Le Cardinal Sarr déplore des 'propos insupportable' du président de la république," Agence de presse sénégalaise, December 30, 2009.

33. Sall was recorded making this statement in a video by Cheikh Fall, "Macky Sall répond sur la relation entre marabouts et president," February 29, 2012, http://www.youtube.com/watch?v=DPZNHPNUAD4 (accessed April 10, 2013).

34. Jean-Emile Charlier, "Le retour de Dieu: L'introduction de l'enseignement religieux dans l'ecole de la Republique du Sénégal," *Education et Societes* 10, no. 2 (2002): 95–112.

35. Both of these reforms were in part driven by the desire to meet international development standards for progress in education. Universal primary education is one of the Millennium Development Goals that Senegal has worked hard to attain, which is no small feat given the country's poverty. State elites justified the policy changes by arguing that increasing religious education will broaden enrollment. The thinking is that religious education in public schools will increase their appeal to Muslim parents, and any move to increase oversight of the *daaras* may be a more pragmatic path to progress than simply wishing that informal education would disappear from urban areas.

36. Kébé interview, June 29, 2010.

37. Quoted in Charlier, "Retour de Dieu," 108. Fatou Kiné Camara pointed out that the religious education available would continue to privilege Muslim and Catholic options over traditional African beliefs (interviewed by David Buckley, Dakar, Senegal, June 23, 2010).

38. Quoted in Charles Gaïky Diene, "Bamba Ndiaye (nouveau ministre chargé des affaires religieuses)," *Wal Fadjri*, January 12, 2010.

39. "Decret No. 2009-1134," *Journal Officiel du Sénégal*, October 14, 2009.

40. Guèye, *Touba*, 281.

41. Abdoul Aziz Kébé, *Argumentaire religieux musulman sur l'equite de genre* (Dakar, Senegal: Ministre de developpement social, la famille et de la solidarite nationale, 2006), 20. Senegal's rate of female genital mutilation has dipped lower than 30 percent and is trending downward among younger women, in comparison to the UNICEF-reported rates of more than 90 percent in neighboring states such as Mali and nearly 80 percent in Gambia.

42. Paul Sanga, interviewed by David Buckley, Dakar, Senegal, June 22, 2010.

43. Abbé Alphonse Seck, interviewed by David Buckley, Dakar, Senegal, June 25, 2010; Assane Diagne interview, June 18, 2010.

44. Villalón, "From Argument to Negotiation," 384.

45. "Collectif pour la défense de la laïcité et de l'unité nationale au Sénégal," 2003, http://www.wluml.org/fr/node/1060 (accessed April 10, 2013).

46. Quoted in Diene, "Bamba Ndiaye."

47. Assises nationales du Sénégal, *Charte de gouvernance démocratique* (Dakar, Senegal: Assises nationales, 2009). The Assises' attention to the restoration of *laïcité* arose in several interviews, particularly with Boubacar Seck of CONGAD.

48. Abbé Jacques Seck, interviewed by David Buckley, Dakar, Senegal, June 25, 2010.

49. Moriba Magassouba, *L'Islam au Sénégal: Demain les mollahs? La "question" musulmane et les partis politiques au Sénégal de 1946 à nos jours* (Paris: Karthala, 1985), 205.

50. Quoted in Pape Modou Lo, "Des imams solidaires à l'église prient pour une alternance politique," *PressAfrik*, January 3, 2010, http://www.pressafrik.com/Des-imams-solidaires-a-l-eglise-prient-pour-une-alternance-politique_a18563.html (accessed April 10, 2013).

51. Assane Diagne interview, June 18, 2010.

52. Quoted in Joseph Diedhiou and Charles Gaïky Diene, "Réaction du Cardinal Théodore Adrien Sarr: Wade au ban de l'église," *Wal Fadjri*, December 30, 2009.

53. Quoted in Cécile Sow, "Un president, un monument et une polemique," *Jeune Afrique*, August 11, 2009.

54. Abbé Alphonse Seck interview, June 25, 2010.

55. U.S. Department of State, "International Religious Freedom Report 2007: Senegal," 2007, http://www.state.gov/j/drl/rls/irf/2007/90117.htm (accessed May 23, 2016).
56. Alphonse Seck interview, June 25, 2010.
57. Kiné Camara interview, June 23, 2010.
58. "Darou Salam: Me Wade réaffirme son appartenance au mouridisme," Agence de presse sénégalaise, February 22, 2012; "Wade à Touba: Plus d 200 millions pour un 'ngiguel,'" Seneweb News, February 15, 2012.
59. Ibrahima Lissa Faye, "En visite à Tivaouane: Wade hué par des jeunes," Press Afrik, February 2, 2012.
60. Ben Abass, "Les petits fils d'el H. Malick Sy exigent la démission d'Ousmane Ngom et des excuses publiques de Wade," PressAfrik, February 22, 2012.
61. "Sénégal: Le gouvernement s'excuse de la 'profanation' de la mosquée," Le Monde, February 19, 2012.
62. Eveques du Sénégal, "Pour quel Sénégal après Mai 1998," in Paroles des eveques 1963–2000 (Dakar, Senegal: Impremerie Saint-Paul, 2005), 203.
63. Kébé interview, June 29, 2010.
64. Youssoupha Mine, "Des imams et le Cardinal Sarr pourraient jouer la médiation pour l'apaisement," Le Populaire, May 7, 2011.
65. Eugène Kaly, "Observation de l'élection présidentielle: L'Église Catholique est satisfaite du déroulement du scrutiny," Le Soleil, March 1, 2012.
66. "Touba: Quatre dignitaires Mourides tenteraient de donner un 'ndigël' au nom du khalife," Seneweb-News, March 13, 2012, http://www.seneweb.com/news/Societe/touba-quatre-dignitaires-mourides-tenteraient-de-donner-un-quot-ndigel-quot-au-nom-du-khalife_n_61446.html (accessed April 10, 2013).
67. Quoted in Abdoulaye Camara, "Dernier Cheikh du 5e khalife des Mourides: 'Wade n'a pas entendu les consignes de Serigne Saliou,'" Walfadjri, October 5, 2010.
68. Boucar Aliou Diallo, "Lobbying avorté de Wade pour une audience auprès de Serigne Sidy Mokhtar Mbacké: Le Khalife dans l'isoloir spirituel à Tawfekh," Le Quotidien, March 7, 2012.
69. Kébé interview, June 29, 2010.
70. Diallo, "Lobbying avorté."
71. Quoted in Mously Ndiaye, "Macky Sall apres sa visite a Tivaouane et a Ndiassane: 'Aucun marabout ne donnera de ndigël dans ce pays,'" Le Populaire, March 13, 2012.
72. Quoted in ibid.
73. See Fall, "Macky Sall," for a video of Sall making these remarks at a press conference.
74. Quoted in Christine Holzbauer, "Entretien: Macky Sall, candidat à la présidentielle au Sénégal: 'Il ne faut pas créer des fractures pour gagner les elections,'" La Croix, March 12, 2012.

75. Pew Forum on Religion and Public Life, *Tolerance and Tension*.

76. Probing any religious-secular divide in public opinion is difficult in Senegal because essentially the entire population both identifies with a religion and identifies religion as very important in their lives. As a statistical matter, I thus focus on the Mouride community and on interfaith comparisons. The nature of the "secular bloc" in Senegal is of broader theoretical interest as well, and I take it up in the chapter's conclusion.

77. Guèye, *Touba*, 287.

78. Kiné Camara interview, June 23, 2010.

79. Alphonse Seck interview, June 25, 2010.

6. SECULAR EMERGENCE IN THE PHILIPPINES

1. *Estrada v. Escritor*, 455 Phil. 411 (Supreme Court of the Philippines, 2003). Many thanks to Pats Alcantara for his generous help in navigating Philippine case law related to religion and politics (interviewed by David Buckley, Quezon City, August 19, 2010).

2. Ahmet T. Kuru, *Secularism and State Policies Toward Religion: The United States, France, and Turkey* (Cambridge: Cambridge University Press, 2009).

3. Ricardo Abad, "Religion in the Philippines," *Philippine Studies* 49, no. 3 (2001): 337–55.

4. Horacio De la Costa and John N. Schumacher, *Church and State: The Philippine Experience*, Loyal Papers (Manila: Loyola Papers Board of Editors, 1978).

5. Christl Kessler and Jürgen Rüland, *Give Jesus a Hand! Charismatic Christians, Populist Religion, and Politics in the Philippines* (Quezon City, Philippines: Ateneo de Manila University Press, 2008).

6. International Social Survey Programme Research Group, *International Social Survey Programme (ISSP): Religion III* (Cologne, Germany: GESIS, 2008).

7. Ibid.

8. Cited in *Pamil v. Teleron*, 86 SCRA 413 (Supreme Court of the Philippines, 1978).

9. Nicolas Villarruz, *Commentaries and Opinions on the Constitution of the Philippines* (Manila: Imprenta Manila, 1935), 120.

10. Quoted in Orlando M. Hernando, "Quezon and the Rule of Law in the Philippines," *Journal of Church and State* 5 (1963): 223.

11. Joaquin G. Bernas, *The Constitution of the Republic of the Philippines: With Annotations Based on Commission Deliberations* (Manila: Rex Book Store, 1987), 105.

12. In *The Church and Its Social Involvement in the Philippines, 1930–1972* (Quezon City, Philippines: Ateneo de Manila University Press, 1988), Wilfredo Fabros provides an extensive overview of Catholic efforts to shape state policy during the commonwealth and early years of independence. Although Catholic views did not

6. SECULAR EMERGENCE IN THE PHILIPPINES 225

always prevail, there were extensive patterns of consultation that emerged during this period.

13. Quoted in Hernando, "Quezon and the Rule of Law," 225.

14. Jorge A. Coquia, "Religious Freedom in the Philippines," *Philippine Studies* 4, no. 1 (1956): 15–30.

15. *Victoriano v. Elizalde Rope Workers Union*, 59 SCRA 54 (Supreme Court of the Philippines, 1974).

16. Peter Gowing, "Mandate in Moroland: The American Government of Muslim Filipinos, 1899–1920," PhD diss., Syracuse University, 1968, 812.

17. Anshari Ali, "Islamic Family Law in the Philippines: A Historical Survey," *Al-Shajarah: Journal of the International Institute of Islamic Thought and Civilization* 6, no. 1 (2001): 114–15.

18. Linda Luz Guerrero, Hamid Barra, Mahar Mangahas, and Vladymir Joseph Licudine, *The Code of Muslim Personal Laws in Practice: What Influential Muslims and Sharia Lawyers Think* (Quezon City, Philippines: Social Weather Stations, 2007), 1.

19. Michael Mastura, "Maguindana on Hopes and Fears from the Constitutional Convention," in *Understanding Islam and Muslims in the Philippines*, ed. Peter Gowing (Quezon City, Philippines: New Day, 1988), 121.

20. Through the Spanish colonial period, church–state relations in the Philippines were shaped by the broader Patronato real de las Indias that governed Spain and its imperial holdings. Under this agreement, the monarch, as patron of the church, was granted legitimate territorial rule and the right to control both major and minor clerical appointments under Spanish control. As Philip II humbly described his power in 1574, "Let no secular person, nor cleric, order, convent, congregation, or community . . . dare to intrude into matters touching [ecclesiastical] patronage" (quoted in John Schumacher, *Readings in Philippine Church History*, 2nd ed. [Quezon City, Philippines: Loyola School of Theology, Ateneo de Manila University, 1987], 9). In practice, this fusion of church and state masked regular tension between religious and secular authorities.

21. De la Costa and Schumacher, *Church and State*, 20.

22. Peter G. Gowing, "The Disentangling of Church and State Early in the American Regime in the Philippines," in *Studies in Philippine Church History*, ed. Gerald H. Anderson (Ithaca: Cornell University Press, 1969), 205. After one tied vote regarding establishment and a second vote broken by the chair and protested by Catholic Church supporters as a piece of procedural trickery, the convention approved Title III, Article 5, in which "the State recognizes the freedom and equality of all religions, as well as the separation of Church and State" (quoted in Schumacher, *Readings*, 279). However, to maintain a unified nationalist front as conflict with the United States loomed, the convention proclaimed in Article 100 that "the execution of Article 5, Title III, is hereby suspended until the meeting of [a postwar] constituent

assembly" (quoted in Schumacher, *Readings*, 279). Even Mabini, notwithstanding his Masonic views, saw the need to engage native clergy in the looming war with the United States, and so the church–state cleavage was temporarily tabled.

23. Quoted in Schumacher, *Readings*, 266.

24. De la Costa and Schumacher, *Church and State*, 30–31.

25. Steven Shirley, *Guided by God: The Legacy of the Catholic Church in Philippine Politics* (Singapore: Marshall Cavendish Academic, 2004), 29–35.

26. Gerald H. Anderson, "Providence and Politics Behind Protestant Missionary Beginnings in the Philippines," in Anderson, *Studies in Philippine Church History*, 286.

27. Quoted in De la Costa and Schumacher, *Church and State*, 57.

28. Frederic Marquardt, "Quezon and the Church," *Philippines Free Press*, August 19, 1954. Quezon professed family motives as well as his relationship with Archbishop Michael J. O'Doherty of Manila for his return to the church.

29. Quoted in *Journal of the Constitutional Convention of the Philippines*, vol. 1 (Manila: East, 1961), 142.

30. Quoted in Hernando, "Quezon and the Rule of Law," 230.

31. Quoted in Schumacher, *Readings*, 204–5. In a brutal piece of irony, as native clergy became better trained, they also became more suspected of disloyalty by Spanish administrators. Three such priests, Fathers José Burgos, Mariano Gomez, and Jacinto Zamora, would be executed after secret military trial in 1872, and other leaders among the native clergy would be intimidated into exile. The three executed priests, in particular Burgos, exerted a substantial influence on the growing nationalist movement in the late nineteenth century (John N. Schumacher, *The Propaganda Movement, 1880–1895: The Creators of a Filipino Consciousness, the Makers of Revolution* [Manila: Solidaridad, 1973]). Nationalist writer and hero José Rizal remarked that he would have become a Jesuit priest if not for the witness provided by the executed priests, who instead inspired him to nationalist action. And although the Katipunan, the armed resistance movement to Spanish rule that emerged near the end of the nineteenth century, is frequently seen as anticlerical because many members were Masons influenced by the republican conflicts in Spain, its password was a contraction of the three executed priests' names: "GomBurZa."

32. Fabros, *The Church and Its Social Involvement*, 15.

33. Mary Dorita Clifford, "Religion and the Public Schools in the Philippines: 1899–1906," in Anderson, *Studies in Philippine Church History*, 301–24.

34. McKinley's famous quote that United States had an obligation to "uplift and civilize and Christianize [the Filipinos]" appeared in an interview with the *Christian Advocate* published in 1903 and may have reflected the phrasing of the president's allies rather than of McKinley himself. Whatever the precise source of the quotation, it seems fair to say that both American Protestant religious leaders and political elites viewed the Catholic Church's influence in the Philippines skeptically.

35. Quoted in V. Ruiz Navarro, *The Philippine Constitutional Convention*, vol. 1 (Manila: General Printing Press, 1934), 113–14.

36. Villarruz, *Commentaries*, 119.

37. Clifford, "Religion and the Public Schools," 308.

38. Taft and his superiors in the McKinley and Roosevelt administrations worked closely with American Catholic leaders such as Cardinal James Gibbons of Baltimore and Archbishop John Ireland of St. Paul to construct a state that was both secular and respectful of Catholic Church institutions (De la Costa and Schumacher, *Church and State*, 38).

39. P. N. Abinales, *Orthodoxy and History in the Muslim–Mindanao Narrative* (Quezon City, Philippines: Ateneo de Manila University Press, 2010).

40. Ibid., 32.

41. Both the Aglipayans and the INC are native Christian movements, inspired in large part by resistance to the close ties between the Catholic Church and Spanish colonizers. Gregorio Aglipay, Catholic priest and revolutionary solider, demanded the Vatican appoint native Filipino bishops and in 1902 broke away from the Catholic Church to form a fully nationalized church, the Philippine Independent Church, commonly known as the Aglipayans (see Schumacher, *Readings*, 317–33). About a decade later, in 1914, the INC was founded as another nationalist alternative to the transnational Catholic Church, this time with a more charismatic structure around the central figure of Felix Manalo (see Albert Sanders, "An Appraisal of the Iglesia ni Cristo," in Anderson, *Studies in Philippine Church History*, 350–65).

42. Clifford, "Religion and the Public Schools," 305.

43. With Catholic archbishop Bernardino Nozaleda opposing the revolution and behind American lines, questions of who should speak for the native Filipino Catholic priests became pressing. One option was to nationalize the church leadership, although doing so would require Vatican approval. In a scene that should ring familiar to students of the Investiture Conflict, a Filipino priest, Father Gregorio Aglipay, appointed a vicar general in place of a bishop captured by the revolutionary forces and thus brought excommunication upon himself. Aglipay argued, "[The revolutionary government] cannot recognize as head of the Filipino clergy a Spanish prelate, since the all-embracing political influence of the clergy on the government is known to all"—in other words, Rome must allow the revolutionaries to appoint their bishops (quoted in Schumacher, *Readings*, 281). This logic drove Aglipay to formal schism in 1902.

44. Quoted in Joaquin G. Bernas, *The 1987 Constitution of the Republic of the Philippines: A Commentary* (Manila: Rex Book Store, 1996), 318.

45. Hernando, "Quezon and the Rule of Law," 226.

46. Quoted in ibid., 227.

47. Quoted in "Mutual Understanding," *Philippines Free Press*, July 23, 1938.

7. SECULAR EVOLUTION IN THE PHILIPPINES

1. Quoted in Carla Gomez, "Bacolod Bishop to SC: Stop Comelec from Removing Poll Tarpaulins in Church," *Inquirer Visayas*, March 1, 2013.

2. Antonio F. Moreno, *Church, State, and Civil Society in Postauthoritarian Philippines: Narratives of Engaged Citizenship* (Quezon City, Philippines: Ateneo de Manila University Press, 2006), 41–68.

3. Robert L. Youngblood, "Church Opposition to Martial Law in the Philippines," *Asian Survey* 18, no. 5 (1978): 505–20.

4. Robert L. Youngblood, "The Protestant Church in the Philippines' New Society," *Bulletin of Concerned Asian Scholars* 12, no. 3 (1980): 22.

5. "Enrile Confirms Break in Military–Church Talks," Foreign Broadcast Information Service—APA, January 25, 1983.

6. Quoted in "Marcos Reassures Clergy," Foreign Broadcast Information Service—PNA, February 4, 1986.

7. It is important to remember that in the immediate aftermath of the martial law declaration, Catholic and Protestant religious elites generally acquiesced to the regime. As Youngblood points out, "Bishop Estanislao Abainza of the United Church of Christ in the Philippines (UCCP), prais[ed] the 'enforced discipline' of the New Society and enjoin[ed] Filipinos not to 'minimize' the 'positive effects' of martial law" ("Protestant Church," 19). This response mirrored the CBCP's statement "recogniz[ing] the right and duty of civil authorities to take appropriate steps to protect the sovereignty of the state" and "ask[ing] our people to remain calm and law-abiding" (CBCP, "Statement of the CBCP Administrative Council on Martial Law," September 26, 1972, http://cbcponline.net/v2/?p=177 [accessed April 10, 2013]).

8. Youngblood, "Protestant Church," 19.

9. Ibid., 23.

10. Ibid., 24.

11. Rina Jimenez David, interviewed by David Buckley, Ortigas, Philippines, June 18, 2014.

12. Quoted in Isabel L. Templo, "The Truth Shall Set Us Free: The Role of Church-Owned Radio Stations in the Philippines," Center for Media Freedom and Responsibility, February 25, 2011, http://cmfr-phil.org/media-ethics-responsibility/ethics/the-truth-shall-set-us-free-the-role-of-church-owned-radio-stations-in-the-philippines/ (accessed June 16, 2016).

13. Constitutional Commission of the Philippines, *Record of the Constitutional Commission: Proceedings and Debates*, 5 vols. (Quezon City, Philippines: Constitutional Commission, 1986), 1:128–29.

14. Ibid., 4:382.

15. Ibid., 4:363–65.

16. See, for instance, 4:326–29.

17. Ibid., 4:329.
18. Ibid., 4:330.
19. Ibid., 4:328.
20. Ibid., 4:368.
21. Ibid., 4:972.
22. Ibid.
23. Ibid.
24. *Republic v. Court of Appeals*, 268 SCRA 198 (Supreme Court of the Philippines, 1997), at 676–80. The Court held, "Here, the State and the Church—while remaining independent, separate and apart from each other—shall walk together in synodal cadence towards the same goal of protecting and cherishing marriage and the family as the inviolable base of the nation."
25. Survey evidence shows that this pluralization at the elite level has corresponded to modest recent growth in pluralism among the general population, as non–Roman Catholics grew from 15 percent of the population in 1998 to 19 percent in 2008 (International Social Survey Programme Research Group, *International Social Survey Programme [ISSP]: Religion III* [Cologne, Germany: GESIS, 2008]).
26. Moreno, *Church, State, and Civil Society*, 266.
27. Daniel Franklin Pilario, "Catholic Movements in the Philippines: Clashes with 'Official' Powers," unpublished manuscript, copy in the author's files.
28. Christl Kessler and Jürgen Rüland, *Give Jesus a Hand! Charismatic Christians, Populist Religion, and Politics in the Philippines* (Quezon City, Philippines: Ateneo de Manila University Press, 2008), 8. See also Katherine Wiegele, *Investing in Miracles: El Shaddai and the Transformation of Popular Catholicism in the Philippines* (Honolulu: University of Hawai'i Press, 2005).
29. Moreno, *Church, State, and Civil Society*, 76–78.
30. As stated in chapter 6, the most recent survey evidence from the ISSP estimates non–Roman Catholic Christians at 7.5 percent of the overall population of the Philippines. This category includes a range of groups, including the INC and Aglipayan communities that have existed for decades.
31. Grepor "Butch" Belgica, interviewed by David Buckley, Quezon City, Philippines, August 18, 2010; Grepor Butch Belgica, *Remove the Evil from Our Midst! Biblical Blueprint for Comprehensive Social Action Against Delinquency and Substance Abuse* (Manila: National Library, 1994).
32. Kessler and Rüland, *Give Jesus a Hand*, 67.
33. Sylvia Claudio, interviewed by David Buckley, Diliman, Philippines, June 27, 2014.
34. *James M. Imbong et al. v. Hon. Paquito N. Ochoa, Jr. et al.*, G.R. No. 204819 (Supreme Court of the Philippines, 2014).
35. Quoted in Ina Alleco R. Silverio, "Non-Catholic Groups Recognize Value of RH Bill to Maternal Health," *Butatlat*, August 10, 2012, http://bulatlat.com

/main/2012/08/10/non-catholic-groups-recognize-value-of-rh-bill-to-maternal-health/ (accessed January 23, 2013).

36. Reverend Rex Reyes, interviewed by David Buckley, Quezon City, Philippines, August 19, 2010.

37. Miriam Defensor Santiago, "Leave No Woman Behind: Why We Fought for RH Bill," CNN December 21, 2012, http://www.cnn.com/2012/12/29/opinion/philippines-reproductive-health-bill-santiago/ (accessed June 16, 2016).

38. Risa Hontiveros, interviewed by David Buckley, Quezon City, Philippines, June 24, 2014.

39. Philip Tubeza, "CBCP Reminds Aquino About Excommunication," *Philippine Daily Inquirer*, September 30, 2010. The particulars of this "threat" were at least in part a result of the media's appetite for conflict on this issue, and the bishop may have been misquoted. Regardless, the episode is one indicator of the sharp religious-secular tensions related to this issue.

40. Conrado de Quiros, "Holy Orders," *Philippine Daily Inquirer*, January 21, 2013.

41. David Balangue, interviewed by David Buckley, Makati, Philippines, June 25, 2014.

42. Mary Racelis and Marita Castro Guevara, interviewed by David Buckley, Quezon City, Philippines, June 30, 2014. Racelis and Castro Guevara were authors of various statements issued by Ateneo de Manila faculty members in support of the RH law over the years of its development and spoke to me at length of the debates at Ateneo over how to respond to the law.

43. Meneleo Carlos Jr., interviewed by David Buckley, Pasig City, Philippines, July 1, 2014.

44. Joaquin G. Bernas, "Bishops at War," *Philippine Daily Inquirer*, August 26, 2012.

45. See, for example, Eric Genilo, "Crossing the Line: Church Use of Political Threats Against Pro–RH Bill Legislators," *Intersect* 24, no. 1 (2010): 28–36; Eric Genilo, John J. Carroll, and Joaquin G. Bernas, "Towards Critical and Constructive Engagement (Talking Points for Dialogue on the RH Bill)," unpublished manuscript, copy in the author's files.

46. Father Eric Genilo, S.J., interviewed by David Buckley, Loyola House of Studies, Quezon City, Philippines, August 13, 2010.

47. Joaquin Bernas, S.J., "Unfinished Debate Over the RH Law," *Philippine Daily Inquirer*, January 14, 2013.

48. Michael Lim Ubac and Philip C. Tubeza, "Church–Gov't Ties Thawing," *Philippine Daily Inquirer*, December 2, 2012.

49. Eleanor Dionisio, "What Difference Can a Manila Archbishop Make?" *Philippine Daily Inquirer*, December 12, 2012.

50. "DOH Exec Eyes Inputs from Church on RH Bill Implementation," *GMA News*, December 21, 2012.

51. Norman Cabrera, interviewed by David Buckley, Quezon City, Philippines, June 19, 2014.

52. Quoted in Paterno Esmaquel II, "Move on, Bishops Urge Critics of RH Law," *Rappler*, April 8, 2014, http://www.rappler.com/nation/54984-cbcp-villegas-reaction-rh-law-upheld (accessed June 16, 2016).

53. Bernardo Villegas, interviewed by David Buckley, Makati, Philippines, July 1, 2014.

54. For one entertaining example, see Joey Ramirez, "Explaining Secular Democracy to Tito," *Rappler*, September 8, 2012, http://www.rappler.com/move-ph/33-editors-pick-moveph/12024-explaining-secular-democracy-to-tito (accessed June 16, 2016).

55. Quoted in de Quiros, "Holy Orders."

56. Genilo interview, June 18, 2014.

57. Barbara Mae Dacanay, "Aquino Declares Eid al Fitr a Holiday," *Gulf News*, August 13, 2012.

58. Father José Magadia, interviewed by David Buckley, Quezon City, Philippines, August 20, 2010.

59. Rey Trillana, interviewed by David Buckley, Philippine Center for Islam and Democracy, Greenhills, Philippines, August 16, 2010; Amina Rasul, interviewed by David Buckley, Philippine Center for Islam and Democracy, Greenhills, Philippines, August 16, 2010.

60. Jeffrey Ayala Milligan, "Teaching Between the Cross and the Crescent Moon: Islamic Identity, Postcoloniality, and Public Education in the Southern Philippines," *Comparative Education Review* 47, no. 4 (2003): 488.

61. Thanks to Amina Rasul of the Philippine Center for Islam and Democracy for highlighting Undersecretary Boransing's work and the ALIVE program. For more information on the ALIVE program, see Lito Dar, "Gov't Focuses on Integration Program for Muslim OSYs," Philippine Information Service, March 27, 2010. For more on Project Madrasa Education, see Jeffrey Ayala Milligan, "Reclaiming an Ideal: The Islamization of Education in the Southern Philippines," *Comparative Education Review* 50, no. 3 (2006): 410–30.

62. It is important to note that although the provision of sharia law protections is not equally made for other religious communities, this does not violate the empirical standard of maintaining principled distance from religious communities. Principled distance requires even-handedness in relating to religious communities but not strict equality of outcome. In this way, Islam–state relations in the Philippines resemble what Alfred Stepan calls "asymmetric federalism," or granting unique group-specific rights and public status in places such as Catalonia and Quebec ("Federalism Beyond the US Model," *Journal of Democracy* 10, no. 4 [1999]: 29).

63. Linda Luz Guerrero, Hamid Barra, Mahar Mangahas, and Vladymir Joseph Licudine, *The Code of Muslim Personal Laws in Practice: What Influential Muslims*

and Sharia Lawyers Think (Quezon City, Philippines: Social Weather Stations, 2007), 4–8.

64. Trillana and Rasul interviews, August 16, 2010.

65. Ralph Recto, "Strengthen Madrasah Education to Promote Peace," speech before the Senate of the Philippines, April 25, 2007.

66. Jesli Lapus, "Increase in the Monthly Allowances of Muslim Teachers in the ALIVE Program," Philippines Department of Education memorandum, March 8, 2010.

67. Catholic Bishops and Educators in Mindanao, "Working Towards a Reconciled Diversity," April 14, 2014, http://www.mindanews.com/around-mindanao/2014/04/14/working-towards-a-reconciled-diversity/ (accessed June 10, 2014).

68. *Ang Bagong Bayani v. Comelec*, 404 SCRA 719 (Supreme Court of the Philippines, 2001). The party-list portion of the legislature, which makes up 20 percent of the House of Representatives, is reserved for underrepresented communities such as indigenous groups and women's organizations, and religious groups are explicitly forbidden by Article 6.5.1 to contest these seats. The constitutional language governing the party list system excludes "the religious sector," and the Supreme Court's decision in *Ang Bagong Bayani v. Comelec* reaffirms the distinction.

69. For example, Cabrera interview, June 19, 2014.

70. On missing a candidate forum scheduled by Quiboloy for the presidential elections of 2010, candidate Benigno Aquino apologized profusely, claiming, "Getting a cold is something that I cannot schedule" (quoted in Gil C. Cabacungan Jr., Michael Lim Ubac, and Norman Bordadora, "Aquino Apologizes; Villar Won't Explain Davao No-Show," *Philippine Daily Inquirer*, March 11, 2010).

71. Eddie Panlilio, written correspondence with David Buckley, August 19, 2010.

72. Cabrera interview, June 19, 2014.

73. Bishop Broderick Pabillo, interviewed by David Buckley, Binodo, Philippines, June 20, 2014.

74. Father John Carroll, S.J., interviewed by David Buckley, Loyola House of Studies, Quezon City, Philippines, August 16, 2010.

75. John Carlos "J. C." de los Reyes, interviewed by David Buckley, Intramuros, Philippines, June 26, 2014.

76. Aries Rufo, "RH and Elections: Pols Knew There's No Catholic Vote," *Rappler*, December 31, 2012, http://www.rappler.com/nation/politics/elections-2013/opinion/18783-rh-and-elections-pols-knew-thereâ%80%99s-no-catholic-vote (accessed June 16, 2016).

77. The term *critical collaboration*, which was also used to describe the church's relationship to the Marcos regime in the martial law period, came up in several interviews with Catholic elites, including Bishop Broderick Pabillo (written correspondence with David Buckley, August 27, 2010). Bishop Pabillo at that time chaired the CBCP's National Secretariat for Social Action-Justice and Peace.

78. Reyes interview, August 19, 2010.

79. Belgica interview, August 18, 2010.

80. Father Roberto Rivera, interviewed by David Buckley, Quezon City, Philippines, August 18, 2010. See also Pilario, "Catholic Movements in the Philippines."

81. See Christl Kessler, "Charismatic Christians: Genuinely Religious, Genuinely Modern," *Philippine Studies* 54, no. 4 (2006): 560–84, for detailed explanation of the variables Kessler uses to construct a more thorough index of charismatic religiosity. Although her remarkably detailed survey design would certainly give more confidence in identifying Charismatics, the "born again" question is the most reliable means of identifying Charismatic-influenced Catholics in the data available from the ISSP.

82. The choice of referent category does not affect the primary finding: Catholics are, if anything, more supportive of benevolent secularism than some religious minorities and certainly not less supportive.

83. David T. Buckley, "'The Punisher' Is Now President-Elect: Can the Church Adapt?" *America*, May 17, 2016.

CONCLUSION

1. Daniel Philpott, "Explaining the Political Ambivalence of Religion," *American Political Science Review* 101, no. 3 (2007): 505–25.

2. Alfred Stepan, "Religion, Democracy, and the 'Twin Tolerations,'" *Journal of Democracy* 11, no. 4 (2000): 39.

3. Jürgen Habermas and Ciaran Cronin, *An Awareness of What Is Missing: Faith and Reason in a Post-Secular Age* (Cambridge: Polity Press, 2011).

4. David Robinson, *Paths of Accommodation: Muslim Societies and French Colonial Authorities in Senegal and Mauritania, 1880–1920* (Athens: Ohio University Press, 2000).

5. Peter M. Haas, "Introduction: Epistemic Communities and International Policy Coordination," *International Organization* 46, no. 1 (1992): 1–35.

6. Mary Fitzgerald, "The Future of Islamic Ireland," *Irish Times*, February 12, 2011.

7. Abdel Zeroug, interviewed by David Buckley, Dublin, May 18, 2011.

BIBLIOGRAPHY

INTERVIEWS

Alcantara, Pats. Interviewed by David Buckley. Quezon City, Philippines, August 19, 2010.
Balangue, David. Interviewed by David Buckley. Makati, Philippines, June 25, 2014.
Belgica, Grepor "Butch." Interviewed by David Buckley. Quezon City, Philippines, August 18, 2010.
Cabrera, Norman. Interviewed by David Buckley. Quezon City, Philippines, June 19, 2014.
Carlos, Meneleo, Jr. Interviewed by David Buckley. Pasig City, Philippines, July 1, 2014.
Carroll, Father John, S.J. Interviewed by David Buckley. Loyola House of Studies, Quezon City, Philippines, August 16, 2010.
Claudio, Sylvia. Interviewed by David Buckley. Diliman, Philippines, June 27, 2014.
Daly, Eoin. Interviewed by David Buckley. Dublin, May 26, 2011.
David, Rina Jimenez. Interviewed by David Buckley. Ortigas, Philippines, June 18, 2014.
De los Reyes, John Carlos "J. C." Interviewed by David Buckley. Intramuros, Philippines, June 26, 2014.

Diagne, Assane. Interviewed by David Buckley. Dakar, Senegal, June 18, 2010.
Diagne, Souleymane Bachir. Interviewed by David Buckley. New York, March 2010.
Genilo, Eric. Interviewed by David Buckley. Quezon City, Philippines, August 13, 2010, and June 18, 2014.
Hogan, Claire. Interviewed by David Buckley. Dublin, May 20, 2011.
Hogan, Linda. Interviewed by David Buckley. Dublin, May 12, 2011.
Holohan, John. Interviewed by David Buckley. Dublin, May 19, 2011.
Hontiveros, Risa. Interviewed by David Buckley. Quezon City, Philippines, June 24, 2014.
Kébé, Abdoul Aziz. Interviewed by David Buckley. Dakar, Senegal, June 29, 2010.
Kiné Camara, Fatou. Interviewed by David Buckley. Dakar, Senegal, June 23, 2010.
Magadia, Father José. Interviewed by David Buckley. Quezon City, Philippines, August 20, 2010.
Martin, Archbishop Diarmuid. Interviewed by David Buckley. Dublin, May 25, 2011.
Mbacké, Khadim. Interviewed by David Buckley. Dakar, Senegal, June 30, 2010.
Morrow, Reverend Dr. Trevor. Interviewed by David Buckley. Dublin, May 17, 2011.
Mullan, Peter. Interviewed by David Buckley. Dublin, May 24, 2011.
Ndiaye, Théodore Ndok. Interviewed by David Buckley. Dakar, Senegal, June 26, 2010.
Nugent, Michael. Interviewed by David Buckley. Dublin, May 16, 2011.
O'Hanlon, Father Gerry. Interviewed by David Buckley. Dublin, May 19, 2011.
Pabillo, Bishop Broderick. Interviewed by David Buckley. Binodo, Philippines, June 20, 2014.
Quinn, David. Interviewed by David Buckley. Dublin, May 25, 2011.
Racelis, Mary, and Marita Castro Guevara. Interviewed by David Buckley. Quezon City, Philippines, June 30, 2014.
Rasul, Amina. Interviewed by David Buckley. Greenhills, Philippines, August 16, 2010.
Regan, Sister Ethna. Interviewed by David Buckley. Mater Dei Institute, Dublin, May 12, 2011.
Reyes, Reverend Rex. Interviewed by David Buckley. Quezon City, Philippines, August 19, 2010.
Rivera, Father Roberto. Interviewed by David Buckley. Quezon City, Philippines, August 18, 2010.
Sanga, Paul. Interviewed by David Buckley. Dakar, Senegal, June 22, 2010.
Scharbrodt, Oliver. Interviewed by David Buckley. Cork, Ireland, May 16, 2011.
Seck, Abbé Alphonse. Interviewed by David Buckley. Dakar, Senegal, June 25, 2010.
Seck, Abbé Jacques. Interviewed by David Buckley. Dakar, Senegal, June 25, 2010.
Seck, Boubacar. Interviewed by David Buckley. Dakar, Senegal, June 22, 2010.
Selim, Ali. Interviewed by David Buckley. Dublin, May 23, 2011.
Trillana, Rey. Interviewed by David Buckley. Greenhills, Philippines, August 16, 2010.
Villegas, Bernardo. Interviewed by David Buckley. Makati, Philippines, July 1, 2014.

Whyte, Gerard. Interviewed by David Buckley. Dublin, May 18, 2011.
Zeroug, Abdel. Interviewed by David Buckley. Dublin, May 18, 2011.

PRINT SOURCES

Abad, Ricardo G. "Religion in the Philippines." *Philippine Studies* 49, no. 3 (2001): 337–55.
Abass, Ben. "Les petits fils d'el H. Malick Sy exigent la démission d'Ousmane Ngom et des excuses publiques de Wade." *PressAfrik*, February 22, 2012.
Abinales, P. N. *Orthodoxy and History in the Muslim–Mindanao Narrative*. Quezon City, Philippines: Ateneo de Manila University Press, 2010.
Ahern, Bertie. "Address by an Taoiseach, Bertie Ahern T.D., at a Reception for Churches and Faith Communities in the Structured Dialogue." Dublin, April 22, 2008.
——. "Speech by an Taoiseach, Mr. Bertie Ahern T.D., at the Inauguration of the Structured Dialogue with Churches, Faith Communities, and Non-confessional Bodies." Dublin Castle, February 26, 2007.
Akenson, Donald H. *The Irish Education Experiment: The National System of Education in the Nineteenth Century*. Studies in Irish History, no. 2. London: Routledge & Kegan Paul, 1970.
Ali, Anshari. "Islamic Family Law in the Philippines: A Historical Survey." *Al-Shajarah: Journal of the International Institute of Islamic Thought and Civilization* 6, no. 1 (2001): 89–123.
Altinordu, Ates. "The Politicization of Religion: Political Catholicism and Political Islam in Comparative Perspective." *Politics & Society* 38, no. 4 (2010): 517–51.
Anderson, Gerald H. "Providence and Politics Behind Protestant Missionary Beginnings in the Philippines." In *Studies in Philippine Church History*, edited by Gerald H. Anderson, 279–300. Ithaca: Cornell University Press, 1969.
Assises nationales du Sénégal. *Charte de gouvernance démocratique*. Dakar, Senegal: Assises nationales, 2009.
Audrain, Xavier. "Du 'ndiggël avorté' au Parti de la Vérité." *Politique Africaine* 96 (2004): 99–118.
Babou, Cheikh Anta. "The Senegalese 'Social Contract' Revisited." In *Tolerance, Democracy, and Sufis in Senegal*, edited by Mamadou Diouf, 125–46. New York: Columbia University Press, 2013.
Barrington, Ruth. "Catholic Influence on the Health Services 1830–2000." In *Religion and Politics in Ireland at the Turn of the Millennium*, edited by James Patrick Mackey and Enda McDonagh, 152–65. Dublin: Columba Press, 2003.
Bauberot, Jean. "The Two Thresholds of Laicization." In *Secularism and Its Critics*, edited by Rajeev Bhargava, 94–136. Oxford: Oxford University Press, 1998.

Beck, L. J. "Reining in the Marabouts? Democratization and Local Governance in Senegal." *African Affairs* 100, no. 401 (2001): 601–21.
Belgica, Grepor "Butch." *Remove the Evil from Our Midst! Biblical Blueprint for Comprehensive Social Action Against Delinquency and Substance Abuse.* Manila: National Library, 1994.
Berger, Peter L. *The Desecularization of the World: Resurgent Religion and World Politics.* Grand Rapids, Mich.: Eerdmans, 1999.
———. *The Sacred Canopy: Elements of a Sociological Theory of Religion.* Garden City, N.Y.: Doubleday, 1967.
Bernas, Joaquin G. *The 1987 Constitution of the Republic of the Philippines: A Commentary.* Manila: Rex Book Store, 1996.
———. "Bishops at War." *Philippine Daily Inquirer,* August 26, 2012.
———. *The Constitution of the Republic of the Philippines: With Annotations Based on Commission Deliberations.* Manila: Rex Book Store, 1987.
———. "Unfinished Debate Over the RH Law." *Philippine Daily Inquirer,* January 14, 2013.
Bhargava, Rajeev. "The Distinctiveness of Indian Secularism." In *The Future of Secularism,* edited by T. N. Srinivasan, 20–53. Oxford: Oxford University Press, 2007.
———. *Secularism and Its Critics.* Themes in Politics Series. Delhi: Oxford University Press, 1998.
Blaydes, Lisa, and Drew Linzer. "Elite Competition, Religiosity, and Anti-Americanism in the Islamic World." *American Political Science Review* 106, no. 2 (2012): 225–44.
Bowman, John. "De Valera on Ulster, 1919–1920: What He Told America." *Irish Studies in International Affairs* 1, no. 1 (1979): 3–18.
Bratton, Michael, E. Gyimah-Boadi, and Robert Mattes. *Afrobarometer Round 3: The Quality of Democracy and Governance in 18 African Countries, 2005–2006.* ICPSR 22981-v1. Ann Arbor, Mich.: Inter-university Consortium for Political and Social Research, 2009.
Brossier, Marie. "Les débats sur le Droit de la famille au Sénégal." *Politique Africaine* 96 (2004): 78–98.
Buckley, David T. "Beyond the Secularism Trap: Religion, Political Institutions, and Democratic Commitments." *Comparative Politics* 47, no. 4 (2015): 439–58.
———. "Demanding the Divine? Explaining Cross-National Support for Clerical Control of Politics." *Comparative Political Studies* 49, no. 3 (2016): 357–90.
———. "'The Punisher' Is Now President-Elect: Can the Church Adapt?" *America,* May 17, 2016.
Buckley, David T., and Luis Felipe Mantilla. "God and Governance: Development, State Capacity, and the Regulation of Religion." *Journal for the Scientific Study of Religion* 52, no. 2 (2013): 328–48.

Byrne, Ciaran, and Shane Doran. "Muslims Give Their Blessing: Vast Majority Very Happy Here, Says Poll." *Irish Independent*, December 19, 2006.
Cabacungan, Gil C., Jr., Michael Lim Ubac, and Norman Bordadora. "Aquino Apologizes; Villar Won't Explain Davao No-Show." *Philippine Daily Inquirer*, March 11, 2010.
Camara, Abdoulaye. "Dernier Cheikh du 5e khalife des Mourides: 'Wade n'a pas entendu les consignes de Serigne Saliou.'" *Walfadjri*, October 5, 2010.
"Le Cardinal Sarr déplore des 'propos insupportable' du président de la République." Agence de presse sénégalaise, December 30, 2009.
Casanova, José. "Civil Society and Religion: Retrospective Reflections on Catholicism and Prospective Reflections on Islam." *Social Research* 68, no. 4 (2001): 1041–80.
———. *Public Religions in the Modern World*. Chicago: University of Chicago Press, 1994.
Catholic Bishops and Educators in Mindanao. "Working Towards a Reconciled Diversity." April 14, 2014. http://www.mindanews.com/around-mindanao/2014/04/14/working-towards-a-reconciled-diversity/.
Catholic Bishops' Conference of the Philippines (CBCP). "Statement of the CBCP Administrative Council on Martial Law." September 26, 1972. http://cbcponline.net/v2/?p=177.
Central Statistics Office of Ireland. *1936 Census of Ireland*. Dublin: Stationery Office, 1936.
———. *2006 Census of Ireland*. Dublin: Stationery Office, 2006.
———. *2011 Census of Ireland*. Dublin: Stationery Office, 2011.
Cesari, Jocelyne. *The Awakening of Muslim Democracy: Religion, Modernity, and the State*. New York: Cambridge University Press, 2014.
Charlier, Jean-Emile. "Le retour de Dieu: L'introduction de l'enseignement religieux dans l'ecole de la Republique du Sénégal." *Education et Societes* 10, no. 2 (2002): 95–112.
Clark, J. A. "The Conditions of Islamist Moderation: Unpacking Cross-Ideological Cooperation in Jordan." *International Journal of Middle East Studies* 38, no. 4 (2006): 539–60.
Clifford, Mary Dorita. "Religion and the Public Schools in the Philippines: 1899–1906." In *Studies in Philippine Church History*, edited by Gerald H. Anderson, 301–24. Ithaca: Cornell University Press, 1969.
"Collectif pour la défense de la laïcité et de l'unité nationale au Sénégal." June 13, 2003. http://www.wluml.org/fr/node/1060.
Collier, David. "Understanding Process Tracing." *PS: Political Science and Politics* 44, no. 4 (2011): 823–30.
Conference Episcopale du Sénégal. *Paroles d'evêques 1963–2000*. Dakar, Senegal: Imprimerie Saint-Paul, 2000.

Constitutional Commission of the Philippines. *Record of the Constitutional Commission: Proceedings and Debates.* 5 vols. [Quezon City, Philippines]: Constitutional Commission, 1986.

Constitutional Review Group. *Report of the Constitutional Review Group.* Dublin: Stationery Office, 1996.

Coolahan, John. "Address for the Launch of the Forum on Patronage and Pluralism in the Primary Sector." Clock Tower, Department of Education and Skills, Dublin, April 19, 2011.

Cooney, John. "Gormley: It's Time Bishops Stopped Interfering." *Irish Independent*, June 18, 2010.

Coquia, Jorge A. "Religious Freedom in the Philippines." *Philippine Studies* 4, no. 1 (1956): 15–30.

Coulon, Christian. *Le marabout et le prince: Islam et pouvoir au Sénégal.* Série Afrique Noire. Paris: Pedone, 1981.

Cruise O'Brien, Donal B. "Le contrat social sénégalais à l'épreuve." *Politique Africaine* 45 (2003): 9–20.

———. *Symbolic Confrontations: Muslims Imagining the State in Africa.* New York: Palgrave Macmillan, 2003.

Dacanay, Barbara Mae. "Aquino Declares Eid al Fitr a Holiday." *Gulf News*, August 13, 2012.

Dahl, Robert Alan. *Polyarchy: Participation and Opposition.* New Haven: Yale University Press, 1971.

Daly, Eoin. "Citizens Should Have Access to Non-sectarian Public Schools." *Irish Times*, May 26, 2011.

———. "The Constitution and the Protestant Schools Cuts Controversy: Seeing the Wood for the Trees." *Irish Journal of Legal Studies* 1, no. 1 (2010): 84–107.

———. *Religion, Law, and the Irish State: The Constitutional Framework in Context.* Dublin: Clarus Press, 2012.

Dar, Lito. "Gov't Focuses on Integration Program for Muslim OSYs." Philippine Information Service, March 27, 2010.

"Darou Salam: Me Wade réaffirme son appartenance au mouridisme." Agence de presse sénégalaise, February 22, 2012.

Daughton, J. P. *An Empire Divided: Religion, Republicanism, and the Making of French Colonialism, 1880–1914.* Oxford: Oxford University Press, 2006.

De Benoist, Joseph-Roger. *Histoire de l'Église Catholique au Sénégal: Du milieu du Xve siècle à l'aube du troisième millénaire.* Dakar, Senegal: Karthala, 2008.

De la Costa, Horacio, and John N. Schumacher. *Church and State: The Philippine Experience.* Loyola Papers. Manila: Loyola Papers Board of Editors, 1978.

De Quiros, Conrado. "Holy Orders." *Philippine Daily Inquirer*, January 21, 2013.

"Decret No. 2009-1134." *Journal Officiel du Sénégal*, October 14, 2009.

Defensor Santiago, Miriam. "Leave No Woman Behind: Why We Fought for RH Bill." CNN, December 21, 2012. http://www.cnn.com/2012/12/29/opinion/philippines-reproductive-health-bill-santiago/.

Deutsch, Karl. "Social Mobilization and Political Development." *American Political Science Review* 55, no. 3 (1961): 493–514.

Diagne, Souleymane Bachir. "A Secular Age and the World of Islam." In *Tolerance, Democracy, and Sufis in Senegal*, edited by Mamadou Diouf, 36–50. New York: Columbia University Press, 2013.

Diallo, Boucar Aliou. "Lobbying avorté de Wade pour une audience auprès de Serigne Sidy Mokhtar Mbacké: Le khalife dans l'isoloir spirituel à Tawfekh." *Le Quotidien*, March 7, 2012.

Diedhiou, Joseph, and Charles Gaïky Diene. "Réaction du Cardinal Théodore Adrien Sarr: Wade au ban de l'église." *Wal Fadjri*, December 30, 2009.

Diene, Charles Gaïky. "Bamba Ndiaye (nouveau ministre chargé des affaires religieuses)." *Wal Fadjri*, January 12, 2010.

Dionisio, Eleanor. "What Difference Can a Manila Archbishop Make?" *Philippine Daily Inquirer*, December 12, 2012.

Diop, G. Nesta. "Avec un seul ministre et quatre députés: Les chrétiens du Sénégal crient leur frustration." *Wal Fadjri*, June 25, 2007.

Diouf, Léon. *Église locale et crise africaine: Le Diocèse de Dakar*. Paris: Karthala, 2001.

Diouf, Mamadou. "Introduction: The Public Role of the 'Good Muslim': Sufi Islam and the Administration of Pluralism." In *Tolerance, Democracy, and Sufis in Senegal*, edited by Mamadou Diouf, 1–35. New York: Columbia University Press, 2013.

"Le directeur de la Sûreté nationale: 'Jean-Paul Dias n'a pas été interpellé à l'intérieur de la cathédrale.'" Agence de presse sénégalaise, April 14, 2006.

Djerejian, Edward. "The US and the Middle East in a Changing World." *U.S. Department of State Dispatch* 3, no. 23 (1992): 444–50.

"DOH Exec Eyes Inputs from Church on RH Bill Implementation." *GMA News*, December 21, 2012.

Driessen, Michael D. "Public Religion, Democracy, and Islam." *Comparative Politics* 44, no. 2 (2012): 171–89.

———. *Religion and Democratization: Framing Religious and Political Identities in Muslim and Catholic Societies*. New York: Oxford University Press, 2014.

Dwyer, Kyle. "De Valera and the Church's Special Position." *Irish Examiner*, January 5, 2013.

"Enrile Confirms Break in Military–Church Talks." Foreign Broadcast Information Service—APA, January 25, 1983.

Esmaquel, Paterno, II. "Move on, Bishops Urge Critics of RH Law." *Rappler*, April 8, 2014. http://www.rappler.com/nation/54984-cbcp-villegas-reaction-rh-law-upheld.

Eveques du Sénégal. "Pour quell Sénégal après Mai 1998." In *Paroles des eveques 1963–2000*, 202–6. Dakar, Senegal: Impremerie Saint-Paul, 2005.

Fabros, Wilfredo. *The Church and Its Social Involvement in the Philippines, 1930–1972.* Quezon City, Philippines: Ateneo de Manila University Press, 1988.

Fall, Cheikh. "Macky Sall répond sur la relation entre marabouts et president." February 29, 2012. http://www.youtube.com/watch?v=DPZNHPNUAD4.

Fatton, Robert. "Clientelism and Patronage in Senegal." *African Studies Review* 29, no. 4 (1986): 61–78.

Faye, Ibrahima Lissa. "En visite à Tivaouane: Wade hué par des jeunes." *PressAfrik*, February 2, 2012.

Finke, Roger, and Rodney Stark. *The Churching of America, 1776–1990: Winners and Losers in Our Religious Economy.* New Brunswick, N.J.: Rutgers University Press, 1992.

Fitzgerald, Mary. "The Future of Islamic Ireland." *Irish Times*, February 12, 2011.

Flynn, Kieran. "Understanding Islam in Ireland." *Islam and Christian–Muslim Relations* 17, no. 2 (2006): 223–38.

Foley, Ellen, and Cheikh Anta Babou. "Diaspora, Faith, and Science: Building a Mouride Hospital in Senegal." *African Affairs* 110 (2010): 75–95.

Foster, Elizabeth. "An Ambiguous Monument: Dakar's Colonial Cathedral of the Souvenir Africain." *French Historical Studies* 32, no. 1 (2009): 85–121.

Fox, Jonathan. *Political Secularism, Religion, and the State: A Time Series Analysis of Worldwide Data.* New York: Cambridge University Press, 2015.

———. *A World Survey of Religion and the State.* Cambridge: Cambridge University Press, 2008.

Galvan, Dennis. "Political Turnover and Social Change in Senegal." *Journal of Democracy* 12, no. 3 (2001): 51–63.

Gay and Lesbian Equality Network (GLEN). *Dail Debates on Civil Partnership.* Dublin: GLEN, 2010.

Genilo, Eric. "Crossing the Line: Church Use of Political Threats Against Pro–RH Bill Legislators." *Intersect* 24, no. 1 (2010): 28–36.

Genilo, Eric, John J. Carroll, and Joaquin G. Bernas. "Towards Critical and Constructive Engagement (Talking Points for Dialogue on the RH Bill)." Unpublished manuscript. Copy in the author's files.

George, Alexander L., and Andrew Bennett. *Case Studies and Theory Development in the Social Sciences.* Cambridge, Mass.: MIT Press, 2005.

Gibbons, John. "Ayatollah Would Have Seen McQuaid as Kindred Spirit." *Irish Times*, August 6, 2009.

Gill, Anthony James. *The Political Origins of Religious Liberty.* Cambridge: Cambridge University Press, 2008.

Gomez, Carla. "Bacolod Bishop to SC: Stop Comelec from Removing Poll Tarpaulins in Church." *Inquirer Visayas*, March 1, 2013.

Gowing, Peter G. "The Disentangling of Church and State Early in the American Regime in the Philippines." In *Studies in Philippine Church History*, edited by Gerald H. Anderson, 203–22. Ithaca: Cornell University Press, 1969.
———. "Mandate in Moroland: The American Government of Muslim Filipinos, 1899–1920." PhD diss., Syracuse University, 1968.
Groupe d'études et de recherches constitutionnelles et politiques (GERCOP). *Étude sur le comportement electoral dans les regions de Thies et Diourbel*. St. Louis, Senegal: Université Gaston Berger, 1999.
Grzymała-Busse, Anna. *Nations Under God: How Churches Use Moral Authority to Influence Policy*. Princeton: Princeton University Press, 2015.
Guerrero, Linda Luz, Hamid Barra, Mahar Mangahas, and Vladymir Joseph Licudine. *The Code of Muslim Personal Laws in Practice: What Influential Muslims and Sharia Lawyers Think*. Quezon City, Philippines: Social Weather Stations, 2007.
Guèye, Cheikh. *Touba: La capitale des Mourides*. Hommes et sociétés. Dakar: Karthala, 2002.
Gueye, Maïmouna. "Code du statut personnel ou Code de la famille." *Le Soleil*, April 23, 2003.
Haas, Peter M. "Introduction: Epistemic Communities and International Policy Coordination." *International Organization* 46, no. 1 (1992): 1–35.
Habermas, Jürgen, and Ciaran Cronin. *An Awareness of What Is Missing: Faith and Reason in a Post-secular Age*. Cambridge: Polity Press, 2011.
Hacker, J. S. "Privatizing Risk Without Privatizing the Welfare State: The Hidden Politics of Social Policy Retrenchment in the United States." *American Political Science Review* 98, no. 2 (2004): 243–60.
Hashemi, Nader. *Islam, Secularism, and Liberal Democracy: Toward a Democratic Theory for Muslim Societies*. Oxford: Oxford University Press, 2009.
Haynes, Jeffrey. *Religion and Politics in Africa*. London: Zed Books, 1996.
Hefner, Robert. "Rethinking Islam and Democracy." In *Rethinking Religion in World Affairs*, edited by Timothy Samuel Shah, Alfred Stepan, and Monica Duffy Toft, 85–103. New York: Oxford University Press, 2012.
Hernando, Orlando M. "Quezon and the Rule of Law in the Philippines." *Journal of Church and State* 5 (1963): 214–34.
Hirschkind, Charles. "Civic Virtue and Religious Reason: An Islamic Counterpublic." *Cultural Anthropology* 16, no. 1 (2001): 3–34.
Hogan, Gerard W. "De Valera, the Constitution, and the Historians." *Irish Jurist* 40 (2005): 291–320.
———. "Law and Religion: Church–State Relations in Ireland from Independence to the Present-Day." *American Journal of Comparative Law* 35, no. 1 (1987): 47–96.
Holzbauer, Christine. "Entretien: Macky Sall, candidat à la présidentielle au Sénégal: 'Il ne faut pas créer des fractures pour gagner les elections.'" *La Croix*, March 12, 2012.

Huntington, Samuel P. *Political Order in Changing Societies.* New Haven: Yale University Press, 1968.

Hurd, Elizabeth Shakman. *Beyond Religious Freedom: The New Global Politics of Religion.* Princeton: Princeton University Press, 2015.

Inglis, Tom. *Moral Monopoly: The Rise and Fall of the Catholic Church in Modern Ireland.* 2nd ed. Dublin: University College Dublin Press, 1998.

International Social Survey Programme Research Group. *International Social Survey Programme (ISSP): Religion III.* Cologne, Germany: GESIS, 2008.

Irish Department of Education and Skills. *Information on Areas for Possible Divesting of Patronage of Primary Schools.* Dublin: Central Printing Office, 2011.

Irish Human Rights Commission (IHRC). *Religion and Education: A Human Rights Perspective.* Dublin: IHRC, 2011.

Jacobsohn, Gary J. *The Wheel of Law: India's Secularism in Comparative Constitutional Context.* Princeton: Princeton University Press, 2003.

Journal of the Constitutional Convention of the Philippines. Vol. 1. Manila: East, 1961.

Kaly, Eugène. "Observation de l'élection présidentielle: L'Église Catholique est satisfaite du déroulement du scrutiny." *Le Soleil*, March 1, 2012.

Kalyvas, Stathis N. "Commitment Problems in Emerging Democracies—the Case of Religious Parties." *Comparative Politics* 32, no. 4 (2000): 379–98.

———. *The Rise of Christian Democracy in Europe.* Wilder House Series in Politics, History, and Culture. Ithaca: Cornell University Press, 1996.

Kébé, Abdoul Aziz. *Argumentaire religieux musulman sur l'equite de genre.* Dakar, Senegal: Ministre du developpement social, la famille et de la solidarite nationale, 2006.

Kenny, Enda. "Remarks on Structured Dialogue." *Dáil Debates* 762, no. 3 (April 24, 2012): 305–8.

"Kenny Defends Attack on Vatican." *Irish Independent*, September 4, 2011.

Keogh, Dermot. "The Constitutional Revolution: An Analysis of the Making of the Constitution." In *The Constitution of Ireland 1937–1987*, edited by Frank Litton, 4–85. Dublin: Institute of Public Administration, 1988.

———. *Ireland and the Vatican: The Politics and Diplomacy of Church–State Relations, 1922–1960.* Cork: Cork University Press, 1995.

———. "The Jesuits and the 1937 Constitution." *Studies* 78, no. 309 (1989): 82–95.

———. *Jews in Twentieth-Century Ireland: Refugees, Anti-Semitism, and the Holocaust.* Cork, Ireland: Cork University Press, 1998.

Keogh, Dermot, and Andrew McCarthy. *The Making of the Irish Constitution 1937: Bunreacht na Héireann.* Douglas Village, Ireland: Mercier Press, 2007.

Kessler, Christl. "Charismatic Christians: Genuinely Religious, Genuinely Modern." *Philippine Studies* 54, no. 4 (2006): 560–84.

Kessler, Christl, and Jürgen Rüland. *Give Jesus a Hand! Charismatic Christians, Populist Religion, and Politics in the Philippines.* Quezon City, Philippines: Ateneo de Manila University Press, 2008.

Kissane, Bill. "The Illusion of State Neutrality in a Secularizing Ireland." *West European Politics* 26, no. 1 (2003): 73–94.
———. *New Beginnings: Constitutionalism and Democracy in Modern Ireland*. Dublin: University College Dublin Press, 2011.
Kuru, Ahmet T. "Passive and Assertive Secularism." *World Politics* 59, no. 3 (2007): 568–94.
———. *Secularism and State Policies Toward Religion: The United States, France, and Turkey*. Cambridge: Cambridge University Press, 2009.
Lapus, Jesli. "Increase in the Monthly Allowances of Muslim Teachers in the ALIVE Program." Philippines Department of Education memorandum, March 8, 2010.
Lerner, Daniel. *The Passing of Traditional Society: Modernizing the Middle East*. Glencoe, Ill.: Free Press, 1958.
Lijphart, Arend. *Patterns of Democracy: Government Forms and Performance in Thirty-Six Countries*. New Haven: Yale University Press, 1999.
Lipset, Seymour Martin. "Some Social Requisites of Democracy: Economic Development and Political Legitimacy." *American Political Science Review* 53, no. 1 (1959): 69–105.
Lo, Pape Modou. "Des imams solidaires à l'église prient pour une alternance politique." *PressAfrik*, January 3, 2010, http://www.pressafrik.com/Des-imams-solidaires-a-l-eglise-prient-pour-une-alternance-politique_a18563.html.
Loimeier, Roman. "Dialectics of Religion and Politics in Senegal." In *New Perspectives on Islam in Senegal*, edited by Mamadou Diouf and Mara Lieichtman, 237–56. New York: Palgrave MacMillan, 2009.
———. "The Secular State and Islam in Senegal." In *Questioning the Secular State: The Worldwide Resurgence of Religion in Politics*, edited by David Westerlund, 183–97. London: Hurst, 1996.
Lust, Ellen. "Missing the Third Wave: Islam, Institutions, and Democracy in the Middle East." *Studies in Comparative International Development* 46 (2011): 163–90.
Magassouba, Moriba. *L'Islam au Sénégal: Demain les mollahs? La "question" musulmane et les partis politiques au Sénégal de 1946 à nos jours*. Collection les Afriques. Paris: Karthala, 1985.
Mahmood, Saba. *Politics of Piety: The Islamic Revival and the Feminist Subject*. Princeton: Princeton University Press, 2005.
Mahoney, James. "Path Dependence in Historical Sociology." *Theory and Society* 29, no. 4 (2000): 507–48.
Mahoney, James, and Dietrich Rueschemeyer. *Comparative Historical Analysis in the Social Sciences*. Cambridge Studies in Comparative Politics. Cambridge: Cambridge University Press, 2003.
Mahoney, James, and Kathleen Ann Thelen. *Explaining Institutional Change: Ambiguity, Agency, and Power*. Cambridge: Cambridge University Press, 2010.
Mane, Jean-Pierre. "Les chrétiens 'zappes' dans la distribution des terres." *L'Observateur*, May 25, 2010.

"Marcos Reassures Clergy." Foreign Broadcast Information Service—PNA, February 4, 1986.

Markovitz, Irving. "The Political Thought of Blaise Diagne and Lamine Guèye: Some Aspects of Social Structure and Ideology in Senegal." Présence Africaine, no. 72 (1969): 21–38.

Marquardt, Frederic. "Quezon and the Church." Philippines Free Press, August 19, 1954.

Martin, David. "Secularization and the Future of Christianity." Journal of Contemporary Religion 20, no. 2 (2005): 145–60.

Martin, Reverend Diarmuid. "Keeping the Show on the Road: Is This the Future of the Irish Catholic Church?" Speech to the Cambridge Group for Irish Studies, Magdalene College, Cambridge, February 22, 2011.

———. "The Relationship Between Church and State in Ireland." Speech to the Mater Dei Institute of Education, March 15, 2011. http://www.dublindiocese.ie/index.php?option=com_content&task=view&id=2333&Itemid=372.

Mastura, Michael. "Maguindana on Hopes and Fears from the Constitutional Convention." In Understanding Islam and Muslims in the Philippines, edited by Peter Gowing, 121–29. Quezon City, Philippines: New Day, 1988.

Mbacké, Khadim, and John O. Hunwick. Sufism and Religious Brotherhoods in Senegal. Princeton: Markus Wiener, 2005.

McDonagh, Patricia. "Muslim Anger at Opposition Calls for School Ban on Hijab." Irish Independent, June 2, 2008.

McGarry, Patsy. "The Changing Face of Faith." Irish Times, May 10, 2008.

McLoughlin, William Gerald. "Pietism and the American Character." American Quarterly 17, no. 2 (1965): 163–86.

Menchik, Jeremy. Islam and Democracy in Indonesia: Tolerance Without Liberalism. Cambridge Studies in Social Theory, Religion, and Politics. New York: Cambridge University Press, 2015.

Milligan, Jeffrey Ayala. "Reclaiming an Ideal: The Islamization of Education in the Southern Philippines." Comparative Education Review 50, no. 3 (2006): 410–30.

———. "Teaching Between the Cross and the Crescent Moon: Islamic Identity, Postcoloniality, and Public Education in the Southern Philippines." Comparative Education Review 47, no. 4 (2003): 468–92.

Milne, Kenneth. "The Protestant Churches in Independent Ireland." In Religion and Politics in Ireland at the Turn of the Millennium, edited by James Patrick Mackey and Enda McDonagh, 64–83. Dublin: Columba Press, 2003.

Mine, Youssoupha. "Des imams et le Cardinal Sarr pourraient jouer la médiation pour l'apaisement." Le Populaire, May 7, 2011.

Moreno, Antonio F. Church, State, and Civil Society in Postauthoritarian Philippines: Narratives of Engaged Citizenship. Quezon City, Philippines: Ateneo de Manila University Press, 2006.

Mozaffar, Shaheen, and Richard Vengroff. "A 'Whole System' Approach to the Choice of Electoral Rules in Democratizing Countries: Senegal in Comparative Perspective." *Electoral Studies* 21, no. 4 (2002): 601–16.
"Mutual Understanding." *Philippines Free Press*, July 23, 1938.
An-Naʿim, Abdullahi Ahmed. *Islam and the Secular State: Negotiating the Future of Shariʿa.* Cambridge, Mass.: Harvard University Press, 2008.
Nasr, Vali. "The Rise of 'Muslim Democracy.'" *Journal of Democracy* 16, no. 2 (2005): 13–27.
Ndiaye, Mously. "Macky Sall apres sa visite à Tivaouane et à Ndiassane: 'Aucun marabout ne donnera de ndigël dans ce pays.'" *Le Populaire*, March 13, 2012.
Ndiaye, Thiané. "Me Abdoulaye Wade lors la rencontre des Imams et oulémas du Sénégal." *Le Messager*, April 27, 2006.
New Ireland Forum. "Public Session: Thursday, 9 February 1984." Dublin Castle, Official Publications Collection, Trinity College Dublin.
———. *Report of the New Ireland Forum.* Dublin: Central Printing Office, 1983.
O'Brien, Carl. "Quinn Presses Orders Over Redress Shortfall." *Irish Times*, July 11, 2011.
O'Donnell, Guillermo A., Philippe C. Schmitter, and the Latin American Program of the Woodrow Wilson International Center for Scholars. *Transitions from Authoritarian Rule: Tentative Conclusions About Uncertain Democracies.* Baltimore: Johns Hopkins University Press, 1986.
O'Reilly, Emily. *Masterminds of the Right.* Dublin: Attic Press, 1992.
Packer, George. "The Moderate Martyr." *New Yorker*, September 11, 2006.
Perreau-Saussine, Emile. *Catholicism and Democracy: An Essay in the History of Political Thought.* Princeton: Princeton University Press, 2012.
Pew Forum on Religion and Public Life. *Tolerance and Tension: Islam and Christianity in Sub-Saharan Africa.* Washington, D.C.: Pew Research Group, 2007.
Philpott, Daniel. "Explaining the Political Ambivalence of Religion." *American Political Science Review* 101, no. 3 (2007): 505–25.
Pierson, Paul. "Increasing Returns, Path Dependence, and the Study of Politics." *American Political Science Review* 94, no. 2 (2000): 251–67.
Pilario, Daniel Franklin. "Catholic Movements in the Philippines: Clashes with 'Official' Powers." Unpublished manuscript. Copy in the author's files.
Pollak, Andy. "President Opens Centre for Islam in Clonskeagh." *Irish Times*, November 15, 1996.
"Protestants Plead for Irish Republic." *New York Times*, April 6, 1920.
Przeworski, Adam. *Democracy and the Market: Political and Economic Reforms in Eastern Europe and Latin America.* Studies in Rationality and Social Change. Cambridge: Cambridge University Press, 1991.
Przeworski, Adam, and John D. Sprague. *Paper Stones: A History of Electoral Socialism.* Chicago: University of Chicago Press, 1986.

Putnam, Robert D., and David E. Campbell. *American Grace: How Religion Divides and Unites Us*. New York: Simon & Schuster, 2011.

Quinn, David. "Atheism a Stranger to Reason." *Irish Catholic*, June 29, 2011.

Quinn, Ruairi. "Launch of Forum on Patronage and Pluralism in the Primary Sector." Irish Department of Education and Skills, Dublin, 2011.

Racelis, Mary, and Marita Castro Guevara. Interviewed by David Buckley. Quezon City, Philippines, June 30, 2014.

Radford, Katy. *Health, Faith, and Equality*. Dublin: Irish School of Ecumenics, 2008.

Ramirez, Joey. "Explaining Secular Democracy to Tito." *Rappler*, September 8, 2012. http://www.rappler.com/move-ph/33-editors-pick-moveph/12024-explaining-secular-democracy-to-tito.

Recto, Ralph. "Strengthen Madrasah Education to Promote Peace." Speech before the Senate of the Philippines, April 25, 2007.

Reynolds, Brigid, Sean Healy, and Conference of Religious of Ireland. *Social Partnership in a New Century*. Dublin: Conference of Religious of Ireland Justice Commission, 1999.

Robinson, David. "French 'Islamic' Policy and Practice in Late Nineteenth-Century Senegal." *Journal of African History* 29 (1988): 415–35.

———. *Paths of Accommodation: Muslim Societies and French Colonial Authorities in Senegal and Mauritania, 1880–1920*. Athens: Ohio University Press, 2000.

Rorty, Richard. "Religion as Conversation-Stopper." *Common Knowledge* 3, no. 1 (1994): 1–6.

Rufo, Aries. "RH and Elections: Pols Knew There's No Catholic Vote." *Rappler*, December 31, 2012. http://www.rappler.com/nation/politics/elections-2013/opinion/18783-rh-and-elections-pols-knew-thereâ%80%99s-no-catholic-vote.

Ruiz Navarro, V. *The Philippine Constitutional Convention*. Vol. 1. Manila: General Printing Press, 1934.

Samb, Djibril. *Comprendre la laïcité*. Dakar, Senegal: Nouvelles éditions africaines du Sénégal, 2005.

Sanders, Albert. "An Appraisal of the Iglesia ni Cristo." In *Studies in Philippine Church History*, edited by Gerald H. Anderson, 350–65. Ithaca: Cornell University Press, 1969.

Schumacher, John N. *The Propaganda Movement, 1880–1895: The Creators of a Filipino Consciousness, the Makers of Revolution*. Manila: Solidaridad, 1973.

———. *Readings in Philippine Church History*. 2nd ed. Quezon City, Philippines: Loyola School of Theology, Ateneo de Manila University, 1987.

Schwedler, Jillian. *Faith in Moderation: Islamist Parties in Jordan and Yemen*. Cambridge: Cambridge University Press, 2006.

Seck, Louis. "Wade demande à ses ministres d'aller recueillir des prières à Touba avant chaque mission importante." *Le Populaire*, January 21, 2011.

Selim, Ali. "Urgent Need for Interfaith Dialogue Based on Mutual Trust." *Irish Times*, April 22, 2008.

"Sénégal: Le gouvernement s'excuse de la 'profanation' de la mosquée." *Le Monde*, February 19, 2012.

Senghor, Léopold Sédar. *Liberté*. Paris: Éditions du seuil, 1964.

——. *Pierre Teilhard de Chardin et la politique africaine*. Paris: Éditions du seuil, 1962.

Shirley, Steven. *Guided by God: The Legacy of the Catholic Church in Philippine Politics*. Singapore: Marshall Cavendish Academic, 2004.

Silverio, Ina Alleco R. "Non-Catholic Groups Recognize Value of RH Bill to Maternal Health." *Butatlat*, August 10, 2012. http://bulatlat.com/main/2012/08/10/non-catholic-groups-recognize-value-of-rh-bill-to-maternal-health/.

Smith, Étienne. "Religious and Cultural Pluralism in Senegal." In *Tolerance, Democracy, and Sufis in Senegal*, edited by Mamadou Diouf, 147–79. New York: Columbia University Press, 2013.

Sow, Cécile. "Un président, un monument et une polemique." *Jeune Afrique*, August 11, 2009.

Stepan, Alfred. "Federalism Beyond the US Model." *Journal of Democracy* 10, no. 4 (1999): 19–34.

——. "The Multiple Secularisms of Modern Democratic and Non-democratic Regimes." In *Rethinking Secularism*, edited by Craig Calhoun, Mark Juergensmeyer, and Jonathan Van Antwerpen, 114–39. Oxford: Oxford University Press, 2011.

——. "Religion, Democracy, and the 'Twin Tolerations.'" *Journal of Democracy* 11, no. 4 (2000): 37–57.

——. "Stateness, Democracy, and Respect: Senegal in Comparative Perspective." In *Tolerance, Democracy, and Sufis in Senegal*, edited by Mamadou Diouf, 205–38. New York: Columbia University Press, 2013.

——. "Tunisia's Transition and the Twin Tolerations." *Journal of Democracy* 23, no. 2 (2012): 89–103.

Stepan, Alfred, and Graeme B. Robertson. "Arab, Not Muslim, Exceptionalism." *Journal of Democracy* 15, no. 4 (2004): 140–46.

Stout, Jeffrey. "The Folly of Secularism." *Journal of the American Academy of Religion* 76, no. 3 (2008): 533–44.

Sullivan, Winnifred Fallers. *The Impossibility of Religious Freedom*. Princeton: Princeton University Press, 2005.

Tanner, Marcus. *Ireland's Holy Wars: The Struggle for a Nation's Soul, 1500–2000*. New Haven: Yale University Press, 2001.

Templo, Isabel L. "The Truth Shall Set Us Free: The Role of Church-Owned Radio Stations in the Philippines." Center for Media Freedom and Responsibility, February 25, 2011. http://cmfr-phil.org/media-ethics-responsibility/ethics/the-truth-shall-set-us-free-the-role-of-church-owned-radio-stations-in-the-philippines/.

Thiam, El Hadji Abdoulaye. "Visite de Mandické Niang au Vatican." *Le Soleil*, March 16, 2010.

"Touba: Quatre dignitaires Mourides tenteraient de donner un 'ndigël' au nom du khalife." *Seneweb-News*, March 13, 2012. http://www.seneweb.com/news/Societe

/touba-quatre-dignitaires-mourides-tenteraient-de-donner-un-quot-ndigel-quot-au-nom-du-khalife_n_61446.html.

Toft, Monica Duffy. "Getting Religion? The Puzzling Case of Islam and Civil War." *International Security* 31, no. 4 (2007): 97–131.

Troeltsch, Ernst, and Olive Wyon. *The Social Teaching of the Christian Churches.* New York: Macmillan, 1931.

Tubeza, Philip. "CBCP Reminds Aquino About Excommunication." *Philippine Daily Inquirer*, September 30, 2010.

Ubac, Michael Lim, and Philip C. Tubeza. "Church–Gov't Ties Thawing." *Philippine Daily Inquirer*, December 2, 2012.

U.S. Department of State. "International Religious Freedom Report 2007: Senegal." 2007. http://www.state.gov/j/drl/rls/irf/2007/90117.htm.

Van Hoven, Ed. "The Nation Turbaned? The Construction of Nationalist Muslim Identities in Senegal." *Journal of Religion in Africa* 30, no. 2 (2000): 225–48.

Villalón, Leonardo Alfonso. "From Argument to Negotiation: Constructing Democracy in African Muslim Contexts." *Comparative Politics* 42, no. 4 (2010): 375–93.

———. *Islamic Society and State Power in Senegal: Disciples and Citizens in Fatick.* African Studies. Cambridge: Cambridge University Press, 1995.

———. "Negotiating Islam in the Era of Democracy: Senegal in Comparative Regional Perspective." In *Tolerance, Democracy, and Sufis in Senegal*, edited by Mamadou Diouf, 239–68. New York: Columbia University Press, 2013.

Villarruz, Nicolas V. *Commentaries and Opinions on the Constitution of the Philippines.* Manila: Imprenta Manila, 1935.

"Wade à Touba: Plus d 200 millions pour un 'ngiguel.'" *Seneweb News*, February 15, 2012.

Walshe, Joseph P. "Secretary's Report to Eamon de Valera on His Visit to Rome." *Documents in Irish Foreign Policy* 5, no. 43 (1937). http://www.difp.ie/docs/1937/Visit-to-Rome-_-Constitution/2189.htm.

Warner, Carolyn, and Manfred Wenner. "Religion and the Political Organization of Muslims in Europe." *Perspectives on Politics* 4, no. 3 (2006): 457–79.

Waterbury, John. "Democracy Without Democrats? The Potential for Political Liberalization in the Middle East." In *Democracy Without Democrats? The Renewal of Politics in the Muslim World*, edited by Ghassan Salame, 23–45. London: Tauris, 1994.

Whyte, Gerard. "Religion and Education: The Irish Constitution." Paper presented at "TCD/IHRC Conference on Religion and Education: A Human Rights Perspective," Dublin, November 27, 2010.

Whyte, John Henry. *Church and State in Modern Ireland, 1923–1979.* 2nd ed. Dublin: Gill and Macmillan, 1980.

Wiegele, Katharine L. *Investing in Miracles: El Shaddai and the Transformation of Popular Catholicism in the Philippines.* Honolulu: University of Hawai'i Press, 2005.

Yeats, William Butler. "Debate on Divorce Legislation Resumed." *Seanad Eireann Debates* 5 (June 11, 1925): 435–44.
Youngblood, Robert L. "Church Opposition to Martial Law in the Philippines." *Asian Survey* 18, no. 5 (1978): 505–20.
———. "The Protestant Church in the Philippines' New Society." *Bulletin of Concerned Asian Scholars* 12, no. 3 (1980): 19–30.

INDEX

Abainza, Estanislao, 228n7
Abinales, Patricio, 147
abortion, 213n23
accommodationists, 28, 96, 100
Aglipay, Gregorio, 227n41, 227n43
Aglipayan Church, 137, 147–48, 149, 153, 227nn41–43
Aglipay v. Ruiz, 140, 141
Ahern, Bertie, 76
AIDS/HIV, 23, 29, 32, 91, 117
Alessi, Francis, 157
Algeria, 3, 13
Alonto, Ahmad Domocao, 158
Ang Kapatiran (Philippines), 169, 173, 174
an-Na'im, Abdullahi, 12
anticlericalism, 28, 216–17n6; benevolent secularism undercutting of, 29, 96, 131; defined, 206n47; in Ireland, 52, 55, 56; in Philippines, 144–45, 152–53;

rationalist theories about, 17–18; in Senegal, 96–97
anti-Semitism, 46, 208n18
Aquino, Benigno, III, 165–66, 167, 169, 170, 232n70
Aquino, Corazon, 159, 161
Arabic Language and Islamic Values Education (ALIVE), 171, 172
Arab world, 86, 191; Awakening of, 16, 19; religious-secular tensions in, 3, 10
assertive secularism, 24–25, 30, 85; Kuru on, 22, 24, 85
Assises nationales du Sénégal, 119
Association des juristes sénégalaises, 109
Association of Major Religious Superiors of the Philippines (AMRSP), 156, 157, 161
Ateneo de Manila University, 136, 165–66, 168
Atheist Ireland, 64, 71

atheists, 62–63. *See also* nonbelievers and "nones"
autonomy, religious, 20, 24–25, 184, 196–97; in Ireland, 53; in Philippines, 141–42, 166; in Senegal, 90, 91, 95, 104, 111, 119, 130

Bacani, Teodoro, 158, 159
Bacik, Ivana, 62
Baha'i, 113
Balangue, David, 168
Belgica, Grepor "Butch," 162, 175
benevolent secularism: alternative theories to, 16–21, 57–59, 100–103, 149–51; ambiguities of, 193–96; anticlericalism undercut by, 29, 96, 131; assessing case studies in, 46–52, 88–93, 138–43; challenges to, 186–87, 188, 196–97, 198–99; and coalition alliances, 28–32, 73, 132, 157–59, 184; conceptualization of, 22–25; and cooperation, 23, 24, 28, 47; defined, 4–5, 21, 22; and differentiation, 22–23; endurance of, 63, 132, 170–71, 181–82; future of, 196–99; institutional effects of, 5, 25–35, 52–57, 93–100, 112–25, 143–49, 150–51; *laïcité* as, 88–93; pious secularism empowered by, 26–27, 53, 94, 184; and pluralization, 164–75; policy makers and, 6–7, 29, 194; and principled distance, 23–24, 114–15; and public opinion, 33–34, 94, 125–30, 175–81; and "public religion," 2, 5, 27, 103, 184; regime threats to, 114–16, 156–57; and religious minorities, 28–29, 33, 72–73, 146–47, 148; religious-secular divide bridged by, 5, 21–22, 26, 32–34, 75, 121, 131, 175, 184, 186, 187–88, 197, 199; and secularism trap avoidance, 21, 26, 99, 186, 196, 199; tensions in, 61, 82, 103–5, 181–82, 190–91, 199; three dimensions of, 47, 60, 92, 105, 190–91; and twin tolerations, 143–44, 186
Berger, Peter, 4, 16

Bernas, Joaquin, 139–40, 158, 168
Bewley, Charles, 53–54
Bhargava, Rajeev, 5, 22, 24, 78, 115
Binchy, William, 77, 216n55
Bishops-Businessmen's Committee on Human Development (BBC-HD), 158, 162, 165–66, 168, 197
Bishops-Ulama Conference, 163, 171
blasphemy, 50, 64
Boland, Gerald, 55
Bonifacio, Andrés, 144
Boransing, Manaros, 171
Buddhism, 66
Burgos, José, 226n31

Cabrera, Norman, 174
Cahill, Edward, 53, 56, 58, 210n41
Calderón, Felipe, 145–46
Camara, Fatou Kiné, 121, 130, 217–18n21
Carlos, Meneleo, Jr., 168
Carroll, John, 168, 174
Casanova, José, 27, 36, 102
Castro, Melvin, 167
Catholic Bishops' Conference of the Philippines (CBCP), 1, 136, 161–62; and RH Law, 154, 165, 166, 167, 168–70, 190, 197
Catholic Church: International Eucharistic Congress of, 56, 58, 148, 210n32; rationalist theories on, 18; role of in Ireland, 35, 44–45, 46, 49, 50, 51, 53–54, 67–69, 83; role of in Philippines, 134–36, 145–46, 150; in Senegal, 88, 98, 111, 123; and Vatican, 53–54, 113–14, 157; Vatican II of, 37, 58, 65, 148, 150.
Catholics for Reproductive Health, 168
Catholic Vote Philippines, 174
Celdran, Carlos, 1, 167
censorship, 49, 59–60
Cesari, Jocelyne, 23
Charismatic movement, 161–62, 175, 176, 177–78, 180, 233n81

Chartre de gouvernance démocratique, 119
China, 14
Christian Irishman, 54
Church-Military Liaison Committee (CMLC), 156–57
Church of England, 14, 22, 46
Claudio, Sylvia, 165
coalition alliances, 21, 26, 99, 186, 196, 199; benevolent secularism encouragement of, 28–32, 132, 157–59, 184; data collection on, 40; institutional effects of, 29–30, 31–34, 63, 82, 143–49; in Ireland, 43, 52, 63, 73, 74–77, 82, 186; in Philippines, 148–49, 152, 157–59, 167–69, 171–72, 181; and principled distance, 23–24, 114–15; and religious integralism, 27–28, 30–31, 94; and religious minorities, 28–29, 33; in Senegal, 100, 118–25, 126–27, 130; and twin tolerations, 143–44, 186. *See also* interfaith relations; religious-secular partnerships
Cocquino, Luigi, 157
Code de la famille (Senegal), 103–5, 130, 187
Code of Muslim Personal Laws, 23, 142, 160, 171
Collectif pour la défense de la laïcité et de l'unité nationale au Sénégal, 119
colonialism, 193–94; Ireland legacy of, 43, 193–94, 209n20; Philippine legacy of, 36, 134, 138, 144, 146–47, 150, 192, 195, 225n20, 226n31, 226n34; Senegal legacy of, 96, 194, 218n22
Colson, Charles, 162
Comité islamique pour la réforme du Code de la famille au Sénégal (CIRCOFS), 27, 110, 113, 119
Committee for Ethics of the Conseil des ONG d'appui au développement (CONGAD), 108, 109
Commonwealth Constitution (Philippines), 28, 149–50, 195; drafting of, 28, 146, 188; on religion-state separation, 133, 138–40, 142–43; on religious education, 151
Conference of Religion of Ireland, 44–45
Conseil supérieur des chefs religieux, 95
Constitution (Senegal), 24, 55, 84–85, 89, 91, 130
Constitution of 1937 (Ireland), 35, 63, 207n6; on Catholicism, 46, 49, 50, 67, 212n16; on education, 48, 213–14n26; on family and marriage, 48; no religion endorsed in, 46, 59, 208n14; on private property, 49; protection for religious minorities in, 46–47, 49, 51, 68, 72; revision of, 67–68; secularity of, 42, 43
contraception, 68, 212–13n18
Coolahan, John, 74
cooperation, religion-state: benevolent secularism theory on, 23, 24, 28, 47; and differentiation, 189–90, 191; in educational realm, 32, 47–48; interfaith relations strengthened by, 32–33; in Ireland, 47–49, 52–53, 64–65, 71, 81, 209n20; in Philippines, 139–41, 146, 153, 159–60, 166, 224–25n12; and principled distance, 188–89, 191; in Senegal, 89, 90–91, 95, 103–5, 116–18
Cosgrave, William, 56
Couples for Christ, 161–62, 175
Cumann na nGaedheal party (Ireland), 56

Dahl, Robert, 10
Dakar, Senegal, 87, 107, 108, 110, 120, 122, 131
Daly, Cahal, 65, 74
Daly, Eoin, 70–71
David, Rina Jimenez, 157–58
Davide, Hilario, 159
de los Reyes, J. C., 174
del Pilar, Marcelo, 144
democracy. *See* religion-democracy relationship

256 INDEX

de Quiros, Conrado, 168
Deutsch, Karl, 16
de Valera, Éamon, 50, 55–56, 59–60, 210n36; and religious leaders, 42, 53–55, 67, 186, 211n51
Dia, Mamadou, 91, 92, 97, 98
Diagne, Assane, 108, 120
Diagne, Blaise, 96
Diagne, Souleymane Bachir, 91, 92
Dias, Jean-Paul, 115
Dièye, Cheikh Abdoulaye, 114
Dièye, Cheikh Bamba, 121
differentiation: benevolent secularism and, 22–23; and cooperation, 189–90, 191; and credible commitment, 28; in Ireland, 47, 49–50, 52, 55–56, 78, 80; in Philippines, 138–39, 153, 156, 159, 166, 173–74; in Senegal, 89–90, 97, 112–14
Dignitatis humanae, 65
Dionisio, Eleanor, 169
Diouf, Abdou, 88
Diouf, Léon, 111
diversity: challenges of, 195–96; in Ireland, 45, 64, 66, 70–71, 74–75, 186, 188–89; limits to internal, 30–31; in Philippines, 135–37, 150, 160–61, 172; in Senegal, 86, 96, 98, 102, 131, 207n55
divorce: Ireland and, 48, 68, 69, 213n21; Philippines and, 141, 142, 160
Djerejian, Edward, 3
Duffy, Gavan, 47
Duterte, Rodrigo, 181, 188

economic development, 149; secularization theory on, 10, 17, 57; in Senegal, 91, 101, 109, 117–18
Educate Together (ET, Ireland), 47, 71–72, 199, 214n27
education and schools: in Ireland, 47–48, 50, 63, 70–72, 73, 76, 193–94, 213–14nn26–27; in Philippines, 139–40, 146, 151–52, 159–60, 171; in Senegal, 116–17, 121, 221n35

Egypt, 13, 19, 27, 89, 191
El Shaddai movement (Philippines), 136, 161, 172–73
Employment Equality Acts (Ireland), 83, 216n60
Enrile, Juan Ponce, 158
Epifanio de los Santos Avenue (EDSA), 156, 158
Esliza, Leoncio, 145
establishment, religious, 27; Ireland and, 46, 49, 50, 53, 54, 59; Philippines and, 36, 138, 144–45; Senegal and, 93–94; Sweden and, 204n19; United Kingdom and, 14, 22, 24, 46
Estanislao, Jesus, 162
Estrada, "Erap," 172–73
Estrada v. Escritor, 138, 141, 160
European Court of Human Rights, 197
European Union, 71

family: Irish constitution on, 48; Philippine code on, 160; Senegal code on, 27, 103–5, 130, 187
Family Planning Organization of the Philippines, 164
Fawzayni, Matlaboul, 111
Federation of Free Workers / Federation of Free Farmers (Philippines), 140
Fianna Fáil (Ireland), 56
Fitzgerald, Mary, 195
FitzGerald, Taoiseach Garret, 63, 68–69
FitzGerald, William, 212–13n18
Forum civil (Senegal), 123
Fox, Jonathan, 21, 32
France, 84–85, 216–17n6
Free State, Irish, 36, 54, 56, 57; Constitution of, 43, 45, 47, 207–8n6
Front pour le socialisme et la démocratie / Benno Jubël (FSD/BJ, Senegal), 114, 121

GABRIELA Women's Party (Philippines), 164
Gambetta, Léon, 85

Genilo, Eric, 168, 169
Gibbons, James, 227n38
Gill, Anthony, 18, 58
Gomez, Mariano, 226n31
Gregg, John, 54
Guevara, Marita Castro, 230n42
Guèye, Lamine, 96–97, 98, 111, 114, 117, 130

Habermas, Jürgen, 12, 190
health care: in Ireland, 59, 209n20; in Philippines, 165–70; in Senegal, 32, 117, 194
Herzog, Issac, 54–55
Hindus, 66
Hobbes, Thomas, 2–3
Hogan, Claire, 72–73
Hogan, Gerard, 46, 49, 212n16, 213n21
Hogan, Linda, 65, 213n23
Holohan, John, 71–72
homosexuality, 61, 69. See also LGBT rights
Hontiveros, Risa, 167
Humanist Association of Ireland, 71
humanists, 45, 64
Huntington, Samuel, 16

Iglesia ni Cristo (INC), 137, 141, 147, 168, 227n41
Indonesia, 3, 86, 198
institutional replacement, 14, 204n19
institutional structure: assessing impact of, 35–38; benevolent secularism's effect on, 5, 25–35, 46, 52–57, 93–100, 112–25, 143–49, 150–51; and coalition alliances, 29–30, 31–34, 63, 82, 143–49, 151; and public opinion, 192–93; significance of, 11, 25–26, 33, 187–88, 194–95
Interfaith Partnership for the Promotion of Responsible Parenthood (Philippines), 167
interfaith relations, 32–33, 190; in Ireland, 63, 74–75; in Philippines, 163,

167, 171–73, 174, 181; in Senegal, 88, 98–99, 107, 113, 119–21, 123–24, 128–29, 130, 187, 190. See also coalition alliances; religious-secular partnerships
international bodies, 197
International Eucharistic Congress, 56, 58, 148, 210n32
international population flow, 131, 155, 185
International Social Survey Programme (ISSP), 41
Ireland, 7, 36, 42–83, 186–87; and abortion, 213n23; alternative explanations of secularism in, 57–59; anticlericalism in, 52, 55, 56; assessing benevolent secularism in, 46–52; British colonial rule in, 43, 193–94, 209n20; Catholic Church role in, 35, 44–45, 46, 49, 50, 51, 53–54, 67–69, 83; censorship in, 49, 59–60; coalitional ties in, 43, 52, 63, 73, 74–77, 82, 186; Constitution of 1922 in, 43, 46, 47, 207n6; contraception in, 68, 212–13n18; cooperation of state and religion in, 47–49, 52–53, 64–65, 71, 81, 188–89; demographic shifts in, 64–65; differentiation in, 47, 49–50, 52, 55–56, 78, 80; diversity in, 45, 64, 66, 70–71, 74–75, 186, 188–89; divorce in, 48, 68, 69, 213n21; educational patronage reform in, 70–72, 76; effects of benevolent secularism in, 5, 52–57; evolution of religion-secular ties in, 75–77; health care in, 59, 209n20; Hindus and Buddhists in, 66; independence of, 45, 46, 207n6; interfaith partnerships in, 63, 74–75; international influences in, 197; Jews in, 45, 47, 49, 51, 54–55, 82, 208n18; LGBT rights in, 69; media in, 63; Mother and Child Crisis in, 59–60; Muslim minority in, 19, 29, 33, 45, 50, 66, 72–73, 74–75, 195; nonbelievers and "no religion" category in, 43, 45, 64–65, 80; Northern, 45, 55–56, 68; pious secularism in,

Ireland (continued)
43, 53–54, 65, 81; political parties in, 56, 211n59; principled distance in, 49–50, 51–52, 59–60, 61, 78, 81, 186; Protestants in, 45, 47, 49, 50, 54, 55–56, 59, 66; public opinion in, 77–81, 193; and religious establishment, 46, 49, 50, 53, 54, 59; religious exemptions in, 47, 82–83, 208n17, 216n60; religious integralism in, 53–54, 59, 60, 61, 69, 173; religious landscape of, 44–45, 64–66; Republicanism in, 55, 76, 211n54; schools and education in, 47–48, 50, 63, 70–72, 73, 76, 193–94, 213–14nn26–27; sexual abuse scandals in, 61, 62, 65; Sikhs in, 214n35; and twin tolerations, 43, 46, 52. *See also* Constitution of 1937
Ireland, John, 227n38
Irish Catholic Bishops' Conference, 44
Irish Human Rights Commission (IHRC), 76–77, 215–16nn53–54
Irish Independent, 75
Irish Labour Party, 56, 211n59
Irish Times, 42, 60, 75, 195
Irwin, J. A. H., 52, 54, 211n51
Islam: Sufi, 86–88, 102. *See also* Muslims
Islam and Christianity in Sub-Saharan Africa, 125
Islamic Cultural Centre of Ireland, 195

Jamaat Ibadou Rahman (Senegal), 110
Jehovah's Witnesses, 24, 141, 196
Jesuits, 46, 168
Jews, 45, 47, 49, 51, 54–55, 82, 208n18

Kalyvas, Stathis, 10, 18, 28, 101
Keane, Ronan, 46, 208n14
Kébé, Abdoul Aziz, 108, 110, 114, 117, 123
Kenny, Enda, 62, 75–76
Kessler, Christl, 163, 177, 233n81
Kissane, Bill, 42, 52, 63, 70
Knights of Columbanus, 45, 56
Kuru, Ahmet, 11, 21, 22, 24, 85, 134

Laffoy, Mary, 50
laïcité: alternative explanations for, 100–103; as benevolent secularism, 88–93; coalition alliances defending, 100, 109, 118–25, 126–27, 130; cooperative dimension of, 89, 90–91, 95, 103–5, 116–18; defined, 91, 92; and election of 2012, 106–7, 122–25; in France, 42, 85; future challenges to, 130–31, 132, 187; instability in, 103–5; and institutional change, 112–18; and interfaith cooperation, 88, 98–99, 107, 113, 119–21, 123–24, 128–29, 130, 187, 190; public opinion in Senegal on, 125–30
Latin America, 27, 155
Laurel, José, 158–59
Lerner, Daniel, 9
LGBT rights, 69, 164
liberalism, 12, 37, 53, 102–3, 150, 184, 190, 195; religious, 19–20, 58
Lijphart, Arend, 10
Lipset, Seymour Martin, 10
Loimeier, Roman, 95, 97–98, 220n12

M23 Movement (Senegal), 122
Mabini, Apolinario, 144, 146
Magadia, José, 170
Mahoney, James, 11, 14
Malik Sy, al-Hajj, 87
Malolos Congress (Philippines, 1898), 134, 144–46, 147, 150, 188, 225–26n22
Manalo, Felix, 227n43
Marcos, Ferdinand, 8, 36, 142, 156–57, 228n7
marriage: in Ireland, 48, 69; in Philippines, 142, 160, 229n24; in Senegal, 98, 130
Martin, David, 27
Martin, Diarmuid, 62, 65, 66, 74, 76
masons and Freemasonry, 56, 96, 144–45, 146, 152, 192, 226n31
Massey, W. H., 54
Mastura, Michael, 142
Mater Dei Institute, 48, 65

Mbacké, Abdou Lahatte, 91–92, 104
Mbacké, Abdou Samath, 114
Mbacké, Amadou Bamba, 87, 94, 198
Mbacké, Kara, 90, 110, 114, 121
Mbacké, Khadim, 91, 108–9
Mbaye, Keba, 104–5
McGarry, Patsy, 75
McGee v. Attorney General, 68
McKinley, William, 146, 226n34
McQuaid, John Charles, 42, 50, 52, 53, 58, 67
methodology: case selection, 35–38, 206–7n51; process tracing, 35–36
Mill, John Stuart, 206–7n51
Milligan, Jeffrey Ayala, 170–71
Mindanao, 5, 36–37, 137, 141–42, 160, 163, 170–72
missionaries: in Ireland, 54; in Philippines, 135–36, 137, 144–45, 147, 150, 156
moderation thesis: as explanation for Irish secularism, 58; as explanation for Philippine secularism, 150–51; as explanation for Senegal secularism, 102–3; imprecision of, 19–21
modernization theory, 10, 37, 149; tenets of, 16–17
Moreno, Antonio, 161
Morrow, Trevor, 211n51
Mosque El Hadj Malick Sy, 122
Mother and Child Crisis (Ireland), 59–60
Mourides, 104, 115, 124, 198; economic power of, 108–9, 110–11; land concessions to, 91–92; political involvement of, 122, 221n23; public views of, 127–30; and Senegal demographics, 86–87; succession struggle among, 110, 220n11; Tidjanns' relationship with, 102
Mullan, Peter, 216n60
multivocality, 11, 26, 30, 102
Muslims: in Ireland, 19, 29, 33, 45, 50, 66, 72–73, 74–75, 195; in Philippines, 36–37, 137, 141–42, 146–47, 149, 155, 163, 170–72. *See also* Sufi brotherhoods

National Citizens' Movement for Free Elections (Philippines), 158, 170
National Commission on Muslim Filipinos, 163
National Commission on the Role of Filipino Women, 164
National Council of Churches of the Philippines (NCCP), 156, 157, 163, 167, 174
National Ulama Conference of the Philippines, 137, 163
Ndiaye, Mamadou Bamba, 115, 117, 119
Ndiaye, Théodore Ndok, 111–12, 115
ndigël, 114, 123, 124
New Ireland Forum, 63, 68–69, 74
Niang, Mandické, 113–14
Niass, Ahmed Khalifa, 120
Niasse, Moustapha, 220n8
Nieva, Maria Teresa, 158
Nolledo, Jose, 158
nonbelievers and "nones," 198–99; in Ireland, 43, 45, 54, 64–65, 80; in Philippines, 158–59, 167
Northern Ireland, 45, 55–56, 68
Norway, 46
Nozaleda, Bernardino, 227n43
Nugent, Michael, 64, 71

O'Brien, Donal Cruise, 90
Odchimar, Nereo, 167, 230n39
O'Donnell, Guillermo, 10
O'Hanlon, Gerry, 65
Ople, Blas, 159
Opus Dei movement, 162
O'Reilly, Emily, 213n23
Osmeña, Sergio, 139

Pabillo, Broderick, 174, 232n77
Pacelli, Eugenio (Pius XII), 53–54
Panlilio, "Among Ed," 172, 173–74

Parish Pastoral Council for Responsible Voting (Philippines), 170, 174
Parti de la solidarité sénégalaise (PSS), 95
Parti de la vérité pour le développement (PVD, Senegal), 90, 114
Parti démocratique sénégalais (PDS), 106
passive secularism, 24, 89, 138, 189
path dependence, 2, 11, 13, 25, 32; benevolent secularism and, 82, 121, 186, 192; of Senegal laïcité, 121, 132, 218n22
Pentecostalism, 17, 27, 66, 91, 162
People Power Revolution (Philippines), 155, 157–59, 160
Perreau-Saussine, Émile, 12
Pew Forum on Religion and Public Life, 41
Philippine Center for Islam and Democracy, 137, 163, 170, 171
Philippine Council of Evangelical Churches (PCEC), 163, 167
Philippines, 8, 133–82, 187–88; Aglipayan Church in, 137, 147–48, 149, 153, 227nn41–43; anticlericalism in, 144–45, 152–53; assessing benevolent secularism in, 5, 138–43; as Catholic country, 1, 135–37, 161; Charismatic movement in, 161–62, 175, 176, 177–78, 180, 233n81; coalition alliances in, 148–49, 152, 157–59, 167–69, 171–72, 181; Constitution of 1987 of, 133, 158, 159–60, 172, 232n68; cooperation of state and religion in, 139–41, 146, 163, 166, 224–25n12; data collection on, 40; differentiation in, 138–39, 153, 156, 159, 166, 173–74; diversity in, 135–37, 150, 160–61, 172; divorce in, 141, 142, 160; education and schools in, 139–40, 146, 151–52, 159–60, 171; election campaigns in, 172–75, 232n70; Family Code revision in, 160; institutional structure in, 143–49; interfaith relations in, 163, 167, 171–73, 174, 181; international influences in, 198; lay Catholic communities in, 161–62; Malolos Congress and Constitution in, 134, 144–46, 147, 150, 188, 225–26n22; Marcos regime in, 156–57, 228n7; marriage in, 142, 160, 229n24; Muslims in, 36–37, 137, 141–42, 146–47, 149, 155, 163, 170–72; nonbelievers in, 158–59; non-Catholic Christians in, 147–48, 161–63, 227nn41–43, 229n30; People Power Revolution in, 155, 157–59, 160; pious secularism in, 145–46, 152, 153, 177–80; pluralization in, 155, 160–64, 180, 182, 229n25; political parties in, 172–73, 232n68; principled distance in, 141–42, 160, 166, 171; Protestants in, 136–37, 146, 147, 148, 156, 157, 158, 167, 198, 226n34; and public opinion, 191–92; public opinion in, 175–81; and religious establishment, 36, 138, 144–45; religious exemptions in, 24, 141–42, 160; religious landscape of, 135–37; religious orders in, 136; Reproductive Health Law in, 154, 165–70, 190, 230n42; secularist bloc in, 164; Spanish colonialism in, 36, 134, 144, 192, 225n20, 226n31; and twin tolerations, 134–35, 143–44; U.S. colonial rule in, 134, 138, 146–47, 150, 192, 195, 226n34. See also Catholic Bishops' Conference of the Philippines; Commonwealth Constitution
Philpott, Daniel, 10–11
pious secularism: benevolent secularism's empowering of, 26–27, 53, 94, 184; in Ireland, 43, 53–54, 65, 81; in Philippines, 145–46, 152, 153, 177–80; religious integralism vs., 27; in Senegal, 94–95, 104, 109–10, 120, 123–24, 125, 129–30
Plunket, William, 54
pluralism: and coalition building, 168–69, 185; and interfaith relations, 35; in Ireland, 50, 71, 164; in Philippines, 144, 151, 155, 160–64, 167, 169, 171, 173, 175,

180–82, 229n25; rationalist arguments on, 18, 101; and secular evolution, 18, 164; in Senegal, 109–12; as worldwide phenomenon, 155, 195
Poland, 210n41
Presence chrétienne, 111, 115, 123
principled distance: benevolent secularism theory on, 23–24, 114–15; and cooperation, 188–89, 191; in Ireland, 49–50, 51–52, 59–60, 61, 78, 81, 186; in Philippines, 141–42, 160, 166, 171; in Senegal, 91–92, 98, 114–16, 127, 217–18n21
private property, 49
Project Madrasa Education (Philippines), 171
Protestants: in Ireland, 45, 47, 49, 50, 54, 55–56, 59, 66; in Philippines, 136–37, 146, 147, 148, 156, 157, 158, 167, 198, 226n34; in Senegal, 113, 131
Przeworski, Adam, 10
public opinion, 33–34, 185; and institutional design, 192; in Ireland, 77–81; in Philippines, 175–81; in Senegal, 125–30, 224n76

Quezon, Manuel, 141, 145, 147, 152
Quiboloy, Apollo, 162–63, 174
Quinn, David, 83
Quinn, Ruairi, 70, 76, 83, 215n49
Quinn's Supermarket decision (Ireland), 82, 208n17

Racelis, Mary, 230n42
Rama, Napoleón, 159
Ramos, Fidel, 158
Rasul, Amina, 163
rationalist and rational choice theories, 37; and credible commitment, 28; as explanation for Senegal secularism, 101–2; as explanation for Irish secularism, 58; as explanation for Philippine secularism, 149–50; pessimism of, 17–19

Rawls, John, 20
Recto, Ralph, 172
Regan, Ethna, 65
religion-democracy relationship, 3, 7, 26, 190; assessing outcomes of, 12–14; future research on, 184–85; rationalist theories on, 17–18; scholarship on, 9–12, 35; tensions in, 2–3, 10, 199
religious exemptions, 24, 205n37; in Ireland, 47, 82–83, 208n17, 216n60; in Philippines, 24, 141–42, 160; in Senegal, 24, 90, 91–92; tensions around, 196–97
religious integralism: benevolent secularism's impact on, 27–28, 30–31, 94; in Ireland, 53–54, 59, 60, 61, 69, 173; pious secularism vs., 27; in Senegal, 94–95
religious liberty: and contemporary religious politics, 6; curtailment of, 14, 29, 58, 156; differentiation and, 22; in Ireland, 46–47, 208n18; in Philippines, 139, 144–45; in Senegal, 86, 89, 113–14, 116; Vatican II on, 58, 65
religious minorities: benevolent secularism and, 28–29, 33, 146–47; and coalition alliances, 32–33;
—in Ireland, 46–47, 50–51, 54, 66, 81, 186; Jews, 45, 47, 49, 51, 54–55, 82, 208n18; Muslims, 19, 29, 33, 45, 50, 66, 72–73, 74–75, 195; other religions, 66, 214n35; Protestants, 45, 47, 49, 50, 54, 55–56, 59, 66;
—in Philippines, 148–49, 161–63, 229n30; Aglipayan Church, 137, 147–48, 149, 153, 227nn41–43; Charismatic movement, 161–62, 175, 176, 177–78, 180, 233n81; Christian revivalists, 163; Muslims, 36–37, 137, 141–42, 146–47, 149, 155, 163, 170–72;
—in Senegal: African religions, 217–18n21; Catholics, 87–88, 98–99, 107, 111–12, 115–16, 117, 123, 127, 190; Protestants, 113, 131

religious moderation thesis. *See* moderation thesis

religious-secular divide: in Arab world, 3, 10; benevolent secularism's bridging of, 5, 21–22, 26, 32–34, 75, 121, 131, 175, 184, 186, 187–88, 197, 199; in Ireland, 81–82, 168–69; in Philippines, 167, 181, 188; rationalist theories on, 17; in Senegal, 131–32

religious-secular partnerships, 37, 63–64, 75–77, 82, 186; in Philippines, 164, 166–67, 169–70, 171, 175, 181–82, 188, 197–98; in Senegal, 107–8, 118–19, 121, 130. *See also* coalition alliances; interfaith relations

Reproductive Health Law (RH Law, Philippines), 154, 165–70, 190, 230n42

Reyes, Rex, 167, 174

Rigos, Cirilo, 158

Rizal, José, 1, 144, 226n31; *Noli me tángere*, 136

Robinson, Mary, 73

Romero, Oscar, 156

Rorty, Richard, 12

Rosales, Gaudencio, 161

Russian Orthodox Church, 18

Sall, Macky, 116, 122, 123, 124

Samb, Djibril, 88, 90

Santiago, Miriam Defensor, 167–68

Sarr, Théodore Adrien, 111–12, 120, 123

Scharbrodt, Oliver, 72

Schmitter, Philippe, 10

Seck, Alphonse, 122, 131

Seck, Boubacar, 109

Seck, Jacques, 119–20

secular emergence, 2, 4, 12, 18, 31; in Ireland, 42–61; in Philippines, 36, 133–53; researching, 39–40; in Senegal, 36, 84–105

secular evolution, 2, 4, 31, 33–34, 40; alternative theories on, 12, 17, 18, 20; characteristics of, 14–15; in Ireland, 36, 62–83; in Philippines, 36–37, 154–82; in Senegal, 36, 106–32

secularism, benevolent. *See* benevolent secularism

secularism trap, 4, 17; alternative theories on, 16, 37, 100, 105, 151; assertive secularism and, 29, 30; benevolent secularism and avoidance of, 21, 26, 99, 186, 196, 199; causes of, 13–14; defined, 3

secularization theory, 9–10, 17, 57, 100–101

Selim, Ali, 72, 73, 74–75

Senegal, 7–8, 84–132, 187; alternative explanations for *laïcité* in, 100–103; anticlericalism in, 96–97; Catholic minority in, 87–88, 98–99, 107, 111–12, 115–16, 117, 123, 127, 190; coalition alliances in, 100, 118–25, 126–27, 130; Constitution of, 24, 84–85, 89, 91, 130; cooperation between state and religion in, 89, 90–91, 95, 103–5, 116–18; demographics of, 86–87; differentiation in, 89–90, 97, 112–14; diversity in, 86, 96, 98, 102, 131, 207n55; economic development in, 91, 101, 109, 117–18; education in, 116–17, 121, 221n35; election of 2000 in, 109, 113, 220n8; election of 2012 in, 122–25; family code in, 27, 103–5, 130, 187; French colonial rule in, 96, 194, 218n22; institutional effects in, 93–100; interfaith ties and partnerships in, 88, 98–99, 107, 113, 119–21, 123–24, 128–29, 130, 187, 190; and international influences, 197–98; land concessions in, 91, 130, 218n22; marriage in, 98, 130; media in, 220n12; party politics in, 89, 95, 109, 110, 114, 187, 217n11; pilgrimage funding in, 23, 91, 117, 131; pious secularism in, 94–95, 104, 109–10, 120, 123–24, 125, 129–30; pluralization process in, 108–12, 220n8; political parties in, 121; principled distance in, 91–92, 98, 114–16, 127,

217–18n21; Protestants in, 113, 131; public health in, 32, 117, 194; public opinion in, 125–30, 224n76; religious diversity in, 102, 131; religious exemptions in, 24, 90, 91–92; religious landscape of, 86–88; street protests in, 107, 111, 116, 122–23; traditional African religions in, 217–18n21; and twin tolerations, 85, 94, 99

Senghor, Léopold Sédar, 8, 36, 98, 105; accomodationist preference of, 96, 218n34; and Catholics, 87, 99; and *laïcité* structuring, 85, 96, 218n31

sharia law, 103–4, 113, 171, 197–98, 231n62

Sikhs, 214n35

Sin, Jaime, 156, 158, 161

Smith, Étienne, 91, 100

Sopi coalition (Senegal), 106, 109, 111

Sow Sidibé, Amsatou, 104

"Special position" clause (Ireland), 54, 67

Stepan, Alfred, 10, 21, 86, 231n62; on multivocality, 11, 26, 30; on twin tolerations, 2, 13, 189

Stout, Jeffrey, 12

Structured Dialogue (Ireland), 76

St. Vincent de Paul Society, 45

Sufi brotherhoods, 95, 97–98, 115, 130, 207n55; calls for religious establishment by, 93–94; economic power of, 108–9, 110–11; and pious secularism, 120; public views of, 127–30; and Senegal political life, 114, 122, 221n23; and Senegal's religious landscape, 86–88. *See also* Mourides; Tidjanns

Sullivan, Winnifred Fallers, 208n17

Sweden, 204n19

Sy al-Ibn, Abdoul Aziz, 123

Taft, William Howard, 146, 227n38

Tagle, Luis Antonio, 161, 169

Tall, El Hajj Seydou Nourou, 99

Tan, Christine, 158

Taylor, Charles, 12

Team Buhay (Philippines), 173

Team Patay (Philippines), 173, 174

Teilhard de Chardin, Pierre, 96

Tendero, Efraim, 167

Thelen, Kathleen Ann, 11, 14

Thiandoum, Hyacinthe, 98–99

Tiadianne Sy, Cheikh, 95

Tidjanns, 104, 122; Mourides' relationship with, 102; and Senegal demographics, 86–87; succession struggle among, 110, 220n11

Tingson, Gregorio, 158

Tocqueville, Alexis de, 12

Touba, Senegal, 87, 92, 104, 108, 109, 110

Touré, Cheikh, 95, 110

Tunisia, 12, 191

Turkey, 3, 13, 24–25, 89, 92

twin tolerations: alternative theories on, 18, 19–20; assessing, 14; benevolent secularism and, 143–44, 186; coalition alliances and, 31, 52; defined, 4, 13; institutional structure and, 5, 11, 26, 31; Ireland and, 43, 46, 52; Philippines and, 134–35, 143–44; Senegal and, 85, 94, 99; Stepan on, 2, 13, 189

Uka, Lugum, 158

Ulama League of the Philippines, 163

Umar Tall, al-Hajj, 87

Union culturelle musulmane (UCM, Senegal), 95, 110

United Church of Christ in the Philippines (UCCP), 136, 228n7

United Kingdom, 14, 22, 24, 46

United States, 6, 52, 102, 210n36; church-state separation in, 22, 46, 89, 133, 208n14; Religious Right in, 20, 192–93

Université Cheikh Anta Diop de Dakar, 110

Vatican II, 37, 58, 65, 148, 150

Verzosa, Alfredo, 146

Villanueva, Eddie, 162, 173
Villarde, Mike, 172
Villegas, Bernardo, 158, 162, 169
Villegas, Socrates, 169

Wade, Abdoulaye, 8, 36, 92, 106, 120; draft constitution of, 112–14; differentiation undercut by, 114–16; in elections, 109, 122–23, 220n8
Wade, Karim, 122
Walsh, Brian, 68
Walshe, Joseph, 53
Waterbury, John, 10
White Vote Campaign (Philippines), 174
Whyte, John Henry, 48, 53, 210n32
Wilson, Paul, 156
women: in Philippines, 164; in Senegal, 117, 222n41. *See also* family

Yeats, W. B., 56
Youngblood, Robert L., 157, 228n7

Zamora, Jacinto, 226n31
Zeroug, Abdel, 195

Religion, Culture, and Public Life
Series Editor: Katherine Pratt Ewing

After Pluralism: Reimagining Religious Engagement, edited by Courtney Bender and Pamela E. Klassen
Religion and International Relations Theory, edited by Jack Snyder
Religion in America: A Political History, Denis Lacorne
Democracy, Islam, and Secularism in Turkey, edited by Ahmet T. Kuru and Alfred Stepan
Refiguring the Spiritual: Beuys, Barney, Turrell, Goldsworthy, Mark C. Taylor
Tolerance, Democracy, and Sufis in Senegal, edited by Mamadou Diouf
Rewiring the Real: In Conversation with William Gaddis, Richard Powers, Mark Danielewski, and Don DeLillo, Mark C. Taylor
Democracy and Islam in Indonesia, edited by Mirjam Künkler and Alfred Stepan
Religion, the Secular, and the Politics of Sexual Difference, edited by Linell E. Cady and Tracy Fessenden
Boundaries of Toleration, edited by Alfred Stepan and Charles Taylor
Recovering Place: Reflections on Stone Hill, Mark C. Taylor
Blood: A Critique of Christianity, Gil Anidjar
Choreographies of Shared Sacred Sites: Religion, Politics, and Conflict Resolution, edited by Elazar Barkan and Karen Barkey
Beyond Individualism: The Challenge of Inclusive Communities, George Rupp
Love and Forgiveness for a More Just World, edited by Hent de Vries and Nils F. Schott
Relativism and Religion: Why Democratic Societies Do Not Need Moral Absolutes, Carlo Invernizzi Accetti
The Making of Salafism: Islamic Reform in the Twentieth Century, Henri Lauzière
Mormonism and American Politics, edited by Randall Balmer and Jana Riess
Religion, Secularism, and Constitutional Democracy, edited by Jean L. Cohen and Cécile Laborde
Race and Secularism in America, edited by Jonathon S. Kahn and Vincent W. Lloyd
Beyond the Secular West, edited by Akeel Bilgrami
Pakistan at the Crossroads: Domestic Dynamics and External Pressures, edited by Christophe Jaffrelot

The Angel Of Poetry

A Poetic Perspective
On Living Through
The Holocaust

by
Brigitte Ringer-Nenner

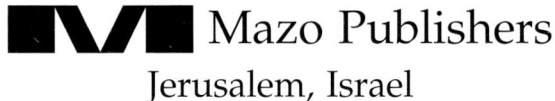 Mazo Publishers
Jerusalem, Israel

The Angel Of Poetry

Copyright © 2003 Brigitte Ringer-Nenner

ISBN 965-90462-1-9

Published by:
■▼■ Mazo Publishers
P.O. Box 36084, Jerusalem 91360 Israel

Website: www.mazopublishers.com
Email: publisher@mazopublishers.com
Tel: (Intn'l) + 972-2-940-0286

Selected German language poems
in this edition were originally included in
"Gedanken und Gedenken"

Design by: Pagemaster

All rights reserved.
No part of this publication may be translated, reproduced, stored
in a retrieval system, or transmitted in any form or by any means,
electronic, mechanical, photocopying, recording or otherwise,
without prior permission in writing from the publisher.

Printed In Jerusalem, Israel

About The Author

Brigitte Ringer-Nenner writes in the language of poetry to express her feelings and thoughts about life as a Jew during the Holocaust (*Shoah*).

Born in 1922, Brigitte lived with her parents and brother in Berlin until November 9, 1938.

It was on this date that the Nazis rampaged through the city, arresting the Jewish men and sending them to the concentration camps, and destroying Jewish property wherever they found it.

Now known as Kristallnacht, the night of the broken glass, the date marked not only the beginning of the Holocaust, but also the Ringer family's struggle to survive.

What follows in this book is Brigitte's poetic record as an eyewitness to the horrors of anti-Semitism.

Brigitte settled in Jerusalem in 1966.

Brigitte, her son Shaul, and her husband Leo

Dedicated
To All The Survivors

I want to dedicate this book to all the survivors who suffered with me through the hell of Bergen-Belsen, including my wonderful parents, Abe' and Anna Ringer, and my beloved brother, Professor Alexander L. Ringer, musicologist, who meanwhile took their memories with them to heaven, before the Throne of God.

Abe' Ringer *Anna Ringer* *Alex Ringer*

I am his sister.
He was my brother.
My only sibling,
There was no other.

When we were children,
We used to fight.
But we made up
Before saying "Good Night!"

My little dolls waited in vain,
Expecting to board his electric train.
But often enough,
He took them along.
And in my heart
I was singing a song.

I loved my brother,
More than I can say.
And wish that I had never
Seen the light of *this* day.

Brigitte's eulogy to her brother,
Professor Alexander L. Ringer
May 2002

Table of Contents

The Angel Of Poetry - Part I	9
A Very Real Story - Part II	12

A Poetic Perspective On Living Through The Holocaust

Too Late	19
Kristallnacht Or Tale Of A Witness	21
Memorial - Levetzow Street - Berlin	23
Amsterdam 1943	25
Memories Of Bergen-Belsen	27
Surviving	29
The Bergen-Belsen Mass Grave	31
Mother	33
Reincarnation Rejected	35
What Is In A Name...?	37
The Wind Over Auschwitz	39
"Life" After The Concentration Camp	41
Pain	43
The Letter	45
To David Irving	47

Brigitte's Poetry in German

Tell Your Story	50
Schreib ein Buch	51
Jew, Where Is Your Country?	52
Wo ist dein Land?	53
My Friend	54
Freund geht auf "Transport"	55
Voyage To Hell	56
Der Höllenzug	57
Aliyah	58
Aliyah	59

50 Years Have Gone By...	60
50 Jahre "Danach"	61
The Concentration Camp	62
K.Z.	63
"Song" Of The Home Country	64
Heimatlieder	65
On The Way To Hell	66
Celle	67
Ein Regentag	69
The Survivors	70
Die Überlebenden	71
Sehnsucht	73
Gebet	75
Mauthausen	77
Hoffnungslosigkeit	79
Die Nachtschwester im KZ	81
Geschehen in Dubnov	83
Letzter Quiz	85
Kind der Spree	87
An G'tt	89
Family Pictures ... Before The Holocaust	92
A Concluding Thought	95

Part I
The Angel Of Poetry

One night, a very long time ago, when I was a nice little girl with blond curls, when I could neither read nor write, the nanny had put me to bed. My mother came and said prayers with me and then turned out the light. And I fell asleep.

All of a sudden, there was light again.

I saw in my room a very beautiful angel, complete with wings and all the trimmings that an angel should have.

I was frightened.

I tried to pull the blanket over my face, but the angel was smiling and said, "Don't be frightened, little girl. God Himself sent me to you. I am the Angel of Poetry. I have the task to accompany you all of your life.

"I know that you cannot yet write what I am going to tell you, but never mind. Soon we will find a solution for that.

"At any rate, I have the order to be at your side, all of your life. And I do enjoy the idea. And now go back to sleep. We will have many occasions to converse.

"Just pay attention to me. I only come at night to visit you. Until you start school to learn how to write what I tell you, you will have to memorize it. Then you will ask your dear father to write it in the morning, as I know him to be a composer himself. He will be very happy to write down the first poems of his little daughter.

At night, the angel was always there for me and happy to help me, especially when I was 10 years old. That is when I wrote my first poem, "Jew, Where Is Your Country?".

So the Angel of Poetry has been with me since that time and even accompanied me during the *Shoah* when I was not yet an angel ... but hardly alive.

One Friday, when I was 15 years old, and on my way home from school, there was a lot of commotion in the street. People were pointing to smoke which seemed to poison the air.

Being a curious child, I followed the smoke. What I saw then, I have never forgotten until this day. The Angel of Poetry came quickly to help me, because the smoke billowed from the burning of my beloved synagogue. The fire had already eaten the biggest part of the building. I started crying, but suddenly, the angel was next to me and said. "Don't cry, write a poem about what you see, so that people for all time will remember it. So at this juncture, I wrote "Kristallnacht." Every year on that date, the 9th of November, the Angel would come to me to remind me to write about this catastrophe, to write another poem, in another language, in English, German and Dutch."

From all of this, you will get an impression of how close the relationship was between the Angel of Poetry and me when I was nearly 16 years old.

But now I must jump to another event, an event that makes me cry as I write about it.

"Dear Angel, please come to me to help me report the facts." It was in 1943 when the Angel of Poetry came to me and said, "I am so sorry. I promised to always be with you, but now I must break this promise because you, my child, are going to hell and angels are not allowed in hell.

"I can only promise you that I shall ask our dear God, who loves you very much, to intervene, so that one day you will be able to leave this hell, alive. You shall write poems about your experiences there."

And so it happened that after several years in the hell of Bergen-Belsen, I survived and could go on writing about it and the Shoah in general.

Thank you, my guardian angel.

*Brigitte and Alex Ringer
with their nanny - 1926*

Part II
A Very Real Story

Dear reader, I thank you for your attention until now. And thus I shall burden you once more with a very real story. Afterwards, even the most realistic among you will agree that only the Angel of Poetry could have accomplished what I am going to tell you, under oath!

When I went to school in Berlin, there was a fashion among girls to write messages to each other in a little diary in order to remember their young friends in later years.

I did not care to remember my colleagues in Nazi uniforms, but I bought such a little diary, red in color, to write my poems inside.

This little red book, with my first poems written inside while the Angel of Poetry was watching, became something very very important in my life and near death.

After the Kristallnacht, my family escaped to Holland.

We were living in Amsterdam when the Gestapo came to our home at 6:00 in the morning, June 20, 1943. We had to hurry. I put only one dress and my red book into a very small suitcase. More time they did not give me.

After this morning, the most unbearable suffering started in the concentration camps, but I made the impossible possible. Everything that I or my parents ever possessed, was lost, except that I managed to protect my little red book, even though the Angel of Poetry could not help me while in the hell of the concentration camp.

After years had passed and the Allies were entering Germany, the Nazis were afraid to keep us much longer, as we were foreign citizens. My father had arranged for us to be citizens of El Salvador. So the Nazis put us on a train, but to where it was going, we did not know. I was very ill with typhoid. There was no place to sit. It was a cattle car. The train went for many days. It only stopped to throw out the dead bodies, the corpses that finally had peace.

After many days, I don't know how many, there was another stop. This time, they shouted to those who were still alive—out! out! out! There was no time to find my suitcase and I could only trust that my Angel of Poetry would somehow find my early work. More I do not remember. I was put on a children's snow sleigh. When I woke up, I found myself incarcerated in another camp. Although it was somewhat better, I remained there for the next 2 years, until I was finally released when the war was over—although not yet for us.

We had to spend another year and a half in Germany until we were allowed to go back to Amsterdam. We had no home and absolutely nothing.

Of course it is quite clear that my red book was gone as I could not grab my suitcase at the last moment when ordered off the train. I don't want to bother you, dear reader, with any more stories, except for one where it is quite clear that my Angel of Poetry was involved.

We finally arrived back in Amsterdam. We had nothing, nothing, nothing any more, not a bed to sleep on, not a chair to sit on. We found some old neighbors. They allowed us to use their attic.

As I was a young girl, I did my utmost to enter life again. I said to my parents that I wanted to go and look to see who in our family might still be alive. I knew that my father had several brothers that lived in Antwerp, Belgium with many children. The trip wasn't very far, only a few hours. I found that most of the family were not alive any more, except for my cousin Shlomo Ringer, who had miraculously survived in an internment camp inside Germany. Also his wife and children were there. I was invited to stay at their house. We were sitting at the table for the Friday night meal. I said to Shlomo, "We have lost absolutely everything, but what bothers me most is the loss of my little red book containing all of my poems from my early childhood. The room went silent. Nobody said a word. Cousin Shlomo got up from the *Shabbat* table and went to a very big library and took out—my red book! I was

*Together after the war...
(L-R) Anna and Abe' Ringer with Shlomo and Liane Ringer .*

in shock, but at this moment I knew that this was the work of the Angel of Poetry. How else could this be explained.

Here is what happened. Shlomo had been deported from Belgium, where the Germans acted differently from those in Holland. Shlomo had also obtained foreign citizenship and therefore he was treated as a foreign national. Instead of being sent to a concentration camp, they sent him to an internment camp where the conditions were better for survival.

It happened that Shlomo was in the group of people who were loaded onto the same train that I was told to get out of.

When Shlomo got off the train, all the luggage was stacked on top of each other to make like a small mountain. They started to call out the names on the luggage so that people could claim their suitcases. Shlomo heard my name called out, so he claimed my suitcase. We have the same last name, so they gave it to him.

Coming from the concentration camp, everything was infested with lice, so the only thing that Shlomo took from the suitcase was my red book, thinking that it would be for a memory of me, a cousin he once had called Brigitte, though he did not know that I was still alive.

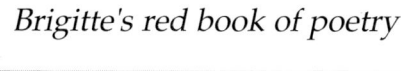

Brigitte's red book of poetry

Opened to the page of her poem "Jew, Where Is Your Country?"

The Angel Of Poetry

A Poetic Perspective
On Living Through
The Holocaust

Too Late

Too late for tears
Over six million souls
And our lost young years.

All I have written
Is frightening true
Still I thank God
To be born as a Jew!

Although my life
Was no garden of roses
I am proud to belong
To the people of Moses.

Kristallnacht
Or
Tale Of A Witness

I am a witness,
For I have seen.
I am a witness
Who lived in Berlin.

I saw those streets
Covered with glass.
I saw the Brown Shirts
Having *viel Spasse. (Fun)*

I saw Jewish men
Dragged out of bed.
Fifty years later
I cannot forget.

I saw those Jews
Hung by the neck.
Heard singing and shouting
Juda Verreck! (Jews Should Die!)

I saw the Temple
In flames, burning high.
I was a child
And asked myself, Why?

I saw the crowds
Watching the show.
I did not hear anyone
Saying "No!"

9th of November, 1988

Memorial
Levetzow Street
Berlin

Where our Temple still should be
A cattle car instead we see.

And next to it a wall in black
Naming those who don't come back.

Names – Names – Names
Their pain forever hidden.

For Jews, Dying Was Not Forbidden!

June 1992

Amsterdam
1943

The 20th of June, who could ever forget?
They came very soon and took me from my bed.
I did not know how to get dressed
With one in my room, who enjoyed the arrest.

Another took parents and brother out.
Speakers were hungry for Jews very loud.
They brought us to a football place
Where yellow stars filled all the space.

In burning sun we stood whole day.
At night they were leading the cattle away.
Hungry and thirsty and trembling of fear,
The cattle cars told us the slaughter is near.

This happened to me in my Twentieth Year.

June 20, 1943

Memories Of
Bergen-Belsen

Full are the overcrowded barracks.
Empty the loudly complaining stomachs.

Loud are the orders, still louder the beating.
Empty the straw mattresses and thus no sleeping.

Full is the tun at night for your need.
Empty the faucet to wash you with speed.

Full are the graves with thousands of dead.
We all wanted to die for a small piece of bread!

Loud are the orders for us to stand still.
Whatever they shout,
We have no more will.

Surviving

As we are growing older
The pain seems to get worse.
Memories of the Shoah
Are like a silent curse.

At times when we were younger
Somehow life has gone on
With ailments and with sorrow
We, now, are left alone.

Nobody will ever understand
No surgeon has learned such wounds to mend
No matter how many pictures are seen
Nobody in future can know what has been.

June 1998

The Bergen-Belsen Mass Grave

I was in a mass grave
But I ventured out.
Too big was the crowd
I said good-bye and be all well.
I cannot stand it.
I go back to the hell.

Of course, at the outside
The hell was not good.
The work was too hard
And long days we stood in mud
Without any moving
Without any food.

I understood my great mistake
And would go back to the mass grave ...
Once I am awake.

Mother

Soon after Brigitte and her family escaped to Holland, her grandparents were able to book passage on a ship to the United States and settle there.

These words express the pain and torment of a grandmother, knowing the suffering and misery that her children would be in the midst of...if they were even still alive.

She is old.
Her hair is white, just like the snow.
In her heart, she has pain.

She is wailing, early til late.
In serious prayer, her lonesome soul is begging
Oh Lord, You Yourself gave them to me,
Please let them go free.

Passes many a night. Mother is waiting.
In the KZ, is need. In the KZ, is no bread.
The executioner waits. In the KZ is death.

Daily, masses are dying.
The mother is grieving.
Still, she is not believing.

The earth is turning.
One year is passing and also the second.
Tomorrow becomes today.

The mother, in her room, is still waiting.
Why should she believe it.
He will not rob her of what He Himself has given.
The Lord will let them live.

Strong will and sad stillness, hoping and waiting,
Staring to heaven, to the only source
Who can refresh the soul.
The struggle is difficult.
But bigger is He.

For her children are free!

Reincarnation Rejected

I dreamt that I was dead
When God one day said,
I think you are worth
To go back to earth.

I cried and I prayed
And that's what I said.
If I have some worth,
"Don't send me to earth."

Please God, understand
Can't be there, I can't.
Whatever I will be,
A man or a tree
Again I must flee
When they step on me...

What Is In A Name…?

They call us "survivors"
As we are on earth

They call us "survivors"
For all it is worth

Who can survive
A corpses life ...?!

The Wind Over Auschwitz

The wind is blowing over Auschwitz
There where the shadows live.

The wind blowing over Auschwitz
Has six million tones.

The wind blowing over Auschwitz
Is part of our future.

The wind over Auschwitz
Blows us to Israel.

"Life" After The Concentration Camp

Some are still alive.
That is true.
But life is for us
Not the same as for you.

Pain

I am suffering.
Suffering pain,
Physical pain
Day and night.

It is a pity
God cannot receive mail.
I would have written Him a letter.

The Letter

Brigitte was inspired to write this poem from her encounters with the sick and dying Jews in the Bergen-Belsen sick barrack.

In addition to her daytime labor in the camp, Brigitte stayed up late into the night helping as best she could when no one else was there for these people, who were all in the process of dying.

There are souls,
They are in heaven.
I knew their bodies
Fifty years ago.

They were suffering.
I was suffering,
And suffered for them.
There was no hope.

They will remember,
Even in heaven,
The hell that was.
They might remember
Two hands in the darkness.

A Note For The Kotel-December 1993

To
David Irving
(Holocaust Denier)

How can you deny,
While knowing the truth
That Hitler erased
Most European Jews?

How can you state
This is not true
When I was there ....
Where were you?

Did you see the mountains of corpses?
Did you ever smell their smell ....?
Mr. Irving, go to hell!
Go to hell.
There is your place
With the purist Aryan race.

June 2000

Brigitte's Poetry in German

Publisher's Note:
   On the following pages, we have included a number of poems that Brigitte wrote in the German language, her mother tongue.
   While some of the poems have been translated, and some have been explained or only titled in English, the poetic strength of her work remains in the original form.

Tell Your Story

Write down your story,
They say to me.

But, for me,
Everything becomes a poem.

Only this way
I can say what I want to say.

So I can also cope with it.
Afterwards I am quiet.

So I can think
What has happened to me.
So I can guide the reader
Until they are very close to this.

What is indescribable,
I then describe.
And so it should remain
That I can tell the story.

Schreib ein Buch

Man sagt: "Schreib ein Buch,
Schreib Deine geschichte!"

Doch mir wird alles
Gleich zum Gedichte.

Nur so kann ich sagen
Was ich sagen will,
So kann ich's ertragen,
Und bin danach still.

Ja so kann ich denken
An was mir geschah,
Die Leser lenken
Bis sie dem ganz nah.

Was nicht zu beschreiben
Beschreibe ich dann...
Und so soll es bleiben,
Damit ich es erzählon kann!

Jew, Where Is Your Country?

Jew, where is your country?
Jew, when I could not find it,
I wanted to ask
What Jews themselves are saying to this.

People are losing their decency.
They have become anti-Semites.
They forbid their country to Jews.

The Germans are driving Jews out of their country.
They want to push them into Poland.
But also the Poles don't want
To have strange blood in their race.

They try to push the Jews into Palestine,
But, it is well known that this too is not a proper place.
There is a constant fight with the Arabs.
They too want to conquer the land.

People are becoming anti-Semites
Just like Germany and Poland.

Berlin, 1933 (At 10 years old)

Wo ist dein Land?

Jude wo ist dein Land?
Als ich es nicht fand,
Wollte ich fragen
Was die Juden selber dazu sagen.
Jude, du hast kein Land
Die Völker verlieren ihren Anstand.
Sie werden Antisemiten,
Sodass sie den Juden das Land verbieten.
Die Juden werden aus Deutschland vertrieben,
Und die Deutschen wollen die Juden nach Polen schieben.
Doch die Polen sind gut auf der Hut,
Auch sie wollen in ihrer Rasse kein fremdes Blut.
Sie lassen die Juden langsam nach Palestina übersiedeln
Doch Palestina ist auch nicht das richtige Land,
Das ist Allen wohl bekannt.
Es hat einen ewigen Kampf mit den Arabern,
Die wollen gerne das Land erobern.
Jude wo ist dein Land?
Den anderen Völkern geht es wie Deutschland und Polen,
Sie werden sich Alle etwas von dem Antisemitismus holen.

My Friend

My friend is going "on a transport."

I don't want to show you
How difficult it is to take leave.

The tears have to keep quiet
Until you have gone away.

What I had missed until now,
My friend, I found with you.

Whatever I had dreamed about,
Destiny is now taking away from me.

Like many others, this friend did not survive.

Freund geht auf "Transport"

Ich will dir ja nicht zeigen
wie schwer der Abschied ist
die Tränen müssen schweigen
bis du gegangen bist

Was ich bisher versäumte
mein Freund fand ich bei dir
was ich mir je erträumte
nimmt jetzt das Schicksal mir

Amsterdam, 1942

Voyage To Hell

Unfortunately at the time, I missed missing the train.
But who could even dream of such a possibility.

Thus, I traveled very deeply into hell.
And there I learned that Mephesto
Is not at all operating alone.

I have suffered and witnessed
What does not exist in our world.
What happened there daily
Makes the Cosmos cry.

Der Höllenzug

Leider habe ich seinerzeit
Versäumt den Zug zu versäumen
Doch von solch einer Möglichkeit
Konnte man nicht einmal träumen

Und so bin ich denn gefahren
In die Hölle tief hinein
Und dort sollte ich erfahren
Mephisto ist gar nicht allein

Hab' erlitten und gesehen
Was es auf der Welt nicht gibt
Was dort täglich ist geschehen
Macht den Kosmos tief betrübt

Aliyah

Enter through the big gate,
It opens up to you forever the holy place.

The goal of all longing
You are allowed to reach.
Over are the anxious years of tears.

Chosen are you.
And you may trust
You will see big things.
And you will find peace.

Kneel down on the holy floor,
From the earth you should drink.
And it should come to your lips,
A prayer for your brethren.

Aliyah

Tritt ein durch die Pforte
Es öfflnet sich dir
Für immer die Tür
Am heiligen Orte

Zum Ziel alles Sehnen
Darfst du gelangen
Vorbei sind die bangen
Jahre der Tränen

Erwählet bist du
Und kannst vertrauen
Wirst Grosses schauen
Und findest Ruh

Knie auf heiligem Boden nieder
Von der Erde sollst du nippen
Und es komm auf deine Lippen
Ein Gebet für deine Brüder

50 Years Have Gone By...

50 years have gone by...
That is a short time
For those who suffered
In concentration camps.
Every day was an eternity.

50 years have gone by...
That is a long time for 6 million
Who went to eternity.

50 years have gone by...
Still it seems very near.

50 years have gone by...
It hurts deeper every year.

50 Jahre "Danach"

50 Jahre sind vergangen
Das ist eine kurze Zeit
Für die, die im KZ gefangen
War jeder Tag die Ewigkeit

50 Jahre sind vergangen
Das ist eine lange Zeit
Für 6 Millionen die gegangen
Auf Mordtransport zur Ewigkeit

50 Jahre sind vergangen
Es ist, als ob es gestern war
50 Jahre sind vergangen
Und es schmerzt tiefer jedes Jahr

Jerusalem 1995

The Concentration Camp

A place which used to be hell
Where every hour has born death.

A place of suffering, dwelling in pain
Designated to finish off life.

A place that was owned by the death hats,
A place that will never be forgotten.

K.Z.

Der Ort der einst die Hölle' war
Wo jede Stunde Tod gebar
Ein Ort der Leiden, Qual und Schmerzen
Bestimmt um Leben auszumerzen
Ein Ort vom "Totenkopf" besessen
Auf ewig sei er UNVERGESSEN!

"Song" Of The Home Country

From my childhood, I remember the song.
Enjoying to do us a lot of wrong.

How good the Jewish blood is tasting,
Not a drop the S.A. shall be wasting.

The Temple is burning, very high.
I, as a child, ask myself, Why?

A warning for Germany...
Today the radical right is murdering like then.
Soon the old songs will be fashionable again.

Heimatlieder

"Die Fahne hoch
Die Reihen fest geschlossen"
Wie gut schmeckt Judenblut
Den Volksgenossen

Tempel brennen lichterloh
"Deutschland ueber alles..." froh
S.A. marschiert den Arm erhoben
Um Vernichtung zu geloben.

Aus meiner Kindheit sind die Bilder
Heute Deutschlands Warnungsschilder!?
Rechts-Radikale morden wieder
Und bald sind neu die alten Lieder.

April 1998

On The Way To Hell

At the time I was so very young,
But the memory is still so alive.
Even today, I, an elderly lady, am
Seeing it exactly as it was before my eyes.

First stopover, Celle,
The city near Bergen-Belsen.
And then by foot into the hell.
Oh, I could not walk anymore!

But just to stand still
During many difficult hours,
With the S.S. and big dogs,
Was strictly forbidden.

When we showed up in Celle,
Coming down from the train,
We walked in the streets.
The living watched from their big buildings.

What could their reaction be
To see such a group of Jews
Wearing stars and all?
What would they have to say?

But they just closed their curtains, half way.

What happened right in front of their windows?
Later they said, ...Absolutely nothing.

Nobody was ever beating his breast.
Nobody had seen anything, ever.

Celle

Auf dem weg zur Hölle
Damals war ich noch so jung
Doch stark lebt die Erinnerung
Jetzt bin ich eine ält're Frau
Und seh' es vor mir ganz genau
Celle, erste Haltestelle ...
Dann der Fussweg in die Hölle

Ach ich konnte nicht mehr gehen
Doch verboten war's zu stehen
Wahrend vieler schweren Stunden
Mit SS und grossen Hunden

Als in Celle wir erschienen
Schlossen halb sich die Gardinen
Man sagte dann: "Nichts war zu sehen"
Was vor den Fenstern ist geschehen
Man schlug sich niemals in die Brust
Denn ... man hat ja nichts gewusst.

It was a rainy Sunday, April 11, 1948 in New York, when Brigitte wrote this love poem to her future husband, Leo Nenner.
Pictured below, they were married August 7, 1949.

*Bridesmaids:
Brigitte's cousins,
Chana and Rachel Ringer
(Daughters of Shlomo Ringer)*

Ein Regentag

Es fallen dicke Tropfen
An diesen grauen Tag
Doch träum ich, dass sie klopfen
Auf unser eignes Dach.

Ich sehe Haus und Herd
Darin ein Feuer brennen,
Und wissend um den Wert
Des Orts den Heim wir nennen,

Sitz ich zu deinem Füssen
Am knisternden Kamin
Und sag: "Du sollst es wissen,
Dass ich jetzt glücklich bin".

Da lösest du vom Buche
Die vielgeliebte Hand,
Auf dass sie tastend suche
Mein Haar - und mein Gewand.

Schon schaut in unser Zimmer
Gott Amor selbst und lacht:
Das habe ich wie immer
Mal wieder gut gemacht.

Er naht mit leisem Schritte
Und löscht das Lampenlicht,
Weilt dann in unsrer Mitte
Bis neuer Tag anbricht.

The Survivors

In our young years,
We experienced thankfully,
That we were still alive.

Now that we are growing older,
The Shoah is following us
Like a silent curse.

With this grieving and pain
Our hearts remain lonely.

No one will ever understand
The reality of what happened to us.

No doctor can help to cope,
To cure the wounds opened to us.

So, in desperation,
We are waiting
For our salvation.

Die Überlebenden

In unsren jungen Jahrën,
Haben dankbar wir erfahren
Dass wir noch am Leben waren

Jetzt nachdem wir älter werden
Will der Schmerz stets stärker werden
Die Grauen die die Shoah schuf
Versolgen uns als stiller Fluch

Mit dieser Trauer und den Schmerzen
Bleiben einsam unsre Herzen
Niemand wird es je verstehen
Was uns in Wirklichkeit geschehen

Kein Arzt kann helfen zu ertragen
Die Wunden die man uns geschlagen
So warten wir in unsrer Not
Auf die Erlösung durch ... den Tot.

Jerusalem

*Brigitte's son, Shaul, (center)
at the Kotel - 1968*

Sehnsucht

Jerusalem Du schöne Stadt
Die uns Gott gegeben hat
Zu Dir sehnet sich mein Herz
An Deiner Mauer ‚klag' ich meinen Schmerz

Um Dich zu sehen allzumal
Möcht ich bezwingen Berg und Thal
Aus Dir, dem Land dem Du geborn
Klingt heraus der Freiheit Horn

Nach Erez sehnet sich mein Herz
Ich hab' erlitten Pein und Schmerz
Nach Ehr' und Freiheit strebt mein Sinn
Zu unserer Heimat zieht's mich hin

Berlin - September 21, 1936

Prayer

Gebet

Ewiger; Du unsre Zuflucht, unser Hort
Sehnsüchtig harr'n wir auf Dein Wort
Mach' unsrem Leiden bald ein Ende
Gib' unsrem Schicksal die erhoffte Wende
Oh, laß Dein Volk nicht untergehn
Laß bald uns wieder bessre Tage sehn
Zu Dir allein fleht jung und alt
Du bist's dem schon der ‚Väter' Beten galt
So gib uns denn den unverdienten Lohn
Wir nahen betend Deinem Thron

Berlin, 22. Juni 1938

Mauthausen Concentration Camp

Mauthausen

(frei nach H. Heine)
(Zum Andenken an meine Jugendfreunde)

Es waren zwei Judenkinder,
die liebten einander gar sehr
Klaus Barbi ist gekommen,
da liebten sie nicht mehr

Es waren zwei Judenkinder,
die liebten das Leben so sehr
Klaus Barbi ist gekommen
da lebten sie nicht mehr

Es waren zwei Judenkinder;
die waren so jung und so schön
Klaus Barbi ist gekommen
man hat sie nie wieder gesehn

Es waren zwei Judenkinder;
die haben wie alle kein Grab.
Man stieß sie zusammen gebunden
vom Steinbruch hoch oben hinab

Amsterdam 1942

Desperation

Hoffnungslosigkeit

Hat man mal einen Traum geträumt
und dieser Traum war schön
so bleibt in jenem Augenblick
ein Stück vom Leben stehn

Und weil man nicht vergessen kann
dreht oft die Zeit zurück
das nennt man dann Erinnerung
so trügt der Schein vom Gück

Amsterdam, 1942

Night Nurse In the Concentration Camp

Die Nachtschwester im KZ

Hab' erhoben heut die Stimme
Seit zwei Jahr zum ersten Mal,
Es war ja gerad' das Schlimme,
Daß mein Herz verhärtet war.

Wenn ich auch geschlossen nächtlich
Hab' der Augenpaare zwei,
Heute frag ich selbstverächtlich:
Fühltest du denn viel dabei?

War doch glücklich, daß ich lebte,
Wenn geschehen Sein Gericht
Und voll Dank mein Herz erbebte
In des Todes Angesicht.

Wollt vergeben mir ihr Brüder,
Daß ich an mein Eigen dacht
Ich besinn mich immer wieder
Der Gedanken in der Nacht.

Heute soll es jeder hören,
Denn ich klag mich selber an;
Es ist schwer sich zu bewähren,
Wenn man selbst verlieren kann.

Weiß, die Welt wird mir verzeihen,
Denn sie ist so schlecht wie ich;
Gott soll auch sein Ohr mir leihen,
Zu dem Schöpfer bete ich...

Biberach, 15. Juli 1945

It Happened In Dubnov

Geschehen in Dubnov

Ich höre ein Wimmern, ein leises Weinen
Am blutigen Ort
Zwischen toten Gebeinen.

Der Wind trägt die Klage
Mit sich fort,
Bis ans Ende der Tage.

Ich bin gefesselt und kann nicht weichen
Und es regt sich etwas
Zwischen den Leichen.

Und ich sehe, o Gott, ach wäre ich blind,
Ein Wesen, das mich anschaut...
Ein Kind!

Sie haben so laut gelacht
Und dann "puff, puff" gemacht
Beginnt der Knabe zu sprechen.

"Das Blut ist so rot
Onkel, bin ich schon tot?"
- Und die großen Augen brechen -

Biberach, 1945

The Last Quiz

Letzter Quiz

Wo muß man nie mehr einsam sein?
Dort wo Gebein liegt bei Gebein
Wo kann man endlich Frieden finden?
Dort wo die Körper schnell entbinden
Wo endet jedes Menschen Not?
Dort wo nur einer lebt ... der Tod.
Wo hört man greifbar noch die Stille?
Dort wo die Ruhe Gottes Wille

A Child
Of The River

Kind der Spree

Sind dies die gleichen Straßen,
die ich gegangen bin,
bevor ich mußt' verlassen
fluchtartig mein Berlin?

Hier wurde unser Tempel
vor meinem Aug' verbrannt,
ich trug noch keinen Stempel
mit Nummer auf der Hand.

Kurfürstendamm in Scherben!
So fing das Ende an,
für Großtransport zum Sterben
war ganz Europa dran.

Sie leben ja noch heute,
die niemals "nein" gesagt,
und die es gar nicht reute,
als wir ins Gas gejagt.

Es fließen meine Tränen,
Erinnerung tut weh,
doch fühlte ich ein Sehnen
weil ich ein Kind der Spree.

Wo ich einst fröhlich spielte
wollte ich nochmals sehn
was ich dabei wohl fühlte...
wer wird es je verstehn?!

(Gedanken zum Berlin-Besuch, Juni 1992)

To God

An G'tt

Täglich fühle ich Dein Walten,
Und ich spüre die Natur,
Ja, ich weiß, wirst ewig halten
Deinem Volk den Treueschwur..

Darum hat auch nicht verzaget
Dein Gebild im höchsten Leid,
Niemals haben sie geklaget,
Nicht einmal im Todesstreit.

Jetzt sind sie dahingegangen
Deine Kinder, groß und klein;
Niemand hat es angefangen,
Zu begraben ihr Gebein.

Immer werden wir beweinen,
Ein Vergessen gibt es nicht.
Vater! Übtest unter Deinen
Doch ein schreckliches Gericht.

Täglich fühle ich Dein Walten
Und verspüre die Natur;
Ja, ich weiß, nicht aufzuhalten
Ist die Rach' im Treueschwur.

Unser Feind er liegt darnieder,
Ist gefällt von starker Hand.
Trotzdem führe uns doch wieder
Heim in das "Gelobte Land".

Reiße aus die Lästerzungen,
Gib uns Arbeit, gib uns Brot,
Und gib Möglichkeit den Jungen,
daß sie leben nach dem Tod.

Täglich fühle ich Dein Walten
Und verspüre die Natur.
Dank sei Dir, Du hast erhalten
Einen Rest, nach deinem Schwur.

Biberach, 15. Juli 1945

Family Pictures...
Before The Holocaust

Author's Note:
When my mother packed her suitcases before our escape to Holland, she included many of our family pictures. After we were captured by the Nazis in Holland, one of our non-Jewish neighbors hid these pictures and kept them safe for us until after the war.

*Brigitte's grandfather, her mother's father,
in front of his department store
Circa 1900*

*Shaul Ringer – Brigitte's
grandfather, her father's father
Krakow, Poland - 1915*

Anna Ringer in Karlsbad *Alex and Brigitte Ringer - 1926*

The Ringer Family with their nanny - 1923

A Concluding Thought

The Angel
Is still at my side.

This gives my heart
The needed pride.

Some say at 80
Life begins.

I must admit
I like such hints.

There is still a lot
I have to say.

From heaven
It seems far away.